FRIENDLY FASCISM

OTHER BOOKS
BY BERTRAM GROSS

The Legislative Struggle:
A Study in Social Combat
The Hard Money Crusade
The Managing of Organizations
Organizations and Their Managing
The State of the Nation:
Social Systems Accounting

EDITED BY BERTRAM GROSS

Action Under Planning
The National Planning Series
A Great Society?
Social Intelligence for America's Future
New Styles of Planning in Post-Industrial America

FRIENDLY FASCISM

The New Face of Power in America

by

Bertram Gross

M. EVANS and Company, Inc.
New York

To My Grandchildren

Library of Congress Cataloging in Publication Data

Gross, Bertram Myron, 1912-
Friendly fascism.

Includes index.
1. United States—Politics and government—1945-
2. United States—Economic policy—1971- 3. Elite
(Social sciences)—United States. I. Title.
JK271.G745 320.973 80-13035
ISBN 0-87131-317-0

M. Evans and Company, Inc.
216 East 49 Street
New York, New York 10017

Design by Robert Bull

Manufactured in the United States of America

9 8 7 6 5 4 3 2 1

Acknowledgments

THE WRITING OF THIS BOOK has been a long voyage of exploration, in the course of which I have learned many new things, changed many old ideas and written far more than there is room to publish in any one volume. Throughout this effort I have been fortunate to receive valuable criticisms, suggestions and other reactions from family members, students, colleagues, editors, and other friends.

I have been particularly helped by the encouragement or ideas given me by the American members of my immediate family—Theodore Gross, Samuel Gross, Larry Gross, David Gross Shulamith Gross, Nora Gross, Edith Lateiner and Isidore Lateiner—and by the Indian branch as well—Kusum Singh, Nisha Singh, Gayatri Singh, Neera Sen and A. N. Sen. Ungrudging support has been provided by an "extended family" of former doctoral students—David Curzon, Itzhak Galnoor, Michael Marien, Herman Mertins, Stanley Moses, David Porter, Michael Springer and David Warner—and of present doctoral students—Frances Cooper and Stephen Frantz.

With apologies to other students too numerous to list, I also wish to thank: Ann Berson, William Byrnes, Randy Crawford, Marjorie Gellerman, Gregory Gerard, John Goetz, Titiana Hardy, Robert Kraushaar, Marilyn Phelan, Sidney Plotkin, Lenore Rasmussen, Maynard T. Robison, Virginia Sherry, Donna Soucy, Mary Stern, Norma Turner and Marcie Waterman.

Let me also express my appreciation for the help received from other colleagues: Carol and Sandor Agocz, Stephen K. Bailey, Blanche Blank, Karen Bogen, Jean Boudin, Leonard Boudin, Philip Brenner, Carlos Ciaño, Robert Chessell, Richard Cloward, Joe Conason, Loretta Curzon, Paul David, John Dixon, G. William Domhoff, Yehezkel Dror, Joel C. Edelstein, Robert Engler, Julian Friedman, Alan Gartner, Corinne Gilb, Max Gordon, Colin Greer, Larry Hirshhorn, John P. Lewis, Robert McGregor, Harry Magdoff, Mary Lou Marien, Max Mark, Donald Michael, S. M. Miller, Mario Monzon, Paul Orentlich, Saul Padover, Alphonso Pinkney, Frances Piven, Frank Riessman, Philip Roos, Peter Salins, Ned Schneier, G. N. Seetharam, Falguni Sen, Chaim Shatan, Derek

Shearer, Hans Spiegel, Julius Stulman, Miguel Teubal, Terri Thal, Edith Tiger, Geoffrey Vickers, Elizabeth Wickenden and Sol Yurick.

Over the years I have been privileged to enjoy encouragement and advice from Peter Mayer, one of the few creative giants in American and British publishing. I have been particularly privileged to have had the editorial help of Maria Carvainis, Peter Steinfels and Fred Graver. Giving more time to this book than Maria or Peter had a chance to do, Fred has proven to me that a brilliant editor can carve out entire chapters, sections and paragraphs without causing too much pain; the secret, of course, is that by going to the roots of what I had been trying to say, he repeatedly pushed me toward reformulating and improving my entire conception. Indeed, it was only through discussions with Fred that I realized something that had been true from the very beginning—namely, that this is a book about democracy.

BERTRAM GROSS

Contents

Introduction: A Patriotic Warning

THIS IS A BOOK ABOUT DEMOCRACY.

It is a book of realism, fear, and hope.

It is about great achievements and tragic failures in America; about maneuverings that could turn the democracy we now know into a new form of despotism. Above all, it is about a more "true" democracy.

As I look toward the future, I see the possibility in America for a more genuine democracy than has ever existed. Economically, socially, culturally, and politically the people of that America would be able to take part—more directly than ever before—in decisions affecting themselves and others and our nation's role in the world. The country would operate in the best sense of a national "honeycomb" of interrelating groups and individuals. On all sides, I see the potentials for that America. "The spirits of great events," in Johannon von Schiller's words, "stride on before the event/ And in today already walks tomorrow." That kind of future, more than material possessions, has always been the vital center of the American dream.

Looking at the present, I see a more probable future: a new despotism creeping slowly across America. Faceless oligarchs sit at command posts of a corporate-government complex that has been slowly evolving over many decades. In efforts to enlarge their own powers and privileges, they are willing to have others suffer the intended or unintended consequences of their institutional or personal greed. For Americans, these consequences include chronic inflation, recurring recession, open and hidden unemployment, the poisoning of air, water, soil and bodies, and, more important, the subversion of our constitution. More broadly, consequences include widespread intervention in international politics through economic manipulation, covert action, or military invasion. On a world scale, all of this is already producing a heating up of the cold war and enlarged stockpiles of nuclear and non-nuclear death machines.

I see at present members of the Establishment or people on its fringes who, in the name of Americanism, betray the interests of most Americans by fomenting militarism, applauding rat-race individualism, protecting undeserved privilege, or stirring up nationalistic and ethnic hatreds. I see pretended patriots who desecrate the American flag by waving it while waiving the law.

In this present, many highly intelligent people look with but one eye and see only one part of the emerging Leviathan. From the right, we are warned against the danger of state capitalism or state socialism, in which Big Business is dominated by Big Government. From the left, we hear that the future danger (or present reality) is monopoly capitalism, with finance capitalists dominating the state. I am prepared to offer a cheer and a half for each view; together, they make enough sense for a full three cheers. Big Business and Big Government have been learning how to live in bed together, and despite arguments between them, enjoy the cohabitation. Who may be on top at any particular moment is a minor matter—and in any case can be determined only by those with privileged access to a well-positioned keyhole.

I am uneasy with those who still adhere strictly to President Eisenhower's warning in his farewell address against the potential for the disastrous rise of power in the hands of the military-industrial complex. Nearly two decades later, it should be clear to the opponents of militarism that the military-industrial complex does not walk alone. It has many partners: the nuclear-power complex, the technology-science complex, the energy-auto-highway complex, the banking-investment-housing complex, the city-planning-development-land-speculation complex, the agribusiness complex, the communications complex, and the enormous tangle of public bureaucracies and universities whose overt and secret services provide the foregoing with financial sustenance and a nurturing environment. Equally important, the emerging Big Business-Big Government partnership has a global reach. It is rooted in colossal transnational corporations and complexes that help knit together a "Free World" on which the sun never sets. These are elements of the new despotism.

A few years ago a fine political scientist, Kenneth Dolbeare, conducted a series of in-depth interviews totalling twenty to twenty-five hours per person. He found that most respondents were deeply afraid of some future despotism. "The most striking thing about inquiring into expectations for the future," he reported, "is the rapidity with which the concept of fascism (with or without the label) enters the conversation." [1] But not all knowledge serves the cause of freedom. In this case the tendency is to suppress fears of the future, just as most people have learned to repress fears of a nuclear holocaust. It is easier to repress well-justified fears than to control the dangers giving rise to them. Thus Dolbeare found an "air-raid shelter mentality, in which people go underground rather than deal directly with threatening prospects."

Fear by itself, as Alan Wolfe has warned, could help immobilize people and nurture the apathy which is already too large in American society.[2] But repression of fear can do the same thing—and repression of fear is a reality in America.

As I look at America today, I am not afraid to say that I am afraid.

I am afraid of those who proclaim that it can't happen here. In 1935 Sinclair Lewis wrote a popular novel in which a racist, anti-Semitic, flag-waving, army-backed demagogue wins the 1936 presidential election and proceeds to establish an Americanized version of Nazi Germany. The title, *It Can't Happen Here,* was a tongue-in-cheek warning that it might. But the "it" Lewis referred to is unlikely to happen again any place. Even in today's Germany, Italy or Japan, a modern-style corporate state or society would be far different from the old regimes of Hitler, Mussolini, and the Japanese oligarchs. Anyone looking for black shirts, mass parties, or men on horseback will miss the telltale clues of creeping fascism. In any First World country of advanced capitalism, the new fascism will be colored by national and cultural heritage, ethnic and religious composition, formal political structure, and geopolitical environment. The Japanese or German versions would be quite different from the Italian variety—and still more different from the British, French, Belgian, Dutch, Australian, Canadian, or Israeli versions. In America, it would be supermodern and multi-ethnic—as American as Madison Avenue, executive luncheons, credit cards, and apple pie. It would be fascism with a smile. As a warning against its cosmetic facade, subtle manipulation, and velvet gloves, I call it friendly fascism. What scares me most is its subtle appeal.

I am worried by those who fail to remember—or have never learned—that Big Business–Big Government partnerships, backed up by other elements, were the central facts behind the power structures of old fascism in the days of Mussolini, Hitler, and the Japanese empire builders.

I am worried by those who quibble about labels. Some of my friends seem transfixed by the idea that if it is fascism, it must appear in the classic, unfriendly form of their youth. "Why, oh why," they retrospectively moan, "didn't people see what was happening during the 1920s and the 1930s?" But in their own blindness they are willing to use the terms invented by the fascist ideologists, "corporate state" or "corporatism," but not fascism.

I am upset with those who prefer to remain spectators until it may be too late. I am shocked by those who seem to believe—in Anne Morrow Lindbergh's words of 1940—that "there is no fighting the wave of the future" and all you can do is "leap with it." [3] I am appalled by those who stiffly maintain that nothing can be done until things get worse or the system has been changed.

I am afraid of inaction. I am afraid of those who will heed no warnings and who wait for some revelation, research, or technology to offer a perfect solution. I am afraid of those who do not see that some of the best in America has been the product of promises and that the promises of the past are not enough for the future. I am dismayed by those who will not hope, who will not commit themselves to something larger than themselves, of those who are afraid of true democracy or even its pursuit.

I suspect that many people underestimate both the dangers that lie ahead and the potential strength of those who seem weak and powerless. Either underestimation stems, I think, from fear of bucking the Establishment. This is a deep and well-hidden fear that guides the thoughts and actions of many of my warmest friends, closest colleagues, and best students. It is a fear I know only too well, for it has pervaded many years of my life.

I fear any personal arrogance in urging this or that form of action—the arrogance of ideologues who claim a monopoly on truth, of positivists who treat half-truths as whole truths, of theoreticians who stay aloof from the dirty confusions of political and economic combat, and of the self-styled "practical" people who fear the endless clash of theories. I am afraid of the arrogance of technocrats as well as the ultra-rich and their high executives. Some of this arrogance I often find in my own behavior. I am afraid of blind anti-fascism.[4]

One form of blindness was suddenly revealed to me in a graduate seminar in which I was trying out the ideas in this book. One of my brightest students asked me a startling question: "Aren't you a friendly fascist yourself, Professor Gross?"

"How can you possibly ask such a question?" I countered.

She replied with a bill of particulars, which she amplified during a few weeks of disconcerting argument.

First, did not the Employment Act of 1946, which I had helped draft and administer, turn out to strengthen the role not only of the President but also of the corporate-government complex?[5]

She then went on to my writings on management. Didn't they all point in the direction of a centrally managed society? She made a special point of my work on social indicators. Would not an Annual Social Report of the President, as I had proposed to Presidents Johnson and Nixon, concentrate more power in the presidential part of an increasingly imperial Establishment?

A strange answer to her rhetorical question came to me in the form of a dream. I saw myself searching for "friendly fascists" through a huge, rambling house. I climbed upstairs, ran through long corridors and opened the doors of many rooms, but found nobody. At last I came to a half-lit room with many doors. I sensed there was someone there, but saw nobody. Striding across the room, I flung open one of the doors—and there sitting at a typewriter and smiling right back at me, I saw MYSELF . . .

I think I now understand the meaning of this dream: For many years I sought solutions for America's ills—particularly unemployment, ill health, and slums—through more power in the hands of central government. In this I was not alone. Almost all my fellow planners, reformers, social scientists, and urbanists presumed the benevolence of more concentrated government power. The major exceptions were those who went to the other extreme of presuming the benevolence of concentrated corporate power, often hiding its existence behind sophistical litanies of praise for the "rationality," "efficiency," or "democracy" of market systems and "free competitive" private enterprise. Thus the propensity toward friendly fascism lies deep in American society. There may even be a little bit of neofascism in those of us who are proudest of our antifascist credentials and commitments.

"You're either part of the solution," wrote Eldridge Cleaver in the 1960s, "or you're part of the problem." By now I think this statement must be both stood on its head and reformulated: "If you can't see that you're part of the problems, then you're standing in the way of attacks on them." It has taken me a long time to concede that I (and my colleagues) have often been a large part of the new Leviathan's entourage. In any case, I no longer am. I no longer regard decentralization or counterbalancing of power as either impossible or undesirable. I see Big Business and Big Government as a joint danger.

For the majority of the population, of course, this is common knowledge. What almost everybody really knows is that the fanfare of elections and "participatory" democracy usually disguises business-government control. Some years ago, a few students popularized this conjugation of the verb "participate":

I participate.	We participate.
You (singular) participate.	You (plural) participate.
He, she or it participates.	THEY decide.

In a world of concentrated, impersonal power, the important levers and wires are usually pulled by invisible hands. To no one is it given to look on many of the faces behind the hands. But everybody knows that THEY include both Big Business and Big Government. In a society dominated by mass media, world-spanning corporations, armies and intelligence agencies, and mysterious bureaucracies, THEY are getting stronger. Meanwhile, the majority of people have little part in the decisions that affect their families, workplaces, schools, neighborhoods, towns, cities, country, and the world. This is why there is declining confidence in the artificial images and rhetorical sales talks of corporate and political leaders and the many institutions which support them.

Some years ago Gunther Anders wrote a warning for the atomic age: "Frighten thy neighbor as thyself. This fear, of course, must be of a special kind: a fearless fear, since it excludes fearing those who would deride us as cowards; a stirring fear, since it would drive us into the streets instead of under the covers; a living fear, not *of* the danger ahead but *for* the generations to come."[6] If fear is to be fearless, stirring, and living, something else must be combined with it—in fact, envelop it.

That something is hope. I am not referring to any deterministic hope rooted in quasi-theological theories of inevitable emancipation through technological progress or proletarian revolution. I am referring to the kind of loving hope that is articulated in rising aspirations and actions toward a truly democratic America in a new world order.

In this hope I am encouraged by many visions of a future participatory democracy. I go along wholly with Alvin Toffler's objective in *Future Shock* of "the transcendence of technocracy and the substitution of more humane, more far-sighted, more democratic planning,"[7] and in *The Third Wave* of creating the "broadened democracy of a new civilization."

As a realistic futurist, however, I start with the past and the present. In part I, "The Roots of Friendly Fascism," I trace the sad logic of declining democrary in First World countries and of rising authoritarianism on the part of a few people at the Establishment's higher levels. For those who have been hiding their heads in the sand, this picture may be a present shock even more painful than Toffler's future shock.

A few years ago, William L. Shirer, whose monumental *The Rise and Fall of the Third Reich* certainly qualifies him as a penetrating observer, commented that America may be the first country in which fascism comes to power through democratic elections.[8] In part II, "The Specter of Friendly Fascism," I document this observation. These chapters provide chilling details on the despotic future that in the present already walks. Unlike Cassandra, I am not mad enough to prophesy what *will* happen. Looking at the future in the light of past trends and current tendencies, I warn against what *could* happen.

The main source of this new-style despotism, I show, is not the frenetics of the Extreme Right—the Know-Nothings, the private militias, the Ku Klux Klan, or the openly neofascist parties. Nor is it the crazies of the Extreme Left. True, either of these might play facilitating, tactical, or triggering roles. But the new order is likely to emerge rather as an outgrowth of powerful tendencies within the Establishment itself. It would come neither by accident nor as the product of any central conspiracy. It would emerge, rather, through the hidden logic of capitalist society's transnational growth and the groping responses to mounting crises in a dwindling capitalist world.

In tracing this situational logic, I try to see the changing crises in America and the world as they are viewed by the leaders of what is now a divided Establishment. I put myself in *their* position as they try to make the most of crises by unifying the Establishment's higher levels, enlarging its transnational outreach, and reducing popular aspirations at home. Without an analysis of this kind, preventive efforts will be myopic, if not blind.

There is an old adage that the cure for the weaknesses of democracy is more democracy. The reason it sounds hollow is that "democracy," like "fascism," is used in many entirely different—even contradictory—ways. When one uses the term to refer only to the formal machinery of representative government, the maxim is a meaningless cliché. Much tinkering with, and perhaps improvements in, democratic machinery might even be expected on the road to serfdom. But if democracy is seen in terms of the decentralization and counterbalancing of power, then the subject for analysis is the reconstructing of society itself.

In part III, "True Democracy," I discuss the endless processes of reconstruction. I show how the forces that have prevented friendly fascism from emerging already could be strengthened in the future. This, also, is not a prediction. It is a statement of what is possible, as well as desirable—and I concede at the start that it now seems less probable than a new despotism. But "in life," as Marvin Harris advises, "as in any game whose outcome depends on both luck and skill, the rational response to bad odds is to try harder." [9]

Fortunately, many people are already making the effort. In reviewing these warm currents, I show that they have an unfolding logic of their own—an alternative logic that includes and goes beyond the traditional American spirit of openness, willingness to experiment, "can do" optimism, and resistance to being pushed around. This is the long-term logic of democracy and of democratic response to crisis. This is a logic that helps define the endless agenda of things to be done and undone. It nurtures non-Utopian visions of true democracy. These are visions rooted in action to reduce the distances between THEM and US, and enlarge citizen activity and decentralized planning in our neighborhoods, cities, and counties. They are action-oriented visions of a country that no longer needs heroes and is led by large numbers of non-elitist leaders who recognize the ignorance of the wise as well as the wisdom of the ignorant.[10] And, above all, there is the vision of America as a true good neighbor in a new world order.

I have written parts of this book in other countries. There I have felt at first hand the fear in people's bones of renewed horrors stemming from American military force, economic penetration, or cultural domination. I have felt equally powerfully the hopes that people elsewhere have for those promises of American life that stand for peace, freedom, and progress. There is reason for these feelings.

As for America, I agree completely with Arnold Beichman that "This is a country in which one has the right to hope." [11] More than that, it is a place where millions of people exercise that right and have reason to do so. I hope that more people will gain the courage to raise their hopes still higher. In this context, and perhaps only thus, it is easier to escape the fear of fear and confront the serious dangers looming ahead. It takes ever-brimming hope—fused with realistic expectations, patience, impatience, anger, and love—to develop the courage to fear, and the sustained commitment to rekindle constantly our best promises.

ONE

The Roots of Friendly Fascism

Arturo Ui, referring to Adolf Hitler:
Let none of us exult too soon,
The womb is fruitful
From which this one crawled . . .

BERTOLT BRECHT,
The Resistible Rise of Arturo Ui

1

The Rise and Fall of Classic Fascism

BETWEEN THE TWO WORLD WARS fascist movements developed in many parts of the world.

In the most industrially advanced capitalist countries—the United States, Britain, France, Holland and Belgium—they made waves but did not engulf the constitutional regimes. In the most backward capitalist countries—Albania, Austria, Greece, Hungary, Poland, Portugal, Rumania, Spain, and Yugoslavia—there came to power authoritarian or dictatorial regimes that boastfully called themselves "fascist" or, as the term soon came to be an all-purpose nasty word, were branded "fascist" by their opponents. The most genuine and vigorous fascist movements arose in three countries—Italy, Germany and Japan—which, while trailing behind the capitalist leaders in industrialization and empire, were well ahead of the laggards.

ITALY, GERMANY, JAPAN

In Milan on March 23, 1919, in a hall offered by a businessmen's club, former socialist Benito Mussolini transformed a collection of black-shirted roughnecks into the Italian Fascist party. His word "fascism" came from the Latin *fasces* for a bundle of rods with an axe, the symbol of State power carried ahead of the consuls in ancient Rome. Mussolini and his comrades censured old-fashioned conservatives for not being more militant in opposing the socialist and communist movements that arose, in response to the depression, after World War I. At the same time, they borrowed rhetorical slogans from their socialist and communist foes, and strengthened their support among workers and peasants.

In their early days these groups had tough going. The more respectable elements in the Establishment tended to be shocked by their rowdy, untrustworthy nature. Campaign contributions from businessmen came in slowly and sporadically. When they entered electoral contests, the Fascists did badly. Thus, in their very first year of life the Italian Fascists suffered a staggering defeat by the Socialists.

In 1920 the left-wing power seemed to grow. Hundreds of factories were seized by striking workers in Milan, Turin, and other industrial areas. Peasant unrest became stronger, and many large estates were seized. The Socialists campaigned under the slogan of "all power to the proletariat."

For Mussolini, this situation was an opportunity to be exploited. He countered with a nationwide wave of terror that went far beyond ordinary strikebreaking. Mussolini directed his forces at destroying all sources of proletarian or peasant leadership. The Fascist *squadristi* raided the offices of Socialist or Communist mayors, trade unions, cooperatives and left-wing newspapers, beating up their occupants and burning down the buildings. They rounded up outspoken anti-Fascists, clubbed them, and forced them to drink large doses of castor oil. They enjoyed the passive acquiescence—and at times the direct support—of the police, the army, and the church. Above all, business groups supplied Mussolini with an increasing amount of funds. In turn, Mussolini responded by toning down the syndicalism and radical rhetoric of his followers, and, while still promising to "do something for the workers," began to extol the merits of private enterprise.

On October 26, 1922, as his Fascist columns started their so-called March on Rome, Mussolini met with a group of industrial leaders to assure them that "the aim of the impending Fascist movement was to reestablish discipline within the factories and that no outlandish experiments . . . would be carried out." [1] On October 28 and 29 he convinced the leaders of the Italian Association of Manufacturers "to use their influence to get him appointed premier." [2] In the evening of October 29 he received a telegram from the king inviting him to become premier. He took the sleeping train to Rome and by the end of the next day formed a coalition cabinet. In 1924, in an election characterized by open violence and intimidation, the Fascist-led coalition won a clear majority.

If Mussolini did not actually march on Rome in 1922, during the next seven years he did march into the hearts of important leaders in other countries. He won the friendship, support, or qualified approval of Richard Childs (the American ambassador), Cornelius Vanderbilt, Thomas Lamont, many newspaper and magazine publishers, the majority of business journals, and quite a sprinkling of liberals, including some associated with both *The Nation* and *The New Republic*. "Whatever the dangers of fascism," wrote Herbert Croly, in 1927, "it has at any rate substituted movement for stagnation, purposive behavior for drifting, and visions of great future for collective pettiness and discouragements." In these same years, as paeans of praise for Mussolini arose throughout Western capitalism, Mussolini consolidated his rule, purging anti-Fascists from the government service, winning decree power from the legislature, and passing election laws favorable to himself and his conservative, liberal, and Catholic allies.

Only a few days after the march on Rome, a close associate of Hitler, Herman Esser, proclaimed in Munich among tumultuous applause: "What has been done in Italy by a handful of courageous men is not impossible here. In Bavaria too we have Italy's Mussolini. His name is Adolf Hitler. . . ."

F. L. CARSTEN [3]

In January, 1919, in Munich, a small group of anti-Semitic crackpot extremists founded the German Workers Party. Later that year the German Army's district commander ordered one of his agents, a demobilized corporal, to investigate it. The Army's agent, Adolf Hitler, instead joined the party and became its most powerful orator against Slavs, Jews, Marxism, liberalism, and the Versailles treaty. A few months later, under Hitler's leadership, the party changed its name to the National Socialist German Workers' Party and organized a bunch of dislocated war veterans into brown-shirted strong-arm squads or storm troops (in German, S.A. for *Sturmabteilung*). The party's symbol, designed by Hitler himself, became a black swastika in a white circle on a flag with a red background.

On November 8, 1923, in the garden of a large Munich beer hall, Adolf Hitler and his storm troopers started what he thought would be a quick march to Berlin. With the support of General Erich Ludendorff, he tried to take over the Bavarian government. But neither the police nor the army supported the *Putsch*. Instead of winning power in Munich, Hitler was arrested, tried for treason, and sentenced to five years' imprisonment, but confined in luxurious quarters and paroled after only nine months, the gestational period needed to produce the first volume of *Mein Kampf*. His release from prison coincided with an upward turn in the fortunes of the Weimar Republic, as the postwar inflation abated and an influx of British and American capital sparked a wave of prosperity from 1925 to 1929. "These, the relatively fat years of the Weimar Republic, were correspondingly lean years for the Nazis." [4]

Weimar's "fat years" ended in 1929. If postwar disruption and class conflict brought the Fascists to power in Italy and nurtured similar movements in Germany, Japan, and other nations, the Great Depression opened the second stage in the rise of the fascist powers.

In Germany, where all classes were demoralized by the crash, Hitler recruited jobless youth into the S.A., renewed his earlier promises to rebuild the German army, and expanded his attacks on Jews, Bolshevism, the Versailles treaty, liberalism, and constitutional government. In September 1930, to the surprise of most observers (and probably Hitler himself), the Nazis made an unprecedented electoral breakthrough, becoming the second largest party in the country. A coalition of conservative parties, without the Nazis, then took over under General Kurt von Schleicher, guiding genius of the army. With aged Field Marshal von

Hindenberg serving as figurehead president, three successive cabinets—headed by Heinrich Bruening, Franz von Papen, and then von Schleicher himself—cemented greater unity between big business and big government (both civilian and military), while stripping the Reichstag of considerable power. They nonetheless failed miserably in their efforts to liquidate the Depression. Meanwhile Adolf Hitler, the only right-wing nationalist with a mass following, was publicly promising full employment and prosperity. Privately meeting with the largest industrialists he warned, "Private enterprise cannot be maintained in a democracy." On January 30, 1933, he was invited to serve as chancellor of a coalition cabinet. "We've hired Hitler!" a conservative leader reported to a business magnate.[5]

A few weeks later, using the S.A. to terrorize left-wing opposition and the Reichstag fire to conjure up the specter of conspiratorial bolshevism, Hitler won 44 percent of the total vote in a national election. With the support of the Conservative and Center parties, he then pushed through legislation that abolished the independent functioning of both the Reichstag and the German states, liquidated all parties other than the Nazis, and established concentrated power in his own hands. He also purged the S.A. of its semisocialist leadership and vastly expanded the size and power of his personal army of blackshirts.

Through this rapid process of streamlining, Hitler was able to make immediate payments on his debts to big business by wiping out independent trade unions, abolishing overtime pay, decreasing compulsory cartelization decrees (like similar regulations promulgated earlier in Japan and Italy), and giving fat contracts for public works and fatter contracts for arms production. By initiating an official pogrom against the Jews, he gave Nazi activists a chance to loot Jewish shops and family possessions, take over Jewish enterprises, or occupy jobs previously held by German Jews.

Above all, he kept his promise to the unemployed; he put them back to work, while at the same time using price control to prevent a recurrence of inflation. As Shirer demonstrates in his masterful *The Rise and Fall of the Third Reich*, Hitler also won considerable support among German workers, who did not seem desperately concerned with the loss of political freedom and even of their trade unions as long as they were employed full time. "In the past, for so many, for as many as six million men and their families, such rights of free men in Germany had been overshadowed as he [Hitler] said, by the freedom to starve. In taking away that last freedom," Shirer reports, "Hitler assured himself of the support of the working class, probably the most skillful and industrious and disciplined in the Western world." [6]

Also in 1919, Kita Ikki, later known as "the ideological father of Japanese fascism," set up the "Society of Those Who Yet Remain."

His *General Outline of Measures for the Reconstruction of Japan,* the *Mein Kampf* of this association, set forth a program for the construction of a revolutionized Japan, the coordination of reform movements, and the emancipation of the Asian peoples under Japanese leadership.[7]

In Japan, where organized labor and proletarian movements had been smashed many years earlier and where an oligarchic structure was already firmly in control, the transition to full-fledged fascism was—paradoxically—both simpler than in Italy and Germany and stretched out over a longer period. In the mid-1920s hired bullies smashed labor unions and liberal newspapers as the government campaigned against "dangerous thoughts," and used a Peace Preservation Law to incarcerate anyone who joined any organization that tried to limit private property rights. The worldwide depression struck hard in Japan, particularly at the small landholders whose sons had tried to escape rural poverty through military careers. The secret military societies expanded their activities to establish a Japanese "Monroe Doctrine for Asia." In 1931 they provoked an incident, quickly seized all of Manchuria, and early in 1932 established the Japanese puppet state of Manchukuo.

At home, the Japanese premier was assassinated and replaced by an admiral, as the armed forces pressed forward for still more rapid expansion on the continent and support for armament industries. As the frontiers of Manchukuo were extended, a split developed between two rival military factions. In February 1936, the Imperial Way faction attempted a fascist coup from below. Crushing the rebels, the Control faction of higher-ranking officers ushered in fascism from above. "The interests of business groups and the military drew nearer, and a 'close embrace' structure of Japanese fascism came to completion," writes Masao Maruyama. "The fascist movement from below was completely absorbed into totalitarian transformation from above."[8] Into this respectable embrace came both the bureaucracy and the established political parties, absorbed into the Imperial Rule Assistance Association. And although there was no charismatic dictator or party leader, the Emperor was the supercharismatic symbol of Japanese society as a nation of families. By 1937, with well-shaped support at home, the Japanese army seized Nanking and started its long war with China.

BREEDING GROUNDS OF FASCISM

Before fascism, the establishments in Italy, Japan, and Germany each consisted of a loose working alliance between big business, the military, the older landed aristocracy, and various political leaders. The origin of these alliances could be traced to the consolidation of government and industry during World War I.

"Manufacturing and finance," writes Roland Sarti about World War I in Italy (but in terms applicable to many other countries also), "drew even closer than they had been before the war to form the giant combines necessary to sustain the war effort. Industrialists and government officials sat side by side in the same planning agencies, where they learned to appreciate the advantages of economic planning and cooperation. Never before had the industrustrialists been so close to the center of political power, so deeply involved in the decision-making process." [9]

United in the desire to renew the campaigns of conquest that had been dashed by the war and its aftermath, the establishments in these countries were nonetheless seriously divided by conflicting interests and divergent views on national policy. As Sarti points out, big-business leaders were confronted by "economically conservative and politically influential agricultural interests, aggressive labor unions, strong political parties ideologically committed to the liquidation of capitalism, and governments responsive to a variety of pressures." [10] Despite the development of capitalist planning, coping with inflation and depression demanded more operations through the Nation-State than many banking and industrial leaders could easily accept, more government planning than most governments were capable of undertaking, and more international cooperation among imperial interests than was conceivable in that period.

The establishment faced other grave difficulties in the form of widespread social discontent amidst the uncertain and eventually catastrophic economic conditions of the postwar world. One of the challenges came from the fascists, who seemed to attack every element in the existing regimes. They criticized businessmen for putting profits above patriotism and for lacking the dynamism needed for imperial expansion. They tore at those elements in the military forces who were reluctant to break with constitutional government. They vilified the aristocracy as snobbish remnants of a decadent past. They branded liberals as socialists, socialists as communists, communists as traitors to the country, and parliamentary operations in general as an outmoded system run by degenerate babblers. They criticized the bureaucrats for sloth and branded intellectuals as self-proclaimed "great minds" (in Hitler's phrasing) who knew nothing about the real world. They damned the Old Order as an oligarchy of tired old men, demanding a New Order of young people and new faces. In Japan, the young blood was represented mainly by junior officers in the armed forces. In Italy and Germany the hoped-for infusion of new dynamism was to come from the "little men," the "common people," the "lost generation," the "outsiders," and "uprooted" or "rootless." Although some of these were gangsters, thugs, and pimps, most were white-collar workers, lower-level civil servants or, declassed artisans and small-business men.

But the fascist challenge did not threaten the jugular vein. Unlike the communists, the fascists were not out to destroy the old power structure or to create an entirely new one. Rather, they were heretics seeking to revive the old faith by concentrating on the fundamentals of imperial expansion, militarism, repression, and racism. They had the courage of the old-time establishment's convictions. If they at times sounded like violent revolutionaries, the purpose was not merely to pick up popular support from among the discontented and alienated, but to mobilize and channel the violence-prone. If at the outset they tolerated anti-capitalist currents among their followers, the effect was to enlarge the following for policies that strengthened capitalism. Above all, the fascists "wanted in."

In turn, at a time of crisis, leaders in the old establishment wanted them in as junior partners. These leaders operated on the principle that "If we want things to stay as they are, things will have to change." Ultimately, the marriage of the fascist elements with the old order was one of convenience. In Italy and Japan, the fascists won substantial control of international and domestic politics, were the dominant ideological force, and controlled the police. The old upper-class structure remained in control of the armed forces and the economy. In Japan, the upper-class military was successfully converted to fascism, but there were difficulties in winning over Japan's family conglomerates, the *zaibatsu*.

Thus, while much of the old order was done away with, the genuinely anti-capitalist and socialist elements that provided much of the strength in the fascist rise to power were suppressed. The existing social system in each country was actually preserved, although in a changed form.

THE AXIS

From the start fascism had been nationalist and militarist, exploiting the bitterness felt in Italy, Germany, and Japan over the postwar settlements. Italians, denied territories secretly promised them as enticement for entering the war, felt cheated of the fruits of victory. Japanese leaders chafed at the rise of American and British resistance to Japanese expansion in China, and resented the Allies' refusal to include a statement of racial equality in the Covenant of the League of Nations. Germans were outraged by the Versailles treaty; in addition to depriving Germany of 13 percent of its European territories and population, the treaty split wide open two of Germany's three major industrial areas and gave French and Polish industrialists 19 percent of Germany's coke, 17 percent of its blast furnaces, 60 percent of its zinc foundries, and 75 percent of its iron ore.[11]

Furthermore, each of the fascist nations could ground their expansion in national tradition. As far back as 1898, Ito Hirobumi, one of the founders of the "new" Japan after the Meiji restoration of 1868, had gone into great detail on Japan's opportunities for exploiting China's vast resources. While the late-nineteenth-century Italians and Germans were pushing into Africa, the Japanese had seized Korea as a stepping-stone to China and started eyeing Manchuria for the same purpose. Mussolini's imperial expansion in Africa was rooted, if not in the Roman empire, then in late nineteenth-century experience and, more specifically, in the "ignominy" of the 1896 Italian defeat by ill-armed Ethiopian forces in Aduwa. Hitler's expansionism harked back to an imperialist drive nearly a century old—at least.

Now, while Japan was seizing Manchuria, Mussolini responded to the crash by moving toward armaments and war. He used foreign aid to establish economic control over Albania, consolidating this position through naval action in 1934. In 1935 he launched a larger military thrust into Ethiopia and Eritrea.

By that time, the Nazi-led establishment in Germany was ready to plunge into the European heartland itself. In 1935, Hitler took over the Saarland through a peaceful plebiscite, formally repudiating the Versailles treaty. In 1936 he occupied the Rhineland and announced the formation of a Berlin-Rome Axis and the signing of a German-Japanese Pact. Hitler and Mussolini then actively intervened in the Spanish Civil War, sending "volunteers" and equipment to support General Franco's rebellion against Spain's democratically-elected left-wing republic.

The timetable accelerated: in 1938, the occupation of Austria in March and of Czechoslovakia in September; in 1939, the swallowing up of more parts of Czechoslovakia and, after conclusion of the Nazi-Soviet Pact in August, the invasion of Poland. At this point, England and France declared war on Germany and World War II began. Japan joined Italy and Germany in a ten-year pact "for the creation of conditions which would promote the prosperity of their peoples." As a signal of its good intentions, Japan began to occupy Indochina as well as China. Germany did even better. By 1941 the Germans had conquered Poland, Denmark, Norway, the Netherlands, Belgium, and France. They had thrown the British army into the sea at Dunkirk and had invaded Rumania, Greece, and Yugoslavia. A new world order seemed to be in the making.

For Japan, it was the "Greater East Asia Co-Prosperity Sphere," and for Italy a new Roman Empire to include "the Mediterranean for the Mediterraneans." And, for Germany, the new order was the "Thousand-Year Reich" bestriding the Euro-Slavic-Asian land mass.

ANTI-FASCIST FAILURES

Only one thing could have broken our movement: if the adversary had understood its principle and from the first day had smashed with extreme brutality the nucleus of our new movement.

ADOLF HITLER [12]

Neither at home nor abroad did fascism's adversaries understand the potentials of the major fascist movements and counter them effectively.

For many years, Mussolini's regime had been supported by American bankers. From 1933 up to the outbreak of World War II Hitler received tremendous financial aid from private British banks and the Bank of England itself. Government appeasement of fascist aggression went back to Western flabbiness in the face of Japan's seizure of Manchuria in 1932, the British negotiation of a 1935 naval treaty with Germany (which recognized Germany's right to rearm), the League of Nation's futile gestures over Mussolini's conquest of Ethiopia, and the general acquiescence to Hitler's occupation and militarization of the Rhineland. In early 1938, the Western powers stood idly by as Hitler's armies, with the help of the local Nazis, swallowed up Austria. Later in the same year the leaders of Britain, France, Germany, and Italy signed the famous Munich agreement, which authorized Germany to absorb the Sudetenland, that part of Czechoslovakia with a significant German population. Neville Chamberlain, the British Prime Minister, returned home announcing "peace with honor" and "peace in our time." Hitler responded by taking over all of Czechoslovakia.

The Western appeasement of fascist aggression was rooted in an unequal balance between interventionists and noninterventionists. The most influential interventionists were those forces committed to continuing dominance by the leading capitalist powers. In Europe their most outstanding spokesman was Winston Churchill, whose main interest was in preservation of the British Empire. In the United States, where old-time statesmen like Henry Stimson had futilely called for sanction against Japan for the seizure of Manchuria, many northeastern corporate and banking groups gradually came around to Churchill's position. As members of a decades-old Anglo-American alliance, they gradually began to see American intervention against Axis agression as reversing the relationship between the two countries and making this an "American Century" in the ultra-frank words of Henry Luce, editor of *Time, Life,* and *Fortune.* These interventionist forces were supported by anti-fascist refugees, the Jewish communities in democratic countries, many liberals and radicals, and—with the exception of the twenty-two months of the

Nazi-Soviet pact between August 23, 1939 and June 22, 1941—all Communist parties and their sympathizers.

For many years the noninterventionists prevailed. Many British, French, and American leaders came to realize that there was a genuine logic in the fascist calls for a revision of the Versailles treaty; they hoped that with limited expansions, the Axis appetites would be satisfied and that with a few minor changes the old order could be maintained. Others were immobilized by the vaunted Nazi superiority in warfare. Still others were genuinely upset by the possibilities of mass destruction inherent in the new-style warfare. In Europe, memories of World War I were too vivid for many Europeans to risk death defending the Spanish Republic or Czechoslovakia, let alone the distant Africans in Ethiopia. In the United States, a March 1937 Gallup poll reported that 94 percent of Americans favored staying out of all wars instead of taking the risks involved in trying to prevent them from erupting or spreading.

One of the most powerful forces behind noninterventionism was widespread Western endorsement of the Axis powers' anti-Russian stance. The Japanese seizure of Manchuria seemed more acceptable if Japan would then be encouraged to continue north and west into Siberia. Germany's drive to the east was more plausible if the Germans would be satisfied with swallowing up the Soviet Union and leave the other powers alone. At best the fascists and communists would bleed themselves to death and the old order would be rescued from the twin specters of communism and fascist expansion. Or else the Soviet regime might be destroyed and Russia "regained." At least the Axis powers and the Soviet Union would both be greately weakened, to the benefit of the Western democracies. Just as the French aristocrats and businessmen as far back as 1935 had sincerely believed "Better Hitler than Léon Blum," top business circles sincerely believed "Better Hitler than Stalin."

The leaders of the Soviet Union would also have preferred an isolationism of their own, standing by while the capitalist powers destroyed themselves in interimperialist warfare. Since this was unlikely, their major strategy was to try to divide the capitalist powers by linking up with one side or another. This was the logic of their Brest-Litovsk peace treaty of 1918, their Rapallo agreement with Germany in 1922, the winning of diplomatic recognition from Mussolini in 1924, the negotiation of trade agreements with the Weimar Republic, and the renewal of these agreements with Hitler in April 1933 (one of the first international acts of recognition of the Third Reich). At the same time, in an effort to develop a buffer zone against eastward German expansion, the Soviet union entered into a number of pacts with its Western neighbors. Nonaggression treaties with China, Poland, the Baltic states, Finland, and France became the prelude to a drive for "collective security against the aggressors" in the League of Nations, spearheaded by Foreign Commissar Maxim Litvinov. After Munich in 1938, as the prospects of collective security seemed dimmer, Stalin went back to the former Soviet policy of closer relations with Germany. Litvinov was replaced by Foreign Commisar Vyacheslav Molotov, who negotiated the Nazi-Soviet Pact of August 1939. A week later Hitler invaded Poland. By the next September, when the Axis of Germany, Italy, and Japan was finally cemented with ten-year pacts, he had conquered Norway, Denmark, Netherlands, Belgium, and France. The Battle of Britain was under way.

FASCIST EXPLOITS

The essence of the new fascist order was an exploitative combination of imperial expansion, domestic repression, militarism, and racism. Each of these elements had a logic of its own and a clear relation to the others.

Imperial expansion brought in the raw materials and markets needed for more profitable economic activity. By absorbing surplus energies as well as surplus capital, it diverted attention from domestic problems and brought in a flood of consumer goods that could—at least for a while—provide greater satisfactions for the masses.

Domestic repression in each of the three countries was essential to eliminate any serious opposition to imperialism, militarism, or racism. It was used to destroy the bargaining power of unions and the political power not only of communists, socialists, and liberals but of smaller enterprises. It helped hold down wages and social benefits and channel more money and power into the hands of big business and its political allies.

Militarism, in turn, helped each of the Axis countries escape from the depression, while also providing the indispensible power needed for both imperial ventures and domestic pacification.

All of the other elements were invigorated by racism, which served as a substitute for class struggle and a justification of any and all brutalities committed by members of the Master Race (whether Japanese, German, or Italian) against "inferior" beings. This may not have been the most efficient of all possible formulae for exploitation, but it was theirs.

No one of these elements, of course, was either new or unique. None of the "haves" among the capitalist powers, as the fascists pointed out again and again, had built their positions without imperialism, militarism, repression, and racism. The new leaders of the three "have nots," as the fascists pointed out, were merely expanding on the same methods. "Let these 'well-bred' gentry learn," proclaimed Hitler, "that we do with a clear conscience the things they secretly do with a guilty one." [13] There was nothing particularly new in Mussolini's imperialism and militarism.

His critics at the League of Nations in 1935, when a weak anti-Italian embargo was voted on, may have seemed shocked by his use of poison gas against Ethiopian troops, but he did nothing that French, British, English, and Dutch forces had not done earlier in many other countries. The Japanese and Germans, however, were a little more original. In China and other parts of Asia, the Japanese invaders used against Koreans, Chinese, Burmese, Malayans, and other Asians even harsher methods than those previously used by white invaders. Similarly, up to a certain point, the Nazi war crimes consisted largely of inflicting on white Europeans levels of brutality that had previously been reserved only for Asians, Africans, and the native populations of North, Central, and South America.

In open violation of the so-called "laws of war," German, Japanese, and Italian officials—to the consternation of old-style officers from the upper class "gentry"—ordered the massacre of prisoners. All three regimes engaged in large-scale plunder and looting.

Since German-occupied Europe was richer than any of the areas invaded by the Japanese or Italians, the Nazi record of exploitation is more impressive. "Whenever you come across anything that may be needed by the German people," ordered *Reichsmarschall* Goering, "you must be after it like a bloodhound. . . ."[14] The Nazi bloodhounds snatched all gold and foreign holdings from the national banks of seized countries, levied huge occupation costs, fines and forced loans, and snatched away tons of raw materials, finished goods, art treasures, machines, and factory installations.

In addition to this unprecedented volume of looting, the Nazis revived the ancient practice of using conquered people as slaves. In doing so, they went far beyond most previous practices of imperial exploitation. By 1944, "some seven and a half million civilian foreigners were toiling for the Third Reich. . . . In addition, two million prisoners of war were added to the foreign labor force." Under these conditions German industrialists competed for their fair share of slaves. As key contributors to the "Hitler Fund," the Krupps did very well. "Besides obtaining thousands of slave laborers, both civilians and prisoners of war, for its factories in Germany, the Krupp firm also built a large fuse factory at the extermination camp at Auschwitz, where Jews were worked to exhaustion and then gassed to death."[15]

Domestic repression by the fascists was directed at both working-class movements and any other sources of potential opposition. In all three countries the fascists destroyed the very liberties which industrialization had brought into being; if more was destroyed in Germany than in Italy and more in Italy than in Japan, it was because there was more there to destroy.

All three regimes succeeded in reducing real wages (except for the significant increments which the unemployed attained when put to work by the armaments boom), shifting resources from private consumption to private and public investment and from smaller enterprises to organized big business, and channeling income from wages to profits. As these activities tended to "de-class" small entrepreneurs and small landowners, this added to the pool of uprooted people available for repressive activities, if not for the armed services directly. Moreover, each of the three regimes attained substantial control over education at all levels, cultural and scientific activities, and the media of communication.

In Germany, however, domestic repression probably exceeded that of any other dictatorial regime in world history. An interesting, although little known, example is provided by Aktion t 4. In this personally signed decree, Hitler ordered mercy killing for hospital patients judged incurable, insane, or otherwise useless to the war effort, thereby freeing hospital beds for wounded soldiers. At first the patients were "herded into prisons and abandoned castles and allowed to die of starvation." Since this was too slow, the Nazis then used "a primitive gas chamber fed by exhaust fumes from internal combustion engines." Later they used larger gas chambers where "ducts shaped like shower nozzles fed coal gas through the ceiling . . . Afterward the gold teeth were torn out and the bodies cremated." Two years later, after about ten thousand Germans were killed in this manner, a Catholic bishop made a public protest and the extermination campaign was called off.[16]

By this time, however, Aktion t 4 had been replaced by Aktion f 14, "an adaptation of the same principles to the concentration camps, where the secret police kept their prisoners—socialists, communists, Jews and antistate elements." By the time he declared war on the United States in December 1941, Hitler extended Aktion f 14 to all conquered territories in his "Night and Fog" (*Nacht und Nebel*) decree, through which millions of people were spirited away with no information given their families or friends. This was an expansion of the *lettres de cachet* system previously used by French monarchs and the tsar's police against important state prisoners. Under this method untold thousands vanished into the night and fog never to be heard of again.[17]

Each of the three regimes, moreover, developed an extra-virulent form of racism to justify its aggressive drive for more and more "living space" (in German, the infamous *Lebensraum*). Italian racism was directed mainly against the Africans—although by the time Italy became a virtual satellite of Nazi Germany, Mussolini started a massive anti-Jewish campaign. Japanese racism was directed mainly against the Chinese, the Indochinese, and in fact, all other Asiatic people and served to justify, in Japanese eyes, the arrogance and brutality of the Japanese troops. The largest target of Nazi racism was the Slavs, who inhabited all of the Eastern regions destined to provide *Lebensraum* for the Master Race.

And during W[illegible]II more Slavs were killed than any other group of war victims [illegible]ious history.

But Nazi [illegible]m went still deeper in its fanatical anti-Semitism. Hitler, of cours[illegible] did not invent anti-Semitism, which ran as a strand through most significant ideologies of the previous century. While a strong strain of anti-Semitism has usually characterized the Catholic church, Martin Luther, the founder of Protestantism, went further in urging that Jewish "synagogues or schools be set on fire, that their houses be broken up and destroyed." [18] Nazi anti-Semitism brought all these strands together into a concentrated form of racism that started with looting, deprived the German Jews (about a quarter of a million at that time) of their citizenship and economic rights under the Nuremberg Laws of 1935, and then—following Martin Luther's advice with a vengeance—led to the arson, widespread looting, and violence of the *Kristolnacht* ("The Night of the Broken Glass") of November 1938. Early in 1939 Hitler declared, in a Reichstag speech, that if a world war should ensue, "the result will be . . . the annihilation of the Jewish race throughout Europe," a threat and near-prophecy that he kept on repeating in his public statements. A few weeks after the Nazi invasion of Russia he started to make it a reality with a decree calling for a "total solution" (*Gesamtlosung*) or "final solution" (*Endlosung*) of the Jewish question in all the territories of Europe which were under German influence. The "final solution" went through various stages: at first simply working Jews to death, then gassing them in the old-style chambers used under Aktion t 4, then using still larger gas chambers capable of gassing six thousand prisoners a day—to the lilting music of *The Merry Widow*—through the use of hydrogen cyanide.

While business firms competed for the privilege of building the gas chambers and crematoria and supplying the cyanide, recycling enterprises also developed. The gold teeth were "melted down and shipped along with other valuables snatched from the condemned Jews to the Reichsbank. . . . With its vaults filled to overflowing as early as 1942, the bank's profit-minded directors sought to turn the holdings into cold cash by disposing of them through the municipal pawnshops." Other recycling operations included using the hair for furniture stuffing, human fat for making soap, and ashes from the crematoria for fertilzer. While a small number of cadavers were used for anatomical research or skeleton collections, a much larger number of live persons—including Slavs as well as Jews—were used in experimental medical research for the German Air Force on the effects on the human body of simulated high-altitude conditions and immersion in freezing water. All in all, of an estimated 11 million Jews in Europe, between 5 and 6 million were killed in the destruction chambers (and work gangs or medical laboratories) at Auschwitz, Treblinka, Belsen, Sibibor and Chelmna, as well as minor camps that used such old-fashioned methods as mere shooting.[19]

FASCIST IDEOLOGIES

The motivating vigor of German, Japanese, and Italian fascism transcended ordinary versions of the carrot (whether in the form of increased profits, power, prestige, or loot) and the stick (whether in the form of ostracism, torture, or sheer terror). Both the leaders of the fascist establishment and the many millions who did their bidding were impelled by sentiments and convictions. Any conflicting values were for many Germans, Japanese, and Italians consigned to the inner depths of conscience, to return only in the face of military defeat and postwar reprisals.

Centrally controlled propaganda was a major instrument for winning the hearts of the German, Japanese, and Italian people. The growth of the control apparatus coincided with the flowering during the 1920s and 1930s of new instruments of propagandistic technology, particularly the radio and the cinema, with major forward steps in the arts of capitalist advertising. "Hitler's dictatorship," according to Albert Speer, "was the first dictatorship of an industrial state in this age of technology, a dictatorship which employed to perfection the instruments of technology to dominate its own people." [20] Apart from technology, each of the Axis powers used marching as an instrument of dominating minds. In discussing this method of domination, one of Hitler's early colleagues, Hermann Rauschning, has given us this explanation: "Marching diverts men's thoughts. Marching kills thought. Marching makes an end of individuality. Marching is the indispensable magic stroke performed in order to accustom the people to a mechanic, quasi-ritualistic activity until it becomes second nature." [21]

The content of fascist propaganda, however, was more significant than its forms or methodology. In essence, this content was a justification of imperial conquest, rampant militarism, brutal repression, and unmitigated racism. Many fascist theorists and intellectuals spun high-flown ideologies to present each of these elements in fascist exploitation in the garb of glory, honor, justice, and scientific necessity. The mass propagandists, however (including not only Hitler, Mussolini, and their closest associates, but also the flaming "radicals" of the Japanese ultra-right), wove all these glittering abstractions into the superpageantry of a cosmic struggle between Good and Evil, between the Master Race which is the fount of all culture, art, beauty, and genius and the inferior beings (non-Aryans, non-Romans, non-Japanese) who were the enemies of all civilization. As the stars and the planets gazed down upon this apocalyptic struggle, the true defenders of civilization against bolshevism and racial impurity must descend to the level of the enemies of culture and for the sake of mankind's future, do whatever may be necessary in the grim struggle for survival. Thus, bloodletting and blood sacrifice became a spiritual imperative for the people, an imperative transcending mere materialism.

This holy-war psychology was backed up by the indiscriminate use of any concept, any idea, theory, or antitheory that was useful at a particular time or place. Liberalism and monarchism, individualism and collectivism, hierarchic leadership and egalitarianism, scientific management and organic spontaneity, private enterprise and socialism, religion and atheism—all were drawn upon as the condition warranted—to polish the image of the nation's leader and play upon the emotions of both establishment and masses. No human interest, drive, or aspiration was safe from exploitation. To help in organizing support of specific groups, promises were made to workers as well as businessmen, peasants as well as landowners, rural folk as well as urbanites, the old nobility as well as the "common man," the old as well as the young, women as well as men. Once, in a Berlin speech before becoming chancellor, Hitler even promised, "In the Third Reich every German girl will find a husband." [22]

DESTRUCTION OF THE AXIS

While Nazi bombs were raining down on England, Colonel Charles A. Lindbergh, the American aviation hero, predicted that England would quickly collapse before Germany's superior equipment and spirit. His author-wife, Anne Morrow Lindbergh, proclaimed that the fascist leaders "have felt the wave of the future and they have leapt upon it . . ." [23]

And yet, as we now know, the wave was weaker than it seemed and was at last to be fiercely fought.

The first weakness was overextension by each Axis country. From the very beginning Mussolini went further in foreign adventures than the Italians—even those in uniform—were willing to accept. The Japanese leaders also suffered from dreams of easy glory. American researchers working for the War Crimes Trials in Tokyo were astounded to find that Japan's warlords had made no serious assessment of their capabilities for an extended war in the Pacific. The Nazis had the greatest blind spot of all. As Lawrence Dennis, America's most articulate fascist, put it, "Hitler and his top inner circle neither took the United States seriously as a possible armed foe in the future nor could they believe that the highly capitalistic United States ever could or would, line up with Communist Russia against Nazi Germany." [24] When the Nazis invaded the Soviet Union, they thought that the Americans would cheer them on or else simply stand by and let the Germans and Russians bleed each other white. By this mistaken position, they created a situation in which they themselves were soon to be bled white by a war on two fronts.

In comparison with the Americans, the Nazis were technologically backward. They did not lack for good scientists. Despite the loss of Jewish physicists who fled the country, the physicists who remained were among the best in the world. What they lacked—in terms that came into usage after the war—was a mature technostructure closely linked with top political and military leadership. In the autumn of 1942, outstanding Allied scientists had the ear of Roosevelt, Churchill, and their generals. The Hitler-Goering-Speer approach to technology was more circumscribed. Actually, it was Albert Speer himself, Hitler's chief aide on armament production, who scuttled the German atom bomb project at the very time the Americans and British were charging ahead at full speed.

Both overextension and technological backwardness, however, were relative matters. They would have hardly been decisive if the adversaries of the Axis had remained aloof or disunited. 1941 was a year of change. As American conservatives began to grasp the possibilities of the American Century and liberals to enthuse over the Century of the Common Man, noninterventionism began to ebb. The Lend-Lease Act gave President Roosevelt complete freedom to provide war material to any country whose defense he deemed vital to the United States. When the Germans invaded the Soviet Union in June, 1941, communists and their sympathizers all over the world switched to full-fledged interventionism. Almost as promptly, Churchill and Roosevelt pledged their support. By December 6, 1941, with help through Lend-Lease, Stalin was able—despite enormous reverses during the previous months—to mount the first Soviet counteroffensive against the German troops. On the following day, December 7, 1941, American noninterventionism was destroyed by the Japanese attack on the American navy at Pearl Harbor. From then, the U.S.-British-Soviet alliance became stronger.

This anti-Axis coalition lasted for fifty months. Its strength derived from the fact that it was grounded on certain limited common interests of the dominant groups in each of the three countries and wholehearted support by almost the entire population of each country. In both the Soviet Union and in Britain the war against the Axis soon became a struggle for national existence. In the United States, where national existence was not threatened, the war brought the Great Depression to an end and united the country in a high fever of activity that led the United States to become the dominant power of the world by 1945.

Thus the coalition was not an alliance against fascism as such. It was a temporary military alliance which, after knocking out the "new Roman Empire," shattered Hitler's "Thousand-Year Reich" (which lasted only twelve years) and destroyed the "Greater East Asia Co-Prosperity Sphere." In so doing, the coalition also destroyed its own reason for being.

INDESTRUCTIBLE MYTHS

One of the great successes of the classic fascists was to concoct misleading pronouncements on their purposes and practices. Anti-fascists have often accepted some of these self-descriptions or added part-truths of their own. The result has been a vast structure of apparently indestructible myths. Today, these myths still obscure the nature of classic fascism and of present tendencies toward new forms of the old horror.

Although the classic fascists openly subverted constitutional democracy and flaunted their militarism, they took great pains to conceal the Big Capital-Big Government partnership. One device for doing this was the myth of "corporatism" or the "corporate state." In place of geographically elected parliaments, the Italians and the Germans set up elaborate systems whereby every interest in the country—including labor—was to be "functionally" represented. In fact, the main function was to provide facades behind which the decisions were made by intricate networks of business cartels working closely with military officers and their own people in civilian government. In Japan, the corporate conglomerates called *zaibatsu* (wealth or money cliques) had already handled affairs along these lines; they merely tightened up.

A still more powerful device was the myth of the great leader who represents all the people and who makes all the decisions. Mussolini called the state a "violin in the hands of a maestro," namely, himself. The tune, however, was developed by the orchestra—namely, the Fascist establishment that unceremoniously dumped him shortly after the allied invasion of Italy. Although Hitler was much more of a top decision-maker, his personal power was won at the price of concentrating on certain matters and leaving huge realms of decision making to others—the well-developed style of today's corporate managers. Hugh R. Trevor-Roper reports on the Nazi establishment this way: "The structure of German politics and administration instead of being as the Nazis claimed, 'pyramidal' and 'monolithic,' was, in fact, a confusion of private empires, private armies and private intelligence services." [25]

In this situation of oligarchic in-fighting the cartels did very well indeed—just so long as they "paid their dues" to the Nazis and supported Hitler's foreign adventures on their behalf. In Japan, of course, the Emperor was the source of all authority and the fountainhead of all virtue—but at the same time largely a figurehead. In all three countries, with their varying degrees of control imposed on capital, corporate accumulation expanded enormously during the war and by war's end (despite the physical damage inflicted on their properties), was more highly developed and productive than ever before.

Since the end of the war, the role of big capital in classic fascism had been obscured by the myth of fascism as a revolt of "little people." This myth confuses an important source of support with the centers of power. There is no doubt that in all three countries the consolidation of the fascist establishment was supported by a psychological malaise that had hit the lower middle classes harder than anyone else. But if one examines the support base of classic fascism, it is hard to avoid the conclusion that the fascists had *multiclass support.* Many workers joined the fascist ranks—even former socialist and communist leaders. To the unemployed workers not represented by trade unions or the socialist movement, fascism offered jobs and security and delivered on this promise. Although the older aristocrats were somewhat divided on the subject, many highly respectable members of the landed aristocracy and nobility joined the fascist ranks. The great bulk of civil service bureaucrats was won over. Most leaders of organized religion (despite some heroic exceptions in Germany and some foot-dragging in Italy) either tacitly or openly supported the new regimes. Leading academicians, intellectuals, writers, and artists toed the line; the dissident minority who broke away or left the country made the articulation of support by the majority all the more important. Hitler enjoyed intellectual support, if not adulation, from the leading academicians in German universities. In Japan, the Showa Research Association brought many of the country's leading intellectuals together to help the imperial leaders formulate the detailed justifications for the New Asian Order. In Italy, fascism was supported not only by Giovanni Gentile, but also by such world-renowned figures as Vilfredo Pareto, Gaetano Mosca, Roberto Marinetti, Curzio Malaparte and Luigi Pirandello. No *Lumpenproletariat* nor rootless little men these!

Attention to the full structure of the fascist establishments has also been diverted by many observers who, as in the old Hindu story about the blind men trying to describe an elephant, have concentrated on separate parts of the beast.

Psychologists have found the essence of fascism in the "authoritarian personality" or the consequences of sexual repression. Ernst Nolte discovers the hidden wellsprings of fascism as a metapolitical outlook, which he terms "resistance to transcendence . . . a lurking, subterranean fear . . . of the inevitable disintegration of national communities, races and cultures." Peter Drucker argues that in revolt against the view of man as an economic unit, people turned toward "new sorcerers" like Hitler and Mussolini who could offer the values of heroism, self-sacrifice, discipline, and comradeship. Hannah Arendt carries this idea further by describing fascism as an extreme form of irrationality produced by man's isolation, alienation, and loss of class identity. She sees anti-Semitism as basic to fascist irrationality, while also maintaining that anti-Semitism was narrowly rational as a part of a conservative struggle to end the threat of liberalism and radicalism. No big capitalist body for these observers! They prefer to concentrate—and often do so brilliantly—on trunk, tail, legs, or ears.

Many communists, in contrast, have seized directly on the "private parts" (if that Victorian euphemism can be used for an elephant) by defining bourgeois democracy as a fig leaf. By an easy step, this leads to a vivid definition of fascism: capitalism in full nudity. Once the fig leaf is removed, the argument has gone, the workers can then see—in the words of the Communist International in 1928—fascism as "a system of direct dictatorship—a terrorist dictatorship of big capital."

This analysis contains at least five oversimplifications. First of all, instead of operating directly, big capital under fascism operated indirectly through an uneasy partnership with the fascist politicos, the military leaders, and the large landowners. If the privileged classes won many advantages as a result of the indispensable support they gave to the fascist regimes in Italy, Japan, and Germany, they also paid a high price. In addition to being subjected to various forms of political plunder, they lost control of many essential elements of policy, particularly the direction and tempo of imperial expansion. Second, the shift from constitutional to fascist capitalism meant structural changes, not merely the removal of a fig leaf. The fascists suppressed independent trade unions and working-class parties and consolidated big capital at the expense of small business. They destroyed the democratic institutions that capitalism had itself brought into being. They wiped out pro-capitalist liberation and old-fashioned conservatism as vital political forces. Third, while classic fascism was terroristic, it was also beneficient. The fascists provided jobs for the unemployed and upward mobility for large numbers of lower and middle class people. Although real wage rates were held down, these two factors alone—in addition to domestic political plunder and war booty—improved the material standard of living for a substantial number, until the whole picture was changed by wartime losses.

Fourth, instead of moving to full nudity, fascism decked itself up in a full-dress costume which obscured all its many obscenities, under the guise of "revolutionary" dynamism and the myths of fascist idealism, spirituality, populist (in German *volkisch*) sentiment, and the omnipotence of the fascist state, party or leader.

Finally, no member of the fascist Axis was reactionary in the traditional sense of "turning back the clock of history" or restoring some form of old regime. Each separately and all three together were engaged in the displacement of old-time reactionaries, as well as of the conservative defenders of the status quo at home or abroad. Through imperialism, militarism, repression, and racism, they aimed at a new order of capitalist exploitation.

The most widespread myth of all, however, is the simple equation "fascism equals brutality." In a masochistic poem about her father, Sylvia

Plath wrote, "Every woman loves a fascist—the boot in the face." Although I refuse to think she was really speaking for every woman, her words illustrate the popular identification of fascism with sadism in any form—from war and murder to torture, rape, pillage, and terrorism. In this sense a brutal foreman, a violent cop, or even a teacher who rides roughshod over his or her students may be called a "fascist pig."

One difficulty with this metaphor is that for thousands of years hundreds of governments have been fiercely brutal—sometimes on conquered people only, often on their own people also. If we stick by this terminology, then many of the ancient Greeks and Hebrews, the old Roman, Persian, Byzantine, Indian, and Chinese empires, the Huns, the Aztecs, and the tsars who ruled Russia were also fascist. Some of these, let me add, also exercised total control over almost all aspects of human life. Indeed, "force, fraud and violence," as Carl Friedrich and Zbigniew Brzezinski have pointed out, "have always been features of organized government and they do not constitute by themselves the distinctively totalitarian operation." [26] But concentrated capital, modern-style government, and constitutional democracy are relatively new features of human history—as is also the kind of Big Business-Big Government alliance that subverts constitutional democracy. Anyone has the constitutional right to pin the label "fascist" or "fascistic" on the brutalities of a Stalin or his heirs in various "Marxist-Leninist" countries, or on the bloodbath inflicted by American firepower on Indochina for a full decade, or even on the latest case of police brutality in a black or Latin ghetto of New York City. This may be a forceful way of protesting brutality. It is much less than a serious examination of the realities of classic fascism or the accumulating tendencies toward new forms of fascism toward the end of the twentieth century.

2

The Takeoff Toward a New Corporate Society

The multinational corporations are unifying world capital and world labor into an interlocking system of cross penetration that completely changes the system of national economics that characterized world capitalism for the past three hundred years.

STEPHEN HYMER [1]

The United States cannot shape the world single-handed—even though it may be the only force capable of stimulating common efforts to do so.

ZBIGNIEW BRZEZINSKI [2]

As long as the economic system provides an acceptable degree of security, growing material wealth and opportunity for further increase for the next generation, the average American does not ask who is running things or what goals are being pursued.

DANIEL R. FUSFELD [3]

AS WORLD WAR II drew to a close, the victories of the anti-Axis forces triggered one crisis after another.

The first was economic jitters. In Washington we all knew that it was only the war that pulled us out of the Great Depression of 1929–39. Might not the war's end bring back the Depression? When Mussolini fell in 1943, postwar planning became high fashion in Washington and London. A year later, when the second front was opened against Germany, politicians began to vie with each other in promising "jobs for all" after the war. When Berlin fell, the British voters threw Winston Churchill out of office, fearing that under Churchill's form of conservative capitalism mass unemployment would return. When the Japanese surrendered, postwar planning went into high gear. I remember being called back from a brief vacation to organize the congressional hearings on full-employment legislation.

The atom bomb detonated another crisis. When Churchill told Lord Moran, his secretary, of the decision to bomb Japan, Moran wrote in his diary with shivering hand:

> I was deeply shocked . . . It was not so much the morality of the thing, it was simply that the linchpin that has been under pinning the world had been half-wrenched out of its socket. [4]

The shock did not disappear. "Every man, woman and child," warned President John F. Kennedy some years later, "lives under a nuclear sword of Damocles, hanging by the slenderest of threads, capable of being cut at any moment by accident, miscalculation or madness."

A more immediate crisis was the loss of one country after another to "Marxist-Leninist" regimes. Even before Hiroshima, Stalin's armies had taken over most of Eastern Europe. Immediately after Hiroshima, the Soviet armies rolled through Manchuria and North Korea. It was only the atomic explosions, which hastened the inevitable surrender of Japan, which kept them from descending into northern Japan. At Hanoi in September 1945 Ho Chi Minh proclaimed the Democratic Republic of Vietnam. In China, Mao Tse-tung's Red Army mobilized the peasants against Chiang Kai-shek, who was supported by the United States and Britain. By 1949 the People's Republic of China was set up and "we"—that is, the capitalist world—lost China. Amaury de Riencourt, the French historian, recorded that in the United States this was felt as "a personal insult" and "a stunning blow" more shocking than the Russian revolution of a generation earlier.[5] During this same period communist resistance movements were deployed in Laos, Cambodia, Thailand, Malaya, Indonesia, the Philippines, Burma, and Northern Iran. And in Italy and France, the capitalism of Western Europe's heartland was threatened by socialist and communist movements, which had won enormous prestige in the struggle against Mussolini and Hitler.

Finally, as though by an uncontrollable chain reaction, the old colonial empires were unravelled. Japan and Italy lost all their colonies promptly. But decolonization—often supported by the United States—also struck the French, Dutch, and Belgians. And after India's independence in 1947, the British Empire—without Churchill to preside over the process—was rapidly liquidated. It was obvious to all observers that by the 1960s political independence would be given to—or won by—almost all the colonies in Asia, the Middle East, Latin America, and the Caribbean.

With old empires breaking into pieces, economic collapse lurking around the corner, and anticapitalist movements gaining power, capitalist leaders faced an unprecedented challenge.

This challenge could not have been met merely by cold, warm, or hot wars against communism and socialism. Nor could it have been coped with by reviving the classic fascist regimes or returning to old-style conservatism, liberalism, or reformism. The logic of the situation called for something much more positive. Under American leadership it was supplied.

During the war thousands of businessmen, political leaders, military officers, and their professional, scientific, and technical aides had grown accustomed to working together on national and world affairs. Some of them were consciously preparing for the "American Century." As the war ended, they won the quick support of major elites in Western Europe and Japan in reconciling the contradictions among capitalist countries, fighting communism and socialism in a more unified manner, and moderating the capitalist business cycle. This is how it happened that they converted a bleak and squalid system from a cataclysmic failure in the 1930s into a formidable, if faulty, "engine of prosperity." [6] Without returning to classic fascism, they developed a new, expanding, and remarkably flexible—even to the point of sharp internal conflicts—structure of business-government partnership. If in the process constitutional rights had been thoroughly suppressed in many dependent countries, civil rights and civil liberties (although not all) were at the same time considerably expanded not only in America, but also in America's newfound allies, the former Axis powers.

THE SUN NEVER SETS ON AMERICA'S "FREE WORLD"

> In the realities of the capitalist system . . . "inter-imperialist or ultra-imperialist" alliances are inevitably nothing more than a truce between wars.
>
> V. I. LENIN [7]

Before World War II the idea of a single leader of world capitalism was a new one. For almost two centuries the dominant pattern had been bitter rivalry and recurring warfare among the capitalist powers. Nor did the business and political leaders of the other capitalist powers respond to the challenge of socialism and communism by trying to thrust leadership into the hands of the United States. They simply sought help in warding off the communist specter at home (and received it) and in trying to keep control of former colonies (which, generally, they did not receive).

For most communist leaders, the idea of an integrated world capitalist bloc was a theoretical impossibility. Even Lenin's close associate Nikolai Bukharin, who first referred to "the formation of a golden international," pointed out that the tendencies towards integration were opposed by fierce capitalist nationalism that would lead to "the greatest convulsions and catastrophes." [8] Lenin was even more vehement on the subject. He argued that before any ultra-imperialism is reached, "imperialism will inevitably explode" and "capitalism will turn into its opposite." [9] After Lenin died and Bukharin was liquidated, Stalin continuously restated the dictum that it was impossible for the major capitalist powers to get together. By the time his message was fully absorbed by loyal followers in many countries, the "impossible"—spurred on by the spread of communism itself—was already taking place.

As American leaders—political, economic, military, and cultural—were preparing for the American Century, they rushed in to extend a protecting arm over the major capitalist countries, fill the vacuums left by their departure from former colonies, and seek decisive influence over all parts of the globe up to (or even across) communist boundaries. In response to each extension of communism, American leadership strove to integrate the noncommunist world into a loose network of constitutional democracies, authoritarian regimes, and military dictatorships described as the "Free World."

For conservative commentators, the word "empire" is more descriptive. It emphasizes the responsibilities of imperial leadership with respect to protectorates, dependencies, client states, and satellites, without suggesting the Marxist connotations of "imperialism." Thus Richard Van Alstyne, George Liska, Amaury de Riencourt, and Raymond Aron have written insightful books, respectively, about *The Rising American Empire* (1960), *Imperial America* (1967), *The American Empire* (1968), and *The Imperial Republic* (1974).

If this be empire, it is very different from—as well as much larger than—any previous empire. First of all, the "imperium" (to use another word favored by conservative observers) is not limited to preindustrial countries. It also includes the other major countries of industrial capitalism: Canada, Japan, the countries of the North Atlantic Treaty Alliance (including Belgium, Britain, Denmark, France, Greece, Iceland, Italy, Luxembourg, the Netherlands, Portugal, Turkey, and West Germany), Spain, Australia, New Zealand, and Israel. In turn, instead of being excluded from America's preindustrial protectorates, the largest corporations in most of these countries share with American corporations the raw material, commodity, labor, and capital markets of the third world.

Then, too, U.S. imperial control is exercised not by American governors and colonists, but by less direct methods, (sometimes described as "neocolonialism"). This has involved the development of at least a dozen channels of influence operating within subordinate countries of the "Free World":

- The local subsidiaries or branches of transnational businesses, including banks
- U.S. foreign military bases, which reached a peak of more than 400 major bases (and 3,000 minor ones) in 30 countries

- The C.I.A. and other intelligence agencies
- U.S. agencies providing economic and military aid through loans, grants, and technical assistance
- U.S. embassies, legations, and consulates
- The local operations of U.S. media (radio, TV, magazines, cinema) and public relations and consulting firms
- The local operations of U.S. foundations, universities, and research and cultural institutions
- Local power centers and influential individuals, friendly or beholden to U.S. interests
- Local armed forces, including police, equipped or trained in whole or part by U.S. agencies
- Subordinate governments—like Brazil, the Philippines, and Iran under the Shah—capable of wielding strong influence in their regions
- Transnational regional agencies such as NATO, the European Economic Community and the Organization of American States
- Agencies of the United Nations, particularly the World Bank and the International Monetary Fund

While these channels of influence have frustrated the efforts of any U.S. ambassador to establish personal control and have pushed final coordinating responsibilities to the level of the White House and the president's National Security Council, the net result has been a remarkably flexible control system in which competing views on strategy and tactics make themselves felt and are resolved through mutual adjustment. When serious mistakes are made, they can be corrected without injury to the dominant forces of a system that can adjust, however painfully, to the loss of any single leader, no matter how prominent. During the Korean War, when General Douglas MacArthur erred in driving through North Korea toward the Chinese border (which brought the Chinese into the war and lost the U.S.-occupied portion of North Korea to the capitalist world), he was promptly replaced. When President Lyndon Johnson erred in overcommitting U.S. troops and resources to the Indochinese war, he was pressured into retiring from the 1968 presidential campaign. Moreover, when new conditions call for new policies, the leaders of transnational corporations may move flexibly where political and military leaders fear to tread—as with corporate initiatives in commercial relations with the Soviet Union, China, and Cuba.

Moreover, the economic functions of subordinate countries now go far beyond those described many decades ago by Hobson and Lenin. Many Third World countries have become, or are about to become:

- Markets for raw materials, particularly wheat produced in the United States, Canada, and Australia
- Sources of trained technicians and professionals who may then move

through the so-called "brain drain" into the skilled-labor markets of the major capitalist countries

- Channels for mobilizing local capital which may then be invested locally under foreign control or repatriated to finance investment in the industrialized countries
- Sources of low-cost labor for transnational subsidiaries which then manufacture industrial goods that are marketed in the major capitalist countries as well as locally

This last point bears special attention. There used to be a time when industrialization—often referred to by the magic word "development"—was seen as the road to economic independence. As it has emerged, however, industrial development has usually been a process of converting preindustrial dependencies into industrial dependencies. Previously, many left-wing revolutionary movements aimed to throw off the yoke of imperialism by joining with the native capitalists in "national revolutions." What has often happened, however, is that the local capitalists have supplanted the old landowning oligarchs in trying to cooperate with, rather than break with, foreign capital. Instead of "ugly Americans" or Europeans meddling in their affairs, many Third World regimes are increasingly manned by Americanized Brazilians, Anglicized Indians and Nigerians, and Westernized Saudi Arabians and Egyptians. As dependent industrialism grows, moreover, its roots spread deeply into the state bureaucracies, in the universities and among the managerial, technical, professional, and intellectual elites. As this happens, military control or the threat of a military takeover becomes somewhat less essential and the military themselves became more civilianized, if not even subordinate to corporate economic interests. Thus a huge infrastructure of dependency is developed which Susanne Bodenheimer sees as "the functional equivalent of a formal colonial apparatus." [10] In fact, external controls are now internalized in domestic institutions, and the new infrastructure may be more powerful than any previous colonial apparatus.

Thus, with the old oligarchies pushed aside by industrial development, the sons and grandsons of the preindustrial chieftains and feudal aristocrats leap from landowning to stockholding, from the protection of ancient privileges to the glory of new privileges as the local agents—at times, even junior partners—of the new industrial oligarchs of the "New World" empire. The lands they still own allow them to keep one foot in the past, thus easing the transition, or better yet, allowing them to move into the new world of chemically fertilized, supermechanized, and superseeded agribusiness.

Moderate nationalization is also being absorbed into the structure of dependent industrialism. On the one hand, in countries where sweeping nationalization had been undertaken earlier—as in Nasser's Egypt, Sukarno's Indonesia, Vargas's and Goulart's Brazil, and the first Peron regime in Argentina—national undertakings are being either placed into private ownership or else run like private firms. On the other hand, nationalization is also being used to directly aid private and foreign capital. The monetary policies of a government-owned central bank, as in India, and the credit policies of investment promotion corporations, as in Mexico and Indonesia, have long served to promote capitalist enterprises. Socialized enterprises in utilities, transportation, communication, and water are being used to subsidize private firms by providing them with essential services at nonprofit or below-cost prices. More nationalization of this type is under way—particularly in basic mineral, forest, and land resources.

Oil, of course, is the biggest issue. In Venezuela, nationalization of currently developed oil reserves, previously scheduled to come into effect by 1983, was completed in 1975—under terms that proved a bonanza to the foreign companies. Similarly, nationalization moved steadily forward in the Middle East, with Libya and Iraq taking the lead and Saudi Arabia and the smaller sheikhdoms trailing behind. But there is little prospect that the nationalization of oil would promote socialization in other sectors, any more than it did during the decades after Mexico's expropriation of foreign oil companies. On the contrary, it seems likely that the bulk of any additional money obtained from the larger share of oil profits will be plowed into private enterprise at home and abroad. This is one of the strange lessons of the oil embargo and price increases of 1973–74 and the spectacular rise since then in the oil income of the oil-exporting countries. Although the embargo was widely regarded as an anti-Western move inspired by the Russians, its long-range effect has been to bring the Arab countries more fully than before into the world capitalist market as well as to foster dependent industrialism in the entire Arab world. More extensive (albeit limited) nationalization will probably have a similar effect, with American and European oil companies beating a slow retreat from extraction, organizing joint private-government refineries and petrochemical complexes, trying to maintain their monopoly on worldwide distribution, and at the same time expanding their operations in natural gas, coal, atomic energy, and any other energy sources that may become profitable.

In some countries of dependent industrialism where capitalist expansion has proceeded most rapidly, the degree of dependence on the First World has lessened somewhat and the native capitalist and political leaders have developed the capability to define themselves as something slightly above the level of mere pawns or clients. Thus the military junta of Brazil has for many years held full status as a "subimperial power," influencing events in Paraguay, Uruguay, Bolivia, and other Latin American countries. "We too can invoke a Manifest Destiny," one of its leaders stated in the early 1970s, "even more so because it does not clash in the Caribbean with that of our older brothers to the North." [11]

Brazil's worldwide position is buttressed not only by its formidable growth rate but also by its purchase of nuclear reactor facilities from West Germany and its ill-concealed intentions of becoming a nuclear power. For all these reasons it was natural for Secretary of State Kissinger in 1976 to reach an agreement to consult with Brazil on all major events of international importance. This agreement has not been abrogated by the Carter administration.

But Brazil is not the only Third World country to seek subimperial status. In Latin America, oil-rich Venezuela may become a close rival. In West Asia, the largest subimperial drive was attempted by Iran under the Shah. Other major aspirants, provided they can achieve greater domestic stability, are Indonesia, the Philippines, and Zaire. In all of these countries, government tends to play a more central economic role than in the First World. From a longer-range view, India has the greatest subimperial potential. Although weakened by the poverty of its vast population and its lack (thus far) of domestic petroleum, India nonetheless possesses an industrial establishment and a science-technology elite far beyond that of Brazil or any other Third World country.

Some of the countries I have just referred to are frequently attacked as "fascist." This attack has also been levied against the regimes of other countries that have little ground for subimperial aspirations—such as Argentina, Bolivia, Chile, Haiti, and Paraguay.

Most of the governments in these countries are crude military dictatorships with few compunctions about wiping out most domestic freedoms in defense of the freedoms of domestic oligarchies and First World interests. Sheer brutality, however, as I have pointed out earlier, does not qualify a regime as fascist; its regime must also be interlocked with concentrated capital. Yet big capital is growing in these countries—albeit in forms that are mainly dependent on First World support and initiatives. Hence these can best be seen as countries of "dependent fascism." In some of the countries, as the domestic oligarchies become more closely linked with transnational capital, the regimes tend to become more sophisticated in drawing velvet gloves over iron fists and in assuming a "friendlier" visage.

THE GOLDEN INTERNATIONAL

Long before World War II, the larger capitalist corporations spread around the world in their efforts to obtain raw materials and sell manufactured products; a few developed manufacturing facilities in other countries. But they did these things in the context of deadly struggle among capitalist nations. After World War II, they reached an entirely new stage of international development by transcending the old limits on the location of activity. They learned how to do almost anything any place—to engage in manufacturing and service enterprises in former colonies, to use foreign subsidiaries to vault over or under trade and credit barriers, to mobilize both equity and loan capital in other countries. The modern transnational corporation not only internationalized production, it became the only organization with resources and scope to think, to plan, and to act in developing global sources of raw materials. This wider scope of planning has given the transnationals the advantage of escaping whatever inhibitions might be imposed by national policies on currency, credit, trade, and taxes, and of allowing them to play national currencies and governments against each other. It has also put them in the strategic position of encouraging and profiting from the larger markets made available through the European Economic Community and other regional arrangements. Within these larger markets the transnationals have worked together (while also competing) to contain left-wing movements, subvert left-wing regimes, and maintain the integrity of the "Free World" empire.

The flexibility of the larger transnationals is enhanced by the fact that most of them have become conglomerates. No longer limited to specific sectors, their business is to get money and power, not make specific products. Competence in producing this or that specific product need no longer be built up over generations; it can be bought. Thus the giant Western oil companies have bought into coal, natural gas, uranium, atomic energy, and solar energy. Some have gone still wider, entering computers, retailing, and engine manufacture. Wide-spectrum transnational conglomerates like ITT and Gulf & Western have brought together scores of subsidiaries in such diverse fields as telephones, mining, sugar plantations, insurance, transportation, hotels, TV, radio, book publishing, movies, and professional athletics. This broad scope of business activities helps insulate them from collective bargaining by labor unions, which traditionally operate within one sector only. As many unionists have lamented, "How can workers strike a conglomerate transnational?" Host countries face similar difficulties. How can a government plug tax loopholes and enforce local regulations when the accounting wizards of the transnational corporations usually provide information only on a consolidated basis and refuse to provide data on specific products?

But no transnational operates as an island unto itself. The legal entity is merely the central node at the heart of a far-flung cluster of supporting organizations. These include subsidiaries, suppliers, distributors, research organizations, and firms (or occasionally individuals) providing banking, legal, accounting, managerial, advertising, and public relations services.

Each large cluster, in turn, usually operates as part of what we may call a constellation, a still larger group of organizations. The typical constellation (of which the cartel is one form) works out policies that become the framework for oligarchic cooperation and competition or—through secret consultations by subordinates, legal counsel, or otherwise—sets output quotas, divides markets, or fixes minimum prices. Many a transnational operates not only within its own cluster but within one or more constellations. In banking, which has usally taken the leading role in transnational expansion, the formal name for a constellation is "consortium" or "group." Sometimes competing constellations that are dependent on each other work together in a duopoly—as in the case of OPEC and the giant Western oil companies through which OPEC enforces its decisions.

In turn, the most dynamic clusters and constellations have learned how to imbed their activities within loose, flexible networks or "complexes" of private and public organizations, institutions, foundations, research institutes, law and accounting firms, and strategically placed individuals. The so-called "military-industrial complex" is no unique institutional form; the "complex" has become the standard mode of structuring the planning and control activities of corporate banking, agribusiness, and mass communications. One of the most important examples is the huge automobile-highway-petroleum-trucking complex. With the help of the Highway Trust Fund set up under the Eisenhower administration, this huge complex has become the major force in undermining mass transportation in American cities, promoting suburban expansion and attaining the "automobilization" of the U.S. economy.

In all the complexes or networks, the older forms of integration—financial groups, cartels, trade associations, interlocking directorates, and interlocking stock ownership—still exist. Indeed, they seem to have expanded. But the new interlocks are wider (covering more sectors and territorial space), deeper (covering more levels of activity) and more flexible. And decision making within the network is far more complex than in the old-style cartel or *zaibatsu*. The older practices of centralized hierarchy (still adhered to by some components) have been incorporated in a more flexible polyarchic system of mutual accommodation. The request "Take me to your leader" cannot be honored. In this new-style, faceless system no one knows his name; he does not exist. The web is spidery, but there is no single spider.

Some of these capitalist complexes are tightly organized, some remarkably loose. Most find ways of using public funds, contracts, or guarantees as an essential part of their operations. All of them have blurred older distinctions between "public" and "private". All have developed increased power by co-opting, or incorporating as valuable appendages, regulatory agencies presumably established to control them, and by influencing research institutions that might otherwise subject them to embarrassing scrutiny. Large transnationals like General Motors, it has often been pointed out, have total annual sales volumes larger than the annual GNP of medium-sized countries. What has been less noted or understood is that the multinational automobile-highway-petroleum complex (within which General Motors plays a vital role) controls far more money, scientists, and technicians than provided for in the entire budget of *any* capitalist country's national government, including the United States itself.

The emerging reality of the Golden International is concretized in a myriad of private, public, and international organizations. The growth of the European Economic Community and its many offshoots has triggered the parallel creation of such powerful business organizations as UNICE (the Union of Industries of the European Economic Community) and FBEEC (the Banking Federation of the European Economic Community). These operations, in turn, have necessitated more active cooperation among First World governments. Thus in the field of international currency the Group of Ten finance ministers—representing the United States, Canada, Japan, Britain, West Germany, France, Sweden, Italy, the Netherlands, and Belgium—has been negotiating to establish a new monetary system in which, as Sylvia Porter put it quite a while ago, "our proud but overburdened dollar will remain a key currency of the world—a first among equals—but . . . will not longer be the sole pivot money around which all other currencies evolve." [11] To those who mistakenly see the international value of the dollar as an unmistakable indicator of American capitalism's strength, this may look like an American retreat. For the American transnational corporations, however, who operate in all the world's media of exchange (including the International Monetary Fund's special drawing rights), this is an advance. Together with their European and Japanese brethren, they provide solid support (and more than occasional guidance) for the complex efforts of the IMF in setting up the new multicurrency, and also aid the World Bank in promoting conditions for profitable capitalist investment in the Third World.

As more transnational organizations of this type are set up, they tend to create more confusion, and the need is greater for strategic coordination. For a while it seemed that this need could be met by intergovernmental organizations such as the Organization for Economic Cooperation and Development (OECD) and the North Atlantic Treaty Organization (NATO). These were informally tied together by small and more secretive informal groups such as the G-5 group of finance or treasury officials from the "top five" countries, or by the annual Bilderberg conferences created "to preserve the Western way of life." [12] But by 1970, it became evident, as first pointed out in public by Zbigniew Brzezinski, that OECD was too narrowly limited to official government representatives. Neither provided a flexible enough framework for complex policy discussions among corporate and business leaders, or even a basis for legitimating the senior-partner status that Japanese and

Western European interests demanded, and which the leaders of the U.S. establishment have been willing to confer. Brzezinski succinctly defined the situation as requiring a new formal structure through which the Americans will "involve Western Europe and Japan" and the new holy trinity could "weave a new fabric of international relations." [13]

Anthony Eden followed up a little later in an article declaring that "The free world now needs its own organization where its leading nations can meet, discuss and deal with political problems which are worthwhile." With a rather clumsy lack of diplomatic skill, he nominated for membership in this working club "the four Western European powers, the United States and Canada, Brazil, Japan and Australia." [14] With much greater finesse, David Rockefeller and other banking leaders designed an organization of "prominent citizens" rather than governments, and limited the geographical scope to what they called the "trilateral world" embracing North America (the United States and Canada), Japan, and Western Europe. Thus the Trilateral Commission came into being in 1973. The commission's membership is mainly high-level bankers and industrialists supported by a sprinkling of enlightened and reliable politicians, public officials, intellectuals, and even union leaders—sixty people apiece from each of the three parts of the trinity. A smaller executive committee has been hard at work organizing task forces and behind-the-scenes discussions by top corporate and government leaders. Its basic task has been to formulate top-level strategy for the leaders of the First World's establishments on such intricate matters as monetary policy, energy, control of the high seas, trade, development, and relations with both communist nations and the Third World. It can do this because, as a *Newsweek* journalist pointed out, it is not "merely a rich man's club" but rather a "remarkable cross-section of the interlocking establishments of the world's leading industrialized nations." [15]

BIG WELFARE FOR BIG BUSINESS

> The federal government is replete with supportive programs—subsidies, research, promotional, contracts, tax privileges, protections from competition—which flow regularly into the corporate mission of profit and sales maximization.
>
> RALPH NADER [16]

Both welfare spending and warfare spending have a two-fold nature: the welfare system not only politically contains the surplus population but also expands demand and domestic markets. And the warfare system not only keeps foreign rivals at bay and inhibits the development of world revolution (thus keeping labor power, raw materials and markets in the capitalist orbit) but also helps to stave off economic stagnation at home.

JAMES O'CONNOR [17]

Although industrial capitalism has always enjoyed government support, the scale and pervasiveness of such support became immeasurably greater after World War II. Indeed, as Ralph Miliband has pointed out, in no previous epoch in the history of capitalism has the capitalist order been more fully accepted by the political leadership and government bureaucracy. In Western Europe and Japan, this acceptance has included socialist parties willing to take on the burdens and honors of trying to manage capitalist societies. In the United States it has extended to the many socialists and crypto-socialists operating under the banner of the Democratic party. Throughout the "Free World," moreover, many communists and revolutionaries often seek popular support as champions of immediate gains for workers through new forms of state intervention. As in the past, this tends to strengthen the hands of more moderate reformers in pushing backward capitalists into grudging acceptance of the larger government help required for a more perfect capitalism.

This state-supported capitalism has been imperfectly labeled by many popular terms which, while containing particles of truth, conceal the genuine nature of the new business-government relationships: "state capitalism," "welfare state," "warfare-welfare state," and "mixed economy." The power of the concept "state capitalism" (or "state monopoly capitalism") is that it stresses the alliance of powerful capitalist forces with the state. But it greatly underestimates the extent to which big business operates on its own, both without the state and beyond the reach of the state. In no country of advanced capitalism is business completely controlled by the state; the state, rather, is subject to business control, although not completely. The relationship is more that of a business-government partnership, with business often serving as the senior, although sometimes silent, partner.

The term "welfare state" also contains a germ of truth. Under pressure from communist regimes and movements, the governments of all major capitalist countries have out-Bismarcked Bismarck in taking over socialist demands and enacting a host of programs to provide state-ordained floors under living and working standards. In a broader sense, however, the "welfare state" idea is fundamentally misleading. The welfare provided is not the general well-being of the people. It is welfare, rather, in the narrow and restrictive sense of public assistance to the poor and other programs (usually financed by the lower and middle classes themselves) to take the rough edge off capitalist exploitation, promote docility among the exploited, and thereby help form a more perfect capitalism. If this be the general welfare it is "subwelfare," the level of which has been grudgingly attuned to the amount of domestic pacification required in a particular country or at a particular time.

Thus, in Britain and Western Europe, with stronger left-wing movements to be contained, the levels of subwelfare have been higher than in the United States, where the productive capacity itself could have supported the highest levels of welfare in the capitalist world. Under President Truman's Fair Deal (1946–52) dramatic proposals for raising the low U.S. levels, although never approved by Congress, helped placate the many liberal leaders who had been less than enthusiastic about the "cold war" and the Korean War. John F. Kennedy's pleas to "get the country moving again" linked a more interventionist attitude at home with one abroad. Although President Johnson's Great Society programs were stunted as money and energy went to the war in Asia, the various initiatives in social security, public assistance, health care, education, housing, job-training, and local uplift were cited by administration spokesmen as they begged for liberal and minority tolerance of intervention overseas. Many of these welfare programs, in fact, subsidized banks and other corporations under the banner of providing them with incentives for "doing good" for the poor. Indeed, in most countries of modern capitalism big business makes at least as much money from welfare as from warfare. Hence there is some logic in using James O'Connor's term "warfare-welfare state."

But to focus attention on warfare-welfare spending alone would be to lose track of the Big Welfare handouts that big business gets or extracts from the normal peacetime activities of the capitalist state. Although it is perfectly true, as conservative economists insist, that "there are no free lunches," there are scores of corporate "free lunchers" who manage to get other people—via government intervention—to pick up all or part of the bill. Although new forms of this fine-tuned intervention are created every year, some of the more conspicuous examples in the United States are:

- The Federal Reserve system, which supports bankers by maintaining high interest rates and bailing out bank failures.
- The nominally progressive federal tax system, which has become a labyrinth of special loopholes that provide many billions of "tax expenditures" (indirect subsidies) for specific companies or groups. For fiscal year 1980 these tax expenditures amounted to over $150 billion—more than 20 percent of direct budget outlays for the same year.
- The Treasury Department, which maintains huge interest-free deposits in large banks while at the same time paying the bank's interest on money lent to the government.
- Billions in direct subsidies that are paid to airlines, the merchant marine, agribusiness and others.

- Federal expenditures for scientific research and development, which have subsidized the growth of capitalism's technological reserve.
- Government guarantees that protect many billions of bank mortgages and foreign investments against losses.
- Government regulations that give the large banks control over the investment of the pension funds of most labor unions.
- So-called regulatory commissions, which help maintain the oligarchic power of the communication media, public utilities, and major transportation interests.
- Government forays into wage-price controls, or "incomes policy," which are used to keep wages down or squeeze out business competitors.

A large amount of corporate planning involves intricate tussles to keep other people's hands out of this bustling free-lunch bazaar while getting as much as possible for one's own "crowd". Sometimes juicy scraps are snatched away by small-time operators whose proclivities for improperly covered lawbreaking may produce enough public scandal to distract attention from those quietly walking away with the lion's share.

There are two other forms of government intervention that tend to give the false impression that the modern capitalist economy is "mixed" in the sense of being less capitalistic than before: central government planning and government ownership. Since World War II, the government of every major capitalist country has engaged in some form of economic planning, albeit sometimes under the label of policy coordination or program integration. The central function of these planning efforts is to strengthen capitalist performance by (1) helping maintain market demand; (2) extending welfare-state programs as a means of doing this while also pacifying protest; (3) designing fiscal, monetary, and regulatory policies to support more profitable corporate operations in specific sectors; and (4) mediating conflicts among various interests in the corporate world. At the local level, this kind of planning has been backed up by zoning regulations, land-use plans, and public improvement programs that have helped subsidize both suburban growth and astronomical increases in urban and suburban land values.

In turn, government ownership and "mixed enterprises" in certain sectors of capitalist society have tended to (1) help corporate capital pull out of less profitable activities and move to greener fields; (2) promote technological rationalization of backward industries; (3) provide government capital for use by private corporate interests; (4) tax the lower classes by selling government-monopolized products at higher prices, or (5) subsidize private business by giving them government goods and services at low prices. In addition, both government planning and government ownership perform the invaluable service of mobilizing liberals, and socialists—and sometimes communist revolutionaries also—behind the policies needed for a more perfect capitalism.

MORE RATIONAL CORPORATE MANAGEMENT

With the coming of science and technology, it is fair to say that we can get ten dollars out of nature for every dollar that we can squeeze out of man.

KENNETH BOULDING [18]

Capitalists have never needed theorists to explain the connection between money and power. It has taken theorists at least a century, to develop the pretense that they are separate.

It has also taken businessmen more than a century to learn how to accumulate capital and power on the largest possible scale over the longest period of time. The older aristocratic traditions of aristocratic life had to be abandoned. The two oldest business commandments—"buy cheap, sell dear" and "let the buyer [or borrower] beware"—had to be expanded to a full decalagogue which included the following: (3) risk other people's money, (4) make money out of shortages, (5) use only those new technologies that are more profitable, (6) shift social costs to others, (7) conceal assets and income, (8) squeeze workers as much as possible, (9) buy political influence, and (10) help build a powerful establishment. Each of these maxims, of course, operated under the umbrella of "anything goes if you can get away with it."

During World War II many corporate planners learned how to get away with much more than had previously been imagined. After the war, corporate planning and control became the central focus of attention for hundreds of colleges or departments of business administration, thousands of management articles and books published every year, and hundreds of thousands of participating in undergraduate and graduate programs and "management development" or "advanced management" seminars, conferences, and discussion groups. With or without the direct help of such formalities, the leaders of the largest corporate institutions became not inert organization men but adaptive innovators in the more rational and unconstrained pursuit of money and power for the owners and managers of large-scale private property. In this pursuit, they now for the first time had the help of a vast array of professional experts in such new technical fields as business policy, organization, finance, production, personnel, and marketing. Many of these subjects correspond to the major departments or course offerings in business schools, as well as to the functional division of labor within the typical corporation structure. Some are rooted in scientific research or advanced theoretical analysis, others in the careful *ad hoc* accumulation of experience. In each, there is a technical jargon that facilitates communication among the technicians in the same field and hinders communication with anyone else; this babel of many tongues becomes still more complicated whenever, as often happens, one specialty is subdivided into many subspecialties. In each area, particularly those allied with the various information sciences, the more creative experts often claim to be *the* management experts capable of either integrating or displacing the work of all the others.

Between the lines of these suitably arcane disciplines a modern Machiavelli can discern a blunter set of "tacit guidelines," as listed in the table, "Elements of Rational Corporate Management." The technical experts take those for granted, dress them up in fancy rationalizations, but openly discuss them only at their peril. Expanding on the older Ten Commandments, these unstated imperatives do not exhaust management techniques. It would be overly cynical to suggest that "managerial economics" or "cash-flow budgeting" or "product design and engineering" amount to nothing more than "make money from shortages," "speculate in international currency," or "plan accelerated obsolescence."

ELEMENTS OF RATIONAL CORPORATE MANAGEMENT

Technical Specialties	*Between-the-Lines: Tacit Guidelines*
Business Policy	
Business-government relations	Mobilize state support, public funds, and political influence
Investment and product-line planning	Extend structure of corporate power
Managerial economics	Make money from shortages
Management information systems	Shift social costs to others
Public relations	Build benevolent image and support the establishment.
Organization	
Organizational development	Promote "profit consciousness"
Reorganization	Weed out undesirables
Decentralization of operations	Provide "cover" for top-level decision makers
Subcontractor-supplier relations	Maintain subcontractor-supplier dependency, build flexible clusters and constellations

Technical Specialties	*Between-the-Lines: Tacit Guidelines*
	Finance
Securities flotation	Risk other people's money
Accounting	Conceal assets, income, bribes, and political contributions
Capital budgeting	Shift costs to external accounts
Cash-flow budgeting	Speculate in international currency
	Production
Product design and engineering	Plan accelerated obsolescence
Research and development	Promote labor-saving technologies
Production scheduling	Minimize costs that cannot be shifted
	Personnel
Labor relations	Maintain work discipline, through "independent" unions where necessary
Human relations	Keep workers docile
Recruitment	Select "dociles," reject "undesirables"
Job analysis	Develop competitive, low-cost stratification
	Marketing
Market research	Manufacture consumer needs
Distribution	Keep prices as high as possible
Advertising	Conceal product defects

But the latter do represent crucial realities that are rarely publicly unacknowledged. Often, I am sure, these tacit guidelines are refined far beyond the rough-and-ready rules here listed and enter the infinite series of well-shrouded mysteries in the realms of high finance and high *politique.* They are the special province not of technicians but of the top-level overseers and exceutives whose task it is to nurture, guide, and coordinate the many technicians needed to help in the accumulation of concentrated power and wealth.

TECHNOLOGY: STARTING, STOPPING, SUPPRESSING

The pressures of World War II unleashed a new burst of technological creativity. The Nazis succeeded in fueling planes and tanks through gasoline made from coal and in developing advanced rocket technology.

The U.S. success with the atom bomb was matched by a whole spectrum of less spectacular achievements, including radar, jet propulsion, computers, and operations research. Instead of subsiding with the war's end, technological inventiveness thrived in the ebullient atmosphere of "Free World" integration and corporate expansiveness. With massive support from military and civilian agencies of government, Big Business once again devoted itself to what Karl Marx has called "revolutionizing the means of production." As had already happened in nuclear physics, theoretical and applied scientists were caught up within a complex network of technological research and development. They became valuable resources to be funded, nurtured, and honored by those who saw the possibility of distilling new power or capital from their findings.

The result was "a new technological revolution" in the methods of collecting, transforming, storing and moving almost all forms of energy, matter and information. There has been a veritable chain reaction in atomic energy: hydrogen bombs, nuclear-powered submarines and icebreakers, electricity production through nuclear fission. Important research is underway on electricity production through nuclear fusion and through the more direct use of solar energy through photovoltaic cells that convert sunlight into electricity, tapping the geothermal heat of the earth itself, and, above all, converting grains and other agricultural products into alcohol and other substitutes for gasoline. Also, as Alvin Toffler reports, "scientists are now studying the idea of utilizing bacteria capable of converting sunlight into electrochemical energy." [19] There have been continuing advances in production of energy from fossil fuels and its instantaneous transmission over vast distances through electrical grids, superconductors and the more spectacular means of lasers and microwaves.

Materials are no longer limited to those found in nature. They are now being created *de novo* either to substitute for such traditional materials as textiles, rubber, steel, aluminum, or paper, or to create entirely new materials, both inorganic and organic. "Just as we have manipulated plastics and metals," reports Lord Ritchie Calder, an eminent science commentator, "we are now manufacturing living materials." [20] Medical technology has been developing new capabilities for eradicating contagious diseases; for facilitating or preventing childbirth; for replacing parts of the body. The new "genetic engineers" have been discovering how to reprogram DNA molecules.

Still more revolutionary changes have been taking place in successive generations of information technologies. The collection of information is now possible through increasingly sophisticated systems, including the more ominous forms of remote electronic surveillance. The processing of information through fantastically rapid computers now facilitates the kind and quantities of calculations never before possible. The transmission, storage and retrieval of information is accomplished in new ways by the widespread advances in telecommunications and electronic coding. Finally, and most disturbingly, the means of control over this great mass has been developed to such a degree that centralized systems can keep tabs on incredible amounts of information over long sequences of widely dispersed and decentralized activities.*

This technological revolution is embodied in the plans and actions of industrial, military and political leaders. It is institutionally orchestrated and financed. One strategic objective has been to maintain the military and economic superiority of the United States and its "Free World" allies. Another has been to nurture the economic health of the largest "Free World" conglomerates, clusters, constellations and complexes by staving off the stagnation that always threatens in the event of a decline in innovation. Whether intended or not, a major result has been to help knit together the leading corporations of the technologically advanced countries and buttress their domination of technologically inferior countries.

The scientists and technologists have become an informal "techno-international" whose members (funded from establishment sources) keep in constant touch with each other and hold frequent international meetings. Having more common interests than the managers and owners of corporate wealth, they play a vanguard role in transcending national boundaries and helping make all corporate kings kin. They draw the new generations of Third World scientists and technologists into the First World culture, thereby fostering a Third World brain drain that turns out to be a continuing brain gain for the Golden International.

These activities are helped immeasurably by a euphoric vision—widely shared among the "knowledge elites", as Daniel Bell calls them—that any problems or crises created by new technologies can be coped with, if not solved, by some new technology.* The euphoria is nourished by technological thrusts and feints in myriad directions, with thousands of technologists or scientists plunging far beyond the realm of what may be immediately feasible. There is thus built up a huge stockpile or reserve of embryonic, nascent, semi-developed techniques, devices, inventions, theories and methodologies—a sort of reserve army of available but unused technologies.

Although the technology reserve is huge and growing, it is no cornucopia from which benefits quickly or automatically flow to meet the needs of humankind. The great bulk of the new innovations are those fostered by the Establishment's "master magicians"—namely, innovations responding to demands for more destructive weapons, more profitable

---

* In "Managing Information and Media" (chapter 12) I discuss how these many technologies may be used in personal surveillance and dossier-building.

* I touch on this subject again in "New Ideologies of Control" in "The Friendly Fascist Establishment" (chapter 9).

products and more labor-saving processes. In these areas, there is some relevance in Goethe's fable of the sorcerer's apprentice, in which the brooms and water pails take off on their own and run wild. In Pentagon-supported innovation, almost anything goes. For the first time in history, military leaders have escaped the traditional fixation on armaments used in past wars and are creatively at work on the weapons of the future. Side by side with this perverse form of creativity, untold billions are still spent on increasingly obsolete weapons of the past—such as tanks and aircraft carriers, both of which are sitting ducks for the new anti-tank and anti-carrier missiles.

In contrast, however, there is only a small amount of research on nutrition, health promotion (as contrasted with disease treatment), physical exercise, home building, mass transportation, the recycling of waste products, energy conservation, total energy systems, and the full use of agricultural products, including wood, in the production of alcohol and other fuels. When protests are made against the neglect of research in such areas, the response is "technological tokenism." Thus, early in 1980 the National Science Foundation proudly announced a new program to promote "approximate technologies." These were excellently defined as follows:

> Appropriate technologies are . . . those which possess many of the following qualities: they are decentralized, require low capital investment, are amenable to management by their users, result in solutions that conserve natural resources, and are in harmony with the environment; they are small or intermediate in scale, take into account site-available natural and human resources and are more labor than capital-intensive.[21]

These qualities, however, are clearly *in*appropriate for the maintenance, let alone the promotion, of large-scale, centrally controlled, labor-saving, energy-intensive operations. They were therefore put on a starvation diet of $1.8 million for fiscal year 1980—that is, about $300,000 apiece for each of six appropriate technology areas. The total budget allotment, it should be noted, was far less than one one-hundredth of one percent of the $47 billion in total spending on scientific research and development.

In covering up the Establishment's unyielding thrust toward inappropriate technology, statisticians have laboriously developed a narrow concept of "productivity" which measures the amount of labor used to yield a given quantity of output, but excludes inputs of capital, energy and materials. If the input of labor goes down relative to output, that demonstrates the forward march of productivity, which has become a fashionable indicator of economic progress. Accordingly, most efforts to measure capital productivity, energy productivity, materials productivity, or "total productivity" (which would take into account capital, energy, and materials as well as labor) have been shunted aside.[22]

In turn, the narrow concept of labor productivity has become the touchstone for a new "supply side" economics, oriented toward more government incentives for business investment and profitability. To the extent that any energy conservation measures replace machinery and fossil-fuel energy with people, this is registered on the "productivity" index as a backward step. The "remedy" is to freeze or suppress any conservation technologies and thereby restore the desired rate of increase in labor productivity. If this results in shortages of energy and capital * and a larger supply of wasted labor, no matter. The net result is continuing progress in the accumulation of capital and power under the control of an immensely sophisticated, albeit divided, Establishment. This progress, as described in the next chapter, is one of the miraculous achievements of modern capitalism.

---

* I discuss these shortages at greater length in the section on "An Abundance of Shortages" in "Friendly Fascist Economics" (chapter 10).

3

The Mysterious Establishment

The good old rule
Sufficeth them, the simple plan
That they should take who have the power
And they should keep who can.

WILLIAM WORDSWORTH

There are no stories or magazine sections [in CBS Evening News, NBC Nightly News, Newsweek, or Time] about what the sociologists call the Social Structure . . . nor about more easily grasped complexes such as the Class Hierarchy or the Power Structure.

HERBERT GANS [1]

MYSTERY HAS ALWAYS HOVERED around the masters of power and wealth.

The oligarchs of agricultural kingdoms wrapped themselves in witchcraft and divinity to conceal their weaknesses and magnify their strengths. They were helped by priests, scribes, courtiers, royal chamberlains, and old-style bureaucrats.

As industrial capitalism acumulated power and wealth, the old mysteries were replaced and dwarfed by the new mysteries of high finance, market manipulations, convoluted and lucrative legalisms, pressure-group politics, and a labyrinth of new bureaucracies. In 1918, Franz Kafka, unhappily embedded in an insurance company job in Prague, pictured the new order as a castle, "hidden, veiled in mist and darkness," a baffling symbol of the industrial establishment as it dominated the life of preindustrial villagers. The socialist industrialists in Russia used the myths of monolithic omnipotence on the part of Party or leader to hide the new mysteries of struggle among powerful forces in the central oligarchy. During the short-lived fascism of Italy, Japan, and Germany, the myths of nationalism and divine or quasi-divine leadership cloaked the fierce tensions within the big business-military-political-bureaucratic establishments.

The building of the "Free World" empire after World War II has resulted in First World establishments that dwarf Kafka's unfathomable castle. Indeed, the Establishment in any of the leading capitalist societies is like a network of many castles—often a few hundred—spread across each country and linked with similar power structures in other countries.

THE CASTLES OF POWER

> *Establishment:* An exclusive group of powerful people who rule a government or society by means of private agreements or decisions.
>
> *American Heritage Dictionary*

The American Establishment is not an organization. Nor is it a simple coalition or network. Like the industrial-military complex, it has no chairman or executive committees.

Like the Golden International, the Establishment is more complicated than any complex. It is a complex of complexes, a far-flung network of power centers, including institutional hierarchies. These are held together less by hierarchical control and more by mutual interests, shared ideologies, and accepted procedures for mediating their endless conflicts.

Like the establishments in other First World countries, the American Establishment is not just a network of State leaders. Nor is it merely a coalition of private governments. It is an interweaving of two structures—polity and economy—that under industrial capitalism have never been independent of each other. It is the modern partnership of big business and big government. As such, it is much looser and more flexible than the establishments of classic fascism. And in contrast with them, above all, it operates in part through—and is to an important extent constrained by—the democratic machinery of constitutional government. Private agreements and decisions—even well-protected secrecy—play a large role in its operations; this adds to the Establishment's inherent mystery. It is why people often refer to it as the "invisible government." Yet many of its agreements and decisions are open to public view. Indeed, so much information is available in public reports, congressional hearings, and the specialized press that anyone trying to make sense of it all runs the danger of being drowned in a sea of excessive information. This, of course, is the problem faced by all intelligence agencies, which usually feed on a diet of 95 percent public data spiced with 5 percent obtained through espionage. Also, as with intelligence and counterintelligence, there are huge information gaps side by side with huge amounts of deliberately deceptive misinformation.

Thus the analysts of national establishments and power structures must bring to available data the same skepticism and creative imagination that Sherlock Holmes or Hercule Poirot brought to the clues left at the scenes of fictional murders. Since the truth of accumulated wealth and power is much stranger than fiction, any analyst must leave many riddles —and murders—unsolved. Besides, there are not many people who try to unravel these mysteries.

Social scientists receive research grants not to study power structures in any comprehensive sense. Those who make the effort—like G. Wilham Dumhoff, C. Wright Mills, and Gabriel Kolko—have had to operate on the fringes of scientific respectability, with more academic obstruction than support. Fortunately, their work has been aided by an equally small number of investigative journalists such as Ferdinand Lundberg and Morton Mintz, and lawyers like Jerry S. Cohen, and Arthur S. Miller, as well as a few other social scientists or journalists who have also helped tear away one or another of the veils that shroud the Establishment.[2]

From all this work, a few points stand forth clearly.

The Establishment has many levels. As shown in the chart, "The National Establishment, USA", these levels may be divided functionally. At the apex of strategic guidance are the "top dogs" of the Ultra-Rich and the Corporate Overseers. Among these are the president of the United States and those who assist him as commander in chief of the armed forces and in other roles. But these people cannot run things by themselves. They have the help of a larger group of "executive managers" who are, in turn, assisted by a much larger number of "junior and contingent members." Below these levels are the rest of the country's social structure—the middle and lower classes of the population in their roles as employees,. self-employed, consumers, taxpayers, homeowners, and tenants.

The number of people actively involved—even at the very top—is too large for any meeting or convention hall. Robert Townsend, who headed Avis before it was swallowed by ITT, has made this estimate: "America is run largely by and for about 5,000 people who are actively supported by 50,000 beavers eager to take their places. I arrive at this figure this way: maybe 2,500 megacorporation executives, 500 politicians, lobbyists and Congressional committee chairmen, 500 investment bankers, 500 partners in major accounting firms, 500 labor brokers. If you don't like my figures, make up you own . . ."[3]

I am convinced his figures are far too small. If there are 4,000–6,000 at the top, they are probably able to deploy at least five times as many in executive management; who in turn operate through at least ten times as many junior and contingent members. My total ranges between a quarter and a third of a million. Even without adding their dependents,

THE NATIONAL ESTABLISHMENT, USA

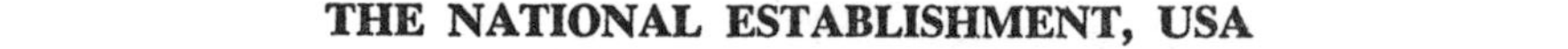

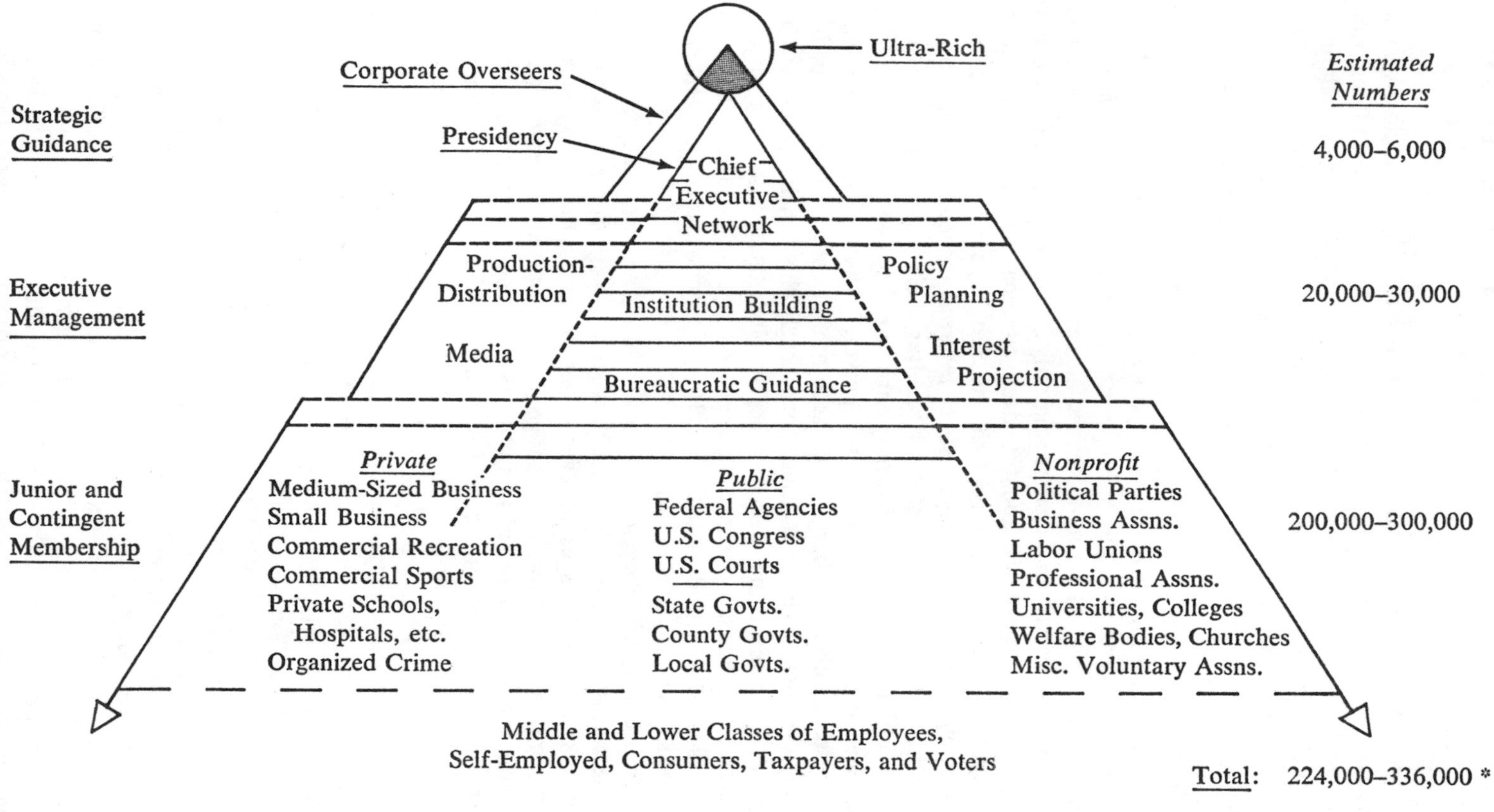

* Less than two tenths of one percent (.002) of the U.S. population and less than two hundredths of one percent (.0002) of the non-communist "free world" under the leadership of the U.S. Establishment.

this is a far cry from a small handful of people. Yet in relative numbers this large number of people is still a "few." A third of a million people numbers less than two tenths of one percent of the U.S. population of about 220 million; and with their immediate family members this would still be less than 10 percent. It is less than one hundreth of 1 percent (.0001) of the "Free World" under the shared leadership of the United States. Seldom if ever has such a small number of people done so much to guide the destinies of so many over such vast expanses of the planet.

There are conflicts at all levels. Most of these are rooted in divergent or clashing interests, values, perceptions, and traditions. Some are minor, others are major. Many minor crises at various points in the Establishment are daily occurrences, surprising only the uninitiated. But "whenever we are prepared to talk about a deep political crisis," as Papandreou observes, "we should assume that the Establishment (as a whole) is undergoing a crisis, either because of *internal* trouble—namely, because some of its members have seen fit to alter their relative position within the coalition—or because of *external* trouble, because another challenger has risen who wants a share of the power." The bulk of these conflicts are resolved through bargaining, accommodation, market competition, and government decision making, particularly through bureaucratic channels. A few more come to the surface through the legislative, judicial, or electoral processes. Coherence is provided not only through these procedures for conflict adjustment but also by large areas of partially shared interests, values, and ideologies.

It is constantly changing. If the Establishment were a mere defender of the status quo, it would be much weaker. While some of its members may resist many changes or even want to "turn the clock back," the dominant leaders know that change is essential to preserve, let alone, expand, power. "If we want things to stay as they are," the young nephew said to his uncle, the prince, in Lampedusa's *The Leopard*, "things have got to change. Do you understand?" Power holders may not understand this at once, but events drive the point home to them—or drive them out. Thus many of the changes occur in the membership of the Establishment which, at any point, may expand or contract. If the Establishment is a target, it is—in Leonard Silk's apt words for the "overall corporate government complex"—a "moving target." [4]

There is no single central conspiracy. I agree with Karl Popper when he says: "Conspiracies occur, it must be admitted. But the striking fact which, in spite of their occurrence, disproves the conspiracy theory is that few of these conspiracies are ultimately successful." Many of them have consequences entirely or partly unintended or unforeseen. Popper adds the observation that the successful ones rarely come to public attention and that there is usually a "situational logic" that transcends any conscious planning. When there is a fire in an auditorium, people do not get together to plan what to do. The logical response to the situation is "Get out." Some will do it in an orderly fashion; others might be rather rough toward people who get in their way. The Establishment often operates this way. Some of its most historic achievements have been forced on it by "fires" that break out suddenly, often unanticipated. The major advances in the welfare state, for example, have historically been opposed by most elements in capitalist establishments who were usually too stupid or nearsighted to realize that these measures would put a floor (or elevator) under market demand, thereby promoting the accumulation of corporate capital and taking the sting out of anticapitalist movements.

THE ULTRA-RICH

> Let me tell you about the very rich. They are different from you and me. . . . Even when they enter into our world or sink below us, they still think that they are better than we are. They are different.
>
> F. Scott Fitzgerald

> If we made an income pyramid out of a child's blocks, with each layer portraying $1,000 of income, the peak would be far higher than the Eiffel Tower, but almost all of us would be within a yard of the ground.
>
> Paul Samuelson [5]

The greatest difference between the Ultra-Rich and the rest of us is that most of them are addicted to sensory gratification on a grand scale. In part, as Ferdinand Lundberg has documented, this gratification takes the form of palatial estates, fabulously furnished town houses, private art collections, exclusive clubs, summer and winter resorts on many continents, membership in social registers, birth and burial under distinctive conditions, etc.[6] It also involves an array of services going far beyond the ordinary housekeepers, cooks, gardeners, masseurs, valets, chauffeurs, yacht captains, and pilots of the large fleet of rich people's private aircraft. But above all, the valets of the ultra-rich also include expert executives, managers, advisers, braintrusters, ghostwriters, entertainers, lawyers, accountants, and consultants. Most of their services are more expensive (and far more sophisticated) than those enjoyed by the emperors, emirs, and moguls of past centuries. Some are freely given in exchange for the privilege of approaching the throne and basking in the effulgent glory of accumulated wealth. Most are paid for by others—eitheir being written off as tax deductions or appearing as expenses on accounts of various corporations, banks, foundations, universities, rsearch institutes, or government agencies. These payments for modern valet service can be unbelievably high. Indeed, one of the earmarks of the Ultra-Rich in America is that they even have millionaires—most of them involved in big business—working for them.

Among the Ultra-Rich, of course, there are the so-called "beautiful people" who nourish their addiction merely by using a little of what accrues to them from fortunes managed by others. These are the "idle rich," the *rentiers* whose hardest work, beyond clipping coupons, is flitting from one form of entertainment to another. There are also a few deviants who betray their class by renouncing their addiction, getting along with small doses only, or actively using some of their money to finance liberal or left-wing causes. The great majority, however, seem to be stalwart conservatives who abstain from idleness by some form of "public service"—that is, by holding the top posts in the most prestigious institutions of philanthropy, higher education, health, culture, and art.

There are also those whose addiction is more powerful; they can satisfy it only by larger and larger doses of money or power. This can be done only by exercising directly or indirectly their roles as overseers, roles legitimized by their personal participation in the management of corporate property. As suggested by overlapping area (shared jointly by the Ultra-Rich and the Corporate Overseers on page 57), this probably comprises a large minority of the Ultra-Rich, in contrast with those lotus-eaters, deviants and "do-gooders" who do not take part in the guidance of national and international affairs.

If you ask how much a yacht costs, J. Pierpont Morgan once said, you're not rich enough to afford one. To this old principle, another may now be added: If you really know how much money you have, then you're not rich. The really rich cannot possibly calculate the present market value of their real estate, stocks, art or jewelry collections, bonds, trust funds, notes, or cash-surrender value of life insurance—and may even have trouble keeping track of many bank deposits in various countries. If a member of the Ultra-Rich is asked a question on total assets or net worth, as Nelson Rockefeller was asked in the congressional hearings before ascending (in reality, "descending") to the vice-presidency, he must use the services of experts on financial statements. For such services, any ultra-rich person or family spends hundreds of thousands of dollars a year (more than the annual income of the ordinary rich) in tax-deductible payments to hide both income and wealth from tax collectors or inquisitive reporters. In particular, corporate lawyers and accountants have made remarkable progress since World War II in the intricate arts of tax avoidance and evasion. Like an old-fashioned lady's hoop skirt, the corporation's annual financial statement conceals far more than it reveals and directly touches no sensitive parts. Reported assets are mere "book values." One set of books is prepared to ward off tax collectors, a second to attract investors, a third to help management decision making. Hidden reserves, slush funds, and political contributions never appear in the first two and are often kept secret from all but a few decision makers who really "need to know." Family accounts are even trickier. Hence, what observers can know about the money of the ultra-rich is unavoidably a combination of the demonstrable and the undemonstrable, the obvious and the conjectural, the known and the unknown.

In 1968 Arthur M. Louis attempted such a combination for *Fortune* magazine.[7] Putting together many combinations of "inside" and public information, he tried to calculate the "centimillionaires," those with a net worth of at least $100 million. The result was an Eiffel Tower like this:

	Number	
	By Level	*Cumulative*
$1 billion to $1.5 billion	2	2
$500 million to $1 billion	6	8
$300 million to $500 million	5	13
$200 million to $300 million	27	40
$150 million to $200 million	26	66
$100 million to $150 million	87	150

Louis readily acknowledges the incompleteness of the list and the downward bias in his estimates: "Some forms of wealth—and some of the Super-Rich themselves—absolutely defy detection." He also gives the names, ages, and some identifying data on the 66 above the $150 million level. Here we see many names associated with America's older fortunes: Rockefellers, du Ponts, Mellons, and Fords. Each of these appear with a few entries for each family: six Rockefellers, five Mellons, three du Ponts, and two Fords. The Kennedy family appears only under the name of the father, Joseph P. Kennedy. Many of the names are relatively obscure, such as Leon Hess of New York, Peter Kiewit of Omaha, William L. McKnight of St. Paul, and E. Clairborne Robins of Richmond. Some of the obscurity seekers have failed in their efforts and—as with the two billionaires at the top of the list, J. Paul Getty and Howard Hughes—have at times become conspicuously notorious.

Although one can only guess how many more people are now at the peak of the Eiffel Tower, there has been a remarkable increase in the number of mere millionaires a little closer to the ground:

1953	1963	1969	1979
27,000	67,000	121,000	520,000 [8]

Part of this steep rise, of course, is the result of inflation—particularly the rising market value of real estate and other fixed assets. But from 1969 to 1979 prices as a whole went up only about 100 percent, as contrasted with a 300 percent increase in the number of millionaires.

For the same period, my guess is that the number of centimillionaires probably rose from 150 to 250 or so. If we could compensate for the downward bias in all these estimates, the total proportion of wealth at these heights would rise. And if we brought together into family units the various persons among whom familial wealth has been distributed to avoid taxes, the number of wealth hoards would decrease and a better picture would be provided on the concentration of money power. The billionaires, let me point out, have a thousand times more money than mere millionaires. It is this difference, I suppose, that let Paul Samuelson, himself a millionaire from the sales of his best-selling textbook *Economics*, to say that "almost all of us" are much nearer the ground. Like most economists, however, Samuelson prefers to write about income, which is less concentrated and a little more difficult to hide than wealth.

Many of the ultra-rich and the rich, of course, report no income whatsoever to the government, since they can escape U.S. income taxes by holding tax-exempt bonds and various foreign investments. What is more, many of the rich pay no taxes at all—or little more taxes than the run-of-the-mill office worker whose taxes are deducted at the source. Yet of those who paid taxes on reported income 1,779 persons reported to the Internal Revenue Service in 1978 that during 1977 they received incomes of $1 million or more. The average of this group was $2 million apiece.

"Wherever there is great property," wrote Adam Smith two centuries ago, "there is great inequality. For one very rich man, there must be at least five hundred poor, and the affluence of the few supposes the indigence of the many." Although totally excluded from establishment texts on economics, including Samuelson's, Smith's observation has become even more relevant in today's "more perfect" capitalism. If I consider the poor in Third World countries as well as in America, the ratio may be even higher than Smith's off-the-cuff estimate. If one concentrates on America, one finds a growing gap between the rich and the poor. Thus Herman Miller of the U.S. Census Bureau has calculated that the dollar gap between the average income of the "officially poor" (those below the government's poverty line) and the "rich" grew from $27,300 in 1959 to $37,700 in 1972. In 1959 the "ratio of rich to poor" was 12.5 to 1.[9] By 1972 it rose, according to Miller's calculations, to 16.3 to 1. But "rich" in this calculation referred to the entire top 20 percent of all the people in Samuelson's Eiffel Tower; this includes millions of people far nearer the ground than Samuelson. If Miller had defined "rich," rather, in terms of millionaires (less than two fifths of one percent) the ratio for 1972 would surely have been much more than 100 to 1 rather than the paltry 16 to 1. If he had focused on the ultra-rich, the ratio would have been far higher than 1,000 to 1. It is this higher group which probably owns over 80 percent of all corporate stock, 90 percent of all tax-exempt state and local bonds, and accounts for about a quarter of America's national wealth and income. If we compare any of these groups with the poor and the indigent, the ratios for income are astronomically high. As for wealth, ordinary arithmetic is not relevant—for large numbers of the lowest income groups have more debts than assets. The only way to picture their position is to dig deep underground cellars beneath the tower.

Apologists for concentrated income and wealth often defend the present structure by claiming that perfectly equal distribution—which nobody has ever seriously proposed—would bring everybody down to a dull level of gray austerity. Thus in 1972 Henry Wallich wrote a guest column for *The New York Times* in which he claimed that the average family income in America was only about $10,000. What he called "average," however, was the median. In other words, half the families got less than $10,000 and half more. But when income is inequitably distributed, the mean average is always much higher than the median average. In 1972, for a family of four, as I pointed out a few days later in the same paper's letter column, it was not $10,000 but almost $17,000.[10] By 1979, the mean income for a family of four was well over $33,000—and for the average family of 3.37 family members over $28,000 before taxes and about $24,000 after taxes. Similarly, if all personal wealth were to be divided by the total population, a family of four would have about $100,000. The reason these figures are so high, of course, is the tremendous amount of income and wealth at the very top. If the money of Henry Ford II, who has received as much as $5 million in one year, is added to that of a Ford assembly-line worker and then divided by two, the average comes out at the millionaire level. The high average does not suggest that the mythical average person is well off. On the contrary, it reveals the enormous amount of money available to gratify the self-indulgent whims and power lusts of the Ultra-Rich.

THE CORPORATE OVERSEERS

> No one can be truly powerful unless he has access to the command of major institutions, for it is over these institutional means of power that the truly powerful are, in the first instance, truly powerful . . .
>
> C. Wright Mills [11]

> Their [a few immense corporations] incredible absolute size and commanding market positions make them the most exceptional man-made creatures of the twentieth century. . . . In terms of the

size of their constituency, volume of receipts and expenditures, effective power, and prestige, they are more akin to nation-states than business enterprises of the classic variety.

RICHARD J. BARBER [12]

If better means more powerful, then the rich and the ultra-rich are truly better than most people. While you and I may work for major institutions, they are part of or close to (sometimes on top of) the cliques that control them. Their family life is also different. For ordinary people, family planning has something to do with control over the number and spacing of children. For the rich, family planning involves spawning trust funds and family foundations that hide wealth and augment control of corporate clusters and complexes. As a result of brilliant family planning, the formal institutions of corporate bureaucracy and high finance have not led to a withering away of the Morgans, Rockefellers, Harrimans, du Ponts, Weyerhausers, Mellons, and other oligarchic families of an earlier era. Nor have they prevented the rise of newer family networks such as the Kennedys. Rather, the nature of family wealth and operations has changed. "Rather than an Irénée du Pont exercising absolute domination, now the [du Pont] family fortune has been passed on to a number of heirs, even as the family's *total* wealth continues to grow. This splitting up of family stock blocks does not mean that capital no longer tends to accumulate. Just the opposite . . . du Pont wealth, and the power of their business class as a whole, is not diminishing, but growing." [13]

The growth of familial power, paradoxically, has been made possible by the sharing of that power with nonfamily members who handle their affairs professionally and mediate inevitable intrafamily disputes. Many of the corporate institutions, moreover, have been built and are guided by people who are merely rich and are ultra-rich only in intent. Whether the heirs of old wealth or the creators of new wealth, they mingle with the ultra-rich in clubs and boardrooms and play an indispensable role in overseeing corporate affairs.

The role of overseer no longer requires total ownership—or even owning a majority of a company's stock. Most corporations are controlled by only a small minority of corporate stockholders. By usual Wall Street calculations, 5 percent stock ownership is enough to give total control; in a few cases, the figure may rise to 10 percent. The larger the number of stockholders, the smaller this percentage. This "internal pyramiding" is carried still further through chains of subsidiaries and holding companies. Thus, strategic control of a small block of holding company stock yields power over a vast network of accumulated power and capital. Many of these networks include both financial corporations and corporations in industry, utilities, communications, distribution, and transportation. Most of the overseers are what Herbert Gans called Unknowns. "How many well-informed people," asks Robert Heilbroner, "can name even one of the chief executive officers—with the exception of Henry Ford II—of the top ten industrial companies: General Motors, Standard Oil (N.J.), Ford, General Electric, Socony, U.S. Steel, Chrysler, Texaco, Gulf, Western Electric? How many can name the top figures in the ten top utilities or banks—perhaps with the exception of David Rockefeller?" [14]

While the names of chief executive officers are a matter of public record, the names of the top stockholders are not. Most wealthy individuals, as Richard Barber has shown, "are tending to withdraw from direct stock ownership to companies and to funnel their investments through institutions, especially pension funds and mutual funds. This latter development has substantially increased the power of institutions—pension funds, banks, insurance companies and mutual funds—in the affairs of even the largest companies." [15] These institutions, in turn, manage their operations through the use of "nominees," otherwise known as "straws" or "street names." Thus, such "street names" as Aftco, Byeco and Cadco are some of the code words used by the Prudential Insurance Company, which tends to hide its interests from the general public.[16]

The major companies controlled by the corporate overseers are the largest concentration of capital in industrial capitalism's two-hundred-year history. An important part of this picture is seen by looking at the 500 largest industrial corporations listed every year in *Fortune* magazine. In 1954, when *Fortune* started this listing, these 500 accounted for half the sales and two thirds of the profits of all industrial corporations. By the mid-1970s these figures rose, respectively, to two thirds of the sales and three quarters of the profits. They have been rising since.

With all the attention given to the 500 industrials, most analysts have tended to neglect *Fortune's* annual listing of 300 additional corporations: 50 each in the six areas of commercial banking, life insurance, diversified financial companies, retailing, transportation, and utilties. If one looks at the entire 800 and selects the top 20, as I have done in the following table "The Apex of the Corporate Apex," one finds that by asset size only five industrials—Exxon, General Motors, Mobil, Ford and IBM—are in this topmost group. At the very top stands American Telephone and Telegraph, while the remaining 16 are all financial corporations.

Since *Fortune* also lists the world's largest industrial corporations (outside of the communist countries), it is also interesting to look at the 20 largest as ranked by annual sales volume. Of these 20, 15 are American. While all 20 companies are huge employers, 13 have more than 100,000 employees apiece scattered all around the world. Of these 13, let it be noted, 9 are American. And only General Motors and Ford employ more than 400,000 people. None of the industrial giants, of course, could operate without support and assistance from the financial giants and the corporations in the other sectors.

THE APEX OF THE CORPORATE APEX

The 20 Largest U.S. Corporations, 1978 *
(Ranked by billions of dollars in assets)

	Assets
1. American Telephone and Telegraph (N.Y.)	103
2. BankAmerica Corp. (San Francisco)	95
3. Citicorp (N.Y.)	87
4. Chase Manhattan Corp. (N.Y.)	61
5. Prudential (Newark)	50
6. Metropolitan (N.Y.)	42
7. Exxon (N.Y.)	42
8. Manufacturer's Hanover Corp. (N.Y.)	41
9. J. P. Morgan & Co. (N.Y.)	39
10. Chemical New York Corp.	33
11. General Motors (Detroit)	31
12. Continental Illinois (Chicago)	31
13. Equitable Life Assurance (N.Y.)	28
14. Bankers Trust N.Y. Corp.	26
15. Western Bancorp (L.A.)	26
16. First Chicago Corp.	24
17. Aetna Life and Casualty (Hartford)	24
18. Mobil Oil (N.Y.)	23
19. Ford Motor (Dearborn, MI.)	22
20. IBM (Armonk, N.Y.)	21

* The 1979 Fortune Double 500 Directory

When one looks at the entire apex, whether defined in terms of 800 corporations or a somewhat larger group, it becomes apparent that a few thousand corporate overseers make strategic decisions on the volume and location of investment, the changing pattern of employment in many countries, the kinds of products that are produced, the level of prices and interest rates, and the content of mass advertising. "Instead of government planning," as Andrew Hacker puts it, "there is boardroom planning that is accountable to no outside agency: and these plans set the order of priorities on national growth, technological innovation, and, ultimately, the values and behaviors of human beings." [17] Boardroom planning is just that; its strategic outlines are never publicly proclaimed nor bureaucratically reported to any central control agency or clearing house outside the boardroom. Specific decisions—such as announced increases in prices or interest rates—may come sharply to the attention of buyers and borrowers, but usually after the fact and in isolation from other aspects of flexible corporate planning. Even in such highly concentrated areas as oil, automobiles, food, and commercial banking, the canny outsider can only learn bits and pieces of what is really going on.

THE APEX OF THE CORPORATE APEX

The World's 20 Largest Industrial Corporations, 1978 **
(Ranked by billions of dollars in sales)

	Sales	# Employees
1. General Motors (Detroit)	63	839,000
2. Exxon (N.Y.)	60	130,000
3. Royal Dutch/Shell Group (England/Netherlands)	44	158,000
4. Ford Motor (Dearborn, MI.)	42	507,300
5. Mobil Oil (N.Y.)	35	207,000
6. Texaco (N.Y.)	29	67,841
7. British Petroleum	27	109,000
8. National Iranian Oil	23	67,000
9. Standard Oil of Ca.	23	37,575
10. IBM (Armonk, N.Y.)	21	325,516
11. General Electric (Fairfield, CT.)	20	401,000
12. Unilever (Brit-Neth)	19	318,000
13. Gulf Oil (Pittsburgh)	18	58,300
14. Chrysler (MI.)	16	157,958
15. ITT (N.Y.)	15	379,000
16. Standard Oil (IN., Chi.)	15	47,601
17. Philips (Netherlands)	15	387,000
18. Atlantic Richfield (L.A.)	12	50,716
19. Shell Oil (Houston)	11	34,974
20. U.S. Steel (Pitts.)	11	166,848

** Fortune World Business Directory, 1979

THE CHIEF EXECUTIVE NETWORK

The most visible actors in modern capitalist establishments are the chief executives of national governments—whether presidents or prime ministers—and a few of their aides. Unlike the Ultra-Rich or the Corporate Overseers, the chief executives—and often their family members also—live in a blaze of publicity. They also wear many hats. In the United States the president is not only commander in chief of the armed forces, chief diplomat, high legislator with prerogatives of both initiative and veto, but also boss of covert operations, party leader, tribune of the people, manager of prosperity, symbol (for better or worse) of public morality, and "leader of the Free World." And wherever he goes, he carries with him the control box whose buttons, when properly pushed, would unleash again the fury of nuclear bombs.

Despite all the glare of spotlights on the presidency, however, no other institution in the country is so thoroughly obscured by carefully prepared clouds of mystery and darkness. During the presidential campaigns, in Nicholas Johnson's somewhat whimsical words, the contest is "waged between two television consultants nobody knows." Afterwards, the public image of the victor—including his face, words, and publicized actions—is a public relations product. But it is not quite correct to say that presidents are sold to the public like soap. In this case the product itself is remarkably active. At the risk of *lèse majesté* one might suggest that all recent presidents have shown the combined talents of huckster and actor.

The focus on the president himself obscures the fact that, in the words of an old-time White House correspondent, "the President is many men." In other words, he is a critical node in a Chief Executive Network of staggering complexity. The more formal elements in the network are the many agencies in the White House Office and the Executive Office of the president: particularly, the National Security Council, the National Security Agency, the Office of Management and Budget, the Council of Economic Advisers, and the various cabinet committees or groups supervised by members of the White House staff. Then there is a large number of official aides and advisers, both military and civilian, and a still larger number of unofficial agents and close associates. From this large mass of people—some of them never appearing on the payroll of the White House, the Executive Office or even the federal government—the president selects the members of the various "inner circles" with whom he consults from time to time or to whom he assigns specific missions. Many of these presidential aides enjoy the protection of well-maintained anonymity. Others are known somewhat in Washington circles or even—as in the case of Henry Kissinger before he became secretary of state—to the broader public. They are then given the special protection of the president's "executive privilege," in accordance with which quaint custom they may make statements to the press but may not be interrogated by congressional committees.

As linchpin of the entire capitalist Establishment, the Chief Executive Network plays a role somewhat similar to that of the Communist party structure in a Marxist-Leninist country. But it holds the Establishment together not by party discipline but through a rather flexible set of linkages with other parts of the system. Each of these linkages is wrapped in extra-special mystery. As a former official involved in the daily workings of the presidency during the Fair Deal and the Korean War, I can attest to my own inability to know what was really going on—or perhaps I should say my ability to appreciate the limits of what I could fathom. This same ability was shared not only by my immediate associates in the President's Council of Economic Advisers and budget office but also, I truly believe, by the president himself.

One part of the mystery is the linkage between the presidency and the Ultra-Rich and the Corporate Overseers. Formally, certain links are provided by such groups as the "President's Club" (executives who contributed $1,000 a year to Lyndon Johnson's campaign chest) or the various business advisory committees that mobilized large sums for the reelection campaigns of Presidents Nixon, Ford, and Carter. On his desk in the Oval Office, President Truman used to have a sign reading "The buck stops here." Another sign at the door of the Oval Office, never written but known to anybody aware of the president's central role in raising money for his party, reads "The buck comes here."

Apart from party financing, there has been increasing interpenetration between the Chief Executive Network and the informal circles at the pinnacles of business wealth and power. During the Johnson administration, special advisory groups from the financial community could be quickly brought into being at the suggestion of any top financial leader or top presidential adviser. The operations of the special Vietnam Advisory Group in 1968 were facilitated by the previous experience of Clark Clifford, then secretary of defense, as both counsel to President Truman many years earlier and then special attorney for Du Pont, General Electric, Standard Oil, TWA and RCA. Under Presidents Nixon, Ford, and Carter, two mutually supporting trends developed: the multiplication of advice-or-action groups in such areas as the promotion of multinational corporations, foreign currency manipulations, the protection of U.S. foreign investments, and the imposition of wage controls or wage guidelines; and increasing interaction between the financial community and presidential staff (many of whom have been "on leave" from business positions). Together, these trends have led to more integration than ever before in American history between top business leaders and the prime movers in the federal government. During the Carter administration, this process of integration was illustrated by acceptance through his executive network of the idea that higher business profits are the central purpose of domestic public policy. Thus at the very moment during the first half of 1979, when commentators were criticizing Carter for ineffectiveness, his administration proved remarkably effective for well-synchronized support of corporate profit making. In an article titled "The Secret Success of Jimmy Carter: Profits Without Honor," I came to Carter's defense by pointing out this achievement, while commenting on the paradox that for political reasons he could not take public credit for it.[18]

An equally challenging mystery is the president's involvement in other countries. This is an arcane world of high and low intrigue, far removed from one's customary picture of government bureaucracy, far closer to the world of adventure fiction, rarely unveiled in the diaries, memoirs, or files of participants. Although ambassadors and consular officials are presidential appointees, they often do little more than provide help to special emissaries (sometimes corporate overlords or their representatives) or "cover" for the chief CIA operative or military officer who organizes a coup d'etat. Indeed, under instructions from President Johnson during the 1960s, the CIA carried on a secret vest-pocket presidential war in Laos. Through its so-called "department of dirty tricks," the CIA provides a vehicle for direct or indirect cloak-and-dagger intervention by the presidency in almost any country of the globe. There is good reason to believe—although I cannot prove—that such intervention continued under President Carter in such diverse countries as, for example, Afghanistan, Pakistan, Bangladesh, India, Angola, Somalia, Italy, Portugal, and Spain.

Less dramatic but more complicated is the network of relations between the presidency and the rest of government—the courts, the Congress, the cabinet departments and independent agencies, and the state, local, and county governments, which receive in transfer payments almost $100 billion a year as a result of legislation, judicial decisions, and executive regulations and interpretations. Looking back through history, one may easily find dramatic confrontations between president and the courts and between president and members, committees, or houses of Congress. But the most grueling, the most baffling, the most endless and the most mysterious confrontations are between the president and his aides, on one side, and the labyrinth of intertwined executive bureaucracies stretching from national agencies through all levels of government down to every county, city, town, and neighborhood in the country. At any point in this labyrinth the president or his aides have some sort of potential influence. At a few points they can dominate—but only for a while. A president is like an oriental potentate with a harem of a thousand wives; the harems of his assistants probably scale down to one hundred and then to a measly ten. While the top man is theoretically free to do anything he wants with any harem member, he has only too few days and nights and too little energy in comparison to the opportunities lying before him. If the metaphor breaks down, it is mainly because in this case the underlings organize alliances of their own and can often outwit the president and his aides—particularly if they can win some support from a few entities in Congress, the external lobbies, and particularly the Corporate Overseers and the Ultra-Rich.

One way in which a president can help influence many government agencies at the same time is to pursue the role of "tribune to the people," a role which is best calculated to succeed when the president is doing what is needed by the Ultra-Rich and the Corporate Overlords. Although this role was anticipated many decades earlier by Andrew Jackson, its first exponent in the twentieth century was Theodore Roosevelt, who seemed at times to brandish his "big stick" on behalf of an aroused populace against the "malefactors of great wealth." The same stick—in weight more like an orchestra conductor's baton—was waved vigorously by Woodrow Wilson, Franklin Roosevelt, Harry Truman, John Kennedy, and Lyndon Johnson. But the chorus they led was not composed of popular masses who at last found a leader. It was made up, rather, of sophisticated upper-class corporate leaders and liberal intellectuals, lawyers, and scholars who favored continuous reforms designed to maintain and strengthen the capitalist order and its imperial structure. Often indeed, it seemed that only a president's voice could speak out loudly and clearly on such reforms as income taxes, antitrust legislation, workmen's compensation, regulatory commissions, social security, labor legislation, and expanded public works. But while the voice was that of the president (and broad assent was often obtained throughout the lower and middle classes), the hands that shaped the creaky machinery of government and usually reaped the longest-run benefits from it were those of the upper-class minorities.

These activities by the Chief Executive Network have been successful only to the extent that presidents have identified themselves with certain values or aspirations of the middle and lower classes. By so doing, Democratic presidents won more support from the "Common Man" in the lower classes, Republican presidents from "Middle America" on Main Street. Still more significant, each president uses his Chief Executive Network as a means of keeping in touch with all of the major institutions and organized groups of American society—particularly those at the middle and lower levels of the establishment. For every geographic, income, ethnic, and religious grouping there is some federal agency, some government policy, some direct or remote tie to some part of the Chief Executive Network. In this symbolic manner there are no longer any Forgotten Men or Forgotten Women in America. Some kind of attention to *all* interests is a prerequisite for adequate servicing of upper-class interests.

As linchpin of the Establishment, the Chief Executive Network often operates at a level of high policy in which apparently unconnected policies help solidify both the Establishment and its popular support. Thus in the early days of the "Free World" empire, President Truman's cold war and military expansion pleased the conservatives, while his Fair Deal proposals (blocked by the conservatives in Congress) placated the liberals. Similarly, as he expanded American military intervention in Vietnam, President Johnson won substantial liberal support by reviving much of the Fair Deal, improving a few of its elements and getting congressional action on them. Under President Carter two apparently contradictory policies—arms control for the liberals and military expansion for the conservatives—were wrapped together in one bundle. Similarly, President Carter's stress on human rights, in addition to restoring some moral tone to U.S. foreign policy, gave ammunition to conservatives for attacking all socialist countries and to liberals for campaigns against U.S.-supported dictatorships in Iran, Nicaragua, Argentina, Chile, and South Korea.

EXECUTIVE MANAGERS

I don't care what the management is so long as it is successful.
MARRINER ECCLES [19]

Karl Marx was one of the first to focus on the expanding role of industrial managers—as distinct from owners—in capitalist enterprise. In every generation since then, observers have rediscovered the same trend. While Marx underestimated the managers, James Burnham and John Kenneth Galbraith went to the other extreme by proclaiming a "managerial revolution" and rule by the "technostructure." But in a complex system the growing importance of some component—like radar instruments in an airplane—does not meant it is in charge. Executive managers are, of course, steering instruments, are used as such, and are particularly valued to the extent that they are self-starting and, subject to vague clues from above, self-steering. Despite some personal stockholdings, the higher executives are "hired executives." Their power and glory derive from service, and subservience, to superiors—above all, from their ability to provide this service most of the time without explicit tutelage. They can be ruthlessly fired if they fail to accumulate the capital that their overseers deem possible.

The most obvious function of executive management is the production and marketing of goods and services for profits. This is the mighty engine that keeps the wheels of capitalism turning, and provides jobs for the great majority of the wage-earning population, the worldly goods for man's consumption or use, and the money and power so essential to satisfy the acquisitive drives of the Ultra-Rich Corporate Overseers. In a still larger sense, moreover, the high executives who manage the domestic and foreign aspects of banking, agribusiness, mining, manufacture, construction, transportation, wholesaling, and retailing also oversee the systematized rewards and punishments embodied in the wages, salaries, and other emoluments received or sought by 70 million private-sector employees. This is a bonding element in the structure of power, one that helps bind the Establishment as a whole to the population's pockets.

To a large extent the mass media are subsidized through the advertising divisions of the larger corporations. Some of the advertising is frankly institutional, associating one or another big-business institution with socially approved values of integrity and public service. But most of it is directly aimed at "soft" or "hard" selling, with "puffery" triumphing over integrity and public manipulation over public service. The entertainment subsidized by advertising provides escape from the strains of the real world or entry into an imaginary world peopled by dramatic symbols of high consumption, excitement, and sexual fulfillment.

The news and commentaries subsidized by advertising provide a more varied agenda, highlighting the rich diversity of views within the public consensus as defined by the Establishment and sharply defining—if not often creating—those subjects generally recognized as public issues. The elite media, in turn, provide the technical, cultural, and recreational materials needed or desired by all the various groupings, currents, and cross currents within the Establishment itself.*

Another executive-management function of vital importance is developing the new or stronger institutions required by any powerful and flexible establishment. This is the major task—rarely recognized—of such superfoundations as Ford, Rockefeller, Duke, Johnson, Lilly, Pew, Carnegie, and Mellon. The avowed purpose and legal justification of these foundations is "philanthropy," the giving of charity to the poor and the helpless; hence their executives are sometimes called "philanthropoids." Before the welfare state, some of the foundations were actually engaged in direct charitable activities. More recently, this function has faded into the background. Most analysts of the growth of American foundations seem agreed on a variety of narrow functions: the avoidance of inheritance taxes; perpetuation of personal or family control over corporate activities through indirect means; extension of power and control into such areas as education, science, technology, the arts, and welfare programs; and creation of a public relations image of "doing good" to help cover up the crudity, violence, lawbreaking, or corruption often associated with the making of the donors' fortunes. All of these are indeed a part of the picture—particularly tax avoidance, without which most of the foundations would immediately crumble and wither away. But emphasis on these points tends to distract attention from the specific ways in which the philanthropoids of the superfoundations have used tax-exempt money in immortalizing corporate control and creating personal and family images: They have financed many of the most prestigious universities, hospitals, scientific laboratories, museums, and social service institutions. During the quarter century after World War II they sparked new initiatives in technical assistance to underdeveloped countries, the development of new government programs at all levels, and the immense expansion of the social and behavioral sciences. While often operating under the guidance of the Corporate Overseers or Ultra-Rich, they contribute to almost all of the institutions of executive management. Also, a major thrust is to promote the still greater expansion of institutions and personnel at the lower levels of junior and contingent membership. They are thus a positive force in promoting the system-strengthening reforms so essential for the sustained growth of a more sophisticated capitalism.

---

* The media deserve much more attention—and they get it in chapter 12, "Managing Information and Minds."

Institution building, in turn, verges over into the closely related function of broad policy planning. It is more diffusely oriented, rather, to the germination, crystalization, and clarification of the wide variety of competing policy options (many of them to be hailed, or adopted, as "reforms" or "revolutions") that may best serve the interests of dominant establishment forces. Hence, there is a wide diversity of emphasis in the conduct of policy planning functions. The values of conservative business and wealth are translated into policy specifics through such groups as the National Association of Manufacturers, the Conference Board, the Chamber of Commerce of the United States, the Business Council, the American Farm Bureau Federation, their sectoral affiliates in areas ranging from automobiles and cotton through machine tools and zinc, and their state and local branches. Still more conservative views are articulated by the American Enterprise Institute and the American Security Council. Policy formulation for the more liberal businessmen and plutocrats is handled by such groups as the Committee for Economic Development, the National Planning Association, the Twentieth Century Fund, and The Brookings Institution, and—in foreign policy—the Council on Foreign Relations and the Foreign Policy Association.

Cutting across both sets of interests are a long succession of *ad hoc* task forces and blue-ribbon commissions (some requested by presidents, to prepare the groundwork for shifts in presidential policy) and a far-flung array of "think tanks" and research institutions. Many of the latter —like RAND, the Systems Development Corporation, the Institute for Defense Analysis, the Centre for Research on Institutions and Social Policy, the Hudson Institute, and the Urban Institute—are wholly or in large part financed by government contracts. Most new policy departures —including the U.S. switch on the admission of China into the United Nations, the use of armed forces in Vietnam, the institution of systems budgeting, federal revenue sharing, and President Carter's cautious "opening" toward Cuba—are initiated only after careful sifting, formulation, and reformulation by one or more of such groups. Sometimes these departures are prepared for by special commissions set up by the president, foundations, or both together.

Throughout this process opportunities are created for people from the junior and contingent level (particularly experts and academics) to make contacts with Corporate Overseers, their aides and the advisers of the chief executive. Executive managers, in turn, meet many people from vastly different ethnic and class backgrounds. These contacts facilitate the selective recruitment of sound "upward-mobiles" into the high-energy staffs at executive levels. With the participation of elected and appointed government officials, they also help crystalize government policy options before they are crystalized within government in operational form.

The nature of this advance preparation—as well as the complexity of the process—is partially suggested in Domhoff's chart "The Policy

THE POLICY FORMULATORS

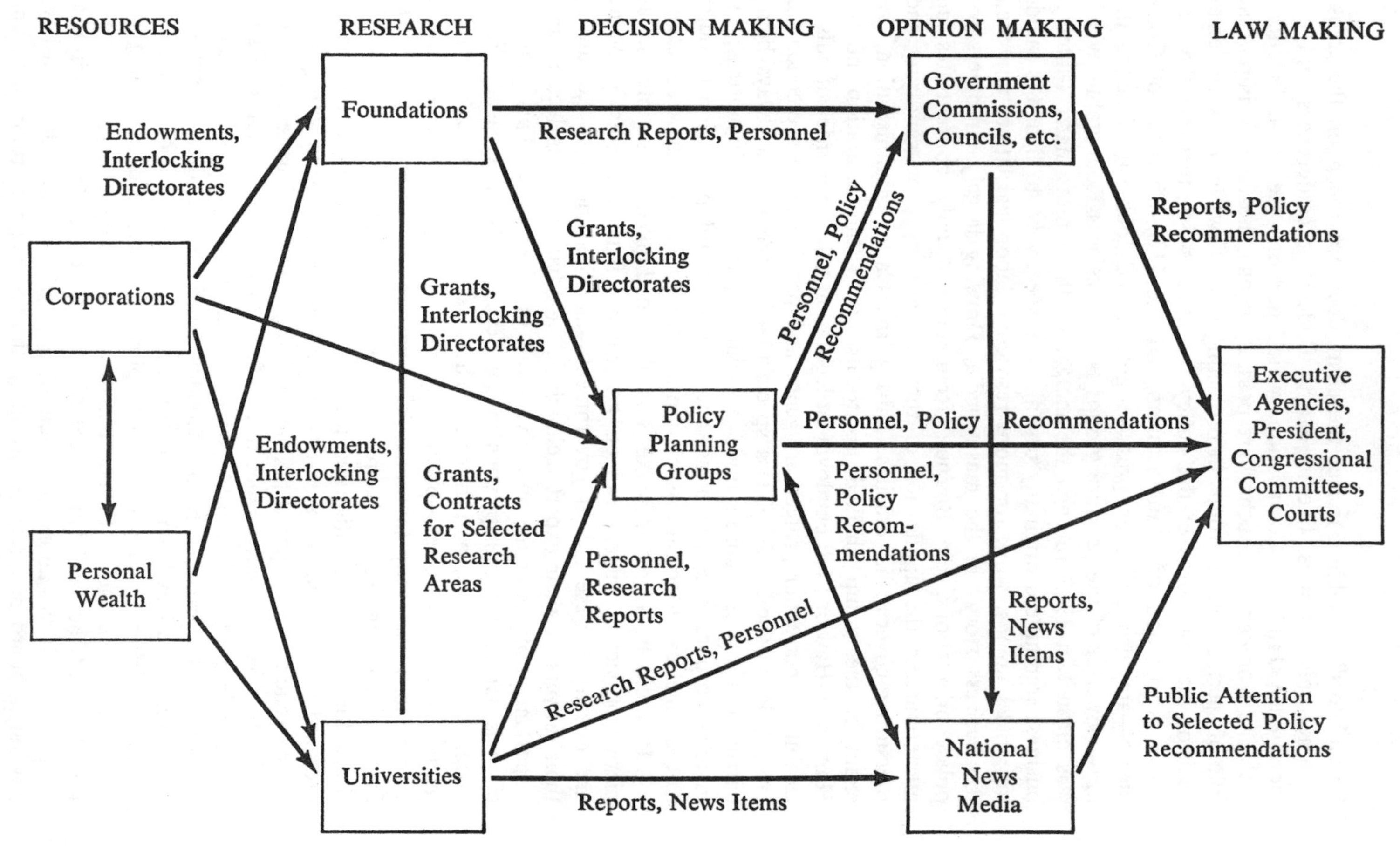

Formulators"[20] (table 6). But the chart does not touch on the transnational policy groups, like the secret Bilderburg conferences and the more open Trilateral Commission, which perform the same functions globally. Nor can any such chart possibly depict the equally important role of special-interest groups in projecting their views into governmental decision making. Some of the policy formulators—particularly the National Association of Manufacturers and the U.S. Chamber of Commerce—are also active as pressure groups and lobbyists. One of the most powerful of the pressure groups is the Business Roundtable, which was created in 1973 through the merger of three more narrow-interest business committees originally organized, respectively, to fight the building trades unions, work for more restrictive labor legislation, and "tell the business story" in the mass media. Drawing largely on others for policy orientations, the Business Roundtable usually concentrates on masterminding the application of these policies by propagandizing and pressuring government officials. During the Carter administration, for example, the group chalked up to its credit the castration of the Humphrey-Hawkins full employment legislation and the murder of bills to establish a consumer protection agency and provide more protection for labor unions. Thousands of less spectacular campaigns are always being carried out by specialized trade associations, *ad hoc* committees, individual corporations, law firms, and such powerful professional bodies as the American Medical Association and the American Bar Association.

It would be a great mistake, however, to think of these interests as merely projecting their views on government from the outside. Many are directly represented in government—as when business executives, their lawyers or their expert technicians, or advisers themselves occupy important positions at the executive levels of government. This phenomenon is particularly conspicuous in the departments of Treasury, State, Defense, Agriculture, and Interior. There is also a reverse flow from many executive agencies—particularly the military and the regulatory commissions—whereby thousands of expert officials prepare themselves for more lucrative private employment through their government work. More formal representation of private interests, mainly corporate, is provided by hundreds of advisory committees that consult with government agencies on proposed policies at early stages, originate many new policies, or veto initiatives that run counter to their perception of Establishment interests. The most powerful of these groups was the Defense Department Industrial Advisory Council consisting of about twenty-five high-level executives from major war contractors. Because of its work in obtaining higher profit rates on cost-plus contracts and promoting the sale of arms abroad, a former Pentagon cost analyst, A. Ernest Fitzgerald, called the IAC "the board of directors of the military-industrial complex." This was an exaggeration, of course. A complex does not have any single board of directors any more than a capitalist ruling class can have a single executive committee. The institutional basis of coherence is much more delicate and complex. Actually, the IAC was dissolved in 1974. It was replaced by a network composed of the Aerospace Industries Association, the National Security Industry Association, and more specialized groups that work closely with the military on a daily basis. The power of the military-industrial complex has not been adversely affected by this change.[21]

On a broader scale, there are also many continuing efforts to bring together the dominant interests in the private, public, and nonprofit sectors. "Every year since 1950, it has been discovered, major business groups join with the American Farm Bureau Federation, the American Bar Association and the American Medical Association for an annual Greenbrier Conference—named after the plush hotel in the resort town of White Sulphur Springs, West Virginia, where they meet—to map out their lobbying strategy for the coming year." [22] Through these and other less formal or more secret processes big business, corporate law, and the biggest farm organizations work out common views on major issues. Ever since World War II these views are projected on to a much wider public through the lavishly funded advertising campaigns of the Advertising Council.

An equally essential but still more complicated function of executive management is provided by the higher-level bureaucrats who guide the operations of the intertwined bureaucratic hierarchies in the private, public, and nonprofit sectors. According to the fairy tales of official sociology or public administration, a top-level bureaucrat is an organization man who takes orders, obeys rules, and competes jealously with all other organizations. As a former bureaucrat of this type in President Truman's office, I reject this stereotype. Many top-level bureaucrats—whether advisers or administrators—are innovative persons who, like Edward Gibbon's "masters of the Roman world," humbly profess themselves the accountable servants of their superiors whose decrees they dictate and obey. Most of them can survive or be successful only by being "wheelers and dealers" who continuously forge and reforge alliances with varied bedfellows—above, alongside and below—in the Establishment. Because many of these officials resist pressures from the Chief Executive Network, the president's aides often see them as being "in business for themselves." Actually, it is this free-wheeling operation that has often done wonders to energize the Chief Executive Network itself and contribute to the more successful performance of the Establishment's business.

This function is probably best illustrated by the rather tough-minded and "independent" bureaucracy in the military services. The Department of Defense and the Joint Chiefs of Staff are the largest employers and spenders in the United States. They must supervise over a million civilian employees, over two million military people, large reserve contingents, and hundreds of huge military contracts, installations, and movements across fifty states, scores of other countries, and on, over and under the high seas. Quite a large number of "high brass" and civilian executives are required to impose some degree of managerial control. But this does not mean that this country's highest-ranking military notables may be ranked (as C. Wright Mills once suggested) alongside the Ultra-Rich, the Corporate Overseers, or the presidency. On all major issues they are subordinate to civilian superiors whose militaristic *machismo* is sometimes bloodthirstier than that of people with battlefield experience; and their eagerness for postretirement jobs with the corporations guarantees an appropriate subservience to civilian overlords.

JUNIOR AND CONTINGENT MEMBERS

> It [the Establishment] may even include leadership or pressure groups of organizations antagonistic or potentially antagonistic to the dominant class and the social order. . . . Their continued participation is dependent upon their continued good behavior.
>
> ANDREAS PAPANDREOU [23]

The lowest levels of the Establishment include the leaders of all the many institutions that directly employ, govern, or feast upon the vast middle and lower classes of workers, consumers, taxpayers, and voters. These private, public, and nonprofit institutions provide the solid foundation for, and operating arms of, Establishment power. As such, they have proliferated enormously in the decades since World War II. As one looks back upon the 1960s especially, one recalls how frequently it was said, in popular and activist parlance, that in one or another of these areas "That's where the action is." And that is where it continues to be: not action to decide the course of national policy at home or abroad, but action to implement it, to absorb the shock of attacks on the Establishment, and to suck upward into the higher ranks those few members of the middle and lower classes capable of proving their usefulness and reliability. Many people suffer from the illusion that the "They" of the Establishment are those juniors closest to them and most visible—namely, immediate employers, officials of schools, hospitals, welfare agencies, and police, and leaders of trade unions, political parties, and churches. Only when they get closer to the action (particularly when they prepare to move upward themselves) do they realize that meaningful participation at this level is contingent, in Papandreou's words, "upon their continued good behavior."

According to the myths of old-fashioned political science, the "separation of powers" endows the Supreme Court and the Congress with power equal to the president's while the federal system reserves for the fifty states all the "powers not delegated to the United States by the Constitution, nor prohibited by it to the States." Beyond the constitutional niceties, political parties are supposed to bring separated parts of government together in organic unity, while also providing the electorate a clear choice among alternative directions. That things do not happen exactly this way under conditions of escalating presidential power is illustrated by continuing outcries for the restoration of congressional authority, the exercise of judicial restraints on executive usurpation, the revival of states' (or local governments') rights, and the building of a responsible party system. The hard-fact content underlying the litany of plaintive calling for this or that reform is that all government below the Chief Executive Network operates most of the time at the junior level. If there is a real, rather than an illusory, tripartite separation among counterbalancing powers, it is not to be found in the formal structure of government. It lies, rather, in the divisions among the Corporate Overseers, the Ultra-Rich, and the Chief Executive network. And to a smaller degree a certain hierarchical separation may be found: between the new Lords at the Establishment's apex, the Lords Temporal of executive management, and the junior and contingent members who comprise the new Commons of the modern capitalist Establishment. Moreover, the old saying "You can't beat City Hall" needs substantial revision. Those who have "beaten" City Hall, the police department, the welfare agency, the university, or any of the junior-level institutions find out that they have captured an empty citadel and end up serving as instruments of, or transmission belts for, higher business and political power.

Another myth elaborately nourished by the more conservative business and political leaders of macrobusiness is the great power of labor unions. Business outcries against the tyranny of Big Labor were particularly strong during the many decades before the New Deal and the government-protected rise of industrial unionism. In recent years, the myth has lingered on—although in a somewhat ethereal rather than full-bodied form. Behind the earthy image of cigar-chomping George Meany lies the power to get a few paltry patches on the sub-welfare state, a few vetoes on issues of marginal importance, a few dedicated friends in elected posts, and many ringing campaign promises that are largely forgotten after elections. Andreas Papandreou's comment about contingent status in the Establishment is particularly relevant to organized labor. While "responsible" trade unions can be immense forces for maintaining the discipline of the work force and nipping socialist movements in the bud, there is always a potentiality for antagonism to "the dominant class and the dominant social order." This potentiality expresses itself whenever a union goes too far in pressing its demands on profits or directly involving itself in matters assumed to be the special prerogatives of management. More broadly, there is also the risk of more widespread unionization. If the proportion of unionized workers in America should rise from 25 percent to the British level of 40 percent, the Swedish of 60 percent, or the Israeli of 75 percent, the payoff in terms of benefits and shared power might be somewhat uncomfortable. These are the reasons, rather than their uncouth manners or backgrounds, why labor leaders' participation in higher affairs is usually "contingent upon their continued good behavior."

There seems to be a general rule that the power of any junior-level group or institution is widely exaggerated during any period in its expansion. Before World War II, the growth of professional management was clearly documented by such astute observers as Walter Rathenau, Adolf Berle, and James Burnham, each of whom then dizzily proceeded to suggest the success of a "managerial revolution" that divorced managers from control by the wealthiest property owners. The rising role of engineers in the processes of production and distribution led Thorstein Veblen to envision an economy in which the engineers became the top managers, replacing both capitalists and politicians. This vision was later embodied in Technocracy, Inc., a movement led by engineers and economists in the 1930s. After the atomic explosions at Hiroshima and Nagasaki, atomic physicists were often hailed as "the new men of power," or attacked as a new satanic priesthood capable of taking society by the scruff of the neck. They were soon outclassed, however, by the economists, who have received much of the credit for the "sophisticated judgments" responsible for taming the capitalist business cycle. The hegemony of the economists, in turn, was challenged during the 1960s by increasing numbers of behavioral or social scientists from sociology, psychology, political science, anthropology, and the newer fields of "computer science" and "systems analysis." After "cracking the genetic code" through their work on DNA and RNA, biologists began to compete with atomic physicists. The only professional groups that have not aspired to more limelight have been the lawyers and accountants; this is possibly to be explained less by inherent professional modesty than by the movement of their most able spokesmen into executive management roles where power, like sex, is best enjoyed when least exhibited in public.

All these many professional specializations have been transcended, however, in magnificent claims for new-style technocrats. Thus Daniel Bell has hailed the broad new class of "knowledge elites," the vast array of experts who are pragmatically empirical in specifying *where* one wants to go, *how* to get there, the costs of the enterprise, and some realization of, and justification for, the determination of *who* is to pay.[24]

In a similar spirit of magnification, John K. Galbraith has acclaimed the role of "the technostructure"—all who bring specialized knowledge, talent, or experience to group-decision making—in providing the "guiding intelligence" or "brain" of large-scale corporate and federal action.[25] Daniel P. Moynihan has pointed out that America has arrived at a "type of decision-making that is suited to the techniques of modern organizations, and which ends up in hands of persons who make a profession of it. . . . They are decisions that can be reached by consensus rather than conflict." [26] Clearly, this style of exaggeration does not discuss the processes of decision making on *which* brains to hire, *what* to do with their products, or *where* the consensus begins and ends. But it does serve the function of morale building throughout the junior levels.

The competition among competing specialties is unnerving, to say the least. Hardly does one group of experts carve out an "ecological niche" for itself than some other group arises to challenge its competence or—as the case with much of systems theory and computer science—to assert general hegemony over all specialized areas. Moreover, the incessant multiplication of expertly defined options for either selection or rejection by those at higher levels inevitably means more of the latter than the former. To this situation must be added the tendency of all junior-level institutions to compete bitterly among themselves for larger shares of scarce resources and, wherever possible to veto the claims of competitors. This is why there is so much empirical backing to the lower levels of the Establishment for David Riesman's view of society as an aggregation of conflicting "veto groups." Also relevant is Daniel Bell's story of the social scientist who runs from his office into the streets shouting "I have a solution! Who has a problem?" When there are more offered solutions than takers, the expert tends to resemble the call girl who stands by the telephone but is seldom called. Perhaps in John Milton's words, "they also serve who only stand and wait."

The very process of waiting or actively seeking to serve, however, has implications. Intellectuals are brought out of the ivory tower and lined up for foundation grants, government contracts, corporate consultancies, or luscious lecture fees. The fallout, or spinoff, from such emoluments helps convert erstwhile intellectuals into technicians no longer interested in ideas for their own sake. "Independent merchants and lawyers, once noted for their forthright views on public affairs," comments Ferdinand Lundberg, "spoke out as the occasion seemed to require. Now that they are gone down the corporate drain, theirs and other voices are frozen in corporate silence." [27] University presidents also once used to speak out with a measure of independence. Under modern capitalism, their voices are "frozen in corporate silence" or else carry the burden of technocratic argumentation within the boundaries of Establishment consensus. Such circumstances help fashion a younger generation of pragmatic mercenaries eager to enter the brains-for-hire market.

At the junior and contingent level, however, the boundaries of Establishment consensus are broad enough to allow generous room for debate not only on minor details but also on established departures from the middle of the road. Heretics on both the Left and the Right are encouraged. Indeed, one minority of the Ultra-Rich has continuously subsidized various left-liberal and radical groups, parties, and publications, while another minority (sometimes larger) has supported various right-wing extremists. One can truly wonder how any institution can long continue to function *outside* of the Establishment. Fundamental dissent is not impossible, but there is no point in denying its difficulty. The very act of institutionalizing—whether in a John Birch Society or a Communist party—tends to bring it into or close to the system, even if only on a contingency basis. Heretics and infidels operating at the Establishment's border only make it easier for the middle-of-the road institutions to put into effect the continuing reforms required for the maintenance and strengthening of modern capitalism.

CONFLICTS AMONG THE FEW

Neither the government nor the Establishment as a whole act unitedly on many fronts. Even the broad general agreements that are often tacitly accepted are usually flawed by clashing interpretations and shifting blocs and coalitions. These divergencies are partly rooted in the sharp rivalries between the producers of military and civilian goods and services; between consumption and investment goods producers; among manufacturers, wholesalers, and retailers; between financial institutions and their creditors; between owners with many interests and executives with narrower interests; among large, medium, and small enterprises; among regional and family groupings; among trade associations with different constituencies; and between self-seeking business interests and presidents (and their staffs) seeking to represent what they presume to be the interests of business as a whole. Above all, when the Ultra-Rich and Corporate Overseers enter the charmed circles of chief-executive power and compete for positions of either open or hidden influence on the high issues of national policy, deep personal drives, propensities and peculiarities—always a part of normal business conflict—become accentuated. Differences over strategy and tactics become inseparably linked with personal ambitions, thereby adding a distinctly human flavor to the changing conflicts among the Establishment's leaders.

These conflicts among the few are not mere imperfections in ruling-class power, imperfections to be ironed out in the course of increased centralization and concentration. Rather, they are an integral part of the process whereby a ruling coalition comes to power and expands its power. Often, as I have shown in chapter 1 on classic fascism, the more powerful a ruling oligarchy, the sharper—and rougher—the conflicts among the oligarchs may become. So long as unity is somehow attained on the most basic matters, internal conflicts may bring new options into the open, thereby avoiding routinization and serving as a vital source of strength. Moreover, there is a vast difference in the nature of conflicts at the lower levels of the American power structure and those at its highest levels. At the lower levels, conflicts are more numerous, intricate, and unresolved. They often constitute what C. Wright Mills described as a "semi-organized stalemate, a way of hampering the more direct expression of popular aspiration," and a form of "divide and rule" through which the few at the very top gain immensely through the divisions among their subordinates. In contrast, conflicts among the very few at the top of the Establishment determine the major public issues in American life—not only when there is a "deep political crisis," as Papandreou suggests, but also in normal times.

Before World War II, the ultra-rich, top business leaders, and the leading contenders for the U.S. presidency were divided on three major issues. During the three decades following World War II, as these issues were partly resolved, they changed their form.

The first issue was the geographical orientation of American economic and political involvement abroad. On the one side stood those who cherished ties with Britain and Europe. Seeing Britain and Europe as the former center of the British Empire and the world, they called themselves "internationalists." Pitted against them were those who favored more aggressive U.S. intervention in Asia and the entire Pacific basin. To the Europe-oriented elites, they were "isolationists" from European affairs or "noninterventionists" in European wars. By the end of World War II, both groups became more world-oriented and the old divisions slowly (and sometimes painfully) faded into the background. The present divisions are among different styles and emphases in the preservation or expansion of the "Free World" empire.

The second issue was the extent of the federal government's intervention into the economy. The basic division has been between the "business conservatives," who favor large-scale help to big business directly, with carefully restricted social welfare programs, and the "big-business liberals," who favor both direct and indirect help to big business, with more central government planning and larger social welfare programs to maintain market demand and dampen class conflict. The New Deal, Fair Deal and Great Society reform measures were, in large part, a victory for the business liberals. By the mid-1970s most of the business conservatives accepted many of these reforms and the entire struggle started all over again with respect to new expansions in government intervention. The most fundamental of these relate to alternative ways of coping with (and benefiting from) stagflation and attaining higher rates of profitability and capital accumulation.

The third issue has been the conflict over which groups shall be more influential among the Ultra-Rich, the Corporate Overseers and the key personnel of the Chief Executive Network. Before and during World War II the dominant element in national affairs was the complex network often referred to as the "Eastern Establishment," and was often attacked by rival financial groups as "*the* Establishment." The dominance of this network over both the Republican party and the Republican presidency was dramatized in the nomination of Wendell L. Willkie (against Senator Robert Taft) in 1940 and of New York Governor Thomas E. Dewey (against Taft) in 1948 and in the election of General Dwight D. Eisenhower in 1952 and 1956. But the huge economic expansion in the postwar period—particularly in oil and defense contracts—brought new business moguls to greater heights of economic and political power. Thus, the presidential nomination of Senator Barry Goldwater in 1964 was a defeat for the northeast liberal corporate wing of the Establishment. But in 1968, with the nomination and election of Richard Nixon, who succeeded in planting one foot firmly in each camp, a new synthesis was achieved. By admitting the new challengers from the West, Southwest and South, the northeastern wing succeeded in maintaining its power. By the 1970s it slowly began to dawn on political commentators that there is no longer any northeastern liberal corporate faction clearly identified with the "Atlantic Alliance" and mild social reform. The top financial, business, and political oligarchs are now increasingly global in their orientations. But they are still divided on how to cope with the expansion of socialism and communism, the crises of stagflation and class conflict, and the side effects of their success in accumulating capital and power. As for the heretical deviations that recurringly crop up within the Establishment itself, they are divided on tactics, but unified on the central necessity of maintaining the Establishment's central values.

PURGES AND CONVERSIONS

> At least 8,000,000 Americans are always under shadow of having to prove their loyalty, if any anonymous, protected informer questions it. Including the families of 8,000,000, about 20,000,000 American citizens are subject to investigative procedures at any time. As people enter and leave investigated employment, the vast total of people who have secret police dossiers compiled about them increases every year.
>
> D. F. FLEMING [28]

After the fall of Japan in 1945, the wartime American Establishment was not yet up to the task of overseeing the reconstruction of war-torn capitalist countries, unifying the noncommunist world, and coping with the old crises of capitalism. At one and the same time, it was necessary to demobilize America's far-flung armies in response to war weariness at home and then to expand and restructure the Establishment as a whole, while infusing large amounts of loyal brainpower into its many levels.

But there were serious obstacles to doing this effectively. Old-time pacifists and noninterventionists—some in important positions of power—began to voice their opposition to the Truman Doctrine, Greek-Turkish aid, the Marshall Plan, universal military training, and other cold-war programs. Moreover, "a war which was defined as a struggle against Fascism . . . tended to reinforce the political predominance of leftist liberal sentiments." Throughout the lower levels of the establishment, there were many thousands of officials, professionals, experts, intellectuals, and artists who, if they had not adopted certain aspects of Communist ideology, were at least sympathetic with America's recent allies, the communists in Russia, China, and Indochina. Among these, there were undoubtedly underground members of various left-wing parties and a larger number of "crypto-socialists" who could no longer accept corporate entitlements to power, privilege, and property and who saw the Democratic party as a vehicle for bringing some form of socialism to America. In 1944, according to one informed estimate, Communist leaders were in control of trade unions with 20 percent of union membership. Leaders with socialist leanings probably accounted for at least another 20 percent.

If these impurities in the establishment had not been eliminated, the unity of the "Free World" might have been undermined at its vital center. Socialism and communism might have expanded more rapidly, and many corporate plans for the accumulation of power and capital would probably have been impaired. Above all, the conflicts at the higher levels of the Establishment might have erupted into differences on fundamental values rather than on tactics and techniques.

In communist countries disloyalty and dissidence within the power structure are usually fought by purges and ideological campaigns led by the Party's dominant faction. In the postwar United States there was no single group with the vision or power to attempt such a cleansing operation. Instead, there developed a veritable orgy of competing purification efforts in which many of the most effective purifiers were themselves branded as traitors or "pinkos" and impelled into still greater demonstrations of their loyalty to the new capitalist order. In this process, immeasurable help was provided by Stalinism in the Soviet Union, which helped convert many noninterventionists and "Asia-firsters" into cold warriors on a global scale and served to disillusion American liberals and radicals concerning the potentialities of any serious alternative to welfare-state capitalism.

The least remembered story on the postwar purification of the American Establishment is the story of what happened to the conservative noninterventionists who objected vigorously to the global expansion of American empire under a military umbrella. As far back as 1943, after the Germans had been defeated at Stalingrad and Allied troops had landed in Italy, influential Senators—backed up by various forces in the business community and the press—were already looking forward to an American withdrawal from Europe at the war's end. Instead of waiting for their blows to fall, President Roosevelt took the initiative. Rather than directly attacking such men as Senators Vandenberg, Taft, Wheeler and Nye, he prodded Attorney General Francis Biddle into a mass indictment of what James McGregor Burns has called "a grand rally of all the fanatic Roosevelt haters." [29] The defendants were charged under the Smith Act of 1940 which (originally aimed at the Communists) prohibited groups from conspiring to advocate the violent overthrow of the government or insubordination and mutiny in the armed forces. With huge amounts of publicity, the great "sedition trial" got under way in the spring of 1944. As a judicial undertaking it was a colossal failure; after seven and a half months, the judge died, and the Justice Department—battered from pillar to post by the civil libertarian counterattacks of the defendants—dropped the case completely. As propaganda, however, it was a great success; it suggested that the real opponents of the administration's policies were—like many of the defendants—anti-Semites, Nazi sympathizers, and fascist fellow travellers. It was thus a factor in preventing unity between right-wing and left-wing opponents of the administration. As suggested by Ronald Radosh, it helped isolate—and push to the right—such liberal critics as Charles Beard, the historian, Oswald Garrison Villard, former editor of *The Nation*, and John T. Flynn, columnist for the *New Republic,* all of whom attacked the drift toward American empire.[30]

Still greater success was attained in converting former "isolationists," some of whom were justifiably afraid of the attacks leveled against them, others of whom were amply rewarded for their switch by being acclaimed as towering statesmen. Thus Senator Arthur Vandenberg of Michigan, one of the most forthright among the earlier noninterventionists, was brought into the counsels of the Roosevelt and Truman administrations and became the widely acclaimed leader of the bipartisan foreign policy consensus on U.S. leadership of the "Free World." At a later date, the same happened with many other conservative leaders, including Senator Everett Dirksen of Illinois. In neither the Vandenberg nor the Dirksen case could this change of heart be separated from the new global orientations of the largest midwest corporations in industry and banking. All such shifts, whether among political leaders or business leaders, were part of a painful process that did not end until the Eisenhower administration. Thus, with the outbreak of the Korean War in 1950, Senator Robert A. Taft of Ohio reluctantly supported Truman's military policies but not his failure to seek a declaration of war by Congress. A year later he rallied the isolationist forces to pass a Senate resolution to keep the President from sending troops to Western Europe without congressional authorization. But the authorization was given. And in 1952, as the Eisenhower forces on the floor of the Republican National Convention shattered Taft's bid for the presidential nomination, the right-wing opponents of "cold war" imperialism went down to their final defeat.

Left wing opposition to the Establishment's global orientation was demolished by a long-drawn-out process of so-called "witch hunting" or "red baiting." The history of these activities has often been associated with the name of Senator Joseph McCarthy of Wisconsin, who from 1950 to 1954—luridly supported by the attention of press, television, and radio—conducted a rabid campaign against "traitors in high places," "egg-sucking phoney liberals," "prancing mimics of the Moscow party line," "top Russian espionage agents" in government departments, and "dilettante diplomats" who "cringed" in the face of communism. Although never supported by evidence, McCarthy's sensational charges helped defeat many Democratic liberals and middle-of-the-roaders in the congressional elections of 1950 and 1952. As a reward, the Senate Republican leadership gave him the chairmanship of the Senate's Permanent Investigations Subcommittee, an ideal springboard for another two years of flamboyant witch-hunting.

Anyone who gives too much attention, however, to the "McCarthyism" of the early 1950s may underestimate the wide-ranging purges that took place in earlier years. Back in 1934, Representative Samuel Dickstein of New York proposed a special House committee to investigate "Nazi activities in the U.S. and other forms of subversive propaganda." As a result, a House committee under the chairmanship of John McCormack of Massachusetts (with Dickstein as vice-chairman) conducted some investigations of Nazi-American and anti-Semitic organizations. When the committee's authority expired, Dickstein tried again, this time teaming up with Representative Martin Dies of Texas, who wanted an investigation of all "un-American" activities. The Dies-Dickstein resolution—with the support of many liberal groups—was passed. This time Dickstein was shoved aside even more completely, not even getting a place on the committee. Under Dies's chairmanship, the new House Committee on Un-American Activities forgot almost completely about pro-Nazis and anti-Semites and launched a vigorous attack on alleged radicals in government, on the more liberal members of President Roosevelt's cabinet, and on the more liberal and radical trade unions then represented by the newly organized CIO.[31] The committee received powerful support from a special "un-American activities" group set up by the U.S. Chamber of Commerce. During the period of the Nazi-Soviet pact (August 1939 to June 1941), as many American communists opposed the Administration's policies of aid to Britain, the Dies Committee stepped up its attack on radicals in government. Although Dies himself was not a conspicuous anti-Hitlerite, he made brilliant political capital out of embarrassing people who had been vigorously anti-Hitler until the Nazi-Soviet pact and then promptly changed their minds. By the time the pact was itself destroyed by Hitler's invasion of the Soviet Union and the American communists had switched their position again, pressure from the business-backed "un-American activities" groups had forced FDR's administration to initiate an Attorney General's list of "subversive organizations" and a new system of "loyalty checks." As the war drew to a close and the Soviet Union changed almost overnight from ally to cold-war adversary, the anti-communist campaign was renewed. In January 1945, the House Un-American Activities committee—through a surprise move by the House conservatives—was made a standing, rather than merely a special, committee. It conducted a free-swinging investigation of Hollywood, the Communist party and various "communist front" organizations. During this period, many innocents were smeared, many careers were wrecked, and some ended up in jail. At the same time, the entire radical movement in America was weakened, as the communists dwindled in number and activity and the left-liberals were increasingly co-opted into cold-war programs. With its left-liberal wing demoralized, the Democratic party lost its congressional majority in the 1946 elections. Many conservative Republicans won their seats by attacking their opponents as "soft on communism." Of these, the most vigorous was Richard Nixon, who won election by unscrupulous smearing of the New Deal Democrat Jerry Voorhis, who himself had been a member of the House Committee on Un-American Activities.

The anti-communist movement, of course, was much broader than Richard Nixon. In 1947 the liberals and socialists in the CIO, conceding the correctness of many of the right-wing charges, started a campaign to de-communize the CIO. Many union leaders who had attained their power through communist support suddenly switched. Where this did not happen, purges were initiated. "By March 1950, every C.P.-dominated union in the C.I.O. was expelled . . . By the mid-fifties the Communists had been reduced to marginal status in the unions—a clump of harried party members here, a scattering of frightened sympathizers there." [32] In the radio and television industries, Hollywood, and many universities, many people with radical connections or leanings (or even relatives) were fired or blacklisted. In the federal government President Truman signed an executive order requiring 2.5 million government employees to undergo security checks. This was soon extended to include 3 million members of the armed forces and 3 million employees of defense contractors.[33] At first, the loyalty boards were obligated to have "reasonable grounds" for dismissing an employee suspected of disloyalty. By 1950, only a "reasonable doubt" was necessary. The cultural impact of this operation was enormous. If only 212 employees were fired, and only 2,000 left voluntarily, one may presume that hundreds of thousands were taught a clear lesson by the clearance experience: namely, to abandon any reservations they had about the Establishment's basic policies and demonstrate at all possible opportunities their dedication to the new "Free World" strategy. On a broader front, this lesson was drummed into actual or potential dissidents by the indictment in 1948 (shortly before the 1948 elections) of Communist party leaders under the Smith Act. This time, in contrast with the earlier trial of the right-wingers, the government won its case. Harry Truman also won the 1948 election. One reason was that he demonstrated his administration's ability to conduct purification operations more efficiently than the various congressional committees on "un-American activities" and "internal security." More important, in presenting his Fair Deal proposals for mild domestic reform, he placated the many liberals and radicals who feared that a combination of cold-war foreign policy and anti-communism at home would mean a halt to the growth of the welfare state. Many former communists became avid Fair Dealers.

During the next few years the purge-conversion processes were accelerated by the loss of China, the first atomic bomb explosion by the Soviet Union, and the exposé of various spy rings in Canada and the United States. Many important second-level experts in the executive branch—among them Lauchlin Currie, Harry Dexter White, and Alger Hiss—were accused of directly or indirectly helping the communists. Of these, Alger Hiss was finally convicted of perjury and jailed. Others were convicted of spying; Julius and Ethel Rosenberg were executed. By 1950, riding the wave of success in their "un-American activities" programs, Richard Nixon and Karl Mundt were able to rise from the House to the Senate. In this election Nixon distinguished himself by using smear tactics even more effectively than in his first House victory four years earlier. He also endeared himself to the right-wing extremists in the Republican party, including many of the "Asia Firsters" who were apoplectic over the loss of China and suspicious of, if not antagonistic toward, those Republicans who favored the Marshall Plan and NATO. Hence, in backing Nixon as Dwight Eisenhower's running mate in 1952, the anti-Taft Republicans in the top corporate levels of the Establishment did something more than bring into the vice-presidency the most vigorous of the anti-communists. They also helped accelerate the conversion of the isolationists and noninterventionists to the globalism of the new "Free World" empire.

PURIFYING IDEOLOGIES

Those who take the most from the table
Teach contentment
Those for whom the taxes are destined
Demand sacrifice
Those who eat their fill speak to the hungry
Of wonderful times to come
Those who lead the country into the abyss
Call ruling difficult
For ordinary folk.

BERTOLT BRECHT

As the takeoff toward a more perfect capitalism began after World War II, popular support of the system was assured in large part by the system's performance—more striking than ever before—in providing material payoffs and physical security. The record of over a third of a century has included the avoidance of mass depression or runaway inflation in any advanced capitalist country, expanded mass consumption, the maintenance or expansion of personal options, no near-war between any advanced capitalist countries and, above all, no world war.

Yet these achievements have depended upon a level of commitment among the elites at the Establishment's lower and middle levels that could scarcely have been forthcoming if either had seriously doubted the legitimacy of the evolving order. This legitimacy was fostered by a three-pronged ideological thrust.

The first prong has consisted of a sophisticated and passionate reiteration in a thousand variations of the simple proposition: *communism and socialism are bad.*

Before World War II there were many small, right-wing movements whose members were driven by nightmares of evil conspirators—usually communists, Jews, Catholics, "niggers" or "nigger lovers"—bent on destroying the "American way of life." During the immediate prewar period, their fears were expressed directly in the Dies Committee's crusade against "pinkos" in the Roosevelt administration. After World War II, these witch-hunting nightmares were transformed into dominant ideology. Professional antiradicalism became entrenched during the brief period of atomic monopoly. It grew stronger in the more frenetic period of nuclear confrontation after Russia acquired atomic bombs. With some toning down and fine tuning, it has maintained itself during the present and more complex period of conflict with socialism and communism. During each of these stages it meshed rather well with anti-capitalist ideology in the Soviet Union, China, Cuba, and other communist countries, thereby providing an ideological balance to parallel the delicate balance of nuclear terror. More specifically, it has given the overall rationale for the extension of America's multicontinental frontiers. It has helped link together the many disparate elements in America's quasi-empire. In large measure, the unity of the NATO countries in Europe had depended on their fear of Soviet communism, and the allegiance of Japan to the United States on the fear of either Soviet or Chinese communism. American aid to "have-not" countries, in turn, has often varied with their ability to produce—or invent—a communist threat on or within their borders. At home, anti-communism has provided the justification needed by the ambitious leaders of the massive military establishment. As Colonel James A. Donovan wrote after retirement from the U.S. Marine Corps, "If there were no Communist bloc . . . , the defense establishment would have to invent one." [34]

Above all, anti-communism has been a valuable instrument in containing pressures for a more rapid expansion of welfare-state measures as opposed to more generous forms of aid to business. In this sense, the ideology of anti-communism has also been anti-socialistic. Although favoring corporate and military socialism for the benefit of businessmen and military officers, the anti-communists have bitterly attacked the "creeping socialism" that aims to benefit the poor, the underorganized, and the ethnic minorities.

The power and the imaginative vigor of anti-communist and anti-socialist ideology has stemmed from its many interlacing currents. At one extreme, there have been those like Senator Joseph McCarthy and Robert Welch of the John Birch Society, both of whom charged that Secretaries of State Dean Acheson and George Marshall were communist agents or dupes. In the middle, people like Acheson and Marshall themselves developed the more influential, mainstream version of anti-communist ideology. By deeds as well as words, they attempted to prove they were more anti-communist than their detractors. Toward the left, many brilliant intellectuals have done their own thing less stridently, demonstrating the inefficiency of communist and socialist practice and the stodginess of communist and socialist doctrine. Each of these currents have been invigorated by significant numbers of former communists and socialists, who have atoned for their former sins by capitalizing on their special knowledge of communist inequity or socialist futility. Each helped publicize many of the Soviet Union's hidden horrors—although the tendency has been less to understand the deformation of Soviet socialism (and its roots) and more to warn against the horrors that would result from any tinkering with the American system.

Thus, like a restaurant with a large and varied menu, anti-communist and anti-socialist ideology has been able to offer something for almost any taste. Each dish, moreover, is extremely cheap. A high price is paid only by those who refuse to select any variety, thus opening themselves to the charge of being "soft on communism." For over a quarter of a century there has been only a small minority—particularly in the realm of government service and academia—willing to pay the price. The result has been a rather widespread conformity with ritualistic anti-communism and anti-socialism and a powerful consensus on the virtues of the established order.

The second prong of the ideological thrust consists of even more sophisticated variations on an equally simple proposition: *the capitalist order is good.* Before World War II one of the weakest links in the established order was the image of the corporation. For its consumers, the corporation said, "The public be damned!" On matters of broad public policy—particularly during the depths of the Great Depression—corporate leaders often distinguished themselves by ignorance and incompetence. There was blantant evidence to support President Roosevelt's epithet "economic bourbons." Even during the 1950s Charles Wilson, a former General Motors president, as secretary of defense, was able to suggest that what's good for General Motors is good for the United States. In short, the large corporation—as the central symbol of capitalism—was selfish, venal, and mean.

To cope with this situation, huge investments were made in public relations campaigns. Some of these campaigns concentrated on the corporate image. Many of them set forth in excruciating detail the infinite blessings of private ownership and free, competitive private enterprise. An exhaustive analysis of the material appears in *The American Business Creed*, by a group of Harvard economists.[35] The essence of this so-called creed (to which no serious corporate executives could possibly have given credence) was the ridiculous assumption that the market was mainly composed of small, powerless firms and that large, powerful corporations were controlled by huge numbers of small stockholders instead of a small minority of large stockholders, managers, or investment institutions.

During the same period, however, a more influential ideology for postwar capitalism was formulated by various groups of pragmatic intellectuals. Their problem was that many corporate managers and their truly conservative economists were traditionally rather blunt in stating that their job was moneymaking, period—no nonsense about social responsibility. Besides, even the most dedicated corporate lawyers often remembered Justice Oliver Wendell Holmes's dictum on the subject: "The notion that a business is clothed with a public interest and has been devoted to the public use is little more than a fiction intended to beautify what is disagreeable to others." Nonetheless, the Advertising Council spent billions over the decades in creating fictional images of business "clothed with public interest." In this they were helped by uninhibited academics like Carl Kaysen, who stated that in the corporate world of Standard Oil, American Telephone and Telegraph, Du Pont, General Electric, and General Motors "there is no display of greed or graspiness:

there is no attempt to push off onto the workers or the community at large part of the social costs of the enterprise. The modern corporation is a soulful corporation." [36] Others have pursued the soulful theme even further by suggesting that the executives of transnational corporations are the real "world citizens" whose efforts may soon usher in a new era of permanent peace.

The third prong in the ideological package is the tacit—but breathtaking—assertion or premise that *capitalism no longer exists.* "A research report of the United States Information Agency," C. L. Sulzberger revealed in a typically incisive column back in 1964, "has ruefully discovered that the more our propaganda advertises the virtues of 'capitalism' and attacks 'socialism' the less the world likes us . . . Most foreigners don't regard 'capitalism' as descriptive of an efficient economy or a safeguard of individual rights. To them it means little concern for the poor, unfair distribution of wealth, and undue influence of the rich." [37] But what the USIA allegedly needed a research report to discover concerning capitalism's image in other countries was already well understood by capitalism's major publicists and spokesmen at home. As far back as 1941, in his "American Century" editorial, Henry Luce used the well-established term "free economic system" instead of "capitalism." The international capitalist market protected by American hegemony became the "free world" and "freedom" became the code word for both domestic capitalism and capitalist empire. In Carl Kaysen's article on the soulful corporation, the nasty word "capitalism" makes not a single entry. Its use would have introduced a jarring note. It would also have violated a powerful norm among economists—namely, that instead of trying to analyze the workings of modern capitalism, capitalism should be discussed mainly in the framework of criticizing Marxian economics or making passing references to the imperfections in Adam Smith's model of perfect competition. When Governor George Romney of Michigan announced that "Americans buried capitalism long ago, and moved on to consumerism," what was really being buried was the old-time conservative defense of capitalism as unadulterated self-interest as superior to socialistic altruism. True believers like Ayn Rand were of no avail in charging that "if the 'conservatives' do not stand for capitalism, they stand for and are nothing" and in proclaiming (like one of her characters in *Atlas Shrugged*) "We choose to wear the name 'Capitalism' printed on our foreheads boldly, as our badge of nobility." [38] The most intelligent spokesmen for the changing capitalist order wear a variety of names on their foreheads.

The first term—and still the most appealing—has been "mixed economy." The persuasive power of this concept stems mainly from lip service to the perfect-competition model as defined in classical or neoclassical ideologies. If capitalism used to be what Adam Smith advocated, the reasoning goes, then capitalism has been replaced by a mixture of private and public enterprise—or even of capitalism and socialism. This mixture blends the (alleged) productive efficiency of the former with the social justice sought by the latter. At the same time, it preserves the beautiful equilibrium of the classical model by providing opportunities for all interests in society to organize in their own behalf. From this competition in both the political and economic marketplaces comes a peaceful resolution of conflicts through the negotiation, bargaining, pressure and counter-pressure, propaganda and counterpropaganda that underlie electoral campaigns and executive, legislative, and judicial decision making. From this confused but peaceful process of political competition among selfish interests there emerges—as though by some invisible guiding hand—the best possible satisfaction of the public interest. Granted, there may be some imperfections in this political marketplace, too much strength at some points and too much weakness at others. But then enlightened government, with the help of Ivy League professors, can come in as a balancing factor and restore the equilibrium.

This pluralistic myth is often reinforced by statistical exercises suggesting that the unfair distribution of wealth and influence was on its way out and the majority of the population had attained "affluence." Thus the mere contemplation of the "objective data" carefully selected under his direction induced the usually self-contained Arthur Burns (later named chairman of the Council of Economic Advisers and the Federal Reserve Board) into the following orgasmic spasm of economic hyperbole: "The transformation in the distribution of our national income . . . may already be counted as one of the great social revolutions in history." [39] With such well-certified "evidence" coming across their desks, former Marxists or revolutionaries were able to explain their conversion to the existing order with something more convincing than diatribes (which often appeared in the form of Trotskyism) against Stalinism and more self-satisfying than the attacks on former comrades made by the former communists who converted to professional anticommunism. By 1960, Seymour Martin Lipset was able to proclaim that "the fundamental political problems of the industrial revolution have been solved." [40] This viewpoint was enlarged by Daniel Bell's sadly joyous funeral oration over the end of socialist or communist ideology in the Western world: "For the radical intelligentsia, the old ideologies have lost their 'truth' and their power to persuade . . . there is a rough consensus among intellectuals on political issues: the acceptance of the Welfare State; the desirability of decentralized power; a system of mixed economy and political pluralism. In that sense, too, the ideological age has ended." [41]

In continuation of the same argument, Bell has moved to replace the old ideologies of competing systems with a new end-of-ideology ideology celebrating the new power of theory, theoreticians, and his best friends. With more wit, passion, and inventiveness than most competing sociologists, Bell has capitalized on the fact that both Western capitalism and Russian socialism have been forms of industrialism. In so doing he defines industrialism loosely as something that has to do with machines, almost completely glossing over the organizational and imperial aspects of industrial capitalism.

This allows him to proclaim the coming of something called "post-industrialism," which is characterized by the increasing relative importance of services as contrasted with goods, of white-collar employment, and of more technical and professional elites. The essence of this allegedly "post" industrialism is "the preeminence of the professional and technical class." This preeminence, in turn, is based on "the primacy of theoretical knowledge—the primacy of theory over empiricism and the codification of knowledge into abstract systems of symbols." The masters of the new theory and symbols are the "knowledge elites" and their domicile is the university, "the central institution of post-industrial society." [42]

With equal wit and a larger audience, Galbraith propounded a similar theme when, in 1968, he claimed that power in the new industrial state has shifted from capital to the "organized intelligence" of the managerial and bureaucratic "technostructure." [43]

For Bell, if the new knowledge elites do not make the ultimate decisions, it is because of a combination of old-fashioned politics and new cultural styles, particularly among younger people who tend to revolt against the rule of reason itself. If these obstacles can be overcome and if enough resources are channeled into R & D and the universities, then man's reason shall at last prevail and rational calculation and control will lead to stable progress. For Galbraith, the remedy was similar, since the system of industrial oligarchy "brings into existence, to serve its intellectual and scientific needs, the community that, hopefully, will reject its monopoly on social purpose." Galbraith's hope lay (at that time) in the wistful presumption that "the educational and scientific estate, with its allies in the larger intellectual community" might operate as a political force in its own right.

Although both Bell and Galbraith have been willing to concede the existence of capitalism (and Galbraith has more recently revealed himself as an advocate of public ownership of the one thousand corporate giants whom he describes as the "planning system," [44] most Establishment social scientists in both the Ivy League and the minor leagues seem to have adopted methodological premises that rule capitalism out of existence. Without the wit, wisdom, or vision of a Bell or Galbraith, they have busied themselves in efforts to provide technical solutions to political, moral and socio-economic problems. The problems they presume to solve—or in Daniel P. Moynihan's more modest terms, to cope with—are defined at the higher or middle levels of the Establishment where decisions are made on which research grants or contracts are to be approved and which professors are to be hired. They are carefully subdivided into categories that reflect the division of labor within the foundations and government contracting agencies.

In turn, the presumably independent "knowledge elites" of the educational, scientific, and intellectual estates—having usually abjured efforts to analyze the morality and political economy of the so-called "market system"—are now rated on their performance in the grant-contract market. The badges of achievement are the research proposals accepted by the Establishment, with the rank order determined by the amount of funds obtained. Alongside the older motto "Publish or perish," (which puts the fate of many younger people in the hands of establishment faithfuls on editorial boards) has risen an additional imperative: "Get a grant or contract and prosper." This imperative also applies to department heads, deans, and college presidents who—like professors—are expected to bring in the "soft money" to supplement the "hard money" in the regular college and university budgets. During the early 1960s the largest amounts of "soft money," came from the government agencies involved in the "hardware" and "software" needed by the military and outer-space agencies, and including the many programs of "area studies" focused on Asia, Africa, the Middle East, and Latin America. Later, with the civil rights and antiwar movements, a minor avalanche of "soft money" was let loose for research, field work, and demonstration projects in the so-called "anti-poverty" and "model cities" programs. The word went quickly around among the new generation of academic hustlers that "Poverty is where the money is." Under these new circumstances, the serious applicant for funds was well advised to steer clear of root causes or systemic analysis. There was no prohibition against proposing research work or field organization designed to challenge the capitalist system, but no applicant has ever been known to openly propose anything so patently "unsound." Moreover, many of the wisest heads in the academic community—whether from profound inner disillusionment or in the heat of professional arrogance—openly advocated the treatment of symptoms only and inveighed against wasting time with the examination of systemic roots of poverty, unemployment, inflation, crime, or environmental degradation.[45]

On a broader scale, methodology became the "name of the game." A new generation of methodologists learned that with unspoken constraints upon the purpose and content of research and theory greater importance must be attached to means and form. Younger people who scorned the catch-as-catch-can methodologies of a Bell, Galbraith, or Moynihan—and were embarrassed by their unseemly interest in turning a good phrase—became the new ideologues of scientific methods. On the one hand, "abstracted empiricists" (as C. Wright Mills called them) became frenetic data-chasers eager to produce reams of computer printouts. On the other hand, enthusiastic model-builders erected pretty paradigms from which hypotheses might be deduced. Both sought verification through the application of methods long proven useful in the natural sciences. In this process, they had the aid and participation of many natural scientists perfectly willing to accept admiration from those naive enough to think that their skills in physics, biology, engineering or mathematics were readily transferable to the analysis of social problems. They also enjoyed the guidance or blessings of old-time radicals who—scorched by the heat of the purges or disillusioned by Stalinism—were eager to build a new God in the image of so-called scientific method. These activities became intensely competitive, with ever-changing cliques and currents providing endless opportunities for innovative nuances in the production of iconoclastic conformity and irrelevant relevance.

Occasionally, the existence of capitalist society has been allowed to enter into the frame of reference—but only marginally. Thus, it has become fashionable for many social science departments to have a well-behaved "Marxist" in residence: an element of good behavior, of course, is to accept the subdivision of mental labor and be a "Marxist" economist, socialist, or political scientist rather than dealing with capitalist society as a whole. A more widespread form of marginal acceptance of capitalist reality is the idea of "putting the profit motive to use in achieving social purposes." The reiteration of this imperative in every area from narcotics control to education has become one of the most effective methods of pledging allegiance to the undescribed and unexamined capitalist order.

Although these many establishment ideologies have not produced any dedicated loyalty or deep commitment to modern capitalism, they have nonetheless been a major factor in the purification process. They have made it possible for purges and induced conversions of dissidents to be reduced in relative significance and conducted on a low-key, routine basis. They have helped absorb some of the activists of the old "New Left" of the 1960s into the Establishment, purify thoughts and behavior during the 1970s, and channel into harmless—if not profitable—ways the resentments and grievances fed by the many crises and traumas of a more perfect capitalism.

4

The Side Effects of Success

So bye bye Miss American Pie
Drove my Chevy to the levy but the levy was dry,
And them good old boys were drinking whiskey and rye,
Singing this'll be the day that I die,
This'll be the day that I die . . .
DON MCLEAN

EVEN IN ITS MORE EXPANSIVE and successful moments a deep malaise corrodes the atmosphere of every advanced capitalist society. "We are very rich," mused Walter Lippmann a little before his death. "But our life is empty of the kind of purpose and effort that gives to life its flavor and meaning." [1] I am always suspicious of statements that throw the word "we" around to cover different kinds of people. For Nelson Rockefeller, up to the moment of his death, life was far from empty. It was full of the hidden flavor and meaning gained by the relentless pursuit of money, power, and sexual gratification. But if Lippmann was referring only to those values of which a person can be openly proud, I am willing to include Rockefeller along with the ordinary rich and the much larger number of un-rich and poor, both young and old, who suffer from the lack of meaning in life.

"If we just enlarge the pie, everyone will get more." This has been the imagery of capitalist growthmanship since the end of World War II—and I once did my share in propagating it. But the growth of the pie did not change the way slices were distributed except to enlarge the absolute gap between the lion's share and the ant's. And whether the pie grows, or stops growing, or shrinks, there are always people who suffer from the behavior of the cooks, the effluents from the oven, the junkiness of the pie, and the fact that they needed something more nutritious than pie anyway.

If this be a failure of "piemanship," it is a special kind—one that illustrates the saying "Nothing fails like success." In all its many forms, both spiritual and material, the malaise of modern capitalism appears side by side with the gains and benefits of capitalist growth and accumulation. None of these forms is often part of central or conscious aims at the Establishment's apex, where dedication to new exploits in a dwindling capitalist world tends to distract attention from—or else, justify—the use of unpleasant or regrettable means, and unpleasant or unintended consequences. Yet these side effects are very real. They spread out in long, interweaving, mutually reinforcing, and incredibly complex sequences of injuries or costs to individuals, families, small groups, organziations, and the entire structure of society.

AN ABUNDANCE OF FRUSTRATIONS

From its very beginnings capitalism has been a dream factory. Since World War II, this factory has produced successive waves of rising aspirations. Its old men have dreamed dreams. Its young men have seen visions. Its political and economic leaders have made promises. No sector of society is immune to the festering sore of a dream deferred or, when it comes true, converted into a nightmare.

A major side effect of increased mass consumption over the years has been to raise aspirations for additional consumption by those who had previously been satisfied with less. As millions of poor people have made more material gains, they have learned to want more—particularly as they see that the gains of other sectors of the population have exceeded theirs. Among blacks, Latins, and Native Americans—some of whom are hopelessly submerged in the underclass—this contrast becomes desperately painful. The pain is not displaced by the humiliations imposed by the welfare system, food stamps, training programs, public housing, and other "uplift" programs. The pain reverberates among the lower- and middle-income workers who are taxed to provide support for people described to them as "loafers" and "spongers." In turn, many people at the middle and higher levels find that skyrocketing prices for highly desired services—household help, good restaurants, taxis, good theatre, a nice cottage at a quiet beach—deny them the affluence to which they think themselves entitled.

At the same time, paradoxically, other aspirations have gone far beyond either the ancient struggle for subsistence or current struggles for more equity in the distribution of material goods. As material needs are met, other values come to the surface. Large sections of the population now aspire to freedom from historic forms of institutionalized injustice. Few black Americans are now willing to tolerate being regarded as subhuman or biologically inferior; many reject jobs that they now see as humiliating and demeaning. Other ethnic groups, stirred out of melting-pot somnolence by the example of blacks, are reasserting ancient traditions and making new demands on the policy. Women increasingly demand liberation from centuries of imprisonment in social roles that presume biological inferiority, physical inability, and mental incapacity. Older people are rejecting the "ageism" that dumps men and women into forced retirement, segregated communities, or nursing-home warehouses without reference to their capabilities for productive work and service.

Moreover, people in all walks of life are becoming interested in satisfactions that transcend the dominant materialisms of the past. They want employment that is fulfilling—not merely full or fair. They want education that liberates the imagination instead of merely giving a certificate. They want to commit themselves to purposes beyond careerism and institutional aggrandizement. They seek new forms of community with others. These higher aspirations have been encouraged by "quality of life" promises by political leaders. At the same time the hard realities continue: racism, ethnic discrimination, male chauvinism, the treatment of young people as children, and older people as waste products. On these cruel rocks, the waves of higher aspirations are repeatedly shattered.

The most dramatic expression of the new hopes was embodied in the counterculture and the New Left of the 1960s. The counterculture touched all forms of artistic expression. It included the theatre of the absurd; pop paintings; rock, acid-rock and folk-rock music; dramatic "happenings," guerilla theatre; psychedelic multimedia dance scenes; "underground" papers; and explicit sexuality in all of the foregoing. But it went much further than previous cultural protest in affecting actual life-styles—from the superficialities of obscene language, hippy or mod clothing, and organic foods to the more fundamental life-style changes of communal living arrangements, liberation from traditional sexual restraints, drug use, and experimentation with mystic experiences and new religious fads. For younger people it provided a "youth culture" that presumed to rebel against the System. For the older people who joined the rebellion, it provided an intimation of regained youthfulness. For both, it provided the illusion that somehow or other—in the euphoric words of Charles Reich—the flower power of a new consciousness would push up through the concrete pavements, through the metal and the plastic, and bring about "a veritable greening of America." [2]

A common element in both the counterculture and the New Left is that some leaders of each became media heroes. In this way they had an impact on American life—the former in changing the nature of mass culture, art, recreation, and sexual mores; the latter in shaking up the administrators and faculties of American universities, awakening American opinion to the horrors of the American war in Indochina, and encouraging black militancy. In so doing, the counterculture became absorbed into the Establishment, functioning more and more as an arm of business operations in entertainment, clothing, foods, and foreign cars, while the

New Left and the many organizations of white and black revolution collapsed into sawdust.

If modern capitalism nurtured new values and aspirations, it has by no means displaced the traditional values of Western civilization and constitutional capitalism. Indeed, under the pressure of social change, many people have gone back to older values, clinging to them more desperately under the threat of confusing new outlooks.

On the one hand, a large part of the lower and middle classes, particularly the many people fighting their way into the lower strata of the Establishment, saw the counterculture or the New Left as perversions of American values and a personal affront. They had grown up and eked their way ahead in rather full acceptance of patriotism, self-discipline, conformity, future preference, and material acquisition. But the counterculture, the New Left and—still more offensive—often their own sons and daughters would desecrate the flag, behave in an undisciplined fashion, violate established norms of clothing, personal appearance, and speech, live for the pleasures of the moment, and turn their backs on many of the established symbols of material well-being. Their neighborhoods and schools were invaded by unfamiliar, low-income blacks—with the invasion often backed up by court order, government action, and high-sounding policy statements by Establishment leaders who themselves lived in exclusive neighborhoods and sent their children to private schools. The permissiveness of the younger generation somehow or other became equivalent to the spread of mugging, burglary, rape, and homicide. This reaction has not been limited to whites alone. Many black parents and grandparents have viewed the revolt of their children and grandchildren as a direct attack on their own values and middle-class aspirations.

On the other hand, the power of the counterculture and the New Left was largely based on the fact that their younger adherents went back to some of the oldest values of Western civilization and American tradition. In many of their actions, they have taken seriously the precepts of the Ten Commandments, the Sermon on the Mount, the Declaration of Independence, and the Bill of Rights. By these standards, they tend to condemn the Establishment, the formalistic traditionalists, and many of their parents as corrupt and complacent hypocrites.

Other older values are common to both of these groups: the ethos of personal autonomy and independence, the desire to participate in decisions affecting one's life, and—to a lesser degree—the dignity of ordinary work. And for both groups these values tend to be perverted by the manipulative nature of large-scale bureaucracy and concentrated wealth and power. The sense of powerlessness and helplessness affects both those industrial and construction workers still indignant against opposition to large military budgets and those still indignant against racism, male chauvinism, militarism, and imperial intervention in other countries. Divided on many specifics, each side clings to certain unspoken common values.

An important source of frustration has always been the Faustian driving force among those committed to the pursuit of money and power. As this pursuit becomes more rational, it feeds upon itself. "The acceptance of wealth (or power for that matter) as the source of self-esteem," Stanislas Andreski has written, "enhances the feeling of insecurity because they are transient possessions which can easily be lost—which may be the reason why people who have acquired them never cease to want more . . ."[3] More is never enough; it becomes ashes in the mouth. The yardstick of money and power does not add much to one's essential self-esteem—especially when one suspects that most of one's closest friends (if the word "friends" can be at all used in this context) are interested mainly in handouts, favors, and deals. Abroad, the top capitalists of other countries are not so eager to go along with American penetration, even in the form of friendly partnerships. At home, as James Reston observes, the leaders in business and the professions "seem unhappy in a system they cannot quite understand or reconcile with their private ideals."[4]

FALLING APART: WORK, COMMUNITY, FAMILY

Turning and turning in the widening gyre
The falcon cannot hear the falconer;
Things fall apart; the centre cannot hold . . .

WILLIAM BUTLER YEATS

In its earlier years industrial capitalism shattered the ancient skills of artisans and craftsmen by fostering an ever more specialized division of labor; this reduced production costs and increased the power of managers. The concentration of production in urban areas and the building of national labor markets went far toward severing human ties to the land; it helped convert the extended family of many interacting relatives into the nuclear family limited to parents and children. These changes, in turn, went so far toward fragmenting human relations that some observers warned that people might be converted—in the words of Emile Durkheim—into "anonymous specks in a cloud of dust."

During the first decades of transnational capitalism, these processes of social fragmentation have undergone a qualitative change. With the new technological revolution, not only physical labor but mental labor as well is being broken down into smaller and smaller parts. As much of the labor force becomes migratory both community and family life decline.

The upsurge of technological innovations after World War II gave rise to many rosy predictions on the nature of work. There would be an end to back-breaking, dangerous, or routine labor. The energies of employees at all levels would be released for leisure and more fulfilling jobs.

It is now possible to see the results. A few million workers are still engaged in labor requiring huge muscular effort, as in mines, foundries, and coke works. This kind of work has been described in a *Wall Street Journal* headline: "Brutal, Mindless Labor Remains a Daily Reality for Millions in the U.S. Mining Coal, Shoveling Slag, Gutting Hogs Pays Bills, But Can Drain Spirit, Hope." [5] But the great majority of modern workers now face the newer hardships of routinized work consisting of minute repetitive fragments. In previous decades, the fragmentation had been done largely by studying the work movements of the best craftsmen and allocating these various movements among less skilled and lower-paid workers; the simplest of these movements were then mechanized. Under the new technological revolution, machines are now designed to do what people could never have done, and people are needed not so much to operate the machines as to serve them.

In this respect there is little difference between factory work and office work, between so-called "blue collar" workers and "white collar" workers. "The office today, where work is segmented and authoritarian, is often a factory," a government report tells us. "Computer key-punch operations and typing pools share much in common with the automobile assembly line." [6]

In the service occupations and retail trade, there are the same tendencies toward specialization and job dilution, whether or not associated with increased mechanization. The basic differences among all these types of work now relate to dangers and pay. In many industrial and construction activities the new technologies have brought new dangers to health, if not to life and limb—through speedier operations, air and noise pollution at the workplace, and the handling of dangerous chemicals and other substances. In contrast, clerical employees and workers in service occupations and retail trade tend to make even less money than laborers.

The basic similarity is the ongoing process of fragmenting work and coordinating the many parts through rules, regulations and hierarchical stratification. Under the impact of this process, employees become increasingly disconnected from the end products to which they contribute and the needs or responses of the consumers who use them. They have only the vaguest idea about the total operations of the organization that employs them or the ongoing dilemmas faced by its managers. As a result, according to Robert Dubin, "the classical distinction between managers and workers has been hardened by the growing gulf of education and knowledge that separates these two classes."[7] This gulf is hardened by widespread hostility and resentment toward management "ripoffs."

But this does not automatically produce the "working class consciousness" which, according to some Marxists, would lead the workers to become the "gravediggers of capitalism." Rather, it leads to the isolation of employees from one another. "The 'large socialized workplaces' which were supposed to generate the 'gravediggers of capitalism,'" John and Barbara Ehrenreich argue, "themselves become the graveyards for human energy and aspirations. The overwhelming response of working people is to withdraw their energy and hopes from the work world and invest them in the only other sphere provided by contemporary capitalism —*private life*."[8]

The work of experts, scientists, and professionals is a major exception. Here, as in the managerial classes, large numbers of men—and, increasingly, women—throw themselves into their work with passionate commitment. Many become work addicts (or "workaholics") capable of giving but grudging attention to private life. In contrast with moonlighters, who take on additional jobs to make money, some of them become what might be called "starlighters," that is, people who extend their regular hours of work beyond any definable limits in order to satisfy their needs for self-expression and creative activity. Needless to say, starlighters may also find that their work addiction pays off in enlarged income and perhaps in diminished frustrations.

But here also the fragmentation process is continuously at work. Every lawyer, physician, engineer, architect, or accountant tends to become a specialist in a small part of the profession—and the number of specializations and subspecializations steadily increases. The same is true of each area of the natural and social sciences, as disciplinary subdivision continuously advances. The decline of the general practitioner in medicine is paralleled by the decline of the generalist in all these fields. These declines are accelerated by the information overload created by the growing volume of publications and research findings in every specialized field. The simplest way to cope with the impossible problem of "keeping up" is to burrow even more deeply into a smaller specialization and ignore relevant information in allied fields. Thus, in the professional and scientific "rat races" the specialized experts may build tight little islands of security, protected against more intruders by a Maginot Line of almost impenetrable jargon. Instead of trying to see the whole woods, he or she focuses on an individual tree, or else a branch, twig or leaf thereof. As with employees at lower levels of the totem pole of status and prestige, the specialists become increasingly isolated from each other, little capable of working together to use their expertise for the common good, and more susceptible to regimentation. The narrow focus of their preoccupations also provides them with an excellent opportunity to ignore —or push deep into the subconscious—the extent to which they consciously or unwittingly help concentrate increased power in the Establishment's leaders.

In changing the nature of work, modern capitalism has uprooted both workers and their managers. With the mechanization of agriculture, the farm population has declined drastically. As former family farmers, tenant farmers, and farm workers have moved to urban areas, the factories of older industrial cities have migrated to rural areas (or other countries) where labor is cheaper and less organized. As black and Latin poor people pour into the central cities, middle-level and upper-level families move to the suburbs—one ring after another. This suburban migration—one of the greatest population movements in history—has burst the boundaries of most cities and created huge metropolitan regions. These, in turn, tend to cluster into megapolitan regions—in the Northeast, the midwest Great Lakes area, and the West Coast. Here are found the headquarters and major regional offices of the huge corporate and government agencies whose operations transcend the boundaries of both urban regions and nations.

While the headquarters tend to stay in the same places, people are on the move. Many Americans have become modern nomads, ever willing to pull up stakes and move elsewhere in search of better jobs, living conditions, or schooling for children. In the brief period of 1975–77, more than one of every four Americans moved from one dwelling to another—half within the same metropolitan area, half elsewhere. Within an area, many are pushed from apartment to apartment or house to house by tidal waves of blight and decay often at their heels. Many poor people are pushed out by redevelopment programs that convert former central-city slums into high-profit real estate developments. These, in turn, bring more well-to-do people back into the "gentrified" central areas. Previously, the perpetual transients were migratory farm workers and derelicts, traditionally referred to as "bums." Today's transients also include technicians, experts, managers, scientists, and academics. For those who stubbornly remain put, in Vance Packard's words "the turnover of people around them is so great that they can no longer enjoy a sense of place." [9] Apart from the embellishments of nostalgic memory, the old neighborhoods (like many old friendships) are rarely what they used to be.

Moving is more than changing one's home. It is also a matter of getting to work. Less than 8 percent of all workers walk to work or work at home. All the rest use some form of transportation other than their feet—and in most cases this is the private automobile. The vast extent of commuting to work is partly shown in the following table:

PERCENT OF WORKERS COMMUTING, 1970 *

	Out of City	Into City	Total
New York City	5.7	18.6	24.3
Chicago	16.8	28.1	44.9
Los Angeles	29.5	38.0	67.5
Philadelphia	12.7	29.1	41.8
Detroit	32.9	41.8	74.7
Houston	9.8	24.1	33.9
Washington, D.C.	19.1	57.5	76.6
Dallas	13.4	34.3	47.7
San Francisco	10.3	39.8	40.1
Boston	23.1	56.7	79.8
Cleveland	25.2	54.7	79.9
Baltimore	25.4	38.1	63.5

* Statistical Abstract of the United States, 1979

What is not shown is the vast amount of time consumed by all this movement, time that might otherwise be available for more enjoyable or productive purposes. Official language tells us that a person "lives" where he or she resides—and "resides" usually means sleeps. But as Richard Goodwin has written in words that apply to women also, "A man works in one place, sleeps in another, shops somewhere else, finds pleasure or companionship where he can and cares about none of these places." [10] The so-called dwelling is merely a "base from which the individual reaches out to the scattered components of his existence." This is what Vance Packard has in mind when he says that America is "becoming a nation of strangers."

The crumbling of community ties is always easier to bear when solace and satisfaction are found in the warmth of family life. Yet the nuclear family seems to be crumbling also. Part of this is evidenced by the dramatic increases that have been taking place in divorce rates since the mid-1960s and the more recent decline in marriage rates. These statistics are buttressed by shakier information on informal separations, illegitimacy, and single-headed families—particularly in lower-income groups.

As with neighborhoods, however, the basic story on fragmentation is told by information not on outright dissolution but on the weakening of human ties. Edward Shorter, an historian of family life, suggests that "Three different aspects of family life today are evolving in directions that have no historical precendent: the definitive cutting of the lines leading from younger generations to older . . . the new instability in the life of the couple . . . [and] the systematic demolition of the 'nest notion' of nuclear family life . . ." [11] Natural "generation gaps" are accentuated by the attenuation of relations with grandparents. Indeed, by consigning their own parents to the cold comfort of retirement communities and nursing homes, many mothers and fathers have denied their children the warmth and shock-absorbing potentials of three-generational contact. They have also prepared the way for their own inevitable classification—in Suzanne Gordon's words—as "unwanted, helpless, ugly and unpleasant" [12]—and burial, before death, in "golden age" warehouses.

In turn, couples who remain married until death does them part tend to become psychologically uncoupled. On the one hand, there is still a tendency for husbands to become rather fully involved in activities outside the house, with only superficial or fluctuating attention to family management and child raising. On the other hand, in a society where monetary values are important, the wife's unpaid activities in procreation, household work, and family management are seriously unappreciated or depreciated. Under these conditions the home, despite its heavy investment in consumer durables, is less of a protective nest than a small-scale motel with an unpaid, unhonored, overworked and increasingly rebellious female manager tending transient guests who may eat or watch TV together but have—as the years go by—less and less in common.

LONELINESS AND ALIENATION

What makes loneliness so unbearable is the loss of one's self.
HANNAH ARENDT [13]

To break or loosen one's bonds with community or family is to gain freedom from the restraints of older values and traditions, from inquisitive neighbors, and from domineering relatives. In the anonymous privacy of the metropolis, one may choose—within the limits of available income—between this or that life style, this or that mate, and this or that form of self-gratification. To "do one's own thing" in this way is an exalted height in the individualistic ideology of capitalism.

But here, as though by invisible hands, anyone may easily be led to break down the very self which was supposed to be liberated. "Detachment from others, from shared existence, is diminution of the self," writes Richard Goodwin, "just as if one were deprived of perceptual capacities or outlets for sexual instinct." [14] With the loss of intimacy, personal commitment and close bonds, the ideal of "I am the master of my fate, I am the captain of my soul" is fatuous. One is in danger of becoming, instead, a soulless victim of fate.

Early industrialism, it was charged by almost all of its critics, tended to reduce individuals to cogs in an imperial system and undermine one's personal sense of identity. Reduced to a set of formal roles, individuals became alienated from other people and from themselves. The same criticism is made more tellingly today. On the more liberal side, Hans Morgenthau writes that people feel they live in "something approaching a Kafkaesque world, insignificant and at the mercy of unchallengeable and invisible forces . . . a world of make-believe, a gigantic hoax." [15] On the more conservative side, George Charles Roche writes that "on every hand he [the individual] meets a denial that the individual is genuinely significant; on every hand he is confronted with vast constitutional amassments that seem beyond his control and his comprehension. He truly lives in 'The Age of Bewilderment!' " [16]

The bewilderment touches almost everything. Throughout the middle and lower classes, people learn that there are mysterious powers that bring about higher taxes, higher prices, diminished job opportunities, and abundant shortages. The promises of politicians—whether liberal, conservative, or radical—to *do something* are discounted. The members of the so-called "silent majority" feel isolated, self-estranged, and powerless—out of touch with themselves, with most other people, with the dominant institutions of society, unsure who "They" are but sure that "They" will somehow or other always manipulate things to their own advantage and "the people be damned!"

The bewilderment is made more painful by its sense of personal helplessness. A government report on work in America describes middle Americans as "alienated from their society, aggressive against people unlike themselves, distrusting of others and harboring an inadequate sense of personal or political efficacy." [17] Among people interviewed by Studs Terkel, the white-collar moan is as bitter as the blue-collar blues: "I'm a machine," says the spot welder. "I'm caged," says the bank teller, and echoes the bank clerk. "I'm a mule," says the steelworker. "A monkey can do what I do," says the receptionist. "I'm less than a farm implement," says the migrant worker. "I'm an object," says the high-fashion model. Blue collar and white collar call upon the identical phrase: "I'm a robot." "There is nothing to talk about," the young accountant despairingly enunciates.[18]

If the young middle manager finds nothing to talk about, the root of his despair may be that he sees useless make-work in executive suites, has too much to complain about, and finds no one to listen. Where can the young corporate accountant bring into the open what he suspects or knows about the use of what Abraham Briloff calls "accounting game plans" [19] to prepare fraudulent balance sheets to hide profits, fleece investors, and camouflage lawbreaking?

"When people begin to feel worthless, abandoned and lonely for the world to which they had grown accustomed," writes Suzanne Gordon, "they understandably begin to withdraw from social contacts." [20] The same withdrawal has been found on the part of other kinds of people who, in a society where people are valued by the price they get for their labor, find that their labor is worthless: those in their thirties or forties who are laid off and then told at employment offices that people over thirty (or forty as the case may be) need not apply; women who after the hard work of raising children try to find paid work outside the home and cannot; young people with high school or college or graduate diplomas who can find no work at all or else nothing faintly approaching what they had been educated to expect. Any serious comparison of steadily employed people with the unemployed shows—as in the survey of the three authors of *The Unemployed*—that the latter "see themselves as undesirable, doubt their own worth, often feel anxious, depressed or unhappy, and have little faith or confidence in themselves." [21] It is no cause for surprise, therefore, when one notes the results of Harvey Brenner's masterful study of the relation between economic instability and admission to mental hospitals. "Instabilities in the economy have been the single most important source of fluctuation in mental hospital admissions or admission rates . . . and there is considerable evidence that it has had greater impact in the last two decades." [22] Other observers have found that the impact is greatest on the poorest people. Poverty means weakness not merely in purchasing power but in other forms of power over the course of one's life. "All weakness tends to corrupt," writes Edgar Z. Friedenberg, "and impotence tends to corrupt absolutely." [23]

But mental hospitalization, like suicide, is an end point on a long, causal chain of breakdowns in social relationships. Whenever one of these points is reached for one person, many others—whether relatives, associates or friends—have already been damaged along the way, and perhaps just as deeply.

For the bulk of the population, breakdown comes in less extreme forms that defy statistical capture. Anxieties and tensions break out in vindictiveness, distemper, child abuse, increased susceptibility to physical illness, alcoholism, addiction, or crime. Still more pervasive is the simple withdrawal of commitment. "Is There Life Before Death?" ran the headline in a student newspaper. "With rising insistence and anguish," writes Margaret Mead, "there is now a new note: Can I commit my life to anything? Is there anything in human cultures worth saving, worth committing myself to?" [24] As those who ask it stay not for an answer, the question hangs ominously in the air. For many, I fear, the answer is, "Very little" or "Nothing."

CRIME: THE DIRTY SECRETS

The law locks up the hapless felon
Who steals the goose from off the common,
But lets the greater felon loose
Who steals the common from the goose . . .

ANCIENT JINGLE

. . . While law enforcers quake in awe
Of felons who transcend the law . . .

AUTHOR'S ADDENDUM

We are not letting the public in on our era's dirty little secret: that those who commit the crime which worries citizens most—violent street crime—are, for the most part, products of poverty, unemployment, broken homes, rotten education, drug addiction, alcoholism and other social and economic ills about which the police can do little if anything.

ROBERT D. DIGRAZIA,
Boston police commissioner [25]

The subject of crime and corruption in the United States is a tangle of dirty secrets: facts that informed insiders know but rarely mention in public.

A dirty little secret is that the police can do very little, if anything, about crime in the streets, which is a side effect of poverty and social fragmentation. Another is that it is the poor more than anybody else who have the most to fear from lower-class crime. The burglary rate in central-city slums, where there is less to be stolen, is at least three times higher than in the suburbs. All victimization rates are higher among blacks than among whites; for murder, the victimization rate is about seven times higher for black women and ten times higher for black men. Outside the area of official statistics, similar differentials are obvious. Vandalism, mugging, rape, and sheer terror have reached scandalous proportions in lower-class schools. In slum and ghetto areas vast numbers of people are victimized by the so-called "victimless crimes" —young men by narcotics addiction, young women by prostitution, and people of all ages by gambling rackets and loans on terms even more extortionate than those of the banks. An important part of this victimization enters the public schools. "Every Monday to Friday," a former high school principal has written, "somewhere in our schools, some students are molested, mugged, assaulted, shaken down or shaken up. Known and unknown drug pushers ply their trade within the school's once-inviolate halls." [26]

This brings us back to the dirty secrets about crime. One of the best kept secrets is the relation between crime and unemployment. Most larceny, burglary, and robbery is a form of self-employment that fills the vacuum created by the lack of jobs. For the young unemployed, "street crime" has the attraction of flexible hours, challenge on the job (instead of routine), fairly good income depending on skill and luck, high prestige among peer groups, no taxes, and the availability of welfare payments, food stamps, and unemployment compensation even while earning criminal income. Despite some risks, this form of self-employment offers possible upward mobility (from small stuff to the bigger rackets). High-class vocational training is provided free, along with board, for those passing through detention homes, jails, and other public institutions.

Another dirty little secret is that the largest proporition of "street criminals" are young blacks. To discuss this fact openly is to make some black people uncomfortable and to underscore the closer relation between street crime and the endemic massive unemployment and underemployment that have confronted young black people for over two decades. A *middle-sized* secret is that most blacks are deeply law-abiding and are much more terrorized by crime in the streets than anyone else. This is also true—although to a somewhat lesser degree—of young blacks, who are themselves terrorized by the active and repetitive law-breaking of a statistical minority among their ranks.

Legitimate concern with crime at the lower depths has other less legitimate functions. It contributes to social fragmentation by creating huge waves of fear and suspicion among people of different ethnic backgrounds. It provides opportunities for the cry of "law and order" to be used by various Establishment forces to justify either illegal or disorderly means of repressing lawful activities by trade unions, minority political parties, and other groups engaged in active resistance to exploitation. Above all, it distracts attention from crime and corruption in higher levels of society.

"Money is the name of the game. Without it you're dead," Gerald Ford is reported to have said while Republican leader in the House of Representatives.[27] Politics is fueled by money and the biggest source of money is business, particularly when business has a pipeline into public treasuries. Some of this money is obtained by elected officials or appointees who "go into business for themselves." The larger part, however, is probably channeled through new-style political machines that have replaced the smaller, tighter machines run by old-fashioned bosses. Although not yet dissected by political scientists, the new machine is an intricate network of government officials, law firms, bankers, and businessmen. It has much more government funds at its disposal and many more favors to dispense than the tighter political machine of a previous era. But like the business complex, it is fluid, hard to pin down, and much harder to bust up or replace.

This combination of private and public corruption spills over into all the many institutions at the junior and contingent levels of the Establishment. Much of this is well-known but rarely commented on in public: the friendship cliques and favoritism in voluntary associations and social service agencies; the foundation officials who give huge sums to universities and then move into cushy jobs thus created; the fee splitting by lawyers and doctors; the padding of bills by hospitals submitting their accounts to insurance funds; the fraudulent claims made by educational institutions, consultants, and research hustlers. Much greater publicity is usually given to corruption in trade unions and the petty frauds perpetrated by recipients of public assistance and unemployment compensation. At a convention session of the Mass Retailing Institute Herbert Robinson charged that bribery runs rampant in retailing: "Ten billion dollars is a conservative estimate . . . The great growth of the economy in recent years has been paralleled by a growth in corrupt business behavior." [28]

Businessmen loudly complain of the money they lose from pilfering by their employees. At the same time, they sanction widespread bribery—and sometimes illegal espionage—in the conduct of their own business. In radio, when disc jockeys are "put on the pad" by record companies, the industry term is "payola." When building contractors win inflated appraisals from the Federal Housing Administration, the best term is "fraud." But, as a Justice Department investigator told the press, it is difficult to trace such frauds because they are "intertwined with the morals of the marketplace." [29] The same "morals" guide the stores that gouge their buyers with high interest rates on credit; the banks with major investments in slum housing that violates local building codes; the contractors and building and financial institutions that manipulate zoning ordinances and land-use plans in order to squeeze maximum profit from land speculation, high-income building, and adroitly designed tax havens. The law is even more brazenly flouted by the so-called law enforcers in the FBI and other branches of the Justice Department who organize burglaries and illegal wiretapping against leaders and participants in dissident movements. The fact that they regard themselves as above the law is not disproved by their claims that illegal action is necessary to protect the national security or fight "organized crime."

The racketeering groups called "organized crime" are not nearly as well organized as any medium-sized corporation. They are merely small or medium-sized networks of businessmen who provide a wide range of illegal services: drugs not readily available from doctors and pharmacies; gambling more exciting or accessible than church benefits, Wall Street, or government betting systems; any form of sexual service other than marriage; and high-interest loans. They are also prone to use considerable violence in controlling competitors and employees. The high demand for their illegal services depends entirely on laws that make certain forms of drugs, gambling, and purchases of sex illegal. Their ability to supply this demand, in turn, depends largely upon the undercover permissiveness, if not enthusiastic cooperation, of legitimate businessmen and government officials at all levels. Despite recurring exposés, thousands of policemen in all the larger cities are "on the pad" of the racketeers. Beyond this, many policemen go very far in expecting money, favors, merchandise, or services from local businessmen. "We wanted to serve others," writes David Durk, a former police officer, "but the department was a home for the drug dealers and thieves . . . Like it or not, the policeman is convinced that he lives and works in the middle of a corrupt society, that everybody is getting theirs, and why shouldn't he . . ."[30]

Police susceptibility to graft is closely connected with morale breakdowns created by "war against crime" rhetoric. To get more funds, police chiefs almost invariably pretend that the main job of the police is to catch criminals and deter lawbreaking. But apart from their illegal cooperation with criminals and lawbreakers, most of the time of the police is dedicated to traffic control, automobile accidents, municipal inspection activities, and internal red tape. Those policemen directly involved in coping with crime are caught in the infuriating bind that even while concentrating on petty crime, they are, by and large, trapped in operations whose failures are always greater than successes. Even petty criminals are rarely obliging enough to be caught in the act. Only a small percentage is arrested after the act, and most of those arrested are never found guilty. Of those who are sentenced, well-to-do people who can afford to hire clever lawyers or subservient judges usually get off with suspended sentences or quick releases through good behavior—or even presidential pardons. Overflowing with poor people (particularly blacks and Hispanics), the jails become training grounds for petty recidivists. Thus even the public records themselves, doctored though they may be to make the picture look less grim, reveal sustained defeat in the so-called "war against crime." The defeated foot soldiers in this phoney war are hemmed in between a criminal-justice system which is criminally corrupt or inefficient, radicals who brand them as pigs or fascists, and intellectuals who see them as incompetent or stupid. Their typical reaction is one of furious resentment, which often finds its expression in the abuse of their duties.

But all the dirty *little* secrets fade into insignificance in comparison with one dirty *big* secret: *Law enforcement officials, judges as well as prosecutors and investigators, are soft on corporate crime.* Modern capitalism requires a legal system to protect private property, enforce contracts, and promote confidence in corporate institutions. On the other hand, the more perfect pursuit of capital and power often requires widespread evasion of the same legal system, let alone of ordinary moral codes. This deep contradiction has worked out in such a way as to tarnish the reputation of government even more than of big business, thereby strengthening corporate defenses against any threat of widespread public ownership.

In his classic *White Collar Crime*, Edwin H. Sutherland reviewed the lawbreaking record of seventy large corporations. He found that the courts or federal administrative agencies had made a total of 980 adverse decisions against them. Their crimes ranged over these areas: restraint of trade; infringement or manipulation of patents, copyrights, and trademarks; misrepresentation in advertising; unfair labor practices; financial manipulation; war crimes; and such miscellaneous activities as unhealthy working conditions, pollution, bribery, fraud, libel, and assault. These crimes had been committed against "consumers, competitors, stockholders and other investors, inventors and employees, as well as against the State." [31]

In analyzing these 980 crimes, Sutherland found these points of similarity with crimes committed by lower-class thieves:

1. Most of the crimes were deliberate rather than inadvertent violations of technical regulations.
2. Most of the offenders were repeaters; there was no effective rehabilitation or deterrence.
3. Illegal behavior by corporations was "much more extensive than the prosecutions and complaints indicate."
4. The businessman-lawbreaker "does not customarily lose status among his business associates."
5. Businessmen customarily feel and express contempt for law and for government "snoopers" charged with law enforcement.
6. Corporate crime is organized informally and formally, through an unwritten consensus on "business ethics," secret agreements and cartels, and formal reward systems for officials who maximize profits and conceal unsavory means.
7. Corporate lawbreaking is shrouded in secrecy, with secrecy facilitated by juggling corporate personalities and brand names and by smokescreens of favorable advertising.

Sutherland also found that muggers, burglars, and racketeers see themselves as criminals and are so defined in the public conception. But corporate lawbreakers do not regard themselves as criminals, and do not customarily associate with "common" criminals. They occupy superior status in society, admired by investigators, prosecutors, judges, and jury members as well as by the media and the public at large. This status is protected by special procedures—such as administrative hearings, consent decrees, and cease and desist orders—that protect them from being treated like ordinary criminals. Another difference is that "the corporate form of business organization also has the advantage of increased rationality" in the use of whatever illegal or unethical means may help maximize pecuniary gain. The corporation "selects crimes which involve the smallest amount of detection and identification . . . [and] in which proof is difficult." Above all, the corporation engages in "fixing" on a scale "much more inclusive than the fixing of professional theft." The corporation's "mouthpieces" and "fixers" include lawyers, accountants, public relations experts, and public officials who negotiate loopholes and special procedures in the laws, prevent most illegal activities from ever being disclosed, and undermine or sidetrack "over-zealous" law enforcers. In the few cases ever brought to court, they usually negotiate penalties amounting to "gentle taps on the wrist." [32]

Although Sutherland covered many decades up to 1944, he merely scratched the surface. Confining himself to manufacturing, mining, and merchandising, he did not try to track down the corporate record in banking, insurance, commmunication, transportation, or construction. Dipping lightly into public utilities, he found that fifteen power and light companies had been found guilty of defrauding consumers or investors in thirty-eight cases. But he withdrew quickly after finding that the perpetrators of fraud in this area were so politically powerful that few cases were ever brought against them. He barely hinted at the massive black marketeering and falsification engaged in during World War II in violation of emergency controls over prices and scarce materials. He stayed away completely from the still larger vast area of criminal profiteering by corporations with large war contracts.

Since 1944, there have been two major changes. On the one hand, there has been a vast increase in the laws needed to provide the business system with larger financial support and protect it against the dangerous consequences that might result from no controls whatsoever over the injuries inflicted on employees, consumers, small investors, and the physical environment. On the other hand, although no one has yet attempted to update Sutherland, it is clear that the scale of corporate crime has risen enormously. From 1945 through 1965 the Federal Trade Commission issued cease and desist orders in almost four thousand cases of business fraud and misleading advertising, and the Food and Drug Administration initiated a much larger number of criminal prosecutions.[33] In 1975 alone Exxon, one of the largest corporations in the world, was defending itself against antitrust charges brought by Connecticut, Florida, Kansas, and the Federal Trade Commission and was charged with three air-quality violations, forty-five environmental violations and fifty-three oil discharge violations.[34] In the wake of the Watergate prosecutions, 150 American corporations admitted having made illegal political contributions from secret slush funds. Lockheed Aircraft and other corporations have confessed to large-scale bribery of officials of foreign governments. For those who study the situation carefully, it is now clear that, in Ralph Nader's words, "corporate economic, product and environmental crimes dwarf other crimes in damage to health, safety and property, in confiscation or theft of other people's monies, and in control of the agencies which are supposed to stop this crime and fraud." [35]

Some things, however, remain unchanged. The few executives ever punished—no matter how lightly—for illegal behavior still complain that they had no choice: they were merely following "standard business ethics." The courts still rule, and the wealthiest stockholders still insist, that the executive's highest responsibility is to maximize long-term corporate profits. "A sudden submission to Christian ethics by businessmen," as one executive has been quoted, "would bring about the greatest economic upheaval in history." [36] Even a slow submission to the much lower level of conduct required by laws and regulations would disrupt the processes of efficient accumulation. More widespreading lawbreaking, in turn, disrupts very little. While a few people are punished by wrist slaps —or, as one observer has put it, by "eyewinks"—most of the executive criminals are unscathed, while their multimillionaire superiors operate through remote-control techniques that provide them with full and complete cover, if not mantles of impeccable respectability.

I am convinced that among the great majority of the people below the Establishment only a small minority break the law. Perhaps this reflects not only ordinary morality but also a scarcity of opportunities. But as we look at the Establishment, the higher we go the more do marketplace norms take over and the greater the opportunities for illegal gain become—from the padding of expense accounts and the inflation of tax deductions to favoritism and corruption in the dispensation of employment and promotions, the awarding of contracts, and the interpretation of rules and regulations. But to find offense ratios of truly staggering proportions one must try to look, as Sutherland did, at corporate crime. Of the seventy corporations he studied, not a single one had a clean record. Half had been found guilty more than ten times. One wonders how much larger this figure would have been if Sutherland could have included the much larger amount of illegal behavior that was never brought formally before the courts or regulatory agencies. One is also entitled to ask how many of the thousand largest corporations today could have a perfectly clean record. The probability of a large corporation's having violated no laws on pollution, product debasement, tax evasion, political contributions, or misrepresentation in advertising may be compared—in the words of Matthew—to the likelihood "for a camel to pass through the eye of a needle" or "for a rich man to enter the kingdom of God." It is still harder to find any case of a millionaire lawbreaker who is sent to jail or kept there as long as someone who has stolen a loaf of bread.

THE EROSION OF AUTHORITY

There aren't any heroes anymore.

WARD JUST [37]

Opinion polls in the United States have repeatedly documented a growing lack of confidence in, if not contempt for, the major institutions of American society.

To some extent this is a youth phenomenon. Young people lose confidence when they sense the contrast between the ideals and the behavior of their elders. But hypocrisy is not perceived only by younger people. Men and women of all ages, colors, and income levels hear cries for "law and order" raised by respectable lawbreakers; by slumlords who violate local building codes; by police departments in collusion with organized crime; by self-proclaimed defenders of morality who regard sex as something evil or dirty and incidentally assist organized crime in maintaining its market monopoly through the present laws on prostitution, gambling, drugs, and pornography; by land developers and speculators who undermine the Supreme Court's rulings on segregation, local government officials who wink at such lawbreaking, and high-minded bankers who finance it; and by the new Suburban Bourbons who talk "liberalese" but have built the lily-white suburbs that encircle our Northern cities; by corporate and public executives who speak unctuously about the environment and accelerate its pollution.

Another dimension of erosion is the decline of authority figures. The titans of big business have retreated into anonymity. Nor are there many trappings of high authority surrounding the "littler giants" of church, school, office or home: minister, priest, rabbi, teacher, professor, the "boss," or Mother and Father. No national heroes have come into being from the ranks of organized labor, educators, students, blacks, or women's liberation. If some Senators become nationally known while investigating Watergate, multinational corporations, the CIA or the FBI, this has been part of a trend toward superficial debunking. It has not brought to national or international attention any genuine leaders with charisma. Roosevelt, Churchill, de Gaulle rise in retrospective stature in comparison with such pigmy-like heirs as Nixon, Ford, Carter, Callahan, Thatcher, Schmidt, or Giscard d'Estaing.

Established doctrines are also faring badly. Even the most ardent reformers are less than enthusiastic with the heritage of past liberal reforms. They are forced to concede the conservative and radical critique that the New Deal, Fair Deal, New Frontier and Great Society overpromised and underdelivered. But neither conservatism nor radicalism have done much better. Conservatives have been increasingly split three ways between free-market, almost anarchist libertarians, strong authoritarians, and the uncouth extremists of the "radical right." Radicals have long since lost confidence in the Soviet Union, which once was accepted as the beacon light of world socialism. Instead, a "thousand flowers" of Marxism and Marxist doctrines come and go, leaving behind them too little serious analysis of the realities of either modern capitalism or the many varieties of socialism now being attempted. A similar decline of confidence may be observed in the promises of science, technology, or expertise. Scientists are increasingly blamed (with something less than full justification) for the destructive uses to which science has been put.

New technologies are increasingly blamed (with more justification) for the plagues of pollution. Although this may be the age of Keynes, the authority of Keynesians and of all economists who promised endless prosperity without inflation has waned. The flamboyant promises made by operations researchers, systems analysists, futurists, and experts in social indicators—all have been punctured. While each of these doctrines or methodologies has certain assets at its disposal and enjoys a coterie of supporters and a broader area of goodwill, each has the greatest of difficulty in meeting the obligations it has previously accepted, even sought to assume. In the accounting sense, therefore, despite their accumulated assets, they tend toward insolvency.

The erosion of authority also affects the institutional structure of the Establishment. Opinion polls tend to show steadily falling public confidence in major corporations, banks and financial institutions, business executives, building contractors, and advertising executives. Higher education, science, and organized religion do not fare much better. The executive branch, the Congress, and even the Supreme Court tend to fare worse.

Although election victories confer formal authority upon the victors, this authority is tarnished by the fact that large numbers of people fail to vote. Thus in 1964 and 1972, respectively, Presidents Johnson and Nixon each won about 60 percent of the votes cast. But of the total voting age population, Johnson won only 38 percent and Nixon only 34 percent; in 1976 Carter's percentage was less than 27 percent. In the nonpresidential election years voter turnout is always lower, and in recent years has been declining. In 1974 elections of the House of Representatives voting participation fell to 36 percent, the lowest since 1944. In many state and local elections it is generally lower, and participation is still lower in primary elections. When nonvoters are asked why they do not vote, the most frequent answer is simply that they do not see candidates worth voting for. Accordingly, as a group of political observers concluded in *Society*, the political system "has forfeited its one high level of diffuse support—the sustaining belief that even if a particular election is deemed unfavorable, at least the system is fair, open and likely to produce favorable outcomes in the future." [38] In 1979, 79 percent of Louis Harris's respondents said that "the rich get richer and the poor get poorer," up from 45 percent in 1966 and 48 percent in 1972. Comments by Harris and other pollsters indicate that most people see the candidates of both parties as contributing to this process of progressive enrichment and impoverishment.

5

The Challenge of a Shrinking Capitalistic World

> There are clear signs that America is being displaced as the paramount country, or that there will be a breaking up, in the next few decades, of any single-power hegemony in the world . . . The American Century lasted 30 years.
>
> DANIEL BELL [1]

THE MALAISE IN FIRST WORLD countries has global roots.

Many top Establishment leaders—particularly in the United States—are frustrated by new events in the world order they helped create and brilliantly led. Having successfully coped with the huge postwar losses of Eastern Europe, China and North Korea, they have more recently been shaken by smaller losses that might augur the continuing shrinkage of the "Free World" and perhaps even its falling apart. They see clear signs, in Daniel Bell's words, that "America is being displaced as the paramount country." Their institutional authority is eroded. They are less able to use tried and tested means of continuing in operation the great engine of prosperity of the postwar Western world.

In 1960, when Daniel Bell first proclaimed the end of ideology, I was inclined to go along with him. It took me many years to realize that the funeral oration came from one of the builders of a new Establishment ideology. In 1975, when Bell announced the end of the American Century, I desperately wanted to believe him. I now see that the American Century is still alive, although unwell. To call it dead is like saying that the Catholic Church was killed by the Reformation.

But when I say it still lives, I am not suggesting it could survive as long as the Catholic Church. Its life expectancy, along with transnational capitalism as a whole, depends not only on the power of the forces against it but also on its adaptation to the unintentional consequences of its own successes.

NEW LOSSES TO COMMUNISM

By 1950, as shown in the table "Growth of National Communism," the "Free World" had shrunk from over 90 to less than 70 percent of the world's population. But concurrently it gained some things that industrial capitalism had never before enjoyed. As stated in "The Takeoff toward a New Corporate Society" (chapter 2), the "Free World" attained a totally unprecedented unity among the leading capitalist powers. This unity was based not only on American political leadership but also on a multicontinental market exploited by giant transnational complexes. Above all, faced by the challenge of communist regimes that had sidestepped the capitalist business cycle, the "Free World" overcame the catastrophic depressions that in the past had always been part and parcel of industrial capitalism. With these new capabilities, under American guidance, it was possible to contain the rising tides of communism and socialism not only in such decisive spots as Western Europe, Japan, and India, but also in many other countries where capitalism was on the defensive.

But only for a while. Wherever military power and right-wing dictatorships became the major instruments of containment, with little or no reforms to improve the living conditions of the people, the barriers proved very shaky and at times unbelievably fragile.

The longest and bloodiest of all containment struggles was in Indochina. It began in 1945 when Ho Chi Minh set up the Democratic Republic of Vietnam. If there had been no containment effort, communist regimes would have probably followed promptly in the rest of Indochina; this could have had important repercussions in such nearby countries as Thailand, Malaysia, Indonesia, and the Philippines. But in 1946 French forces intervened, fighting the communists until decisively defeated eight years later at Dien Bien Phu. The U.S. government quickly moved in to fill the vacuum by supporting an anticommunist state in South Vietnam. Under Presidents Eisenhower and Kennedy, U.S. help gradually increased. As this involvement became massive under President Johnson and was extended to Cambodia under President Nixon, "national honor" and presidential prestige began to hang in the balance. By 1972, when it was already clear that a U.S. victory was no longer possible, Nixon guaranteed his election to a second term by toning down the U.S. conflict with the Soviet Union and China and beginning the long-drawn-out process of withdrawing American forces from South Vietnam and liquidating the military draft. In early 1975, communist regimes won control in all of Vietnam, Cambodia, and Laos. The United States had to accept what Richard Nixon had in 1970 called unacceptable—namely, the "first defeat in its proud one hundred and ninety-year history."

In the meantime, lots of things had been happening in other countries.

One of the most important was in Cuba. In January 1959 the American-supported Cuban dictator, Fulgencio Batista, was overthrown by guerrilla forces under Fidel Castro. There then started a long process toward nationalization of major business enterprises and full socialization of Cuban society. But small though this island of nine million people was in the world arena, the "Castro shock" to the U.S. Establishment was enormous. There was never any doubt as to whether or not "we had Cuba." The Castro example might be followed, it was feared, in other Caribbean or Latin American countries, undermining the sphere of influence so laboriously established in more than a century of the Monroe Doctrine and many decades of economic investment. The island itself could even become a base for Soviet forces or missiles. The United States responded to this challenge by a series of limited actions: an attempted invasion by anti-Castro refugees, a trade embargo, a naval quarantine to force the removal of launching pads, infiltration of Cuba to disrupt the economy and assassinate its leaders, and many steps to prevent or suppress similar socialist or communist tendencies in the rest of the Western Hemisphere. Although some of this effort was successful, it failed on three scores: the invasion was defeated at the Bay of Pigs; Castro and his associates escaped assassination; and by the mid-1970s Cuba was firmly established as a viable communist nation ninety miles off the coast of world capitalism's proudest citadel.

In 1974, on the eve of the American defeat in Vietnam, another communist wave started in Africa. In Portugal, the old Salazar dictatorship was overthrown by military officers radicalized by years of failure in fighting liberation movements in Portugal's African colonies. By 1976 communist regimes took power in these colonies—Mozambique, Guinea-Bissau, and Angola. Similar regimes had previously been established in the Congo and Benin. Shortly thereafter, the old feudal monarchy in Ethiopia, the second largest country of Africa, was replaced by a Marxist-Leninist government. Nor were West Asia and Asia immune to these trends. By the late 1970s communist-style regimes were in power in both South Yemen and Afghanistan.

Thus by 1980, the total number of communist regimes reached twenty-five, almost twice the number that had existed in 1950. Their share of the world's population was about a billion and a half. If this was not a large percentage rise (from 31 percent in 1950 to 36 percent in 1980), it nonetheless suggests the possibility of continuing increases during the 1980s. There is reason to suppose that the rate of communist expansion may accelerate during the 1980s. In Africa, for example, where the conflicts with white-dominated South Africa, Southwest Africa, and Rhodesia are becoming much hotter, the major liberation movements are all led by outspoken foes of capitalism. If and when these countries become (to use their African names) Azania, Namibia, and Zimbabwe, they will probably be governed by Marxist regimes. Similar specters of

GROWTH OF NATIONAL COMMUNISM
TABLE 8

	Population[a] (Millions) 1920	1950	1980	Land Area[b] (Thousands of square kilometers) 1978
Soviet Union	143	193	259	22,402
Europe				
Albania	—	1	3	29
Bulgaria	—	7	9	111
Czechoslovakia	—	12	15	128
East Germany	—	17	17	108
Hungary	—	9	11	93
Poland	—	25	35	313
Rumania	—	16	22	238
Yugoslavia	—	16	22	256
	—	103	134	1,276
Asia				
Afghanistan	—	—	17	647
Cambodia	—	—	9	181
China	—	463	958[c]	9,597
Laos	—	—	3	237
Mongolia	—	1	2	1,565
North Korea	—	9	17	121
Vietnam				
North	—	13	—	
All	—	—	47	332
	—	486	1,053	12,680
Western Asia				
South Yemen	—	—	2	333

	Population [a] (Millions) 1920	1950	1980		Land Area [b] (Thousands of square kilometers) 1978
Africa					
Angola	—	—	6 [d]		1,247
Benin	—	—	3		113
Congo	—	—	1		342
Ethiopia	—	—	29		1,222
Guinea	—	—	5		246
Guinea-Bissau	—	—	1		36
Mozambique	—	—	10		783
	—	—	57		3,989
Western Hemisphere					
Cuba	—	—	10		115
Oceania	—	—	—		—
Total Population	143	782	1,515	Total Land Area	40,795
Total Countries	1	13	25		
[e] World Population	1,813	2,501 [e]	4,208	World Land Area	135,830
Communist Nations as Percent of World	8%	31%	36%		30%

Notes:

[a] Estimates under "1980" are for midyear 1978 (or, where this is not available, mid-1977) and are taken from the *Monthly Bulletin of Statistics*, April 1979, United Nations: New York.

[b] Land area estimates refer to total surface area, including inland waters. Taken from *Statistical Yearbook, 1977*, New York: United Nations 1978.

[c] *New York Times*, 12 July 1979, p. A-12.

[d] For 1972.

[e] *Statistical Yearbook, 1975*.

social revolution loom ahead in other parts of the world. Before the year 2000—if current tendencies continue—the ratio between capitalism and communism may well shrink from 65:35 to 50:50. The implications of such a shift are enormous.

But if the shrinkage of the capitalist world has thus far been accompanied by its unification, the expansion of the communist world has been characterized by multipolarity and divisiveness. The myth of a communist monolith headed by the Kremlin or of a Moscow-Peking Axis (as fostered by the secretaries of state under Eisenhower, Kennedy, and Johnson) was nonsense from the beginning. Communist unity was badly shaken as far back as 1948, when Tito first proclaimed Yugoslavia's independence from Moscow. It was weakened as well as strengthened by the Russian troops sent into Hungary in 1956 and Czechoslovakia in 1968. It was shaken still further as strains developed between the two communist giants, the Soviet Union and China, in the 1950s and 1960s, and eventually broke out into both mutual name-calling and border conflicts in the 1970s. The idea that all communist countries would live in loving peace with each other was itself laid to rest during the more recent wars between Vietnam and Cambodia, China and Vietnam, and Ethiopia and the Eritrean Liberation Front.

If unity among the communist nations, particularly between China and the Soviet Union, should somehow be restored, the threat to capitalism would be much stronger. In fact, it might be decisive in strengthening the extremely divided radical forces in India, which itself accounts for at least one sixth of the world's population.

But strangely enough, disunity has by no means eliminated the communist challenge. While communist movements may be encouraged by international support, their basic power stems from their nationalist roots in countries where people have long suffered from oppression and exploitation. They are thereby far stronger than they would be if they were—or even appeared to be—mere pawns on a chessboard whose pieces were moved by a distant communist power. Thus all of the newest communist regimes—whether in Angola, Ethiopia, or Mozambique—must strongly assert their independence from Moscow, even though, without exception each has been dependent on Soviet arms and military and economic aid in order to take power, survive, and consolidate itself. My personal guess is that before the end of the 1980s, Communist China, strengthened by the new aid pouring in from the leading capitalist powers, will itself become a new source of aid to communist movements in many parts of the world.

The most threatening of all the new spectres of communism, however appear not in the Third World but on the southern flank of European capitalism itself—namely, in Portugal, Spain, France, and Italy. In Portugal, a complex social upheaval was touched off when its armed forces, disillusioned by years of fruitless efforts against the guerrilla independence movements in the African colonies, overthrew the Caetano government in April 1974. In March 1975 the Armed Forces Movement instituted a more radical regime, which, although deeply divided into many shifting factions, seemed agreed on the desirabliity of building some kind of socialist society. In Spain, after the demise of Franco, Socialist and Communist groupings have come to the forefront after many years of repression. In France, strong Communist and Socialist parties, although still divided on many issues and engaged in electoral jockeying, did unite in a popular front movement that in the late 1970s came a hair's breadth from winning the presidency in a national election. In Italy, a still more powerful Communist party has achieved important footholds in major cities and provinces and has been moving toward an "historic compromise" through which they might enter the Italian government along with the Christian Democrats. In each of these four countries, the official Communist party is dynamic, well-organized, rooted in national culture and traditions, and capable of working with many other anticapitalist groupings. The Portuguese Party is the only one to be embarrassed by close adherence to Soviet policies and strategies. The others have demonstrated independence from Soviet positions and disagreement with the approach of the Portuguese Communists. The "loss" of Portugal to the "Free World" would be a much greater blow than the loss of Portugal's former colonies; this would be a crack near the heartland itself. The loss of either Spain or France or Italy would be more than a crack. And the loss of all four countries together with their strategic geopolitical positions and their combined populations of almost 150 million people would mean an historical change in the entire structure of world capitalism.

CREEPING SOCIALISM

While "capitalism" is regarded as an unpleasant term in the United States, where "free enterprise" and other euphemisms are used to describe the system, many Americans fail to realize that "socialism"—also unpopular in the United States—is one of the most popular political catchwords in the rest of the world. The leaders of communist regimes say that their task is to build socialism as a transitional stage before their countries can enter into true communism, when the "dictatorship of the proletariat" will no longer be necessary. The leaders of many Third World countries, such as India, join in waving the banner of socialism as they expand the physical and corporate infrastructure of industrial capitalism. In Western Europe, as Michael Harrington has brilliantly demonstrated, there has been a long tradition of socialist parties taking the responsibility of "running capitalism." [2] Indeed, after World War II the takeoff toward transitional capitalism in all of Western Europe was facilitated by welfare-state programs that helped maintain market demand and submerge class struggles and nationalization programs, and in turn helped subsidize the private corporate sectors. Both socialist ideals and socialist parties have helped strengthen capitalism.

But the popularity of socialist ideals and the appeal of socialist parties has other implications also, implications that may prove dominant over the long run. The first implication is that the short-range steps that may stave off social revolution may also constitute major (albeit confusing) breaks with the capitalist world. Conservatives and reactionaries have long argued that any socialist parties, even such mild reformists as the West German Social Democrats and the British Laborites, are a "camel's nose under the tent." Just a litle socialism, they argue, will lead to a lot of socialism and the end of capitalism. There is some genuine merit in this view.

In the Third World, for example, as shown in the table, "Socialistically Inclined Third World Countries," there are at least a dozen countries whose regimes embody not only the nose and head but at least one hump of the camel. Their total population adds up to over 138 million people. At least four of these countries (Iran, Libya, Algeria, and Iraq) have strategic importance because of their petroleum resources. Jamaica and Guyana contain important bauxite deposits. Somalia is strategically located in geopolitical terms, while Tanzania and Zambia exercise strategic politico-economic influence. Other observers would probably add four or five countries to this list.

None of these regimes is communist in the sense of being "Marxist-Leninist" or pledging themselves to "scientific socialism." Yet the first nine on the list—those in Asia, Western Asia, and Africa—share certain features with communist regimes, particularly one-party politics and tight control of the press and other media. In contrast, the three small countries in the Western Hemisphere—Guyana, Jamaica, and Nicaragua—are politically more similar to Western democracies.

They are also countries whose leadership and people have been among those most influenced by Fidel Castro's advice, Cuban technical assistance, and above all, Cuban example in combating destitution, illiteracy, ill health, and the American "Colossus of the North." In turn, the influence of these three countries, particularly Nicaragua, has been felt among the people in the neighboring Central American dictatorships of Guatemala, El Salvador, and Honduras, and in the Caribbean dictatorship in Haiti. There is a strong possibility that the 1980s will sooner or later see the Caribbean as a socialist sea and Central America as a socialist isthmus. This would not mean Cuban or other Marxist-Leninist style of socialism. It would, however, mean a new series of "losses" to capitalism.

Another implication—or aspect—of socialism's popularity in the world is that it is related to the narrowing of the historic breach between evolutionary and revolutionary socialism. In many parts of the world

SOCIALISTICALLY INCLINED THIRD WORLD COUNTRIES

	Population in 1980 (millions)	Land Area (thousands of square kilometers)
Asia		
Burma	32	676
Western Asia		
Algeria	19	2,382
Iran	35	1,648
Iraq	12	435
Libya	2	111
Syria	8	185
Africa		
Somalia	3	638
Tanzania	17	945
Zambia	5	753
Western Hemisphere		
Guyana	1	215
Jamaica	2	11
Nicaragua	2	130
12	138	8,129
Percent of world's total:	3.3%	6.0%

communist parties previously dedicated to revolution as *the* path to socialism have both accepted the possibility of a peaceful path to socialism and rejected one-party dictatorship as the necessary foundation for building socialism in societies long operating within the framework of constitutional capitalist democracy. This change of position has allowed them to take the position that their socialism would be quite different from that of all communist regimes thus far established. It has also brought them much closer to the socialist and social-democratic parties. Thus the strength of what has been called "Eurocommunism" also adds to the strength of "Eurosocialism." And insofar as Western Europe is concerned, whatever probability there is for communist party regimes, the probability is much greater that socialist governments may not merely run capitalism but may in actuality run or walk away from it.

THIRD WORLD DEMANDS

The First World's difficulties with expanding communism and socialism are increasingly augmented by the rising demands of Third World countries.

The term "Third World," of course, has no meaning except by reference to the "First World" of developed capitalism and the "Second World" of communism. By my classification, as shown in the table, "An Overview of the Three Worlds," it refers to almost eighty countries embracing about half of the world's population. But if one wants to include in this category the seventeen pre-industrial countries of the divided communist world, including China, the number of countries rises higher and the proportion of the population moves from 50 to 75 percent. This broader definition, however, blurs the vital distinction between countries with communist and noncommunist regimes. The larger number can better be described, by the terminology of development, which has given us a sequence of labels from "underdeveloped" (regarded as objectionable by many), "developing" (regarded as an exaggeration by others) to "less developed countries" or LDCs—the last now the United Nations' official label for the majority of its members.

No matter what definition one uses, however, the variety of countries referred to is enormous. Some are still largely primitive, tribal societies like Mali and Oman. Traditional feudal hierarchies—among them Saudi Arabia, Pakistan, and Paraguay—comprise the majority. Then there are those, like India and Brazil, that are well advanced in the transition to modern industrialism although still containing feudal or even tribal elements. They also vary considerably on the extent of democratic constitutionalism. Even when one excludes (as in my table) the "people's democracies" of communism, only a minority operate along the lines of capitalist democracy. The great majority are authoritarian or dictatorial in nature, often with central power openly exercised by a military junta. Economic variations are even more striking. Some are oil-rich countries with a relatively high level of national income per capita (usually enjoyed by a small entrenched minority). Others are in the middle range of national income. A third group is desperately poor.

Despite these vast differences, however, the Third World countries have been remarkably united in making three demands on the First World: an end to colonialism, neocolonialism, and imperialism; more economic and technical aid on better terms; and improved trade relations with the developed countries.

The first demand arose in the immediate years after World War II, in the effort to accelerate decolonization and eliminate the dwindling minority of surviving colonies. The native leaders of former colonies then attacked neocolonialism. By this, they meant either the maintenance of colonial traditions and procedures after liberation or the indirect economic and political pressures exerted by the former colonial power, the United States, or transnational corporations. In many cases, this attack was made by the very leaders who themselves were the people responsible for preserving colonial mentality or serving as submissive, if not servile, cooperators with First World powers. Anti-imperialism became a form of rhetoric available to both its opponents and its friends. The general adoption of this rhetoric, however, has had political implications. Many of the most reactionary collaborators with neocolonialism or imperialism often joined with other Third World countries in attacking American intervention in Vietnam and Cuba and supporting the liberation movements against the Portuguese and in such countries as South Africa, Namibia, and Rhodesia.

The demand for more aid, an even more powerful unifying force, was associated with the growth of the "nonaligned" movement. During the 1950s and the early 1960s, when the confrontation between the United States and the Soviet Union became extremely sharp, a group of Asian leaders started to organize a "third force" to act as a buffer zone between capitalism and socialism. Their successive conferences on the subject (Colombo in 1954, Bandung in 1956, Belgrade in 1961) were sharply denounced as a betrayal of the "Free World" by the American Secretary of State, John Foster Dulles. "If you are not *with* us," Dulles proclaimed in essence, "you are *against* us." What Dulles failed to realize (apart from the fact that his attack helped unify them) was that many of the nonaligned countries were very much *for* capitalism and the "Free World." In India, for example, socialist rhetoric was helpful in placating left-wing parties and getting them to go along with the massive public-sector assistance to the Birlas, Tatas, and other large capitalist conglomerates. But much more was needed: a large infusion of foreign capital and technology. This was obtained under Nehru's inspired leadership by an adroit playing of the Soviet Union against the capitalist countries. The more help they received from the Soviet Union (in return for which small favors were given on the world political arena), the easier it was to raise more funds from First World countries, the World Bank, and the International Monetary Fund. The more help from these, the easier it was to get arms, a huge steel plant, and public sector assistance from the Soviet Union. As many other countries operated according to the same logic (or were inspired by Nehru's example), "Third Worldism" became a tried and trusted method of mobilizing resources in the form of loans, grants, military aid, and technical assistance. To help legitimate India's and other Third World demands for resources, Nehru developed the questionable idea that war is caused by poverty. This idea was warmly embraced by the richer countries who were themselves both the ammunitions makers for the world and the stockpilers of atomic weapons. In return, many Third World countries went through the motions of going along with the still more questionable idea that poverty is caused by overpopulation, despite the evidence that high birthrates and large families are often the only way that poor people can fight poverty. Thus First and Third World countries often found themselves collaborating in antipoverty programs that, like most development programs, enriched Third World elites, and in population-control

AN OVERVIEW OF THE THREE WORLDS
TABLE 10

World	Type	Population Millions	Population %	GNP %	Establishment Structure	International Context
THIRD WORLD	Primitive				Localized tribal/clan domination	
	Traditional				Feudal hierarchies, military juntas	
	Transitional (including socialist and capitalist)				Shifting business-landowning coalitions, with powerful military forces and large bureaucracies	Many clients, satellites or junior partners of First World capitalism; some genuinely "nonaligned"; some strongly socialist or socialistically inclined; most capitalist with feudal vestiges and socialist rhetoric
	Total	2,063	49	10–15		
SECOND WORLD	Pre-industrial Communist				Party leaders, state functionaries, military	Nationalist oriented, polycentric; established with USSR aid but in some cases opposing USSR leadership
	Industrial Communist				Same as above, but with more professionals and technocrats	Associated with COMECOM and Warsaw Pact, under varying forms of USSR leadership
	Total	1,519	36	20–25		

FIRST WORLD	High-technology capitalist				Loose but tightening business-government partnerships served by competing parties, military, professionals, technocrats.	Cooperating through OECD and NATO, with support of IMF and World Bank, in promoting transnational capitalist expansion under U.S. leadership
	Transnational capitalist				Same, with "trilateral" interlocking among national establishments and with Third World partners, satellites, and clients.	
	Total	630	15	60–70		
	Grand Total	4,208	100	100		

programs that had little or no effect in reducing family size. These programs, however, were doubly helpful to the richer people in the poor countries. In addition to getting better and more subsidized birth-control help for themselves, they have received ideological protection against any charge that it was they themselves, by exploiting and repressing the lower classes, who helped cause poverty among the wretched of the earth.

From the earliest days of the Third World's campaign for more aid, it was clear that trade and aid were closely connected. Better trading relations with the First World would be just as helpful as aid and, insofar as aid was directed toward increasing Third World exports, would bring such aid to successful fruition. But it soon became apparent that the terms of trade were often weighted against Third World countries, while First World tariffs and quotas would often deny the Third World access to the huge First World Markets. After years of agitation, the United Nations Conference on Trade and Development was established to help rectify matters through international agreements. A more effective means of changing the terms of trade was found in the early 1970s as the Organization of Petroleum Exporting Countries, OPEC, began to force steady increases in the price of petroleum. In 1974, shortly after OPEC's success in raising crude-oil prices, the president of Algeria, Colonel Houari Boumedienne, delivered a stirring address at the United Nations in which he asked all "Third World" countries to take control of their own resources and work together to change the international terms of trade in their favor. The result was a United Nations declaration calling for a "new international economic order" (NIEO) that would end the exploitation of the "Third World" by Western capitalism. A subsequent declaration by the UN General Assembly, by then often dominated by Third World countries, put it this way:

> The new international economic order should be founded on full respect for the following principles:
> —Full permanent sovereignty of every state over its natural resources and all economic activities . . .
> —Just and equitable relationship between the prices of raw materials, primary commodities, manufactured and semi-manufactured goods exported by developing countries and the prices of raw materials, primary commodities, manufactures, capital goods and equipment imported by them.[3]

The newness behind these euphemisms boils down mainly to two matters: Third World demands to nationalize foreign companies and to get higher prices for their exports while paying less for their imports. Neither of these demands are in themselves either socialist or Marxist-Leninist. For the most part they express the long-term interests of the richest native capitalists and those political leaders and feudal aristocrats who—like the Japanese rulers of a previous era—see public enterprise and enlarged trade as instruments in the transition to industrial capitalism. Nonetheless, these demands have usually won the enthusiastic support of both communists and socialists. The reasons for this, rarely stated in public, are important. For many anticapitalists, as for Marx, Engels, and Lenin in earlier periods of history, the growth of industrial capitalism, its technological capabilities, and its proletariat is a precondition for genuine socialism. Equally important, a major communist and socialist strategy in fighting imperialism or neocolonialism has long been to unite with native capitalists against foreign domination—even at the risk of building the power of the native capitalists who are then to be fought. And from a more global perspective, support for the NIEO can help play LDC capitalists against First World capitalists, thereby diminishing "Free World" unity. Both the Soviet Union and China, each in its own way, have tried to do this.

For First World capitalism, the sum total of these three demands represents a complicated challenge. The complication has been compounded by the growth of the nonaligned movement to include over ninety countries by the time of its Havana conference in 1979. Although many of its newer members include resolutely capitalist countries like Venezuela or right-wing dictatorships, as in Pakistan, communist Cuba and the new communist countries among the LDC's have played a major role in shifting the definition of "nonalignment" to anti-imperialism. It should be noted that the most outspoken conflict at the Havana conference was between two communist leaders: Castro of Cuba, who wanted more open acknowledgment of Soviet support for Third World demands, and Tito of Yugoslavia, whose political *raison d'être* had for thirty years been opposing Soviet interventon in the affairs of other communist countries. The resolution of the conflict, of course, was greater emphasis on struggles against imperialism. To the extent that this struggle is carried out more effectively, the result will be some further advances of communism and socialism and greater independence from First World hegemony on the part of the more vigorous regimes of Third World capitalism.

DETENTE: A COOLER COLD WAR

I am repeatedly amazed by the way in which the catchwords "cold war" and "détente" have served to confuse, rather than illuminate, the long history of capitalist-communist conflict. First of all, cold war was no invention of the 1950s. As Henry L. Roberts has pointed out, it has marked the major capitalist powers' relations with the Soviet Union ever since the early 1920s when hot intervention by American, British, French, and Japanese forces was ended.[4] At that moment the cold war was launched through Western arms and money for anti-bolshevik rebellions and covert sabotage, followed by protracted economic blockade. The Russians responded for a while by unsuccessful support for revolutionary movements in Europe and by more successful efforts to break the economic blockade. During World War II the cold war was put into cold storage, to be brought out again after the communist expansion in Eastern Europe and China. Détente—that is, the cooling down of the cold war—was originally a communist invention. Once in power, the leaders of every communist revolution—from Lenin to Ho Chi Minh, Mao Tse-tung, and Castro—wanted peace on their borders, freedom from subversion and sabotage, and a chance to import capitalist technology. The first formal calls for détente came after Stalin's death with Krushchev's suggestions for "peaceful coexistence" or "peaceful competition." These calls struck a responsive chord in the boardrooms of many large corporations—more in Western Europe than in the United States—which were more interested in profitable undertakings than in conformity with the cold war slogan "you can't do business with the communists." By the late 1960s, as the sources of dynamic growth in the "Free World" became weaker, more and more corporations began to explore the expanding communist markets. Many American corporations moved in to "leapfrog" their Western European competitors and associaates. This effort was buttressed by President Nixon's highly dramatized visits to Moscow and Peking, visits that despite the Vietnam War cast him in the role of world peacemaker and guaranteed his reelection in 1972.

As interpreted by Brezhnev on the Soviet side and Presidents Nixon, Ford, and Carter, détente has never meant an end to conflict or competition between capitalism and communism. Its essential element has been the avoiding of nuclear warfare, which would mean untold destruction for both the United States and the Soviet Union, as well as other countries. This is a mutual interest of vast importance. But it is not inconsistent with ideological conflict and reciprocal strategies of covert intervention, containment, rollback, or the use of business ventures, diplomatic offices, and cultural interchanges as covers for espionage. Nor is it inconsistent with economic, military, or technical assistance to various governments, movements, and parties throughout the world. In the real sense of the idea that détente is a two-way street, each side does all of these.

Who gains the most is a question that thus far can have no answer. Insofar as the avoidance of nuclear war is concerned, there is a sense in which the capitalist powers have more to gain. A third World War would unquestionably mean an end to capitalism. Although the survivors of such a war might well envy the dead, as Krushchev once said, I tend to agree with Mao Tse-tung's view that only communist or other thoroughly collectivist regimes of some type could possibly survive the wreckage of nuclear conflict. Also, in a paradoxical sense that would certainly be a surprise to either Marx or Lenin, the communist countries have come to the rescue of First World countries by supplying large new markets to supplement declining Free World demand. More efficient exploitation of these markets also provides opportunities for capitalizing on the many divisions in the communist world.

On the communist side, détente could be a decisive force for economic progress if it should be accompanied by reduced military expenditures. This would facilitate more rapid progress in overcoming shortages of consumer goods and moving toward the long-promised and long-postponed age of socialist abundance. Progress toward this goal would also be advanced by fuller access to capitalist technology. In a still larger sense, any cooling of the cold war renders less effective the formidable capitalist ideologies depicting communism as a totalitarian horror and socialism as the road to either communism or bureaucratic inefficiency and stultification. Finally, wherever capitalist-communist tensions lessen the greater the likelihood that First World unity—which came into being in a high-tension period—will be impaired.

INSTABILITY AT THE TOP

> I sometimes wonder what use there is in trying to protect the West against fancied external threats when the signs of disintegration within are so striking.
>
> GEORGE KENNAN [5]

During the more immediate aftermath of World War II the normal tensions among the world's major capitalist forces were contained both by the exigencies of internal reconstruction and by the vast business opportunities created by U.S. leadership in building multicontinental markets. Although some vigorous competition began to reappear among Western European countries, and between Japan and Western Europe, and resentment began to develop against American efforts to penetrate both, the competition and the resentment were powerfully contained by the dynamics of American hegemony in military power, trade, technology, and control of transnational institutions and world finance. Increasingly, this hegemony was symbolized less in America's surplus of atomic overkill and more in the "gold-dollar" system whereby for all members of the International Monetary Fund the U.S. dollar was "as good as gold."

Gradually, however, the tensions reasserted themselves. Western Germany and Japan both made huge advances in exports. British, Swiss, and Dutch multinational corporations picked up steam. With the United States giving major attention to military and space technologies, European and Japanese companies surged ahead impressively in many areas of civilian technology. With this resurgence of competition, the barriers to international trade and investment became somewhat higher. In many cases, the strengthening was directly aimed at reducing American dominance.

Paradoxically, America's financial dominance was reduced most significantly by American efforts to maintain military invincibility. During the 1960s the costs of "policing the free world" rose significantly, with American expenditures on the prolonged Vietnam War added to the "normal" expenditures on American military bases around the world and military aid to junior partners and client states. The foreign costs of this policing were met by a huge outflow of American dollars, which in due course converted Europe's postwar "dollar shortage" into a "dollar surplus." The central banks of Japan and Western European countries accumulated far more dollars than their countries or companies wanted to use. Under these circumstances the suspicion arose that the United States was getting real goods and services, plus ownership of industrial facilities in every European country, in exchange for pieces of green paper that were no longer "as good as gold." First France and then other countries started to cash in their paper for gold, thus contributing further to the shakiness of the dollar. By 1971, under the influence of rising imports and the disappearance of the U.S. trade surplus, the outflow of dollars—as measured in all the various indices on the balance of international payments—became enormous. Of such materials, the so-called "international monetary crisis" was born.

In formal terms, the essence of the crisis has been the replacement of controlled exchange rates by "floating currencies." This has meant the devaluation of the dollar, upward revaluation of other currencies (particularly the Japanese yen and the West German mark), a flight to gold that sent the price of gold up to hitherto unknown heights, and recurring speculative attacks upon the dethroned dollar by American transnationals and other wolfpack speculators in the First World. The American government's response to this crisis has been threefold: (1) to withdraw from Indochina and seek greater European armaments to supplement America's military burden in Europe; (2) to seek more foreign income by encouraging more foreign investment by American transnationals; and (3) to reestablish a surplus in foreign trade. Among the weapons in the last two of these steps have been a variety of protectionist measures—import charges, tariffs, preferential measures, quotas, etc.—that threaten the access of other capitalist countries to America's huge domestic markets. The power of these weapons has resided in the fact that for all First World competitors of the United States in the world trade struggle, access to the U.S. market is of vital importance. Beyond this, while no longer exercising financial, trade, or even technological supremacy, the U.S. lion is still the most powerful single force in the world market. A whole series of "Nixon shocks" have been given to many countries—particularly to Japan, whose government had been stubbornly resisting American efforts to buy into (let alone swallow up) Japanese firms or establish Japanese subsidiaries of American transnationals. In turn, other counries have responded with their own forms of protectionism wielded against the United States or each other. Although it would be farfetched, in my judgment, to assert that a full-fledged trade war has begun, there is no doubt that initial skirmishes have been fought. The possibility of sharper conflicts in the future clearly exists.

Moreover, along with détente—and to some extent as an objective factor supporting détente—an important change has been taking place in the composition of First World trade. This is highlighted in the following estimates from *The Wall Street Journal*: [6]

Regions of Europe	European Market Shares (by %)			
	1970		1990	
Capitalist				
Northwest	49		33	
South	6		12	
Total		55		45
Communist				
Soviet Union	32		39	
Eastern Europe	13		16	
Total		45		45

By these estimates, the communist sector of Europe is expected to attain by 1990 the 55 percent level of the capitalist sector in 1970. This means that capitalists in the Northwest countries (mainly West Germany, France, Britain, and Italy) would seek to expand their business in the growing markets of the Soviet Union and Eastern Europe. It also suggests greater market importance for the southern region (defined as Spain, Portugal, Greece, and Turkey), which is politically less stable than the North and more apt to move directly toward socialism, communism, or some intermediate stage presaging the replacement of capitalism at a later date. The future of Japan in the First World alliance raises even more complex questions. Suffering more than any other major capitalist country from the energy crisis, Japan can most easily find the oil it needs from the two neighboring communist giants, China and the Soviet Union. Beyond this, Japan is in a remarkably favorable situation not only to supply both with "advanced" technologies but also to exploit their gigantic markets. While this means competition with all First World countries, it may mean above all a loosening of ties with the United States and less dependence on American markets.

Thus, while the first postwar wave of communist and socialist expansion helped unify the First World, the more recent shrinkage of the capitalist world has tended to create internal tensions. It also promotes a wave of speculations about the future. Thus, without going along with Bell's funeral oration for the American Century, Mary Kaldor in *The Disintegrating West* places her bets on a complete breakup of the "Free World." She even goes so far as to suggest that Europe might be politically unified and that a European supergovernment could—as Germany, France, and England did in the past—be ready to go to war with other capitalist powers.[7] I think this is highly improbable. In any case, to approach such questions, I suggest, it is imperative to look again at the older crises of capitalism—world war, class conflict, and the business cycle—as they are reappearing in new forms. That is my task in the next chapter.

6

Old Crises in New Forms

> The calm is on the surface. Underneath, crisis-laden tendencies and contradictions not only continue to exist but to multiply and are sure to erupt into the open in the historically near future.
>
> PAUL M. SWEEZY [1]

BY THE END OF WORLD WAR II, the armed forces of America and Britain, with Russian help, smashed the Italian, German, and Japanese regimes of classic fascism. After the war, the leaders of America, Western Europe, and Japan made giant strides in coping with the business cycle, class conflict, war among capitalist powers, and the domestic threats of socialism and communism—that is, with the old crises of capitalism which were at the root of classic fascism.

Nowhere was morale higher than among Establishment economists in the United States. In protracted orgies of self-congratulation they praised their capabilities in fine-tuning the economy—some through fiscal policy, others by trying to control the money supply. By 1970, hailing the National Bureau of Economic Research for its diligence in collecting figures on economic fluctuations, Paul Samuelson joyously proclaimed that the bureau "had worked itself out of one of its first jobs, namely, the business cycle." [2] Most of Samuelson's less eminent colleagues supported his judgment that neither unemployment nor inflation presented serious dangers. Thus along with ideology and the American Century, the business cycle also was given a premature burial. In turn, the very idea of class conflict was beyond the pale of serious discussion. As for war, the ancient enmities among Western European nations subsided. And despite the cold war, fears of World War III slowly faded and military spending as a percent of the GNP began to decline.

Paul Sweezy, a neo-Marxist, was one of the first to see that old problems were boiling beneath the surface. Unlike more orthodox Marxists, often ready to predict the system's imminent collapse, Sweezy noted both the decline of the "New Left" of the 1960s and the new combination of "cyclical boom and secular stagnation." But no economists—liberal, radical, or conservative—were prepared for the more disconcerting events of the 1970s, particularly the full emergence of stagflation—the two-misery mixture of stagnation and inflation—and its interconnection with OPEC, the energy crisis, and war dangers in Western Asia. On their part, corporate and military leaders were better prepared respectively, for the threats of class conflict and nuclear war. Yet these preparations have in large part helped intensify the problems they were designed to solve.

By the beginning of the 1980s it became clear that a dangerous beast does not vanish when caged—nor a storm disappear when people find shelter, nor dynamite when defused. The return of old crises in new forms seemed to suggest that the cage door was being pried open, the shelters being slowly flooded, and the fuse in danger of being reignited. Thus the leaders of "free world" capitalism—in Western Europe, Japan, and Oceania as well as North America—now face challenges at home that add immeasurably to the perils of social fragmentation, eroded authority, and a shrinking capitalist world.

UNTAMED RECESSION

> No sane political figure is going to say a kind word for recession—but the universally avoided truth is that there is at present no better way to increase productivity in plants, to turn impulse buyers into careful shoppers at supermarkets, and to cut seriously into rising living costs.
>
> WILLIAM SAFIRE [3]

During the first thirty-five years after World War II the United States witnessed eight minor economic contractions: two under Truman (beginning in 1946 and 1949), three under Eisenhower (1953, 1957, and 1960), one under Nixon (1970), one under Ford (1974), and one under Carter (1979–80). To explain their brief and relatively mild nature, people invented one new word and two new theories. The word was *recession,* which replaced *depression* and stressed the limited nature of the evil. The first theory was the Keynesian "fine tuning," through which professionally advised governments would manage fiscal and monetary affairs in such a way as to promote rising (albeit mildly undulating) total demand and avoid any serious decline in jobs and output. The attractiveness of the theory was based on much more than Lord Keynes, who was probably rolling over sadly in his grave as his name was bandied about by upstarts who selected from his writings a few things out of context. The neo-Keynesians also—for the most part—performed the service of understating the contributions to market demand of the Korean and Vietnamese wars. Their learned memos helped conceal the enormous expansion of labor reserves behind the official figures on unemployment and "labor force." Above all, they distracted attention from the large body of government and corporate policies rather finely tuned toward the accelerated accumulation of corporate capital through more full-bodied support for corporate profitability at home and abroad. All this helped inflate the egos and career opportunities of certified Keynesians.

By the early 1970s the reputation (but not the egos or job openings) of the Keynesians was punctured by recurring recession and continuing inflation. Into the vacuum rushed a new group of self-styled "post-Keynesians" who tried to shift attention from the "demand" side to the "supply" side. The supply-side policy advisers advocate action on such a variety of issues as productivity, capital formation, technology, labor supply, bottlenecks, and government regulation. Underlying this large menu, however, is a common theme that does not differentiate them too much from the pre-post Keynesians: namely, the promotion of corporate profitability. But like the Keynesians, most of them prefer to discuss surrogates of profits rather than coming into the open on a politically delicate subject. Only the true-blue conservatives wear the badge of capitalism on their foreheads and openly stress the role of profitability in accumulating capital and power.

Another common element uniting most Keynesians and post-Keynesians is the ridiculous but politically powerful idea that a recession coming at the time of a Nixon, Ford, or Carter administration is created by it. All that is needed, it is thereby hinted, is a smarter crowd in the White House. Only the Marxists and the dyed-in-the-wool conservatives accept the business cycle as alive and operating. Although Establishment leaders can spin this wheel faster or slower, they cannot justly be given the blame or credit for inventing it.

Corporate leaders, of course, take the cycle for granted and incorporate it into their longer-range plans, which often cover two, three, or more full cyclical swings. In so doing, I believe they often recognize one of the basic contradictions of capitalism, long ago noted by Karl Marx: *Trying to maximize profits tends to undermine profitability.*[4] This undesired (although sometimes anticipated) consequence takes place to the extent that ebullient profitmaking (1) undermines mass purchasing power, thereby lowering the capacity to consume relative to expanded productive capacity, (2) nurtures overexpansion in some areas and neglect of others, thereby creating bottlenecks, (3) provides opportunities for organized workers to raise some wages to the point where they squeeze some profits, or (4) nurtures speculative activities that cannot be maintained. Although competing theorists make a big to-do about one or the other of these, all these factors—and sometimes a few more—are usually at work at the same time.

Since economic downturns have long been regarded as inevitable as sleep or winter, it is only natural that the smartest capitalists long ago learned how to make a virtue of necessity by "riding the business cycle." A corporation did not have to be very smart to make money in boom periods. With depressions, a minority of ultra-clever operators long ago learned how to force competitors to the wall, pick up depression bargains in stocks, land, and companies, and put wages through the wringer. Since World War II, as deep depression was converted into moderate recession, this one-time cleverness became standard operating procedure. "It's not that we look favorably upon depressions or recessions," states Walter Grinder in *Business Week*. "It's just that they are necessary after a bout of antisocial overinvestment in capital, engendered by expansionary monetary policies."[5] Like sleep, recessions now tend to serve as a period of recuperation from, if not cure for, previous excesses. During this refreshing pause, plants are closed, unprofitable products dropped, and employees fired. As conditions for renewed profitability are created, the larger corporations move ahead with their long-range plans. If winter has come, can spring be far behind?

The answer is "perhaps." There is no dearth of new technologies in modern capitalism's vast technology reserve, nor any lack of new tricks whereby government can subsidize profits. But the new world environment is not as favorable as it used to be. The spread of communism, socialism, and crude-oil capitalism—as well as the instabilities in the First World—have created new difficulties for transnational expansion. Under these conditions a First World return to ebullient growth might require putting the majority of its home population through a tighter wringer than any capitalist establishment has thus far been able to operate.

THE HIDDEN UNEMPLOYED

The current definition of unemployment captures only the tip of the iceberg of potential workers; it is itself part of a grand cover-up of the shortage of jobs.

FRANK FURSTENBERG, JR.
AND CHARLES A. THRALL [6]

During a recession, many things—like GNP, income, profits, wages, or even oil imports—go down temporarily. But one thing goes up: unemployment. The height of these unpleasant upswings in various periods, as officially measured in the United States, has been reported like this:

PERCENTAGES OF "LABOR FORCE"

Prewar Depression		Postwar Recessions					
1933	1939	1949	1954	1958	1961	1971	1974
24.9	17.2	5.9	5.5	6.8	6.7	5.9	8.5

These reports are limited to those actively seeking work; they do not include the much larger number of unemployed people who are able and willing to work for pay but are not at the moment seeking jobs—some of them because they already know there are none to be found. Nonetheless, by some mysterious magic, these numbers—routinely publicized every month—have assumed great importance. In Establishment politics, the number of officially estimated job seekers has become enshrined as the measure of full employment. It is as though the number of unmarried men and women over 18—now around 50 million people—should be reduced to those who actively sought a mate during the last four weeks.

It was not always thus. During World War II, full employment was first defined as a shortage of labor—a situation when more employers were seeking workers than there were workers seeking jobs. Toward the end of the war, the Roosevelt administration set a full employment goal: 60 million peacetime jobs. With less attention to numbers, the original full-employment bills drafted in 1944 defined full employment in terms of Roosevelt's Economic Bill of Rights "the right to a useful and remunerative job in the industries or shops or farms or mines of the Nation." This right was to be guaranteed by federal action which, after promoting private employment, would provide "last resort jobs" for anyone the private sector could or would not hire.

Thirty years later, through Rep. Augustus Hawkins and the Congresional Black Caucus, this principle was restated more strongly in the first versions of the Humphrey-Hawkins Full Employment and Balanced Growth Bill. In this measure full employment was defined as "a situation under which there are useful employment opportunities for all adult Americans willing and able to work." Once again, this desirable goal was to be attained by a government guarantee. In addition, as a guide for government planning, specific quantitative numbers were to be set forth every year for the total number of full-time and part-time jobs. Thus, if the legislation had been enacted in its original form, the full-employment goal for 1984 might be—for example—around 125 million jobs: perhaps 20 million full-time or part-time jobs that might not otherwise be available.

In both 1944 and 1974 the supporters of this far-reaching approach argued that it would go far toward reducing poverty and social tensions and would also assure business of stable markets and more stable profits. In both periods big business and conservative opponents opposed it on the ground that it would require more government intervention into economic affairs, which was undoubtedly correct. What really rubbed them the wrong way, however, was that this kind of intervention threatened the rate of profit by curtailing low-wage employment and creating conditions under which individual employees and unionized workers would have more bargaining power to increase wages, improve working conditions, or even enter the sacred precincts of managerial decision making.

Thus the idea of guaranteeing human rights was ruthlessly stricken from the bills finally enacted as the Employment Act of 1946 and the Full Employment and Balanced Growth Act of 1978. In place of human rights to useful paid employment came a whole series of ceremonial rites in which the operational definition of full employment soon became "whatever level of official unemployment is politically tolerable." Over the years this level constantly rose:

ESTABLISHMENT DEFINITIONS OF FULL EMPLOYMENT: UNEMPLOYMENT AS PERCENT OF LABOR FORCE

1940s	1950s	1960s	1970s	1980s
2–3%	2–4%	3–4.5%	4–5.5%	6–?%

The apologists for this continuing redefinition were quick with justifications. Many of the new job-seekers, they argued, were women seeking paid work outside the home, or young people with little or no work experience. Others were black, Hispanic, or members of other minorities. In contrast with prime-age, white males, these no-account people, they argued, should not be taken into account. Subtract them from today's overall figure of 6 or 7 percent and one gets right back to an old-time 3 to 4. The explanation, however, as distinct from the apologetics, is that the higher levels have thus far proved to be politically tolerable. Thus in many of the largest cities of the country official unemployment often reached 9, 10, or 11 percent without political explosions. One basic reason has been the growth of huge government transfer payments to the unemployed and the poor: unemployment compensation, public assistance, food stamps, rent subsidies, and training programs. These payments helped make unemployment tolerable both to business, by helping maintain market demand, and to the unemployed, by helping them get along at minimal levels of subsistence. Without this money, shopkeepers and landlords would have long ago protested the bite of recession, and the unemployed would have been loudly protesting, if not rioting, in the streets, banks, and government offices.

The handling of the transfers, moreover, often helped establish the idea that certain groups of people were not entitled to jobs. Thus the recipients of public assistance have been officially classified as "unemployable"—even though field surveys have proved that most mothers receiving "aid for dependent children" are able to work and would prefer decent jobs if they were available. Indeed, as Furstenberg and Thall have demonstrated, the official unemployment definition itself has helped bolster a "job rationing ideology" which helps indoctrinate older people, women, and younger people with the idea that they are not entitled to a job. This ideology is supported by the grim fact that in a job-scarcity anyone who gets or holds onto a job might feel that he or she is taking it away from someone else.

By massaging the official figures, one can learn a lot more about what different people can tolerate. Black job seekers in America usually outnumber others by two to one; their official unemployment rate is always at a serious recession level. For teenagers as a whole, the figure is much higher. For black and Hispanic teenagers it bursts the confines of recession and hits levels which, by any standard, are those of catastrophic depression.

When one goes beyond the officially reported job seekers, hard facts are harder to get, but the situation is obviously grimmer. Literally, countless millions of people are no longer looking for what experience has proved cannot be found; these are often termed "dropouts from the labor force." Some of them are older people with many years of work experience who are "pushed out" by the motto "No applications accepted from people over 40." Others—mainly women and minorities—are impeded by institutionalized bias; they are in fact "kept outs." A vague idea of how much all this adds up to is provided when a few job openings are advertised—whether for street cleaners, construction workers, or even assistant professors—and the applicants outnumber the openings by astronomical ratios. If ever directed to do so, the U.S. Employment Service could get a complete unemployment index covering everyone able and willing to work by simple expedient of advertising that such-and-such jobs were really available (part time as well as full time) for such-and-such types of people. This, of course, is what the government would have been obliged to do if either of the original full-employment bills of 1944 or 1974 had been enacted without prior castration. In the absence of such a job guarantee policy, a statistical estimator faces as much difficulty as getting an index on nasal congestion, middle-age loneliness, or teenage orgasm.

My own estimate is that the total number of people not working for pay but able and willing to work has generally been at least three times the number of reported job seekers—even between recessions. For 1978 that gives us a figure of about 18 million people. In recessions, of course, the number rises. If Karl Marx were alive today, he would call this "the relative surplus population" or "the reserve army of the unemployed." To this surplus, he would have to add the dependent family members of the unemployed, those who work for a while and then are laid off, those who suffer from permanent insecurity in their jobs, and those whose job insecurities are rooted in their provision of illegal services. But no matter how the surplus is estimated, I doubt whether he would still use the army metaphor. Here there are no commanding officers, no guiding strategy or tactics, no discipline—merely casualties, and most of these come from battle among the nonemployed over who will get a scarce job first or be fired last.

THE NEW INFLATION: HYENA'S DELIGHT

> There is neither system nor justice in the expropriation and redistribution of property resulting from inflation. A cynical "each man for himself" becomes the rule of life. But only the most powerful, the most resourceful and unscrupulous, the hyenas of economic life, can come through unscathed . . . Inflation is a tragedy that makes a whole people cynical, hardhearted and indifferent.
>
> THOMAS MANN [7]

> A spectre is haunting the major industrial nation of the free world . . . That spectre is the grim visage of inflation.
>
> GENE KORETZ [8]

Before World War II, inflation in capitalist societies tended to be violent and temporary. For wartime governments, inflation of the money supply was the quickest way to mobilize resources for war by taxing the masses. In Germany during the 1920s, as Franz Neumann has shown, the creation of runaway inflation "permitted unscrupulous entrepreneurs to build up giant economic empires at the expense of the middle and working classes." In other countries, unplanned speculative booms—whether in boom towns or times—facilitated the sudden growth of great fortunes in the hands of Thomas Mann's "economic hyenas." But sooner or later the inflationary bubbles always burst, with most prices falling sharply and the general price level drifting downwards before any "reflation." During any periods of actual contraction, business and government leaders sought ways and means of preventing prices from falling or "reflating" enough to encourage recovery.

After World War II, modern capitalism entered a new era of the sustained use of mildly inflationary stimulants. Among these were military expenditures, particularly those connected with the Korean and Vietnam wars. These, in turn, were major sources of federal deficits, which pumped additional purchasing power into the economy. The same support for demand was obtained by increasing civilian expenditures (favored by more of the liberals) and reducing taxes (favored by most conservatives). In either case the rising national debt became a valued source of direct profits by the banks holding government securities. Rapidly rising municipal and state debt, also an effective stimulant, became an invaluable form of tax evasion by the wealthy. Corporate debt rose still more rapidly. But the most massive debt increases have been in home mortgages, installment loans, and other forms of consumer credit; together they went rather far in filling the large gap between the actual income of the middle and lower classes and the incomes that would have been necessary to buy the goods and services that could be produced through the expanded productive capacity of private business.

During the first twenty-five years after World War II, except for a brief price splurge when war price controls were suddenly removed, all these measures never pushed prices up as high as 6 percent a year. Most Establishment leaders felt that mild price increases of 2 or 3 percent a year were a good tonic. In this sense, they were all inflationists—both the conservatives who inveighed against inflation and the liberals who regarded anti-inflation talk as an indirect attack on social spending, wage increases, and high employment.

But in the 1970s something new burst onto the scene. Before then, the rate of price increases had always slowed down during a recession. But in 1974–75 and again in 1979, the general price level misbehaved: *it rose during recession.* These figures show how:

Percent Changes from Previous Year	1974	1975	1979 (2nd quarter)
Decline in GNP, constant dollars	−1.4	−1.3	−2.3
Increase in GNP price measure	9.7	9.6	9.3
Increase in consumer prices	12.2	7.0	12–13 (est.)

Economic Indicators, December 1979

This misbehavior proved immensely embarrassing to all varieties of Establishment economists. "The economy is not working the way it's supposed to," they complained. Not being able to tame it, they tried to name it. One name was *slumpflation,* which hinted that after the slump was over ebullient growth would be restored. The name that has stuck—without yet entering the dictionaries—is *stagflation.* More realistically, this word suggests a stagnant economy in which, when recession passes, inflation will continue, and perhaps accelerate, but growth will be sluggish despite inflationary stimulants.

Most people in America—especially those whose heads have not been shrunken or brainwashed by immersion in Establishment economics —know intuitively that the new inflation is a *profit inflation.* They have seen the price of oil pushed up by OPEC, have cringed under the impact of rising prices for gasoline, heating oil, and natural gas, and have accurately sensed the fact that the American oil companies have worked hand in glove with OPEC and made huge profits from well-designed, well-exploited—and therefore real—shortages. They know that the burgeoning prices of food, medical care, and housing have similar roots, being nurtured by government policies to curtail agricultural output, put floors under prices, subsidize the doctor–drug-company–hospital complex, raise interest rates, and encourage land speculation.

The Establishment notables know all this. Indeed, they have a term for it—administered prices (or oligopolistic price setting)—which is not to be uttered in polite society. Publicly, they offer two explanations: demand pull and cost push. In discussing demand, they level their fire at the purchasing power created by wage increases, government's social programs, the federal deficit, and the money supply. They leave out the insatiable demand for profits by transnational corporations with long-term expansion plans they prefer to finance through the larger cash flows won by higher prices. They also tend to exclude the higher demand created by military spending and inflated consumer credit. They define the money supply in terms of current prices alone, studiously avoiding even the barest hint that during inflation the value of money goes down and that the *real* money supply contracts. In complaining about higher costs, they concentrate their fire on rising wages (which in real terms have been declining and by 1979 fell below those paid in West Germany, the Netherlands, Sweden, and Belgium) and falling labor productivity (which always falls when there is a decline in the volume of production). They carefully avoid the costs of capital embodied in higher profits, interest rates, and rents—and in the rising emoluments of the corporate overseers and executive managers.

While both of these explanations avoid direct attention to profits, the explainers are usually united in their less publicly expressed conviction that a central objective of public and private policy under capitalism should be the promotion of higher profits. This is very close to the historical driving force of industrial capitalism since its beginnings about two hundred years ago. But there is a difference: the growing ability of powerful sellers, usually with open or covert government support, to increase profits by raising prices and get away with it even when demand is falling. There is also a difficulty: *making more money by pushing prices up reduces the value of the money made.*[9] This adds an additional twist to the old contradiction that profit maximization tends to undermine profitability. It gives the producers of inflation an interest in trying to modulate the inflation they produce.

One way to do this is to put a lid on wages. This is done through wage-price policies that—in the words of an associate of President Nixon —"zap labor" while being soft on business. This is being done throughout the First World, not only in the United States. As a result, wage increases in general lag behind prices during stagflation, indirectly contributing to corporate profitability. When some militant and well-organized unions succeed in catching up with prices, or even getting a little ahead, the employers usually succeed in passing the additional labor costs on to the consumer in the form of higher prices. This usually accelerates the drive to squeeze wages still more in the unorganized sectors.

Another way to modulate inflation is to play the business cycle by bringing recession sooner and trying to make it a little deeper and longer. This is the celebrated "tradeoff" policy which, although sometimes disavowed, dominates the White House, corporate boardrooms, Wall Street, the OECD, and the International Monetary Fund. This policy rests on the long-observed fact that under present-day capitalism prices are pushed up when employment is high and an economy is racing along and that a truly serious economic decline will tend to push many, if not all, prices down. The policy dictates that recession and unemployment are the easiest way to prevent runaway inflation. Although this policy would require a deep depression to bring inflation down to the old-time levels of 2 to 4 percent a year, it does dampen inflationary surges a little. Accordingly, never have so many bankers, business leaders, and even sane political leaders said so many kind words for recession.

The kindest words of all come from the bankers who, with the help of the Federal Reserve Board, have been raising interest rates—that is, the prices they charge for credit. This is probably even more inflationary than raising the price of oil; higher interest rates enter into the costs of all economic activities relying on credit. One of the bankers' justifications is that they are merely adjusting to inflation. Yet the spread between the interest rates they pay and those they charge has steadily been increasing. Moreover, as the following figures show, as prices rose four times between 1945 and 1979, various interest rates rose by multiples of 12, 17 and 32: [6]

Prices	1945	1979	Increase, in multiples
Consumer price index (1967 = 100)	51.3	227.5 (Nov.)	4.43
GNP price measure (1972 = 100)	37.92	167.2 (3rd Quart.)	4.41
Selected Interest Rates			
Federal Reserve Bank discount rate (N.Y.)	1.0	12 (Dec.)	12
Prime commercial paper, 4–6 months	.75	13.01 (Dec.)	17.34
3-month Treasury bills	.38	12.2 (Dec.)	32.1

Economic Report of the President, January 1979
Economic Indicators, December 1979

If rising interest rates and other factors should push inflation still higher, the hyenas of economic life—to use Thomas Mann's words—can come through unscathed. During the long-lived virulent inflation in Latin America, the First World's transnational corporations have long ago learned the mysterious arts of appreciating capital under conditions of depreciating currencies and massive unemployment. This capability can readily be transferred to the home country. And if the consequence—whether sought or unanticipated—is more unemployment, the side effect will be to enhance the hyenas' future profitability by dampening wage increases, undermining union power, and engulfing many islands of small-business competition.

"Sweet are the uses of adversity," says the Duke in Shakespeare's *As You Like It*, putting the best possible face on his misfortune in being banished to the Forest of Arden. In today's capitalist jungles the uses of adversity are still sweeter when other people, not the corporate elites, suffer the misfortunes of recession and inflation.

THE DYNAMITE OF CLASS CONFLICT

> In the United States resistance to work seems to reach acute proportions from capital's point of view.
>
> STEPHEN HYMER [10]

> Socialism Is No Longer a Dirty Word to Labor
>
> HEADLINE, *Business Week* [11]

Class conflicts since World War II would certainly have been more open, bitter, and prolonged if not for the successes of American-led capitalism in maintaining "First World" leadership, limiting war, moderating the business cycle, and achieving substantial economic growth through more efficient exploitation of people and resources on a global scale.

As it is, class conflict has tended to be submerged, unclear, and sporadic—indeed, even more under control than empire, war, or the business cycle. The greatly enlarged working classes have been divided into five different labor markets: capital intensive, labor intensive, public, nonprofit, and underclass. They are also divided along racial, religious, national, sectional, and regional lines. Since the nineteenth century conceptions of the working class can no longer be automatically applied to late twentieth-century realities, many observers seem to have concluded that the obvious absence of sharp class-consciousness means that there are no underlying class interests and, in fact, no working class at all. Many unions or union leaders see their role in narrow and parochial terms, with little or no interest in organizing all classes of workers, combating the many forms of exploitation outside wage-and-salary bargaining, or seeking any significant changes (other than securing their own positions at the junior and contingent level) in the Establishment. Outside the Marxian minority in America, Daniel P. Moynihan was one of the few people to point out—as he did at the time of the 1967 riots in Detroit—that class interests are still influential in America.

Nonetheless, the perception of exploitation exists. It is expressed in the popular language of complaint by blue-collar, white-collar, and technical workers who feel they have been "ripped off," "shafted," or "screwed" by employers, banks, landlords, supermarkets, and politicians. With more job insecurity, more inflation, more onerous taxation, more military adventurism, the resentment against ripoffs deepens. It reveals itself in many forms of alienation and resistance that are promptly seen by the more farsighted leaders of corporate capital as serious obstacles to efficient accumulation.

In the early nineteenth century organized workers often fought the domination of industrial capitalism's new machinery by wrecking the machines. The new Luddites in the modern working classes often fight mechanization by informal or formal efforts to prevent the introduction of labor-displacing machinery or work routines. In some industries this has been rather successful. In others, the unions have cooperated with corporate mechanization programs in return for somewhat higher positions for a privileged, well-protected, and declining union membership.

The most insidious form of resistance is simple individual withdrawal from efficient work. This withdrawal takes the form of tardiness, early leaving, prolonged coffee breaks, or lavatory visits. Still more serious are high—and often rising—rates of absenteeism and turnover. Thus Harry Braverman reports that "The Fiat Motor Company, Italy's largest private employer with more than 180,000 employees, 147,000 of whom are factory workers, [has] had 21,000 employees missing on a Monday and a daily average absenteeism of 14,000." [12] Throughout the 1970s these conditions became more acute in almost all First World countries. As for the United States, he reports: "At the Chrysler Corporation's Jefferson Avenue plant in Detroit, a daily average absentee rate of 6 percent was reported in mid-1971, and an annual overall turnover of almost 30 percent . . ." Many companies that have fared better than Chrysler in maintaining profitability have been plagued by equally serious absenteeism and turnover.

Somewhat less measurable are the many negative forms of slowdown or "featherbedding" on the job—although a 1972 Gallup poll reported that 57 percent of their respondents thought "they could produce more each day if they tried" and that this figure rose to 70 percent for professionals and businessmen and 72 percent for 18–29-year-olds. Still less measurable—and more disruptive—are such deliberate acts as defective work, pilfering, and sabotage.

The strike, or work stoppage, of course, is the most direct form of resistance to exploitation on the job, and the classic form of class conflict. But the outbreak of many strikes does not necessarily mean that class struggle is coming into the open. Strikes may be precipitated by *agents provocateurs* working for the employers, may be timed in such a way as to coincide with corporate desires to slow down production, or may be "won" by union leadership which then sells out its members. Successful strikes by workers in capital-intensive industries may provide employers with excuses for raising prices to levels that go far beyond what may be needed to cover increased labor costs and thereby impose new burdens of price exploitation on all workers. "Strikes conducted in the state sector by state workers," as James O'Connor points out, "lead either to increases in prices or higher taxes or to lower real wages for the tax-paying working class—or both . . . [They] therefore always hold a potential for dividing the working class . . ." [13]

Nonetheless, the strike threat is always taken seriously by the leaders of corporate capital—and, from their viewpoint, properly so. Despite the cooperative spirit of old-style union management, rank-and-file workers—particularly younger ones or those who come from agricultural backgrounds and have not yet been fully socialized into the acceptance of company or trade-union discipline—are often extremely aggressive. Throughout the First World, O'Connor reports, "there has been a noticeable shift from national, official and centrally directed and controlled strikes to short, local, unofficial slowdowns and strikes." In the state sector, moreover, union militancy—whether by official leadership or rank-and-file pressure—"clearly has the potential for radicalizing both state employees and their organization." This radicalization has even extended to police forces and the uniformed armed services themselves, the very instrumentalities of traditional control over radicals. Sometimes, these forms of resistance—although rooted in antagonism created by the Establishment—serve Establishment interests by being redirected against ethnic minorities, women, younger people, the unemployed, and other exploited people, including the clients or recipients of state services. As countervailing forces (and a threat to the upper levels of the Establishment), there are tendencies toward what O'Connor calls "the developing relationship between state workers and state dependents . . . between teachers, students, and office and maintenance personnel, between welfare workers and welfare recipients, between public health workers and people who use public health and medical facilities, and between transport workers and the public served by public transit."

But the largest steps toward more open and bitter class conflict in the United States have been taken by corporate leaders. In the South and the Southwest—particularly in textiles—they have fought bitterly against the spread of unionism. In the West, they have spared no efforts in preventing the unionization of agricultural workers. Throughout the country they have been successful in slowing down unionization drives among white-collar and service workers. Above all, they have gone in for union busting in a big way—even in areas where previously unions had been formally accepted by management.* In response, some of the most old-time and most conservative leaders of the American trade unions have been accusing corporate leaders of "waging class warfare."

In response to employers, proclaims the *Business Week* headline referred to earlier, "Unions That Used to Bait 'Commies' and 'Kooks' Now Join Forces with Socialists." More and more union leaders—particularly among the machinists, government employees, auto workers, textile workers, and steelworkers—publicly identify themselves as socialists. In 1979 the building trades workers, long regarded as the most conservative element in organized labor, took a full-page advertisement in the newsletter of the Democratic Socialist Organizing Committee. In one of his last public statements before resigning from leadership of the AFL-CIO, George Meany called for the nationalization of the oil industry if "the monopoly fails to adequately serve the public interest." Many more unions now call for government controls over prices (and other forms of income) and investment, and more worker participation in management decision making. Above all, militancy seems to be rising in union relations with employers. If stagflation continues to undercut real wages and working conditions, the class consciousness of employers may be met by more class cohesiveness among employees. In this way, the dynamite of class conflict may be ignited.

LIMITED WAR

> Every man, woman and child lives under a nuclear sword of Damocles, hanging by the slenderest of threads, capable of being cut at any moment by accident, miscalculation or madness.
>
> PRESIDENT JOHN F. KENNEDY,
> September 1961

During the so-called "Hundred Years' Peace" (1815–1914), all wars among the Great Powers were minor, short, or localized. General peace was preserved in an environment of unending limited war.

---

* I discuss this more fully in "The Friendly Fascist Establishment" (Chapter 9).

The period since 1945 has also been one of limited war. Whatever military action has taken place—whether in Korea, Indochina, the Middle East, Africa, or Latin America—has been geographically limited. Although the devastation has been ghastly, no nuclear weapons have been used.

But limited war has created a baffling problem for the leading capitalist powers, particularly the United States: A reduction in military stimulants to economic expansion and capital accumulation. The present condition of the American industrial establishment, writes David Bazelon, "is unthinkable without the benefit of the capacity-building expenditures of the past twenty years induced by war and preparedness measures." [14] The U.S. Arms Control and Disarmament Agency has thought about this in terms that are themselves unthinkable to most Establishment economists: "It is generally agreed that the great expanded public sector since World War II, resulting from heavy defense expenditures, has provided additional protection against depression, since this sector is not responsible to contraction in the private sector and has provided a sort of buffer or balance wheel in the economy." [15]

Strangely enough, the use of military-growth stimulants in the United States also served to stimulate growth in the two major capitalist societies with relatively small military budgets: Japan and West Germany. An important part of U.S. military expenditures spilled over into both Japan and West Germany in the form of both procurement of supplies and payments for the maintenance of U.S. installments. More indirectly, the U.S. concentration of war-related technology (which includes advanced computerization, communication systems, and electronic controls) gave the largest corporations in other leading countries of the "Free World," particularly Japan and West Germany, an opportunity to catch up with, or plunge ahead of, the United States in civilian technologies and thereby make spectacular advances in world trade.

As the United States began its slow withdrawal from Indochina in 1969, military expenditures began to level off and then—while prices for military goods were still rising—to fall by almost $4 billion from 1969 to 1972. As a proportion of total GNP, military spending fell even more drastically—from 9.1 percent in 1967 and 1968 to around 6 percent in 1979. Expenditures for "international affairs" (closely related to military expenditures) also declined. The size of the U.S. armed forces fell from over 3.5 million in 1968 to 2.1 million in 1979. In other words, the military slowdown under conditions of deescalation and détente deprived the American economy of a defense against recession that had been provided during the 1960s. This was one of the factors in the recessions that began in 1970, 1974, and 1979. In each case unemployment rose. In 1975, the total end to the hugely destructive war in Indochina was a retrogressive economic force, as unemployment in the United States and other capitalist countries rose to the highest levels since the Great Depression.

The response of the industrial-military portion of the Establishment has been prompt, publicly warning against the great perils of becoming weaker than the communist enemy and privately warning against the disastrous economic effects of the slowdown. The positive action has been in two directions: the expansion of new and costly weapons systems and the sale of arms to other countries. Under conditions of détente, however, the two of these together were insufficient to restore defense spending to the proportions of GNP reached during Indochinese wars. Thus the American industrial establishment was subjected to a slow withdrawal of the stimulus to which it had become accustomed. The NATO countries were subjected to a sharp decline in the vigor of the Soviet "threat," which was the official *raison d'être* for NATO's existence. The capitalist world was subjected for a while to the "threat" of a peaceful coexistence in which the economic stimulus of war and preparedness would no longer be available at the level to which it had become accustomed. With any decline in détente, of course, these conditions change.

UNLIMITED OVERKILL

The dominant logic of "Free World" militarism in a period of limited warfare has been slowly developing during the 1970s. If unlimited warfare is "dysfunctional," then two lines of operation are indicated.

The first has been to channel a larger portion of military resources into weapons systems produced by the largest military contractors, even though this means a dwindling number of people in the armed services. The result has been a continuous increase in "overkill" capabilities whose actual use would surely destroy capitalism itself but whose production and deployment contribute to the maintenance of a capital accumulation. Overkill itself is matched by various forms of "overdelivery": globe-circling missiles in addition to bombers; multiple warheads on a single missile (MIRVs); launchings from roving submarines, ocean-floor emplacements and eventually satellite space stations; ocean explosions to produce *tsunamis* (tidal waves); antiballistic missiles that would themselves emit vast radiation dosages over the territory presumably defended; and, more recently, cruise missiles that could be launched from submarines, planes, or ships, fly at radar-eluding altitudes, and maneuver around defensive fire. Less publicized, and often excluded from official estimates of nuclear megatonnage, is the armory of "tactical" nuclear weapons. These include huge numbers of air-to-ground, ground-to-air, and ground-to-ground missiles, of which over seven-thousand are stationed in Europe for use by NATO forces. The average yield of these weapons, acording to Robert NcNamara as far back as 1964, was about 100 kilotons, about five times greater than the strength of Hiroshima's Little Boy. Moreover, considerable "progress" has been made in developing the biological, chemical, physiological, and nuclear instrumentalities that could offer the prospect, in the words of a high U.S. Navy official, of attaining "victory without shattering cities, industries and other physical assets." [16] The extent of this progress was revealed by the announcement in 1977 of the "neutron bomb" and its promotion for NATO use.

The second has been a massive escalation of arms sales and government-subsidized arms gifts to Third World countries. In the United States, this program—which represents a huge stimulus to American industry—reached $11.2 billion in fiscal year 1977, and then, under the Carter administration rose to $13.5 billion in fiscal 1979. This activity has been paralleled by similar arms exports from other "First World" countries. A large part of these exports has gone to the Middle East, thereby recycling "petrodollars" for such countries as Iran and Saudi Arabia. A considerable part of the U.S. exports, in contrast to those from most other First World countries, have gone to Israel, as well as to Third World regimes threatened by domestic upheaval. Moreover, a large number of countries have received indirect arms aid in the form of nuclear plants producing the plutonium that could be used for atomic bombs. This implies a widening nuclear capability that is bound to be translated into the wider stockpiling of nuclear weapons and the development of smaller-scale balances of nuclear terror as counterparts to the primary balance of nuclear terror existing between the United States and the Soviet Union. The logic for such counterparts has been vigorously set forth by Robert Tucker in an article in which he argues that "a nuclear balance between Israel and the major Arab states would have a stabilizing effect." [17] Without the help of Tucker's advice, similar "stabilizing balances" have already been developing between China and the Soviet Union and India and China; with the help of expanded export of arms and nucelar plants, they might well develop between many other much smaller nations. Back in 1969 Hasan Ozbekhan of the Systems Development Corporation predicted that "within the next 20 years all the main underdeveloped nations will be in possession of [nuclear] weapons, and of limited, but perhaps sufficient, delivery capabilities." [18] It now seems that Ozbekhan overestimated the time it would take; he also was not able in 1969 to predict more recent developments in the manufacture of "suitcase bombs," small nuclear weapons that could be "delivered" by simply leaving a suitcase in a building, a street, or a reservoir. Thus, by the late 1970s even more than in 1961, when President Kennedy used the quaintly old-fashioned "sword of Damocles" metaphor, men, women, and children in many parts of the world have lived under the threat of some kind of war—perhaps even of the colossal blasts, raging firestorms, and devastating radiation of nuclear war or the less-known evils of bacteriological warfare.

Moreover, since President Kennedy's warning, there have been many mini-accidents. Some of them have involved the leakage of nerve gas from proving grounds, storage tanks, or disposal facilities. Since 1958 there have been over sixteen American accidents with nuclear weapons. Known as *Broken Arrow*, these have involved fires, collisions, and crash landings of nuclear-equipped planes—as well as accidental release from bomb bays.[19] In the realm of accident prevention, several missile crewmen have been arrested on narcotics charges, including the use of LSD. Although no catastrophe has yet occurred, the "accidental explosion of one or more nuclear weapons in the next 10 years," as reported by a research team at Ohio State University, "is not improbable." [20] If this is the American record, it is reasonable to assume that similar mini-accidents —whether smaller or larger—have occurred in other countries also. Nor are miscalculations impossible. An accident may be seen as an act of sabotage or aggression. In the case of actual attack, the wrong country may be perceived as the attacker. Retaliatory strikes may go astray and hit at unintended spots. Tactical moves could logically ascend the escalation ladder and lead to all-out war as an involved series of rational moves and equally rational countermoves add up to collective madness.

The freedom from general warfare that the world has enjoyed since 1945 is sometimes attributed to the delicate balance of terror widely known as MAD, the acronym for Mutual Assured Destruction. Since this term was invented in the 1960s, the escalation of both the arms race and the arms trade has unquestionably moved from MAD to MADDER. The direction of this movement unquestionably suggests that some involved series of supposedly rational moves and equally rational countermoves might well add up before the century's end to the collective madness of MADDEST.

TWO

The Specter of Friendly Fascism

Cassandra:
Cry, Trojans, cry! lend me ten thousand eyes
And I will fill them with prophetic tears . . .
Troilus:
Cassandra's mad . . .

WILLIAM SHAKESPEARE,
Troilus and Cressida

Often do the spirits
Of great events stride on before the event
And in today already walks tomorrow.

JOHANN VON SCHILLER,
Wallenstein

7

The Unfolding Logic

The logic of events is driving [the rulers of the Third World] toward more modern and more efficient forms of dictatorship and all modern dictatorships are bound to have fascist features to some extent.

WALTER LAQUEUR [1]

HOW ARE THE LEADERS of the "Free World," the Golden International, and the U.S. Establishment responding to the challenges that face them?

If one looks at any particular area, the prompt reply may be: "With cautious confusion." When one looks at this or that part of the U.S. Establishment, one can see reactionaries trying to "turn back the clock of history," conservatives who seem to favor the status quo and liberals who seek some system-strengthening reforms.

But as I survey the entire panorama of contending forces, I can readily detect something more important: *the outline of a powerful logic of events*. This logic points toward tighter integration of every First World Establishment. In the United States it points toward more concentrated, unscrupulous, repressive, and militaristic control by a Big Business-Big Government partnership that—to preserve the privileges of the ultra-rich, the corporate overseers, and the brass in the military and civilian order—squelches the rights and liberties of other people both at home and abroad. That is friendly fascism.

There is, of course, no master plan, no coordinated conspiracy. There is no predestined path, leading step by step to a sudden seizure of power by friendly fascists. I emphasize these points, if only because it is easy for a confusion to arise. By trying to make my *analysis* systematic and explicit, I may give the impression that the *reality* will be equally systematic and explicit.

On the contrary, the powerful leaders of the capitalist world have no single secret flight plan. In fact, the major navigators are in constant dispute among themselves about both the direction and the speed of flight, while their most redoubtable experts display their expertise by nitpicking at each other over an infinity of potentially significant details.

At any particular moment First World leaders may respond to crisis like people in a crowded night club when smoke and flames suddenly billow forth. They do not set up a committee to plan their response. Neither do they act in a random or haphazard fashion. Rather, the logic of the situation prevails. Everyone runs to where they think the exits are. In the ensuing melee some may be trampled to death. Those who know where the exits really are, who are most favorably situated, and have the most strength will save themselves.

Thus it was in Italy, Japan, and Germany when the classic fascists came to power. The crisis of depression, inflation, and class conflict provided an ideal opportunity for the cartels, warmongers, right-wing extremists, and rowdy street fighters to rush toward power. The fascist response was not worked out by some central cabal of secret conspirators. Nor was it a random or accidental development. The dominant logic of the situation prevailed.

Thus too it was after World War II. Neither First World unity nor the Golden International was the product of any central planners in the banking, industrial, political, or military community. Indeed, there was then—as there still is—considerable conflict among competing groups at the pinnacle of the major capitalist establishments. But there was a broad unfolding logic about the way these conflicts were adjusted and the "Free World" empire came into being. This logic involved hundreds of separate plans and planning committees—some highly visible, some less so, some secret. It encompassed the values and pressures of reactionaries, conservatives, and liberals. In some cases, it was a logic of response to anticapitalist movements and offensives that forced them into certain measures—like the expanded welfare state—which helped themselves despite themselves.

Although the friendly fascists are subversive elements, they rarely see themselves as such. Some are merely out to make money under conditions of stagflation. Some are merely concerned with keeping or expanding their power and privileges. Many use the rhetoric of freedom, liberty, democracy, human values, or even human rights. In pursuing their mutual interests through a new coalition of concentrated oligarchic power, people may be hurt—whether through pollution, shortages, unemployment, inflation, or war. But that is not part of their central purpose. It is the product of invisible hands that are not theirs.

For every dominant logic, there is an alternative or subordinate logic. Indeed, a dominant logic may even contribute to its own undoing. This has certainly been the case with many strong anticommunist drives —as in both China and Indochina—that tended to accelerate the triumph of communism. If friendly fascism emerges on a full scale in the United

States, or even if the tendencies in that direction become still stronger, countervailing forces may here too be created. Thus may the unfolding logic of friendly fascism—to borrow a term from Marx—sow the seeds of its destruction or prevention. But before turning to this more hopeful subject in Part Three, it is first imperative to look carefully at the unfolding logic itself.

MAKING THE MOST OF CRISES

> The symbol for "crisis" in Chinese is made up of two characters whose meanings are "danger" and "opportunity." To me, that precisely describes the present situation.
>
> JOHN D. ROCKEFELLER III [2]

A few years before his death, John D. Rockefeller III glimpsed—although through a glass darkly—the logic of capitalist response to crisis. In *The Second American Revolution* (1973) he defined the crises of the 1960s and early 1970s as a humanistic revolution based mainly on the black and student "revolts," women's liberation, consumerism, environmentalism, and the yearnings for nonmaterialistic values. He saw these crises as an opportunity to develop a *humanistic* capitalism. If the Establishment should repress these humanistic urges, he wrote, "the result could be chaos and anarchy, or it could be authoritarianism, either of a despotic mold or the 'friendly fascism' described by urban affairs professor Bertram Gross."

Before his book was completed, one of Rockefeller's consultants visited with me at Hunter College. We discussed tendencies toward friendly fascism, not humanistic capitalism.* I made my case that friendly fascism would be a despotic order backed up by naked coercion as well as sophisticated manipulation. Above all, I warned that the various crises in American society provided opportunities for Establishment leaders to do things that would accelerate—often unintentionally—the tendencies toward a repressive corporate society. This warning was not reflected in Rockefeller's book.

The better schools of business management train their students not merely to adapt to the stresses of corporate life but to anticipate challenges before they materialize. The best ones stress the shaping of the crises that may open up new horizons. In national politics, crisis management and crisis exploitation have become well-established modes of leadership.

---

* In "The Democratic Logic in Action," (chapter 20) I discuss the possibility of humanistic capitalism, but in terms that are quite different from Rockefeller's.

At the higher levels of transnational capitalism, therefore, it is only logical for many corporate and political leaders to respond to challenges by creative efforts to perfect their accumulation of capital and privilege.

If *you* were a billionaire, a corporate overseer, or a top executive and dedicated entirely toward advancing your own interests and those of your family members and associates, how would you respond to specific crises of the kind outlined in the previous three chapters? If *you* were a behind-the-scenes adviser to one of the above, what would you propose? I can answer this question by simply observing the behavior (not the public pronouncements) of Establishment notables as they try to make a virtue of necessity or enjoy the sweet adversity of other people's misfortunes. But one can get almost identical answers to putting one's self in their position. Performed as a mental exercise (however unpleasant), the logical result of this is a series of general recipes like the following.

Responding to the Side Effects of Success. Consider a certain amount of frustration as contributing to a stabilizing cynicism and apathy. Nonetheless, tone down overly high aspirations, especially among the lower levels of the Establishment. In turn, provide for tighter integration and higher expectations at the Establishment's top levels. Publicly lament restlessness, family breakdown, alienation, and other forms of social fragmentation. But recognize that these powerful tendencies deepen the apathy that represents mass consent to governance by the Establishment's upper levels. Remedy any resulting absenteeism, turnover, and low productivity with human relations programs conveying a sense of employee "participation." Resist regulations that shift to the polluters and makers the cost of antipollution and consumer protection measures; instead, use pressures for protecting people and nature as an excuse for higher prices and more public subsidy. Respond to crime and corruption by expanding "law and order" drives against street-level and middle-level lawbreaking. Direct attention away from the crimes of corporate and government elites; sanitize these activities by legislative and judicial action exempting the elites from scrutiny and prosecution. If necessary, substitute coercion and new forms of authoritarianism for declining public confidence in the authority of leaders, institutions and doctrines.

Responding to the Challenge of a Shrinking Capitalist World. Try to prevent formation of new socialist or communist regimes, overthrow those that are formed, and do profitable business with those that cannot be overthrown. Extend efforts to absorb communist regimes into the world capitalist economy. Undertake the delicate task of absorbing the new crude-oil capitalists and the more powerful Third World regimes into the middle levels of the Golden International. Try to integrete the strategies and policies of the governments and larger corporations of the Trilateral World and the many international agencies that serve them, particularly the World Bank and the International Monetary Fund.

Responding to New Forms of the Old Crises. In the name of "full employment," job creation, and "supply side" economics, promote new forms of open or hidden payments to big business. In the name of combating inflation, cut social expenditures and promote recessions that lower real wages and weaken labor unions. Hold forth the promise of greater profitability in the future. Dampen class conflicts by sharing the spoils of Third World exploitation with parts of the home population. If exploitation of the Third World is less successful, resort to firmer treatment at home. In either case, "divide and conquer" by co-opting the leaders of potential opposition and nurturing class fragmentation and ethnic conflicts. Try to keep actual warfare limited to small geographical areas and non-nuclear weapons. While calling for a balanced budget, expand arms exports (including the nuclear power plants that enable the proliferation of nuclear war capabilities) and the stockpiling of overkill while striving for "first strike" superiority. Reap the benefits from arms production as a factor in overcoming economic stagnation and a guarantee of profitable growth in the industrial-scientific-military complex. Seek larger armed forces, draft registration and conscription as instruments of military intervention, relief of unemployment, and promotion of militarist discipline in society.

CONSOLIDATING POWER

> *Lippmann:* The breakdown of forms of authority is a much deeper and wider process in modern history than the Vietnam War . . . The destruction of that threatens to produce the chaos of modern times.
>
> *Steel:* You see this as leading to authoritarianism or fascism?
>
> *Lippmann:* It's absolutely one of the things that will occur . . .
>
> RONALD STEEL [3]

Back during the early days of World War I, Robert Michels, the German sociologist who later supported Mussolini's fascism, formulated his famous "iron law of oligarchy." [4] As any organization grows, he held, the more dominant force will be a small minority at the top. Today's crises and future threats, genuine or conjured, only promise to accelerate what—in deference to the superior technologies of the present—might be renamed the "steel and plastic law of oligarchy." The word "law," of course, is always deceptive. It promises a regularity, a uniformity, an inescapability, which I do not accept. Even within the logic of the passage to friendly fascism there is room for surprises, reverses, and variations.

Behind all the varied and conflicting responses to different crises, however, there is a broad and almost all-encompassing unity: the effort to consolidate oligarchic power. A new round of miraculous exploits would be incompatible with too much conflict, chaos, or anarchy within or among the national Establishments. These Establishments must be reshaped and redeployed. This is what President Nixon had in mind when he told C. L. Sulzberger that the trouble with the country was the weakness and division among "the leaders of industry, the bankers, the newspapers . . . The people as a whole can be led back to some kind of consensus if only the leaders can take hold of themselves." [5]

This, of course, is the fundamental insight underlying the creation and the operations of the Trilateral Commission. Where this logic is heading is suggested in *The Crisis of Democracy*, a sophisticated call for oligarchic integration. This study was prepared for the commission by three social scientists. Samuel Huntington of the United States finds a "democratic distemper" in the United States caused by an upsurge of egalitarian values and an "excess of democracy." Michael Crozier of France holds that "European political systems are overloaded with participants and demands," while the Communist parties of the area "are the only institution left in Western Europe where authority is not questioned . . ." Joji Watanuki of Japan finds that "in comparison with the United States, where the 'democratic surge' can be regarded as already having passed the peak, in Japan there is no sign of decline in the increasing tide of popular demands, while at the same time the financial resources of the government are showing signs of stagnation." Together, the three seem to agree that "the principal strains on the governability of democracy may be receding in the United States, cresting in Europe, and pending in the future for Japan." Huntington argues that the challenge of communist threats, inflation, unemployment, commodity shortages, and frustrated aspirations can best be met by *less,* not *more,* democracy. "Democracy will have a longer life," suggests Huntington, "if it has a more balanced existence." [6] The essence of such balance is to respond to the erosion of authority by more authoritarian government.

This unusual bluntness, as Alan Wolfe points out, shattered "a taboo of American society, which is that no matter how much one may detest democracy, one should never violate its rhetoric in public." [7] As a result, when the report was formally discussed at a Trilateral Commission conference at Kyoto, Japan, in May 1975, various commission members denounced the report as too pessimistic. While some of this disagreement may have been for the public record only, some of it undoubtedly reflected the sincere attachment of old-fashioned conservatives to the liberal proprieties. Also, some top- and middle-level members of First World establishments may have trembled at what might happen to them with a tightening of oligarchic concentration and control. Even the dissenters, however, did not contradict the trilateral report's assumption of a need for greater consolidation and coordination within and among national establishments.

To discard the remaining liberal checks on growing oligarchies may be a difficult and heart-rending decision for many such individuals. It may be facilitated by a deepened sense of impending threats to the system, like those that appeared to loom up during the 1960s. Writing in the *National Review* toward the end of that decade, Donald Zoll provided an example of the possible rationalizations. Responding to the turmoil of the antiwar and civil rights movements, Zoll argued in a spirit of rueful advocacy that in the face of truly serious crisis, conservatives must consider *expediential fascism.* They should contemplate abandoning the "traditional rules of the game" by "candidly facing the necessity of employing techniques generally ignored or rejected by contemporary Western conservatives." He therefore urged "political approaches that are totalitarian in nature [though] not quite in the original fascist sense that puts all aspects of life under political authority, at least in the general sense that political theory can no longer restrict itself to general conditions and procedural rules." His alternative to "totalitarian radicalism" would be a totalitarian conservatism uninhibited by "liberal proprieties as to method." Zoll confessed that this "might imply common cause with the Radical Right or even some form of expedential fascism—hardly an appealing association."[8] But if the alternative to expedential fascism is to "let America die," then—according to Zoll's logic—better fascist than dead.

A similar note of urgency is trumpeted by General Maxwell Taylor who, in contrast with Zoll's response to internal dangers, warns mainly against external dangers. "How can a democracy such as ours," he asks, "defend its interests at acceptable costs and continue to enjoy the freedom of speech and behavior to which we are accustomed in time of peace?" Although his answer is not as candid as Zoll's, he replies that such traditional and liberal properties must be dispensed with: "We must advance concurrently on both foreign and domestic fronts by means of *integrated national power responsive to a unified national will*"[9] (my italics). Here is a distressing echo of Adolf Hilter's pleas for "integration" (*Gleichschaltung*) and unified national will.

THE CAT FEET OF TYRANNY

> I believe there are more instances of the abridgement of the freedom of the people by gradual and silent encroachments of those in power than by violent and sudden usurpations.
>
> JAMES MADISON[10]

It is hard to grasp the unfolding logic of modern capitalism if one's head is addled by nightmares of spectacular seizures of power. The combined influence of institutional rigidities, traditional concepts of constitutional democracy, and rifts among powerful elites is so great that friendly fascism could hardly emerge other than by gradual and silent encroachments. Like the tyranny referred to in a *New York Times* editorial, it "can come silently, slowly, like fog creeping in 'on little cat feet.'" [11] Many of the most important changes would be subtle shifts imperceptible to the majority of the population. Even those most alert to the dangers would be able to see clearly, and document neatly, only a few of these changes. Indeed, some important social and economic innovations in manipulation or exploitation (coming in response to liberal or radical demands) might well be hailed as "progress." In other cases, dramatic exposure, attack, and hullabaloo could have smokescreen consequences, blurring and sidetracking any effort to uncover root evils.

Hence I deliberately avoid the high-charged attention-attracting drama of predicting the decade, year or circumstances of a sudden seizure of power by the friendly fascists. Like Oliver Wendell Holmes, I have almost no faith in "sudden ruin." Although friendly fascism would mean total ruin of the American dream, it could hardly come suddenly—let alone in any precisely predictable year. This is one of the reasons I cannot go along with the old-fashioned Marxist picture of capitalism or imperialism dropping the fig leaf or the mask. This imagery suggests a process not much longer than a striptease. It reinforces the apocalyptic vision of a quick collapse of capitalist democracy—whether "not with a bang but a whimper," as T. S. Eliot put it, or with "dancing to a frenzied drum" as in the words of William Butler Yeats. In my judgment, rather, one of the greatest dangers is the slow process through which friendly fascism would come into being. For a large part of the population the changes would be unnoticed. Even those most alive to the danger may see only part of the picture—until it is too late. For most people, as with historians and social scientists, 20–20 vision on fundamental change comes only with hindsight. And by that time, with the evidence at last clearly visible, the new serfdom might have long since arrived.

MANY PATHS

When the experts of the Rand Corporation or the Hudson Institute prepare step-by-step scripts for future events, the effect is to heighten the drama—and perhaps the saleability—of their work. But the single-track scenario is a highly misleading device. It violently oversimplifies the immense complexity of historical change. It obscures the vast possibilities for accident, spontaneity, and the unpredictable conjuncture of simultaneous action on many apparently different fronts. The logic of events cannot be explained by any simple-minded syllogism or simplistic assumption of unified action along one clear path.

It would be easier to grasp the unfolding logic of modern capitalism if the most powerful leaders in capitalist society could readily agree on the flight plan toward a still more perfect capitalism. As it is, the major navigators are in constant dispute among themselves about both the direction and speed of flight, while their most redoubtable experts prove their expertise by nitpicking at each other on an infinity of potentially significant details. Besides, with weather conditions often turbulent and changing, forward motion sometimes creates more turbulence, and these are situations in which delays or even crashes may occur. Thus, in the movement toward friendly fascism, any sudden forward thrust at one level could be followed by a consolidating pause or temporary withdrawal at another level. Every step toward greater repression might be accompanied by some superficial reform, every expansionist step abroad by some new payoff at home, every well-publicized shocker (like the massacres at Jackson State, Kent State, and Attica, the Watergate scandals or the revelations of illegal deals by the FBI or CIA) by other steps of less visibility but equal or possibly greater significance, such as large welfare payments to multinational banks and industrial conglomerates. At all stages the fundamental directions of change would be obscured by a series of Hobson's choices, of public issues defined in terms of clear-cut crossroads—one leading to the frying pan and the other to the fire. Opportunities would thus be provided for learned debate and earnest conflict over the choice among alternative roads to serfdom . . .

The unifying element in this unfolding logic is the capital-accumulation imperative of the world's leading capitalist forces, creatively adjusted to meet the challenges of the many crises I have outlined. This is quite different from the catch-up imperatives of the Italian, German, and Japanese leaders after World War I. Nor would its working out necessarily require a charismatic dictator, one-party rule, glorification of the State, dissolution of legislatures, termination of multiparty elections, ultranationalism, or attacks on rationality.

As illustrated in the following oversimplified outline, which also points up the difference between classic fascism and friendly fascism, the following eight chapters summarize the many levels of change at which the trends toward friendly fascism are already visible.

Despite the sharp differences from classic fascism, there are also some basic similarities. In each, a powerful oligarchy operates outside of, as well as through, the state. Each subverts constitutional government. Each suppresses rising demands for wider participation in decision making, the enforcement and enlargement of human rights, and genuine democracy. Each uses informational control and ideological flimflam to get lower- and middle-class support for plans to expand the capital and power of the oligarchy and provide suitable rewards for political, professional, scientific, and cultural supporters.

A major difference is that under friendly fascism Big Government would do less pillaging *of*, and more pillaging *for*, Big Business. With

CLASSIC FASCISM	FRIENDLY FASCISM, U.S.A.
Drives by capitalist laggards to build new empires at the expense of leading capitalist powers.	Drive to maintain unity of Free World empire, contain or absorb communist regimes, or else retreat to Fortress America.
A tight Government-Big Business oligarchy with charismatic dictator or figurehead, and expansionist, scapegoating, and nationalistic ideologies.	An integrated Big Business- Big Government power structure with new technocratic ideologies and more advanced arts of ruling and fooling the public.
Liquidation or minimization of multiparty conflict and open subversion, with little use of democratic machinery and human rights.	Subtle subversion, through manipulative use and control of democratic machinery, parties, and human rights.
Negative sanctions through ruthless, widespread, and high-cost terror; direct action against selected scapegoats.	Direct terror applied through low-level violence and professionalized, low-cost escalation, with indirect terror through ethnic conflicts, multiple scapegoats, and organized disorder.
Ceaseless propaganda, backed up by spies and informers, to consolidate elite support and mobilize masses.	Informational offensives backed by high-technology monitoring, to manage minds of elites and immobilize masses.
Widespread benefits through more jobs, stabilized prices, domestic spoils, foreign booty, and upward mobility for the most faithful.	Rationed rewards of power and money for elites, extended professionalism, accelerated consumerism for some, and social services conditional on the recipients' good behavior.
Anxiety relief through participatory spectacles, mass action, and genuine bloodletting.	More varied relief through sex, drugs, madness, and cults, as well as alcoholism, gambling, sports, and ultraviolent drama.
Internal viability based on sustained, frantic, and eventually self-destructive expansion.	Internal viability based on careful expansion, system-strengthening reforms, multilevel co-optation, and mass apathy.

much more integration than ever before among transnational corporations, Big Business would run less risk of control by any one state and enjoy more subservience by many states. In turn, stronger government support of transnational corporations, such as the large group of American companies with major holdings in South Africa, requires the active fostering of all latent conflicts among those segments of the American population that may object to this kind of foreign venture. It requires an Establishment with lower levels so extensive that few people or groups can attain significant power outside it, so flexible that many (perhaps most) dissenters and would-be revolutionaries can be incorporated within it. Above all, friendly fascism in any First World country today would use sophisticated control technologies far beyond the ken of the classic fascists.

While the term "friendly" is useful (indeed invaluable) in distinguishing between the old-fashioned and the modern forms of repressive Big Business-Big Government partnerships, the word should not be stretched too far. The total picture provided by the following eight chapters may be thought of as a cinematic holograph of horror—all the more horrifying if the reader finds himself or herself entranced, if not captured, by its compelling logic.

Despite my emphasis on the United States, this unfolding logic is not strictly American. It may be discerned in the other "Trilateral" countries (Canada, Western Europe, and Japan) and in the closely related capitalist societies of South Africa, Australia, New Zealand, and Israel. In all the more developed capitalist societies, corporate oligarchies tend to transcend the nation-state, while in the less developed ones—often with the rhetoric of socialism—State control plays a more decisive role in fostering the growth of big capital and its entry into the larger world of the Golden International. Moreover, the emergence of neofascism in the First World will often continue to be blurred by denunciation of old-style autocracies and military dictatorships as "fascist" in accordance with the colloquial identification of fascism with simple brutality or oppression. Often, the germ of truth in such denunciations is that under dependent fascism old-style dictatorship may often serve to nurture the growth of big capital. On the other hand, when genuine neofascism emerges it may be associated with a relaxation of crude terror and the maturation of more sophisticated, effective, and ruthless controls.

A major factor, of course, is the historic pattern of relationships within the big-business community and between big business and government. Thus, in Japan, the logic of oligarchic integration in response to economic adversity is much more compelling and feasible than in the United States—so much so that many American business leaders look longingly at the pattern of what they like to call "Japan, Inc." On the other hand, it is distinctly possible that the Japanese may plunge far ahead of the Americans in the creation of a tighter power structure. In Japan, *Business*

Week has reported, "vast empires are growing, embracing scores of companies in a dozen or more businesses, each company nominally independent, but with increasingly centralized management, and often bound together by ties that go back a century to the original zaibatsu. . . . All the groups are drawing more tightly together today in the face of economic diversity—consolidating resources and integrating management." [12] Similar tendencies may also be found in Germany; there the resurgence of Nazi-style parties, fashions, and cults must also be taken into consideraiton. The United States, in turn, may outpace all the others in exploiting ethnic conflicts and organized disorder. Also, big capital in America, already more transnational than the Japanese, has a flying head start in making the leap towards an international capitalist Establishment with de-Americanized Americans as the first among the senior partners. This possibility is underscored by the Americans' low-key leadership through the Trilateral Commission in articulating—as Richard Falk has put it—the "general recognition by the elites in the most powerful states that there is an emergent crisis of unprecedented proportions that involves, in particular, the capacity of capitalism to adapt to the future." Americans on the commission have vigorously insisted "that national governments are not necessarily capable on their own of working out the adaptations that are necessary to sustain the existing elites in power in these three centers of global wealth." Thus, as Falk has explained, the Trilateral Commission operates "as a geo-economic search for a managerial formula that will keep this concentration of wealth intact, given its nonterritorial character and in the light of the multiple challenges to it." [13]

As an American traces the many paths to friendly fascism, he or she may find—as Theodore Draper did in commenting on my first article on the subject many years ago—an "uncanny resemblance to present-day America." [14] Those from Canada, Japan or Western Europe may find distressing similarities with their own countries. The reason is that I offer facts on a present "in which already walks tomorrow" and judgments concerning a possible future clearly suggested by present trends.

In so doing, I may have underestimated the evils of friendly fascism and overstated the present facts and tendencies relating to America's world orientation, establishment, informational management, rewards and punishments, and modes of system maintenance. These are empirical questions; I stand ready to be corrected by any superior presentation of the indicators. Also subject to an empirical challenge is my analysis in the following eight chapters of the various paths toward repression and exploitation by a new corporate society. Speculation and conjecture have their place, of course, and I have used both. But so do informed judgments on demonstrable—albeit controversial—indicators and trends. I should be more than delighted if someone can demonstrate that there is little or no motion along any or most of the paths through which I trace the unfolding logic of friendly fascism.

8

Trilateral Empire or Fortress America?

THE UNFOLDING LOGIC of friendly fascism is reasonably clear. But the specific manner in which it takes place will be greatly affected by the changing nature of the Golden International.

Indeed, the future of the Golden International itself may prove open to serious question. Not only have the crises and traumas of Western capitalism, old and new, created considerable uncertainty. The outlook is further clouded by obscure conflicts within the ruling circles of the major powers—and among the various movements that challenge the capitalist empire. These uncertainties suggest that even the most logical policies may often give rise to totally unintended consequences.

Nonetheless, I see two broad alternatives: (1) a breakup of the "Free World" empire or (2) its reconstruction in more mature form. During the 1970s it was possible to see tendencies in both directions at once. This apparently contradictory situation takes each tendency out of the realm of pure speculation. It suggests that either may be a viable alternative under circumstances that may arise.

As for the 1980s, the two tendencies will continue to coexist for a while. But either could become dominant. My own judgment is that the latter is more likely. Indeed, any contraction of world capitalism (unless it becomes cataclysmic) would seem to reinforce transnational integration and the resilience of the Golden International—exactly as the loss of Eastern Europe and China after World War II was a factor in the birth of the "Free World" itself. Remodeled under pressure, the "Free World" might then, conceivably, be capable of reexpansion, effectively absorbing various communist regimes back into the capitalist world order.

AMERICAN RETRENCHMENT

> Dr. Kissinger has, of course, been wringing his hands at the prospect of a Marxist take-over of Europe . . . His nightmare scenario envisions a European domino effect, with one country aping another, with cuts in military budgets, with participation in

> NATO a mockery, until the United States, disgusted, distrustful, disillusioned, withdraws to "Fortress America" leaving Europe to the Russians.
>
> VICTOR ZORZA [1]

The relation between anticapitalist advance and intercapitalist conflict is a splendid example of circular causation.

On the one hand, communist or socialist advance promotes various conflicts among the major capitalist countries. When a communist or semicommunist regime is established, the political and corporate leaders of various First World countries compete with each other in the effort to establish themselves in the communist markets. This undermines the unity of those very First World efforts to undermine or overthrow new anticapitalist regimes. On the other hand, conflict among capitalist interests in the First World facilitates the use of divide-and-conquer strategies by anticapitalist regimes and movements.

Moreover, the internationalization of capital itself promotes new forms of intercapitalist conflict. In a penetrating study for the Soviet Union's institute of World Economics, Margarita Maximova, while quietly burying the old Lenin-Stalin thesis of inevitable war among the capitalist powers, has carefully described the many conflicts (much short of war) that are promoted by the very process of the internationalization of capital. "The chief means and methods of cooperation between monopolies of different capitalist countries and groups of countries," she writes, "are simultaneously the forms of inter-imperialist rivalry and struggle." [2] Maximova meticulously ticks off the many conflicts among the corporations, the dominant political leaders, the smaller and larger capitalist powers, the West German and French rivals for European leadership and, above all, between the Americans, West Europeans, and the Japanese. The smaller the scope of capitalist operations in the world and the more concentrated the world capitalist oligarchy, the less room there is at the top and the more there is to fight about.

One of the strongest tussles of all has been described by Sankar Ray, an expert Indian observer: "A new polarization between international corporations of European origin and those of American and Japanese domination is the most noticeable financial element in the investment situation in Europe." [3] This polarization has led to new mergers by corporations from different European countries: Dunlop-Pirelli (UK and Italy), Philips-Ignis (Netherlands and Italy), Fiat-Citroen (Italy and France), and others. As a result, the share of European corporations in European markets has increased, although the U.S.-based corporations have maintained their lead in the appropriation of profits from their operations in Europe. This conflict spills over into corporate strategies for dealing with both Third World countries and communist regimes.

And as I have already pointed out in "The Challenge of a Shrinking Capitalist World" (chapter 5), much of the confrontation between the First and Third worlds is a polarization between the entrenched capitalist forces of North America, Western Europe, and Japan and their new capitalist challengers—particularly the crude-oil capitalists—from Western Asia, Asia, Latin America, and Africa. Although the capitalist aspects of this conflict are obscured by anticapitalist or semisocialist rhetoric, it is likely that this form of polarization may become much more significant than any of the conflicts within the First World itself.

If, during the 1980s, American leadership should be strengthened, socialist and communist advances will unquestionably be opposed—in one form or another—by a more united First World. Yet the entire nature of this conflict has already been altered by a certain amount of retrenchment.

From a radical viewpoint, Gabriel Kolko finds the source of this retrenchment in America's military defeat in Vietnam: "The essential problem for the U.S. is . . . its lack of a military equivalent that can stop healthy Third World forces that have defeated American interests and power repeatedly in the postwar era."[4] A middle-of-the-roader like Robert W. Tucker advocates a "new isolationism," pointing out that for U.S. security there is no longer any need for the vast system of alliances and commitments built up during the cold war era. Our difficulty in the past, says Tucker, is that the U.S. wanted "paramount influence," not mere security; today paramount influence simply costs too much and should no longer be sought. On the more extreme right, James Burnham and many others lament the collapse of the American will. The refusal to send troops to Angola was a signal that in the face of communist liberation movements, "the West will remain as inert as putty."[5] With the overthrow of the Shah of Iran and the Somoza regime in Nicaragua, these laments have mounted. Irving Kristol complains that "Congressional neo-isolationist liberals have no compunction about cutting the military budget, restricting the government's freedom of action in foreign affairs, and generally following a course of mindless appeasement . . ."[6]

Peter Berger explains this unwillingness by suggesting that there is an unconscious convergence between intellectuals favoring a more modest American posture in the world and corporate elites who like to do business with stable dictatorships. The corporations, he suggests, are impressed not only by the stability of communist regimes but also by the fact that communist markets are untroubled by coups, terrorism, aggressive trade unions, inflation, or complex tax regulations. "A sovietization of Western Europe," he argues, "is becoming less unthinkable to the American business elite."[7] Accordingly, it is becoming less self-evident to the economic elite that American economic interests necessitate the preservation of democracy in Western Europe and the expensive deployment of American military power to that end. This corporate "flabbiness" ties in with and supports "wide-spread weariness with foreign commitments, a fear of Vietnam-like episodes in the future and considerable disillusionment with patriotic rhetoric about America's mission in the world." Thus, Daniel P. Moynihan's 1976 departure from his post as U.S. ambassador to the United Nations was interpreted by some—and presented by Moynihan himself—as an illustration of the U.S. government's unwillingness to maintain the burden of Free World leadership and speak out bluntly against any form of communist advance. With left-wing delight, middle-of-the-road sorrow, and right-wing horror, America's retrenchment has been widely seen as steady, if not headlong, retreat.

But when Victor Zorza writes about a withdrawal to "Fortress America," he knows that he is not referring to any headlong retreat, let alone the complete dissolution, of empire. The idea of "Fortress America" was first originated just before World War II. At that time the so-called isolationists opposed American military intervention in Europe by insisting that the United States should be content with dominion over the Americas—then defined to include Canada, Latin America, and the Caribbean as well as the continental United States itself. Since then, with the admission of Alaska and Hawaii as states, American boundaries were extended far into the Pacific. Also, the islands of Guam, Wake, and Midway and the vast Micronesian trust territory include a chunk of Oceania as large as the continental United States. According to C. L. Sulzberger, the withdrawal of military forces from Vietnam makes this "haphazard empire" off the coasts of Asia all the more important to the United States.[8] If dominion can be maintained over Canada, Latin America, and the Caribbean, this enlarged and well-fortified fortress would be no small potatoes.

A "TRUE EMPIRE"

> The Vietnam war . . . may well come to rank on a par with the two world wars as a conflict that marked an epoch in America's progress toward definition of her role as a world power . . . If the United States comes out of the military confrontation in Europe with a sharpened sense of how to differentiate its role and distribute the various components of national power in the different areas of the world, it will have transcended to the crucial and perhaps last step toward the plateau of maturity. It will then have fulfilled the early hopes of its spiritual or actual founders and will have become a true empire.
>
> GEORGE LISKA[9]

Although American hegemony can scarcely return in its Truman-Eisenhower-Kennedy-Johnson form, this does not necessarily signify the end of the American Century. Nor does communist and socialist advance on some fronts mark American and capitalist retreat on all fronts. There are unmistakable tendencies toward a rather thoroughgoing reconstruction of the entire "Free World." Robert Osgood sees a transitional period of "limited readjustment" and "retrenchment without disengagement," after which America could establish a "more enduring rationale of global influence." [10] Looking at foreign policy under the Nixon administration, Robert W. Tucker sees no intention to "dismantle the empire" but rather a continued commitment to the view that "America must still remain the principal guarantor of a global order now openly and without equivocation identified with the status quo." He describes America as a "settled imperial power shorn of much of the former exuberance." [11] George Liska looks forward to a future in which Americans, having become more mature in the handling of global affairs, will at last be the leaders of a *true empire.*

The current tendencies toward the recreation of American hegemony in new forms once more illustrate the motto "If we want things to stay as they are, things will have to change." A new world situation has been created by the growing economic and military strength of the communist nations, the new militancy of many Third World countries, the rather successful reconstruction—with American help—of capitalism in Western Europe, and the slow but steady internationalization of capital.

Under these new conditions the breakup of the "Free World" empire would be a virtual certainty without sustained leadership by the American establishment. "For better or worse," as Zbigniew Brzezinski puts it, "the United States is saddled with major responsibility for shaping" the future of the world order. [12] For George Liska, this means that the United States must become the active center of a dynamic "global equilibrium." [13] For both, as for all recent U.S. presidents, America must never become a "pitiful, helpless giant." Rather, it must try to remain economically and militarily Number One in the world. "With Kennedy," Brzezinski has written, "came a sense that every people had the right to expect leadership and inspiration from America, and that America owed an almost equal involvement to every continent and every people." [14]

But America's "debt" to the rest of the world, by this line of thought, cannot be paid by routinized maintenance of the kind of American leadership symbolized by Kennedy or his immediate successors. If the capitalist world is to be held together, some things will have to change. The most significant is that the American-led empire must be less American. If the United States cannot shape the world single-handed, other hands must be found and strengthened. The American-led structure of power must be remodeled by converting some clients, satellites, and pawns into allies in a multi-tiered alliance that has room for many junior and senior partners.

In the past, America's role in the world has often been defined as model for the world, as missionary bringing salvation to the heathen, as crusader, and as world policeman. The newly emerging role is that of "Free World Manager." This new role is a far cry from the old-fashioned style of the highly visible, domineering robber-baron or tycoon. It conforms, rather, with the more modern style of the behind-the-scene guidance system attuned to the realities of flexible oligarchy and vast, decentralized operations.

As the new role grows, it does not rule out (and might even reinforce) the old roles of model, missionary, crusader, or policeman. More hands and brains are mobilized to do the manager's bidding and take his advice on what and how to bid. American levels of consumption and American affluence become the model for elites in other capitalist countries, and American styles of large-scale business management become the model for their plutocrats, big-business leaders, executives, and technicians. America's media are the new missionaries of the modern world, with TV shows, films, magazines, and popular music bringing "culture" to the heathen who might otherwise have eked out their lives minus "Kojak," "Bonanza" or "The Incredible Hulk." American corporations—backed up by universities, research institutes, foundations, and political action committees—have been mounting a technological crusade that does much more than win markets, raw materials, and accumulated capital; it also sucks the best and brightest of other countries into the American brain drain or else employs them in their local subsidiaries. Police functions are vastly enlarged through the sound business principle of combining U.S. strategic guidance with decentralized operations by the military and paramilitary forces of many nations.

The greatest impediment to true empire is that the capitalist drive for boundless acquisition is geographically bounded by the continuing expansion of socialist or communist regimes. Under these circumstances the expansive drives of the Golden International must be confined within a dwindling capitalist world—unless something can be done about the boundaries themselves.

The most obvious "something"—which has largely determined the nature of the cold war since the early 1920s—has been the twofold strategy of trying, on the one hand, to "roll back" communist regimes by intervention and subversion of economic blockades and, on the other hand, to contain communist expansion beyond the existing boundaries. Since these strategies have not proved sufficient, the logic of the situation increasingly calls for a new strategy of penetrating, or vaulting over, established boundaries and absorbing the people and resources of communist nations into the capitalist world economy. This logic breaks down into four closely related parts.

The first part focuses on capitalizing on and widening, if possible, the conflicts among the many regimes of national communism. The biggest threat to the capitalist world would be not a worldwide communist conspiracy directed from Peking or Moscow but a loose alliance of nationally rooted anticapitalist regimes and movements capable of integrating their economic and political resources to strengthen existing communist and socialist regimes and support anticapitalist movements in both the First and Third Worlds. The obvious capitalist counter-strategy, therefore, has been to forestall this kind of alliance by providing various kinds of support for "dissident" communist regimes. This has been attempted with varying degrees of success through First World economic support for Yugoslavia, through broader Western efforts to "build bridges" to Eastern Europe, and—more recently—through closer economic relations with China. Whatever successes have thus far been attained have been facilitated by Soviet insistence upon a primordial Russian hegemony in the entire communist world. As a result, the possibilities exist for a capitalist divide-and-conquer strategy to counter the divide-and-conquer strategy used by communist regimes and movements in the Third World. Indeed, in the many years since Kissinger first stated that the primary task of American leaders was "dividing the USSR and China,"[15] these possibilities have been growing. The most dramatic, of course, is highlighted by references in the American media to "playing the China card." In a less dramatic sense, there has already been a lot of playing with the Yugoslavia card—and possibilities exist for finding and exploiting many other such cards by the end of the 1980s, in Africa, West Asia, and Latin America, as well as Asia.

The second motion toward integration attempts to do more business with most communist regimes. Naturally, this means setting aside the cold war doctrine of "You can't do business with the communists," and limiting economic blockades to a few regimes that might still be regarded as shaky or to a few products that are regarded as "military secrets." Of course, even during the hottest of the cold-war years, many corporate giants of the West were doing the kind of business with the communists that official doctrine held should not be done. With the official split between the Soviet Union and China, it became increasingly apparent that by expanding this business Western corporations ran much less risk of being branded "traitors to the capitalist class." Nonetheless, a doctrinal revision protected their political flanks: capitalist business with Communist countries would contribute to the liberalization of the communist regimes. Behind this rationalization there glimmered the tough-minded doctrine of seeking more liberal communist attitudes toward capitalist penetration of communist markets, capitalist use of raw materials from communist countries, and long-term agreements to assure long-term capitalist profit-making.

During the next decade, at least, this kind of communist liberalization can play a role in helping the First World manage the capitalist business cycle. It is one of the supreme ironies of world history that the very communist regimes that represent the greatest threat to Western capitalism are already beginning to provide the markets and raw materials necessary for capitalist survival. Or to put it another way, the same capitalist forces that have consistently tried to overthrow or undermine communist regimes are now forced by the logic of events to develop business with the communists in a way that helps ease the capitalist crisis, reverse capitalist trade deficits, and moderate the capitalist business cycle. From this point of view, the drift of economic activity from the capitalist to the communist regions of the world can been seen not merely as a danger but—in Rockefeller's term—as an opportunity to be exploited.

The third movement in this logic promotes capitalist hegemony over communist economies or, to put it another way, fosters, if possible, dependent communist industrialism. In an address to U.S. ambassadors in Europe in December 1975, the State Department's counsellor, Helmut Sonnenfeldt, formulated this logic with semi-straight-talk bluntness by urging that the West use commercial sales to the Soviet Union and Eastern Europe "to draw them into a series of *dependencies and ties with the West.*" [16] The opportunity to do this is provided in the first instance by communist eagerness—first evident in the Soviet bloc and now still more evident in China—to import Western capitalist technologies, particularly in the area of mining, manufacturing, computers, and automatic control systems. Thus, in their long-term planning, the communist leaders give increasingly high priority to the "scientific-technological revolution" which requires long-term help from the transnational corporations of the First World. This dependence on the West goes beyond mere hard-goods technology. With the aid of Western management and accounting firms, such as Arthur Anderson and Co. of Chicago, Soviet enterprises have been plunging furiously into the use of the most advanced techniques of corporate planning and control. Computerized systems of automated control are being rapidly developed wherever feasible. American computer languages are being installed—COBOL for the economists, ALGOL for the engineers, and FORTRAN for the scientists. While old timers warn against the import of capitalism under the guise of neutral management technologies, the majority of the higher party leaders maintain that their dependence on capitalism will be a temporary expedient only and that in due course, a more advanced communist industrialism will catch up to the West in all areas where it now lags and plunge ahead into the worldwide scientific and technological superiority.

Could the further integration of communist economies into the world capitalist market mean "creeping capitalism" within the communist world? The Chinese Communist leaders have no hesitation in answering this question with a resounding "yes." They excoriate the Soviet leaders as

State-capitalist revisionists who have deserted socialist ideals and are using the Soviet Union's superpower status as a means of building "social imperialism" in the Third World. In turn, the Soviet leaders pillory both Mao and his less-Maoist successors for abandoning the proper style of building socialism and creeping back to capitalism.

From the First World's viewpoint, however, a fully successful creeping capitalism throughout the communist world—no matter how much it might be temporarily acclaimed in such spots as Yugoslavia—would be a mixed blessing. The emergence of a vigorous and well-integrated capitalist society within the present boundaries of communism would present new and formidable rivals to the now dominant capitalist societies; it could well destroy even the most mature American hegemony and bring back the era of deadly intercapitalist rivalry. The exploitative interests of First World capitalism would be better served by a dependent communist industrialism whose leaders would not compete with the West in the bitter struggle for superprofits but who would, instead, serve as intermediaries for the more effective, albeit limited, exploitation of their resources and people by transnational corporations of the First World.

Finally, the fourth step toward integration has more to do with socialist movements and socialistically inclined regimes. Here the logical strategy is rather obvious: to maintain or promote the long-standing dissensions among the two major wings of anti-capitalism, socialism and communism. This present some difficulties at a time when many official communist parties have given up their revolutionary heritage or convictions and come very close to the principles of evolutionary socialism. This phenomenon is found not only within the so-called Eurocommunist parties of Spain, Italy, and France but also in the communist parties of Japan, England, and various other countries. It has led to growing calls for a reuniting of socialists and communists. If this should happen, the result might be that socialist-communist coalitions would take on the mixed responsibility, as I suggested earlier, of both running capitalism and running—or walking—away from it and toward socialism. The obvious antidote is for strong support of those self-styled socialist (or social democratic) regimes, as in West Germany, will have nothing to do with communists and are dedicated to the managing of capitalism. In the case of such other socialistically inclined regimes—as with the last Labor party government in England and the Manley regime in Jamaica—the antidote is to give them the kind of support, through the International Monetary Fund and other agencies, that promotes unemployment and austerity, and gives "socialism" a bad name. In the case of Jamaica, Manley's rhetorical tilts toward Cuba and revolutionary socialism do little to maintain popular support. If the socialistically included governments of Jamaica or Nicaragua should take the quantum leap toward full socialism (no matter how different they might do it in comparison with the Cuban style), then the immediate First World reaction, I presume, could be a return to the good old strategy of economic squeeze and open or covert subversion.

ALTERNATIVE OUTCOMES

Debate over domestic policies in the United States often takes place with sublime remoteness from the conflicting tendencies I have just been discussing. And when the broad alternatives are touched upon, the discussion is often couched in a cloudy meta-language limited to high ideals and timeless abstractions.

Thus those who favor the withdrawal of U.S. support from South Africa or Chile, to take but two examples, often suggest that this would be a victory for black people, working class people, socialists, and Third World supporters in the United States. Those who favor the restoration of American hegemony in the Third World often argue that American retrenchment would mean an end to everything of value in the country—even to the point of its being conquered by the advancing communist or socialist world. A sophisticated consultant to the Department of Defense, Professor Robert L. Pfaltgraff, Jr., concedes that even with a retreat to Fortress America, "American military power, at substantially lower levels than that of the Soviet Union, may be adequate to *deter* an attack against the United States and would enable the United States to survive in a largely hostile world." But this survival would not take place, he insists, "without major changes in its living standards and in its political institutions—at a cost unacceptable to most Americans." [17] The implication, of course, is that with a unified "Free World" under more mature American leadership, there need be no major changes in living standards and institutions, and no unacceptable costs.

Although one can only speculate on these alternatives, this is an unavoidable kind of speculation; it enters into all serious debates on foreign political and economic policies, and on military budgets, the deployment of armed forces, and the nature of the controlled or uncontrolled arms race.

I shall make a few brief observations only.

First of all, a major additional shrinkage of the capitalist world means in the first instance less opportunities for the Golden International to exploit the resources of other countries, less resources for easing difficulties at home, and an intensification of stagflation and all the internal conflicts associated with it. This would accelerate tendencies toward a less friendly, indeed, an unfriendly fascism.

Second, if movement toward a true trilateral empire takes place without large-scale military involvements, then enough resources could be extracted from the rest of the world to maintain U.S. living standards and perhaps even return to a somewhat higher level of growth for another decade or more. This movement could take place, as I have already suggested, even with a certain amount of additional shrinkage in the capitalist world. It is one of the premises for my suggesting the greater probability of friendly, rather than unfriendly, fascism.

Neither alternative, however, can be regarded as an end point. From a long-range viewpoint, each could trigger new coalitions of power that might change the outlook substantially. Under certain political conditions, the very withdrawal of American military power, which is branded "the new isolationism" by militarists, might be accomplished in the context of a new, and true, internationalism. One can even conceive of a "Free World" coalition which, with different coalitions in power in Western Europe, Japan, and America, would work toward a major easing of tensions with the Second World, a serious deescalation of the arms race, and a degree of tolerance concerning the drives for national capitalism or pre-industrial socialism in Third World countries. But these possibilities relate to the alternative logic (itself promoted by the unfolding logic of friendly fascism) set forth briefly in Part Three. Most specifically, they relate to the potentialities for a fundamental restructuring of friendly fascism's emerging power structure..

9

The Friendly Fascist Establishment

> Caesarism can come to America constitutionally without having to break down any existing institution.
>
> AMAURY DE RIENCOURT [1]

> Oceania has no capital and its titular head is a person whose whereabouts nobody knows.
>
> GEORGE ORWELL, *1984*

THE UNFOLDING LOGIC OF FRIENDLY FASCISM, as I have shown, is responding to crises by actions that consolidate power. But what kind of power structure would emerge?

This question would be easy to answer *if* the processes of transition from the present Establishment were entirely new, *if* they eliminated all conflicts at the Establishment's higher levels, *if* they led to a static state, *if* they concentrated power in the hands of a single transcendent person or group, or *if* they led to more visibility and less mystery.

None of these "ifs" apply. The processes of Big Business-Big Government integration have been going on for some time despite (or even because of) the divisions stemming from government-supported expansion. Their acceleration takes place unevenly, with detailed changes that are unforeseeable at any particular point and with broad international orientations that are even more unpredictable. Movement toward greater oligarchic unity on broad policy is accompanied (as with the classic fascists of Germany, Italy, and Japan) by deep internal infighting among the oligarchs. As it emerges, oligarchic integration is dynamically changing. It is rooted in institutional networks of increasing mystery and declining visibility. If it should ever fully emerge, everyone—even those in high positions—would be hard put even to start answering the question "Who are THEY really?"

As I have already stressed, a friendly fascist power structure in the United States, Canada, Western Europe, or today's Japan would be far more sophisticated than the "caesarism" of fascist Germany, Italy, and Japan. It would need no charismatic dictator nor even a titular head. As I have already suggested, it would require no one-party rule, no mass fascist party, no glorification of the State, no dissolution of legislatures, no denial of reason. Rather, it would come slowly as an outgrowth of present trends in the Establishment.

From the viewpoint of their capability to maintain or strengthen the accumulation of capital and power, the present capitalist Establishments have all shared—in varying degrees—certain institutional weaknesses:

Insufficient cohesion
A discredited or flabby chief executive
Dampened militarism
Discredited right-wing extremism
The erosion of older Establishment ideologies
Linguistic foulups

In the United States these weaknesses can be met and Establishment power enhanced without any wholesale purges or profound restructuring of institutions. The takeoff toward a new corporate society began some time ago. All that is now needed is acceleration of the retooling processes already under way.

FROM FLOUNDERING ESTABLISHMENT TO SUPER-AMERICA, INC.

A great empire and little minds go ill together.
EDMUND BURKE

The transition to a remodeled "free world" or to the smaller empire of a "Fortress America" involves much more than learning the lessons of Vietnam "errors" and post-Watergate morality. It requires great minds, as Edmund Burke thundered while the small minds of King George III's court were losing the American colonies. It requires leaders who are not only well selected and well socialized, but also are constantly growing rather than frozenly servile to technical models or temporarily useful ideologies.

Many years ago the Japanese made technological headway by copying American gadgets and technologies. More recently, American leaders have been looking to Japan as a model for the U.S. Establishment. In 1972 the U.S. Department of Commerce published a best-selling "guide for the American businessman," *Japan, the Government-Business Relationship*. Eugene J. Kaplan, the report's author, spells out how Japan's "rolling consensus" restructured the computer, auto, and steel industries. "Japan, Incorporated," he explains, "is not a monolithic system in which government leads and business follows blindly. It is rather more of a participatory partnership . . . Economic decision-making is dominated by the political leadership, the business community, and the administrative bureaucracy." [2]

Some observers have claimed that America, Inc. already exists. This is the view of Morton Mintz and Jerry S. Cohen in their well-documented book under that title. The same view has been set forth by the noted constitutional lawyer, Arthur S. Miller, in his *The Modern Corporate State: Private Governments and the American Constitution.* Both books reveal many facts and trends in which "already walks tomorrow." If one really believes that "America, Inc." and the "modern corporate state" have *already* arrived, then what is slowly emerging might deserve the label "Super-America, Inc." Many critical changes have not yet occurred. They are still around the corner or even on a farther-off horizon. When and if they materialize, it is likely that the Japanese—as well as the Germans and the Italians—may once again look to America as a model.

John B. Connally has long been one of the most outspoken proponents of America, Inc. In discussing the matter with a reporter from the *Wall Street Journal,* he once said that although nobody can foresee the exact changes that "are going to have to take place in American society," there will have to be a "transformation of traditional business-labor-government relationships." According to Richard F. Janssen, the reporter, these changes would include:

> Turning antitrust policy inside out so that in many cases the government would encourage mergers instead of discourage them. More long-range government planning for the economy. Much more federal assistance to key industries—along with much more influence over them. Diverting many young people away from the universities and into vocational training. Convincing—or compelling—unions to abandon lengthy strikes.[3]

But Super-America, Inc. would have to be much broader in scope than the Connally model, with its tilt toward protectionism and rough treatment of First World allies. More thoroughgoing integration of First World Establishments, while playing Second World regimes against each other and co-opting Third World regimes, would be the strategic principles. Only on this basis could the Golden International be strengthened and, in turn, provide reciprocal strength to the American Establishment. The new rolling consensus, in short, must roll over national boundaries.

But global reach requires a firm domestic base. In a simpler world, as Henry Kissinger has pointed out, the foreign ministers of the Austrian and British empires were always frustrated, and at times undone, by domestic opposition. In commenting on empires as diverse as those of Rome, Spain, the Ottoman, and Britain, George Liska finds that "a precondition of success [was] to insulate the internal consumer economy from the cost of external activities by supporting the latter from extraordinary sources." Whether or not this could be done during the remaining years of the century, a number of institutional changes would be necessary at the higher levels of the Establishment.

First, there is still progress to be made in integrating various regionally based interests into the American Establishment and integrating the American Ultra-Rich, Corporate Overseers, and executive managers into the Golden International. These orientations would also have to be shared by a somewhat larger number of well-selected scientists, researchers, intellectuals, and labor leaders.

Another change—and this might be somewhat extraordinary—would be the development of a rolling consensus that could operate successfully without too many calls for heads to roll. I suppose this means a Japanese (or German) style of ego-integration or ego-shrinking, which would make it possible for such remarkably able people as, for example, John Connally, Henry Kissinger, Zbigniew Brzezinski, and Daniel P. Moynihan to work together in constructive harmony with more retiring folk like Cyrus Vance and Harold Brown. To the extent that this can be done, the upper-level bureaucrats will get the signals and work more cooperatively to adjust their competing views. There would still be a need for what Kissinger calls "black channels." No bureaucracy, cluster, constellation, complex, or Establishment could operate without strange labyrinths of unofficial communication. But it is exactly these many informal channels that carry much of the blood through the arteries of the Japanese system. The same is true of the transnational complexes that animate the Golden Internatonal. Above all, on the Big Business side of the emerging partnership, decreased visibility is one of the prices of power; and this has generally been true in the bureaucracy as well. From my own experience in the federal government, I can reliably report that I was never so influential on vital matters as when I operated strictly behind the scenes, with my face known only to insiders and my name never appearing on the multitudinous official documents I wrote. As for higher-ups, it is not enough that they enjoy the protection of shock absorbers in the form of aides who can be thrown to the dogs when doing so may be useful. Decreased visibility is also required—so that there will be less risk of losing face or head. With but few exceptions, the new rulers must be faceless oligarchs.

Third, the new rolling consensus could scarcely take place without an interim period of executive turbulence. Greater cohesion among the leaders of Big Business, the Ultra-Rich, and the Chief Executive network requires executive managers with unprecedented abilities in attaining and maintaining greater profitability in the face of—and often by means of—recurring crises. With the vast banking expansion of the 1960s and early 1970s, according to *Business Week*, "a new generation of bankers was taking over, and where the men they had succeeded had been pussycats, they were tigers: bold, aggressive, and not only willing but literally obliged to seek out profit opportunities." [4] But that was merely a transitional period during which state-chartered banks "went national" and transnational, moved into every variety of financial services, and then through new-style holding companies plunged into the leasing of industrial equipment. For the most part the bankers of that period were merely tiger cubs, not yet fully at home in global operations or in the formulation of the financial policies to guide the operations of the mergers they presided over or the use of the equipment they owned. Under mature oligarchy the bank executives would no longer be cubs. Friendly fascism would see a new generation of management "tigers" handling the top executive problems not only of finance but of production and distribution, communication, policy planning, institutional building, and national security as well. Neither long experience nor high-class education and executive development exercises, nor even the proper family connections would be enough to prepare managers for these tasks. The most basic requirement would be success in surviving recurring shakeups and fighting the battle of the executive suites in a manner that wins the confidence of the Ultra-Rich.

The turbulence of these battles is an essential part of the processes of integration at the very top; it helps separate the tigers from the mere men. While turbulence also reflects some of the continuing cleavages within competing circles of the Ultra-Rich, at a lower level it serves to prevent direct confrontation at the top—just as the world's superpowers may often conduct a conflict indirectly through war between satellite or client states. In this way the owners and top political leaders may reap the considerable benefits of trial-and-error learning, while the costs of the errors are levied against their hired help. The top executives are the "fall guys," always susceptible to summary dismissal when "guilty" of mistaken policies designed to serve (or even dictated to them by) their chiefs. Under such circumstances, executive emoluments become more enormous than ever before. The cost of high-class help—even if it brings top executives into the millionaire class—is a pittance compared to the enormous monetary gains accruing to the Ultra-Rich. Under friendly fascism, could top executive escape control by their controllers, or even seize power from them? There is little danger of it. Precisely because they would operate on longer leashes than before, they could have enough rope to hang themselves or prove themselves; in this basic sense, they would be better controlled than ever. And as before, only a tiny minority could ever "make it" into the rarefied heights of the plutocratic stratosphere.

Fourth, a basic path for the training and selection of management "tigers" in broad policy planning is what Alvin Toffler calls "ad-hocracy." Such great national associations as the U.S. Chamber of Commerce, the National Association of Manufacturers, and the American Bankers Association adjust too slowly to the transition from semi- to mature oligarchy. The same is true of the Committee for Economic Development, the Council on Foreign Relations and "think tanks" like the Rand Corporation and the Hudson Institute. "Throwaway organizations," *ad hoc* teams, and informal, often secret committees, are increasingly needed to withdraw people from institutional slots and give them broader perspectives. As Toffler points out, "this process, repeated often enough, alters the loyalties of the people involved; shakes up lines of authority; and accelerates the rate at which individuals are forced to adapt to organizational change." [5] In this manner, the established policy organizations are given new guidelines. Indeed, some of them—like the famed Council on Foreign Relations—remain as hollow shells of their former selves. By the time the political science textbooks get around to identifying them as agencies of high-policy formulation, they have little more to do than acquaint middle-level executives and technicians with the essentials of policies formulated elsewhere.

A RIGHTEOUS PRESIDENCY

> I cannot lay too great stress upon the high ethical righteousness of the whole oligarchic class. This has been the strength of the Iron Heel.
>
> JACK LONDON, *The Iron Heel*

> The corporate state, American style, exemplifies a politico-legal form of syzygy.
>
> ARTHUR S. MILLER [6]

The word "syzygy" has long been a winning ploy in word games like Scrabble or Ghosts. Few people know its major meaning: the conjunction of two organisms without either of them losing its identity. When Arthur S. Miller uses the term to refer to the American-style corporate state, he helps us remember that both Big Business and Big Government—despite their fusion in operations—retain certain special identities.

For the Chief Executive, a conspicuous exception to the general principle of facelessness, this is particularly vital. Under the full-fledged oligarchy of friendly fascism, the Chief Executive network would become much more powerful than ever before. And the top executive—in America, the president—would in a certain sense become more important than before. But not in the sense of a personal despotism like Hitler's.

Indeed, the president under friendly fascism would be as far from personal caesarism as from being a Hirohito-type figurehead. Nor would a president and his political associates extort as much "protection money" from big-business interests as was extracted under Mussolini and Hilter. The Chief Executive would neither ride the tiger nor try to steal its food; rather, he would be part of the tiger from the outset. The White House and the entire Chief Executive network would become the heart (and one of the brain centers) of the new business-government symbiosis. Under these circumstances the normal practices of the Ultra-Rich and the Corporate Overlords would be followed: personal participation in high-level business deals and lavish subsidization of political campaigns, both expertly hidden from public view. What would be "abnormal" is a qualitative forward leap—as previsioned by John Connally back in 1972—toward a business-government government relationship that breaks all precedent in promoting mergers, supporting American-based transnationals abroad, and preventing any serious losses that business might sustain through expropriation abroad, rising wage demands or prolonged strikes at home, changing conditions in markets and technology, recession, inflation, or even managerial errors.

This transformation would require a new concept of presidential leadership, one emphasizing legitimacy and righteousness above all else. As the linchpin of an oligarchic establishment, the White House would continue to be the living and breathing symbol of legitimate government. "Reigning" would become the first principle of "ruling". Only by wrapping himself and all his agents in the trappings of constitutionality could the President succeed in subverting the spirit of the Constitution and the Bill of Rights. The Chief Executive Network, Big Business, and the Ultra-Rich could remain far above and beyond legal and moral law only through the widely accepted image that all of them, and particularly the president, were fully subservient to law and morality. In part, this is a matter of public relations—but not the old Madison Avenue game of selling perfume or deodorants to the masses. The most important nostrils are those of the multileveled elites in the establishment itself; if things smell well to them, then the working-buying classes can probably be handled effectively. In this context, it is not at all sure that the personal charisma of a president could ever be as important as it was in the days of Theodore or Franklin Roosevelt, Dwight Eisenhower, or John F. Kennedy.

It is no easy task to erect a shield of legitimacy to cloak the illegitimate. Doing so would require the kind of leadership that in emphasizing the long-term interests of Big Business and the Ultra-Rich would stand up strongly *against* any elements that are overly greedy for short-term windfalls. Thus in energy planning, foreign trade, labor relations, and wage-price controls, for example, the friendly fascist White House would from time to time engage in activities that could be publicly regarded as "cracking down on business." While a few recalcitrant corporate overseers might thus be reluctantly educated, the chief victims would usually be small or medium-sized enterprises, who would thus be driven more rapidly into bankruptcy or merger. In this sense, conspicuous public leadership would become a form of followership.

Another requirement would be the weaving of comprehensive linkages to all political currents and major interest groups in American society, including those still opposed to the oligarchy in principle or representing potential sources of future opposition. For every ethnic, religious, sectional, or geographic grouping, for every faction or fraction in conservative, liberal, reactionary, or radical movements, there must be direct or indirect liaison and, for many of their leaders, at least the illusion of access to the "top." This would be the kind of broad-minded totalitarianism that a Nixon, Ford, or Carter administration, and particularly such narrow-gauged assistants as H. R. Haldeman, John Ehrlichman, and Hamilton Jordan could never comprehend. It would provide an "open door" presidential leadership that in fact, makes the White House a more effective instrument on behalf of the "closed door" power of the Corporate Overseers and the Ultra-Rich.

REMOLDING MILITARISM

> Overgrown military establishments are under any form of government inauspicious to liberty, and are to be regarded as particularly hostile to republican liberty.
>
> GEORGE WASHINGTON

> The Institute [for Land Combat] has thus far identified almost 400 possible wars (385 to be exact) for the years 1990 and about 600 new weapons and other pieces of equipment with which to handle these conflicts.
>
> PAUL DICKSON [7]

During the 1970s, as its forces slowly retreated from the Asiatic mainland, the U.S. military establishment seemed to dwindle. Even with veterans' and outer-space expenditures included, war spending declined as a portion of the GNP. Conscription ended in 1973. All proposals for overt military intervention in the Third World—whether in Angola, West Asia, Afghanistan, the Horn of Africa, the Caribbean, or Central America—were sidetracked. From an earlier high of 3.5 million people in 1968, the active military fell to 2 million at the beginning of the 1980s.

But in real terms the military establishment is enormous, much more than most people know. To the 2 million on active duty must be added another 2 million in the reserves, and a million civilians in the defense department. This 5-million-figure total is merely the base for a much larger number of people in war industries, space exploration, war think-tanks and veterans' assistance. Behind this total group of more than 12 million—and profiting from intercourse with them—stands an elaborate network of war industry associations, veterans' organizations, special associations for each branch of the armed services, and general organizations such as the American Security Council and the Committee on the Present Danger. But there is something else that George Washington could never have dreamed of when he warned against an overgrown military establishment and that Dwight D. Eisenhower never mentioned in his warning against the military-industrial complex: namely, a *transnational military complex*. This American-led complex has five military components beyond the narrowly defined U.S. military-industrial complex itself:

1. The dozen or so countries formally allied with the United States through NATO
2. Other industrialized countries not formerly part of NATO, such as Spain, Israel, Japan, Australia, and New Zealand
3. A large portion of the Third World countries
4. Intelligence and police forces throughout the "Free World"
5. Irregular forces composed of primitive tribesmen, often operating behind the lines of the Second World countries [8]

All these forces are backed up by a support infrastructure which includes training schools, research institutes, foreign aid, and complex systems of communication and logistics.

If there is one central fact about this transnational military complex at the start of the 1980s it is *growth.* Paradoxically, every arms-control agreement has been used as a device to allow growth up to certain ceilings, rather than prevent it. And since those ceilings apply only to selected weapons systems, growth tends to be totally uncontrolled in all other forms of destruction. In the United States, total military expenditure has started to move upward at a rate of about 5 percent annual growth in real terms—that is, after being corrected for the declining value of the dollar. A drive is under way to register young people for a draft, while also providing alternative forms of civilian service (at poverty wages) for people objecting to military service on moral, religious, or political grounds. New weapons systems are being initiated—particularly the MX missile, which holds forth the promise of a "first strike" capability against the Soviet Union. Major steps are being taken to increase the military strength of all the other components of the transnational complex—

particularly through the expansion of both tactical and strategic nuclear weapons in Western Europe and the beefing up of the defense forces and nuclear capabilities of the Japanese. Above all, despite some internal conflicts on when and where, the leaders of the U.S. Establishment have become more willing to use these forces. Richard Falk of Princeton University presents this thesis: "A new consensus among American political leaders favors intervention, whenever necessary, to protect the resource base of Trilateralistic nations'—Europe, the United States and Japan—prosperity and dominance." [9] This has required strenuous propaganda efforts to overcome the so-called "post-Vietnam syndrome," that is, popular resistance to the sending of U.S. troops into new military ventures abroad. Equally strenuous efforts are made to convince people in Western Europe that as East-West tensions have been relaxing and East-West trade rising, the West faces a greater threat than ever before of a Soviet invasion.

The logic of this growth involves a host of absurdities. First of all, statistical hocus-pocus hides the overwhelming military superiority of the "Free World." One trick is to compare the military spending of the United States with the Warsaw Pact countries but to exclude NATO. Another trick is to compare the NATO countries of Europe with the Warsaw Pact countries, but to exclude the United States. Still another is to exclude not merely Japan, but also the huge Chinese military forces lined up on China's border with the Soviet Union. Any truly global picture shows that while the geographical scope of the "Free World" has been shrinking, its military capability has been expanding. This expansion has been so rapid that there may even be good reason for the nervous old men in the Kremlin to feel threatened.

Second, much of this expanding military power involves nothing more than overkill. Thus just one Poseidon submarine carries 160 nuclear warheads, each four times more powerful than the Hiroshima bomb. These warheads are enough, as President Carter stated in 1979, "to destroy every large and medium-sized city in the Soviet Union." Pointing out that the total U.S. force at that time could inflict more than fifty times as much damage on the Soviet Union, President Carter then went on to raise the level of overkill still higher.

Third, the advocates of new interventionism foster the delusion that military force can solve a host of intertwined political, economic, social, and moral problems. This delusion was evidenced in the long-term and highly expensive U.S. support for the Shah of Iran and the Somoza dictatorship in Nicaragua. As U.S. strike forces are being prepared for intervention in West Asia (whether in Saudi Arabia, Libya, or elsewhere) the presumption is that military action of this type would preserve the availability of petroleum for the West. What is blindly lost sight of is the high probability—and in the judgment of many, the certainty—that any such intervention would precipitate the blowing up of the very oil fields from which the deep thinkers in the White House, Wall Street, and the Pentagon want to get assured supplies.

Yet in the words of Shakespeare's Polonius, "If this be madness, yet there is method in it." It is the not-so-stupid madness of the growing militarism which is an inherent part of friendly fascism's unfolding logic. "Militarism," Woodrow Wilson once pointed out at West Point in 1916, "does not consist of any army, nor even in the existence of a very great army. Militarism is a spirit. It is a point of view."[10] That spirit is the use of violence as a solution to problems. The point of view is something that spills over into every field of life—even into the school and the family.

Under the militarism of German, Italian, and Japanese fascism violence was openly glorified. It was applied regionally—by the Germans in Europe and England, the Italians in the Mediterranean, the Japanese in Asia. In battle, it was administered by professional militarists who, despite many conflicts with politicians, were guided by old-fashioned standards of duty, honor, country, and willingness to risk their own lives.

The emerging militarism of friendly fascism is somewhat different. It is global in scope. It involves weapons of doomsday proportions, something that Hitler could dream of but never achieve. It is based on an integration between industry, science, and the military that the old-fashioned fascists could never even barely approximate. It points toward equally close integration among military, paramilitary, and civilian elements. Many of the civilian leaders—such as Zbigniew Brzezinski or Paul Nitze—tend to be much more bloodthirsty than any top brass. In turn, the new-style military professionals tend to become corporate-style entrepreneurs who tend to operate—as Major Richard A. Gabriel and Lieutenant Colonel Paul I. Savage have disclosed—in accordance with the ethics of the marketplace.[11] The old buzzwords of duty, honor, and patriotism are mainly used to justify officer subservience to the interests of transnational corporations and the continuing presentation of threats to some corporate investments as threats to the interest of the American people as a whole. Above all, in sharp contrast with classic fascism's glorification of violence, the friendly fascist orientation is to sanitize, even hide, the greater violence of modern warfare behind such "value-free" terms as "nuclear exchange," "counterforce" and "flexible response," behind the huge geographical distances between the senders and receivers of destruction through missiles or even on the "automated battlefield," and the even greater psychological distances between the First World elites and the ordinary people who might be consigned to quick or slow death.

Some people see the drift from MAD to MADDEST exclusively in terms of hard-goods technology. By this reasoning, the ultimate logic of expanding militarism would be a doomsday machine brought into operation by the spiraling arms race. I see the trend in broader terms. The spirit and viewpoint of militarism spreads a subtle poison that can permeate every aspect of life, erode civil liberties, and promote not only police repression but also private terrorism in areas of tension among ethnic groups. They enable establishment leaders to deflect attention from social injustice and racism at home by stirring up hostility toward imagined enemies abroad. When I use the term MADDEST, it is not just to warn against nuclear, bacteriological, or chemical holocaust, it is to pinpoint the effectiveness of the new militarism as a whole and its deadly nature as an emerging part of the friendly fascist power structure.

THE RESTRUCTURING OF THE RADICAL RIGHT

> Leadership in the right has fallen to new organizations with lower profiles and better access to power . . . What is characteristic of this right is its closeness to government power and the ability this closeness gives to hide its political extremism under the cloak of respectability.
>
> WILLIAM W. TURNER [12]

> By 1976 the New Right had helped to elect almost 25 percent of the U.S. House of Representatives.
>
> SASHA LEWIS [13]

With stagflation, alienation, and frustration a growing part of life in Western Europe, many neofascist groups are openly rearing their heads. A so-called "World Union of National Socialists" boasts branches in many countries. The members of its British branch wear Nazi uniforms and distribute Nazi literature. The German neo-Nazis specialize in desecrating Jewish cemeteries. Its French members vow to "exterminate all Jews and generalize the system of apartheid throughout the world." The Italian neo-fascists practice open terrorism.

In the United States, there is also a resurgence of what might be called—in the American tradition—"Know Nothing nut power." Small groups of Nazis parade in public. The Ku Klux Klan organizes in the North as well as the South, and has units among American soldiers and policemen. Secret groups throughout the country launch attacks against both blacks and Jews. "The vision of a fascist future may seem idle," write two reporters, Joseph Trento and Joseph Spear, "but Willis Carto, now in his mid-forties, is working every day to make it come true. And more frightening than the remote possibility Carto will realize his dream is the current power of the (Liberty Lobby) apparatus he has built to bring himself and his ideas into power." [14] The Falangist Party of America openly proposes "an authoritative, one-party government." Claiming that frustrations "need a channel," it argues that "the Falangist can cut the two-party system to ribbons with the inflation issue." [15]

Although most of these right-wing extremists avoid open identification with the classic fascists, the similarities with the early fascist movements of the 1920s are clear. Small clusters of highly strung, aggressive people think that if Hitler and Mussolini (both of whom started from tiny beginnings) could make it into the Big Time under conditions of widespread misfortune, fortune might someday smile on them too.

I doubt it. Their dreams of future power are illusory. To view them as the main danger is to assume that history is obliging enough to repeat itself in unchanged form. Indeed, their major impact—apart from their contribution to domestic violence, discussed in "The Ladder of Terror," (chapter 14)—is to make the more dangerous right-wing extremists seem moderate in comparison.

The greatest danger on the right is the rumbling thunder, no longer very distant, from a huge array of well-dressed, well-educated activists who hide their extremism under the cloak of educated respectability. Unlike the New Left of the 1960s, which reached its height during the civil rights and antiwar movements, the Radical Right rose rapidly during the 1970s on a much larger range of issues. By the beginning of the 1980s, they were able to look back on a long list of victories. Their domestic successes are impressive:

- Holding up ratification of the Equal Rights Amendment
- Defeating national legislation for consumer protection
- Defeating national legislation to strengthen employees' rights to organize and bargain collectively
- Undermining Medicare payments for abortions
- Bringing back capital punishment in many states
- Killing anti-gun legislation
- Promoting tax-cutting programs, such as the famous Proposition 13 in California, already followed by similar actions in other parts of the country
- Promoting limitations on state and local expenditures, which in effect (like the tax-cutting measures) mean a reduction in social programs for the poor and the lower middle-classes
- Undermining affirmative-action programs to provide better job opportunities for women, blacks and Hispanics
- Killing or delaying legislation to protect the rights of homosexuals

They have also succeeded in getting serious attention for a whole series of "nutty" proposals to amend the Constitution to require a balanced federal budget or set a limit on the growth of federal expenditures. By the beginning of 1980, about 30 State legislatures had already petitioned the Congress for a Constitutional convention to propose such an amendment; only 34 are needed to force such a convention, the first since 1787. The major purpose of this drive, however, was not to get a Constitutional amendment. Rather, it was to force the president and Congress to go along with budget cutting on domestic programs.[16] By this standard it has been remarkably successful.

On foreign issues, the Radical Right came within a hair's breadth of defeating the Panama Canal Treaty and the enabling legislation needed to carry it out. They have been more successful, however, on these matters:

- Reacting to the Iranian and Afghanistan crises of 1979 with a frenetic escalation of cold war
- Helping push the Carter administration toward more war spending and more militarist policies
- Making any ratification of the SALT II treaty dependent on continued escalation in armaments
- Preventing Senate consideration, let alone ratification, of the pending UN covenants against genocide, on civil and political rights, and on economic, social, and cultural rights

In a vital area bridging domestic and foreign policy, they provide a major portion of support for the drive to register young people for possible military service and then, somewhat later, reinstitute conscription.

Almost all of these issues are "gut issues." They can be presented in a manner that appeals to deep-seated frustrations and moves inactive people into action. Yet the New Right leaders are not, as the Americans for Democratic Action point out in *A Citizen's Guide to the Right Wing,* "rabid crackpots or raving zealots." The movement they are building is "not a lunatic fringe but the programmed product of right wing passion, plus corporate wealth, plus 20th century technology—and its strength is increasing daily." [17]

This strength has been embodied in a large number of fast-moving organizations:

American Legislative Exchange Council (ALEC)
American Security Council
Americans Against Union Control of Government
Citizens for the Republic
Committee for Responsible Youth Politics
Committee for the Survival of a Free Congress
Committee on the Present Danger
Conservative Victory Fund
Consumer Alert Council

Fund for a Conservative Majority
Gun Owners of America
Heritage Foundation
National Conservative Political Action Committee
National Rifle Association Political Action Committee (PAC)
Our PAC
Public Service PAC
Right To Keep and Bear Arms Political Victory Fund
Tax Reform Immediately (TRIM)
The Conservative Caucus (TCC)
Young Americans for Freedom/The Fund for a Conservative Majority

Many of these groups, it must be understood, include nonrabid crackpots and nonraving zealots. They are often backed up—particularly on fiscal matters—by the National Taxpayers Union and many libertarian groups which may part company from them on such issues as the escalation of war spending or the return of military conscription.

All of them, it should be added, seem to be the recipients of far more funds than were ever available to the less respectable extremists. Much of this money unquestionably seeps down, as the ADA insists, from corporate coffers. Some of it unquestionably comes from massive mail solicitations by Richard Viquerie, who has been aptly christened the "Direct Mail Wizard of the New Right." Since 1964, when he was working on Senator Goldwater's campaign for the presidency, Viguerie has been developing a mailing list operation which puts the New Right into touch with millions upon millions of Americans.

Today, the momentum of the Radical Right is impressive. It has defeated many well-known liberal candidates for reelection to national, state, and local offices. Having helped elect a quarter of the members of the House of Representatives in 1976, it looks forward to much greater influence by the mid-1980s. Like the American labor movement, which has always supported some Republicans as well as many Democrats, the Radical Right has no firm commitment to any one party. Its strength among Democrats is much larger than that of labor among Republicans. It supports candidates of the two major parties and is closely associated with small-party movements, which sometimes have a decisive impact on electoral or legislative campaigns. Its biggest success, however, is that many of its positions which first sounded outrageous when voiced during the Goldwater campaign of 1964 are now regarded as part of the mainstream. This is not the result of Radical Right shifts toward the center. On the contrary, it is the result of a decisive movement toward the right by the Ultra-Rich and the Corporate Overseers.

The unfolding logic of the Radical Right, however, is neither to remain static or to become more openly reactionary. "We are no longer working to preserve the status quo," says Paul Weyrich, one of its ablest leaders. "We are radicals working to overturn the present power structure." [18] To understand what Weyrich means, we must heed Arno J. Mayer's warning—based on his study of classic fascism—that in a time of rapid change "even reactionary, conservative and counter-revolutionary movements project a populist, reformist and emancipatory image of their purpose." [19] More populism of this type can be expected: in a word, more attacks on the existing Establishment by people who want to strengthen it by making it much more authoritarian and winning for themselves more influential positions in it.

There is also a role in all this for left-wing extremists. Bombings, assassinations, or kidnappings by purported revolutionaries can serve as valuable triggering mechanisms for repressive action. Under such circumstances, official violence can take the garb of antiviolence, even though it may be far more extensive than required for the simple squashing of terrorists. With good luck, the friendly fascists can rely on the spontaneous initiatives of "revolutionary" wild men. If this is not forthcoming, they may not hesitate to spark such violence through the use of *agents provocateurs.**

NEW IDEOLOGIES OF CENTRAL POWER

> For any imperial policy to work effectively . . . it needs moral and intellectual guidance . . . It is much to be doubted that the United States can continue to play an imperial role without the endorsement of its intellectual class . . . It is always possible to hope that this intellectual class will . . . help formulate a new set of more specific principles that will relate the ideals which sustain American democracy to the harsh and nasty imperatives of imperial power.
>
> IRVING KRISTOL [20]

During the late 1960s and early 1970s Kristol clearly saw that "a small section of the American intellectual class has become a permanent brain trust to the political, the military, the economic authorities." These are the men, he reported, who "commute regularly to Washington, who help draw up programs for reorganizing the bureaucracy, who evaluate proposed weapons systems, who figure out ways to improve our cities and assist our poor, who analyze the course of economic growth, who reckon the cost and effectiveness of foreign aid programs, who dream up new approaches to such old social problems as the mental health of

---

* See discussion in "The Ladder of Terror," chapter 14.

the aged, etc., etc." But unfortunately, he lamented, the majority of the intellectuals refused to accept these responsibilities. A new class had arisen—mostly pseudo-intellectuals—composed of people alienated from an established order that refused to provide them with enough power or recognition.

Kristol's lament was picked up by a brilliant group of neoconservatives who, clustering around such magazines as *Commentary* and *The Public Interest* and the Basic Books publishing house, levied fierce and unrelenting attacks on this new class of irresponsibles. At the same time an equally brilliant group of somewhat more old-fashioned conservatives developed around William Buckley's *The National Review*, *The American Spectator*, the Arlington publishing house, and the Conservative Book Club. Together, these two new streams of intellectual activity have many elements in common. Some of their most brilliant practitioners are former Marxists, communists, or left-leaning liberals. Having seen the error of their own ways, they are particularly scornful of those bemused intellectuals who have not yet seen the light and—in Norman Podhoretz's term—"broken ranks." They have remarkable access to corporate funds, large and small foundations, and a host of new prosperous research centers and institutes. They have strong footholds in colleges and universities. Indeed, as *Business Week* pointed out in 1979, "major corporations . . . now underwrite at least 30 academic centers and chairs of free enterprise." [21]

Peter Steinfels has pointed out in *The Neoconservatives* that the Kristol-Podhoretz-Moynihan-Bell intellectuals consistently ignore the realities of corporate power.[22] So do the new intellectuals among the more old-fashioned conservatives. By so doing, whether consciously or not, both groups contribute to its increased concentration at the higher levels of both the U.S. Establishment and the Golden International.

One way of doing this is merely to reinforce the older ideologies concerning the badness of socialism and communism and the goodness—or nonexistence—of capitalism. This has led to oft-repeated odes on the pristine beauty of automatic market forces in comparison with the deadly hand of inefficient and corrupt government bureaucracy. The invisible hands of corporate bureaucracies—as well as the multitudinous assists they get from government—are kept invisible.

The routinized reiteration of this older conservative doctrine, however, is buttressed by a new ideological reformaton that emphasizes the excellence of hierarchy, the wonders of technology, and the goodness of hard times. In *The Twilight of Authority*, Robert Nisbet makes an eloquent call for a return to the old aristocratic principle of hierarchy: "It is important that rank, class and estate in all spheres become once again honored rather than, as is now the case, despised or feared by intellectuals." [23] If democracy is to be diminished and if rank, class, and estate are once again to be honored, the intellectuals at the middle and lower levels of the establishment must be brought into line on many points. Those who advocate a somewhat more egalitarian society must be pilloried as "levellers" who would reduce everybody to a dull, gray uniformity. They must be convinced that the ungrateful lower classes whom they hope to raise up are, in fact, genetically and culturally inferior. They must be flattered into seeing themselves as part of a society in which true merit, as defined by the powerful, is usually recognized and rewarded. The power of the Ultra-Rich and the Corporate Overlords must be publicly minimized and the endless plutocratic search for personal gratification must be obscured by lamenting the self-gratifying hedonism of the masses.

Arguments along these lines by Arthur R. Jensen, Edward Banfield, R. J. Hernstein, and Daniel Bell have not yet won the day—not by any means. Indeed, the Watergate debacle of the Nixon administration proved rather embarrassing to those who had hinted that the America of 1973 was led by its best men. But the devotees of meritocratic hierarchy have nonetheless commanded a remarkable degree of attention, often staking out the territory for intellectual combat. The largest battles on this front still lie ahead. A sweeping victory for the advocates of hierarchy would be one of the conditions marking the advent of friendly fascism.

In the face of so many unhappy complications with nuclear energy and pollution, the earlier glorification of "knowledge elites" and science-based technology is losing much of its vigor. The existing order must be justified by more convincing affirmation of the wondrous benefits attainable through the ongoing technological revolution. Just what form these may take is not entirely clear. Three hints are provided by current developments in technology assessment, systems analysis of social problems, and *avant garde* techniques of social control.

Technology assessment itself has been invented as a new "soft" technology. It promises to cope with the second-order and third-order consequences of new technologies that threaten environmental degredation and resource depletion. "None of this has to be," Daniel Bell tells us. "The mechanism of control are available as well." [24] These mechanisms are to be found in the scientific assessment of all possible impacts of new technologies before they are introduced. It was more or less assumed that this assessment could be done "neutrally"—apart from considerations of basic values, economic interests, or political power. But this very emphasis on neutrality is in fact part of a "technological" ideology. It evades realities like those revealed in Philip Boffey's study, *The Brain Bank of America* (and not mentioned by Bell)—for example, that the National Academy of Engineering (an authoritative source for both the theory and practice of technology assessment) is packed with industry-paid assessors who have persistently "parroted the line of corporate interests." [25]

While faith in technology assessment provides a front-line of defense against any attack on the financial oligarchy's use of destructive "hard" techniques, systems analysis—also hailed by Bell as an historic advance—suggests the possibility of technical solutions to almost any social problem. Ida Hoos paraphrases the sales talk of the system analysts: "Do you want to launch a rocket, run a bank, catch a crook? Do you want to improve the efficiency of a fire department, a library, a hospital? The 'scientific methods' of operations research, systems analysis and the like provide the tools whereby you can proceed 'rationally.'"[26] Although these claims are essentially irrational, credibility is given by elaborate kowtowing to the mythology of presumed success in outer-space technology and military systems and the magic-laden symbolism of computer-based mathematical models. According to Ida Hoos, the boom in systems analysis can be explained this way: "Merchandised as a Space Age speciality, a precise and sophisticated set of tools, systems analysis has become the stock-in-trade of practically any individual or organization seeking a government grant or contract or engaged in a project. Its language is the life line of everyone who aspires to make his work appear systematic or technically sophisticated . . . Contrary to being an instrument of innovation, the system approach is essentially reactionary."[27]

Technology assessment, systems analysis, and similar developments serve to restore the public's wavering confidence in technology. They promise to solve technology's problems by more technology. At the same time, old-fashioned innovation continues unabated: breakthroughs in biology and new developments in medicine keep alive humanity's hope of escaping its most basic ills, if not death itself, through science. A society moving toward friendly fascism would be particularly taken with *avant garde* technologies of social control. B. F. Skinner has provided a vivid preview, attracting a national audience for his vision of utopia through a "science of behavior" and a centralized program of conditioning.[28] José Delgado has proposed widespread "behavior control" through electrical stimulation of the brain.[29] And a host of more modest proposals employing drugs, behavior therapy, and screening have been taken quite seriously. It is hard to discern the real promise, or threat, of these lines of research. Ideologically, they distract attention from the political or economic dimensions of social problems. The emphasis on the technological wonders to be gained from the natural or social sciences depoliticizes the establishment's technicians and facilitates stigmatization of social critics as "Luddites." All these tendencies would be exacerbated under friendly fascism, while the long-run possibility of actually adding new instruments of control to the establishment's armamentarium would be carefully pursued.

A successful transition to friendly fascism would clearly require a lowering of popular aspirations and demands. Only then can freer rein be given to the corporate drives for boundless acquisition. Since it is difficult to tell ordinary people that unemployment, inflation, and urban filth are good for them, it is more productive to get middle-class leaders on the austerity bandwagon and provide them with opportunities for increased prestige by doing what they can to lower levels of aspirations. Indeed, the ideology of mass sacrifice had advanced so far by the end of the 1970s that the most serious and best-advertised debate among New York liberals on the New York City fiscal crisis rested on the assumption that the level of municipal employment and services *had* to be cut. The only questions open for debate were "Which ones?" and "How much?" This ideology—although best articulated in general form by political scientists like Samuel Huntington and sociologists like Daniel Bell—also receives decisive support from Establishment economists.

Religious doctrines on the goodness of personal sacrifice in this world have invariably been associated with promises of eternal bliss in the next world. Similarly, the emerging ideologies on the virtues of austerity are bound to be supplemented by visions of "pie in the sky by and by." In their most vulgar form these ideologies may simply reiterate the economistic notion that reduced consumption now will mean more profitability, which will mean more capital investment that in turn will mean increased consumption later. In more sophisticated form, these ideologies take the form of a misty-eyed humanism. While moving toward friendly fascism we might hear much talk like Jean-Francois Revel's proclamation that "The revolution of the twentieth century will take place in the United States" or Charles Reich's view that the counterculture of the young will, by itself, break through the "metal and plastic and sterile stone" and bring about "a veritable greening of America." Indeed, work at such "think-tanks" as the Rand Corporation and Hudson Institute increasingly foregoes its old base in economics and related "dismal" disciplines for straight and unadulterated "humanism," the rhetorical promotion of which seems directly related to their involvement in dehumanized and dehumanizing technologies.

As with the ideologies of classic fascism, there is no need for thematic consistency in the new ideologies. An ideological menu is most useful when it provides enough variety to meet divergent needs and endless variations on interwoven melodic lines. Unlike the ideologies of classic fascism, however, these new ideologies on market virtue, hierarchic excellence, wondrous technology, and the goodness of hard times are not needed to mobilize masses to high peaks of emotional fervor. In contrast, they help prevent mass mobilization. Yet their growing function is to maintain the loyalty of intellectuals, scientists, and technicians at the Establishment's middle and lower ranks, thereby minimizing the need for systemic purges. On this score the two streams of conservative ideology have been remarkably effective. They have taken over the most commanding heights on the intellectual fronts, reducing to a "small section" those anti-Establishment intellectuals who try to swim against the main currents. Indeed, through a remarkable dialectic, the opponents of the so-called "new class" have themselves become a dominant new class of intellectuals who provide the moral and intellectual guidance on the harsh and nasty imperatives of imperial survival in the era of the stagflation-power tradeoff and the movement toward Super-America, Inc.

TRIPLESPEAK

During the take-off toward a more perfect capitalism, the debasement of the language moved no slower than the abasement of the currency through creeping inflation. The myths of the cold war gave us the imagery of a "free world" that included many tyrannical regimes on one side and the "worldwide communist conspiracy" to describe the other. The "end of ideology" ideologies gave us the myth of all-powerful knowledge elites to flatter the egos of intellectuals and scientists in the service of a divided Establishment. The accelerating rise of scientific and pseudo-scientific jargon fragmented social and natural scientists into small in-groups that concentrated more and more on small slices of reality, separating them more than ever before from the presumably unsophisticated (although functionally literate) working-buying classes.

In the early days of this process, George Orwell envisioned a future society in which the oligarchs of 1984 would use linguistic debasement as a conscious method of control. Hence the Party Leaders imposed *doublethink* on the population and set up a long-term program for developing *newspeak*. If Orwell were alive today, I think he would see that many of his ideas are now being incorporated in something just as sophisticated and equally fearful. I am referring to the new *triplespeak:* a three-tiered language of myth, jargon, and confidential straight talk.

Unlike Orwell's *doublethink* and *newspeak,* triplespeak is not part of any overall plan. It merely develops as a logical outcome of the Establishment's maturation, an essential element in the tightening of oligarchic control at the highest levels of the Golden International. Without myths, the rulers and their aides cannot maintain support at the lower levels of the major establishments, and the might itself—as well as the legitimacy of empire—may decay. Jargon is required to spell out the accumulating complexities of military, technological, economic, political, and cultural power. Straight talk is needed to illuminate the secret processes of high decision making and confidential bargaining and to escape the traps created by myth and jargon.

Herein lie many difficulties. With so much indirection and manipulation in the structure of transnational power, there is no longer any place for the pomp and ceremony that helped foster the effulgent myths surrounding past empires—no imperial purple, no unifying queen, king, or imperial council, no mass religion or ideology to fire the emotions of dependent masses. Hence the symbolic trappings of past empires must be replaced by smaller mystifications that at least have the merit of helping maintain the self-respect and motivations of the elites at the middle and lower levels of the national Establishments. Thus the operating rules of modern capitalist empire require ascending rhetoric about economic and social development, human rights, and the self-effacing role of transnational corporations in the promotion of progress and prosperity. The more lies are told, the more important it becomes for the liars to justify themselves by deep moral commitments to high-sounding objectives that mask the pursuit of money and power. The more a country like the United States imports its prosperity from the rest of the world, the more its leaders must dedicate themselves to the sacred ideal of exporting abundance, technology, and civilization to everyone else. The further this myth may be from reality, the more significant it becomes—and the greater the need for academic notables to document its validity by bold assertion and self-styled statistical demonstration. "The might that makes right must be a different right from that of the right arm," the political scientist, Charles Merriam, stated many years ago. "It must be a might deep rooted in emotion, embedded in feelings and aspirations, in morality, in sage maxims, in forms of rationalization . . ." [30]

Thus, in 1975 and 1976, while the long right arm of the American presidency was supporting bloody dictatorships in Chile, Brazil, Indochina, and Iran (to mention but a few), Daniel P. Moynihan, the U.S. ambassador at the United Nations, wrapped himself in the flag of liberty and human rights. His eloquent rhetoric—deeply rooted in emotion and embedded in feelings and aspirations—set a high standard of creative myth-making.[31] At that time, his superiors in Washington failed to realize that Moynihan's approach was, in Walter Laqueur's terms, "not a lofty and impractical endeavor, divorced from the harsh realities of world endeavor, but itself a kind of Realpolitik." [32] Within two years, however, the next president, Jimmy Carter, seized the torch from Moynihan's hand and, without thanks or attribution, set a still higher standard by clothing the might of his cruise missile and neutron bomb in human-rights rhetoric even more deeply rooted in morality, sage maxims, and forms of rationalization.

Domestic myths are the daily bread of the restructured Radical Right and the old-style and new-style conservatives. Many of the ideologies discussed in the last section of this chapter serve not only as cover-ups for concentrated oligarchic power. They provide code words for the more unspoken, mundane myths that define unemployed people as lazy or unemployable, women, blacks and Hispanics as congenitally inferior to other people. Presidential candidates invariably propagate the myth that Americans are innately superior to the people of other countries and that therefore they have a high destiny to fulfill in the leadership of the world's forces for peace, freedom, democracy, and—not to be forgotten—private corporate investment and profitability. Trying to flatter the voting public as a whole, they ascribe most of America's difficulties to foreign enemies or a few individuals at home—like Richard Nixon—who have betrayed the national goodness. Not so long ago, General Westmoreland went much further when, to reassure the more naive members of the American officer corps, he soberly declared that "Despite the final failure of the South Vietnamese, the record of the American military of never having lost a war is still intact." [33] With the arrival of friendly fascism, myths like these would no longer be greeted, at least not publicly, with the degree of skepticism they still provoke. Instead, the Establishment would agree that the domestic tranquility afforded by these convenient reassurances qualified them, in contrast to more critical, less comforting diagnoses, as "responsible." As old myths get worn out or new myths punctured, still newer ones (shall we call them "myths of the month"?) are brought into being.

The momentum of jargon would not abate in a friendly fascist society but move steadily ahead with the ever-increasing specialization and subspecialization in every field. New towers of Babel are, and would be, continuously erected throughout the middle and lower levels of the Establishment. Communication among the different towers, however, becomes increasingly difficult. One of the most interesting examples is the accumulation of complex, overlapping, and mystifying jargons devised by the experts in various subdivisions of communications itself (semiotics, semantics, linguistics, content analysis, information theory, telematics, computer programming, etc.), none of whom can communicate very well with all the others. In military affairs, jargon wraps otherwise unpleasant realities in a cloak of scientific objectivity. Thus, "surgical strike," "nuclear exchange," and even the colloquial "nukes" all hide the horrors of atomic warfare. The term "clean bomb" for the new neutron bomb hides the fact that although it may not send much radioactive material into the atmsophere it would kill all human life through radiation in a somewhat limited area; this makes it the dirtiest of all bombs. Similarly, in global economics the jargon of exchange rates and IMF conditions facilitates, while also concealing, the application of transnational corporate power on Third World countries. The jargon of domestic economics, as I have already shown, hides the crude realities of corporate aggrandizement, inflation, and unemployment behind a dazzling array of technical terms that develop an esprit de corps which unites the various sectors of Establishment economics.

Rising above the major portion of jargon and myth is *straight talk,* the blunt and unadorned language of who gets what, when and how. If money talks, as it is said, then power whispers. The language of both power and money is spoken in hushed whispers at tax-deductible luncheons or drinking hours at the plushest clubs and bars or in the well-shrouded secrecy of executive suites and boardrooms. Straight talk is never again to be recorded on Nixon-style tapes or in any memoranda that are not soon routed to the paper shredders.

As one myth succeeds another and as new forms of jargon are invented, straight talk becomes increasingly important. Particularly at the higher levels of the Establishment it is essential to deal frankly with the genuine nature of imperial alternatives and specific challenges. But the emerging precondition for imperial straight talk is secrecy. Back in 1955, Henry Kissinger might publicly refer to "our primary task of dividing the USSR and China." * By the time the American presidency was making progress in this task, not only Kissinger but the bulk of foreign affairs specialists had learned the virtues of prior restraint and had carefully refrained from dealing with the subject so openly. It may be presumed that after the publication of *The Crisis Democracy*, Samuel Huntington learned a similar lesson and that consultants to the Trilateral Commission will never again break the Establishment's taboos by publicly calling for less democracy. Nor is it likely that in discussing human rights the American president will talk openly on the rights and privileges of American-based transnationals in other countries. Nor am I at all sure that realists like Irving Kristol, Raymond Aron, George Liska, and James Burnham will continue to be appreciated if they persist in writing boldly about the new American empire and its responsibilities. Although their "empire" is diligently distinguished from "imperialism," it will never be allowed to enter official discourse.

For imperial straight talk to mature, communication must be thoroughly protected from public scrutiny. Top elites must not only meet together frequently; they must have opportunities to work, play, and relax together for long periods of time.

Also, people from other countries must be brought into this process; otherwise there is no way to avoid the obvious misunderstandings that develop when people from different cultural backgrounds engage in efforts at genuine communication. If the elites of other countries must learn English (as they have long been doing), it is also imperative for American elites to become much more fluent in other tongues than they have ever been in the past. In any language there are niceties of expression—particularly with respect to money and power—that are always

---

* Referred to in chapter 8, "Trilateral Empire or Fortress America."

lost or diluted if translated into another language. With or without the help of interpreters, it will be essential that serious analysis, confidential exchanges, and secret understandings be multilingual. Thus, whether American leadership matures or obsolesces, expands or contracts, English can no longer be the lingua franca of modern empire. The control of "Fortress America" would require reasonable fluency in Spanish by many top elites (although not necessarily by presidents and first ladies). Trilateral empire, in turn, imposes more challenging—but not insuperable—linguistic burdens.

10

Friendly Fascist Economics

The worst is yet to come.

IRVING KRISTOL [1]

There is a subtle three-way trade-off between escalating unemployment together with other unresolved social problems, rising taxes, and inflation. In practice, the corporate state has bought all three.

DANIEL FUSFELD [2]

WHAT WILL DAILY LIFE be like under friendly fascism?

In answering this question I think immediately of Robert Theobald's frog: "Frogs will permit themselves to be boiled to death. If the temperature of the water in which the frog is sitting is slowly raised, the frog does not become aware of its danger until it is too late to do anything about it." [3]

Although I am not sure it can ever be too late to fight oppression, the moral of the frog story is clear: as friendly fascism emerges, the conditions of daily life for most people move from bad to worse—and for many people all the way to Irving Kristol's "worst."

To Fusfeld's trio of more unemployment, taxes, and inflation, however, we must also add a decline in social services and a rise in shortages, waste and pollution, nuclear poison and junk. These are the consequences of corporate America's huge investment in the ideology of popular sacrifice and in the "hard times" policies that have US "pull in the belts" to help THEM in efforts to expand power, privilege, and wealth.

MORE STAGFLATION

Money to get power, power to protect money.
Slogan of the Medici family

Capital has always been a form of power. As physical wealth (whether land, machinery, buildings, materials, or energy resources), capital is *productive* power. As money, it is *purchasing* power, the ability to get whatever may be exchanged for it. The ownership of property is the power of *control* over its use. In turn, the power of wealth, money, and ownership has always required both protection and encouragment through many other forms of power. Businessmen have never needed theorists to tell them about the connection. It has taken economic theorists more than a century to develop the pretense that money and power are separate. Indeed, while Establishment militarists persistently exaggerate the real power of destructive violence, the same Establishment's economic policymakers increasingly present destructive economic policies as though they have no connection with power.

The vehicle for doing this is becoming the so-called "tradeoff" policy. The more conservative Establishment notables argue that the way to fight inflation is to curtail growth, even though the inescapable side effect is recession and higher unemployment. Their more liberal colleagues politely beg to differ, arguing that the way to cope with unemployment is to "reflate" the economy. For scientific support, both sides habitually refer to a curve developed by A. W. Phillips on the relation between unemployment and changing money rates in England from 1861 to 1957. Giving modern support to part of Karl Marx's theory on the "reserve army of the unemployed," Phillips showed that when more people were jobless, there was less chance of an increase in money wage rates. Phillips also made a sharp distinction between wages and prices, mentioning prices only to point out in passing that a wage increase does not by itself require a proportionate increase in prices.[4] On this side of the Atlantic, Paul Samuelson and various colleagues applied Phillips's curve to prices instead of wages, and hiding their biases behind Phillips's data, developed the current tradeoff theory.

In its more virulent form at the beginning of the 1980s, this theory means the following: Recession is needed to bring the rate of inflation down below the double-digit level—that is, to less than 10 percent. The most naive backers of the theory suggest that once this is done, the "back of inflation will be broken," inflationary expectations will be buried, never to rise again, and the country can return to the good old days of Lyndon Johnson and Richard Nixon.

Many liberal opponents of this theory, in turn, accept on good faith the credentials of the self-styled inflation fighters. Apparently operating on the premise that economic policymaking is a technical exercise in puzzlesolving, they argue that the conservatives are simply mistaken in their understanding of economic behavior, and in failing to see that untold millions may be injured by pro-recession policies. In my judgment, however, the liberals who take this view fail to understand or face up to the nature of Establishment power.

In a world of many divergent objectives that must be reconciled with each other, the leaders of any Establishment are continuously engaged in complex juggling acts. Whether developing global investment policies or apportioning economic or military aid around the world, everything cannot be done at the same time. Above all, in planning for corporate profitability, compromises must continuously be made. Profitability in one area is often accompanied by unavoidable losses in another. Short-term profits must often be sacrificed in the interest of the greater profitability that can come only from the fruition of long-term investment programs. Above all, the maintenance or strengthening of the power to protect future profitability often requires the sacrifice of some present, even future, profits. Neither market power nor the political power supporting it are free goods. They too cost money—and in periods of stagflation they tend to cost more money than before.

Toward the end of 1979, more than 100 corporate executives attended a meeting of the Business Council at Hot Springs, Virginia. Almost to a man, they enthusiastically supported the recessionary policies of the Federal Reserve Board and the Treasury. "The sooner we suffer the pain," stated Irving S. Shapiro, chairman of Du Pont, "the sooner we will be through. I'm quite prepared to endure whatever pain I have to in the short term." Steven Rattner, the reporter for *The New York Times*, pointed out that signs of suffering were nowhere in sight: "The long black limousines and private jet planes were still evident in abundance." Rattner also suggested that Shapiro was apparently referring not to any loss in his personal income but rather to the "pain" that might be inflicted on Du Pont's profits.[5]

How much profit a company like Du Pont might lose in the short run is a matter of conjecture. Unlike American workers, a giant corporation can engage in fancy tax-juggling that pushes its losses on to ordinary taxpayers. Unlike middle-class people, the Ultra-Rich billionaires and centimillionaires can shift the costs of recession or social expenditures to the lowly millionaires, who in turn can pass them along to the middle classes. Above all, the hyenas of economic life can get theirs from recession as well as inflation.

Any serious effort to control stagflation—either its recession side or its inflation side—would require serious limitations on both Big Business and the support given to it by Big Government. Any such limitations, in turn, would have to be backed up by a broad anti-Establishment coalition including, but not limited to, organized labor. The other side of this coin may now be seen in stark clarity: The price of preventing any such coalition and of preserving, if not expanding, Establishment power, is to choose continuing stagflation as the price that must be paid to protect future profitability. The real tradeoff by the big-time traders is not between price stability and high employment. Rather, it is the sacrifice of both in order to curtail union power, dampen rising aspirations among the population at large, and take advantage of both inflationary windfalls and recessionary bargains.

Indeed, not only the U.S. Establishment but the Golden International as a whole has in practice accepted the realities of continuing stagflation (with whatever ups and down may materialize in the proportions of combined inflation and unemployment) as the new economic order of the "Free World." This has long been the operating doctrine of the International Monetary Fund in Third World countries. It is now emerging as a doctrinal strategy for the 1980s in the entire First World.

In the 1960s and early 1970s no one ever dreamed that Americans could become accustomed to levels of either inflation or official unemployment as high as 6 or 7 percent a year. As the Big Business-Big Government partnership becomes closer, the levels previously regarded as unacceptable will—like the hot water to which a frog has become accustomed—be regarded not only as normal but as objectives of official policy. Indeed, 8 percent unemployment is already being regarded as full employment and 8 percent inflation as price stability. Under the emerging triplespeak—in a manner reminding us of "War Is Peace" and "Freedom Is Slavery" in Orwell's *1984*—the norm for unemployment could reach and the norm for inflation far exceed the double-digit level of ten apiece. When the two are added together, this provides what I call a "limited misery index"—limited because no similar arithmetic value can be given to such things as job insecurity, crime, pollution, alienation, and junk. The so-called "tradeoff" theory merely tells us that either of the two elements in the index may go down a little as the other one goes up. What the tradeoffers fail to point out is that despite fluctuations the long-term trend of the two together is upward. Thus in the opening months of the 1980s, even without correcting for the official underestimation of unemployment, the limited misery index approached 20. Under friendly fascism it would move toward 30. . . .

MORE MONEY MOVING UPWARD

As the limited misery index creeps or spurts ahead, a spiraling series of cure-alls are brought forth from the Establishment's medicine chest. Logically, each one leads toward the others. Together, apart from anyone's intentions, the medicines make the malady worse.

To cure inflation, interest rates are raised. This cannot be done by bankers alone. Intervention by central banks, acting on their behalf, is necessary. This results in a quick upward movement in prices and a further increase in government spending on new debt service. The companion step is to cut government spending on most social services—education, health, streetcleaning, fire and police protection, libraries, employment projects, etc. The deepest cuts are made in the lowest income areas, where the misery is already the sharpest political resistance tends to be less organized.

To cure stagnation or recession, there are two patent medicines. The first is more Big Welfare for Big Business—through more reductions in capital gains taxes, lower taxes on corporations and the rich, more tax shelters, and, locally, more tax abatement for luxury housing and office buildings. These generous welfare payments are justified in the name of growthmanship and productivity. Little attention is given to the fact that the major growth sought is in profitability, an objective mentioned only by a few ultra-Right conservatives who still believe in straight talk. Less attention is given to the fact that the productivity sought is defined essentially as resulting from investment in capital-intensive machinery and technology that displace labor and require more fossil fuels. The second patent medicine, justified in terms of national emergencies with only sotto voce reference to its implications for maintaining employment, is more spending on death machines and war forces. This, in turn, spurs the growth of the federal deficit.

To keep the deficit within limits and provide enough leeway for alleviation of the worst cuts in social services, higher taxes are required. This is done by a hidden national sales tax. The preparations for this have already been made by preliminary legislative action toward the imposition of the so-called Value Added Tax (VAT), already in force in France and England. VAT takes a bite out of every stage of production. At the end of the line, this means higher prices for consumers. . . . And so the dismal round continues—higher interest rates, cuts in social services, more tax subsidies for Big Business, and higher sales taxes hitting the middle- and lower-income groups.

Over the short run (which may be stretched out longer than some expect), the net effect of this cycle is to move purchasing power upward toward the most privileged people. This compensates in part for the paradox that making money by raising prices reduces the value of the money made. Over the longer run, however, it intensifies the older contradiction of capitalism, namely, that profit maximization undermines the mass purchasing power required for continued profitability.

AN ABUNDANCE OF SHORTAGES

Be not afraid of great shortages. Some benefit from shortages that are borne naturally. Some achieve shortages by cooperative work, and some have shortages thrust upon them.

An adaptation of Maria's letter to Malvolio in WILLIAM SHAKESPEARE'S *Twelfth Night*

Back in 1798, in his *Essay on the Principle of Population*, Thomas Malthus argued that population tends to grow faster than the food supply. Devastating shortages of food are inevitable, he argued, unless population growth is curbed. For Malthus the major curbs, in addition to sexual continence, were poverty, starvation, pestilence, and war. Today's neo-Malthusians have modernized his thesis. Conceding that food supply has been increased by modern technology, they argue that further growth of production and population will bring back the Malthusian nightmare. According to Herman Kahn, they claim that "the world is entering so severe a period of international scarcity of major agricultural goods that mankind may have to come to grips with the decision of who shall eat and who shall not (the triage decision)," a decision presumably to be made by the major grain-exporting nations.[6] The triage decision refers to the practice of overworked medical staffs in wartime who may divide the wounded into three groups: those who can no longer be helped (and must be allowed to die), those who can get along without help, and those who can be saved by quick help. The implication is that with growing shortages of food, the same grim choices will have to be made. With somewhat less grimness, the sons of Malthus now argue that desperate shortages of all nonrenewable minerals (bauxite, cobalt, copper, chromium, columbium, iron ore, lead, manganese, molybdenum, nickel, tin, tungsten, and uranium, etc.) are around the corner. The greatest fury of all surrounds fossil fuels (coal, natural gas, and petroleum) which, unlike metals, cannot be recycled after they are burned for fuel or transformed into such new products as fertilizer, plastics, textiles, dyes, or dynamite. Because these fossil-fuel deposits will eventually be depleted, the major energy reserves of modern civilization will disappear with them.

In rebuttal, anti-Malthusians argue convincingly that the limits of growth lie not only decades ahead but many centuries in the future. Herman Kahn and his associates at the Hudson Institute estimate that the resources of the planet, although limited, are enough to support a world population of 15 billion people by the year 2176 at a per capita national product of $20,000, or two and a half times the U.S. per capita product in 1976.[7] Barry Commoner estimates that "in round numbers, some 350 billion barrels of domestic crude oil are available to us . . . At the present rate of oil consumption (slightly more than six billion barrels per year), this amount would take care of *total* national demand for oil without any imports for a period of fifty to sixty years." [8] Herman Kahn makes a similar estimate for the entire world supply of oil and gas.

There are also vast proven reserves of coal in the United States. Herman Kahn cautiously estimates that "potential U.S. resources of oil, gas and coal are sufficient to supply the energy needs of this country for more than 150 years." [9] Both Commoner and Kahn point out that within the next fifty years it would be both technologically and economically feasible to replace nonrecoverable fossil fuels with alternative energy sources: nuclear fission (with all its attendant dangers), solar energy in many forms, geothermal energy and eventually, perhaps, nuclear fusion.

But most debates about resource depletion versus resource sufficiency tend to obscure one of the most fundamental facts of life: *Whenever things that many people want are in short supply, those who control the supply have important power over those who want some.* For many centuries this principle was used by feudal landlords, kings, merchant capitalists, and colonial exploiters. In India under the British, for example, crop failures that resulted in widespread famine were occasions for joyous profiteering by landlords and colonial officials, who were able to sell food at extortionate prices. Under modern industrial capitalism, this principle survives in a new form. The new technologies that make abundance possible have the potentiality of abolishing scarcity. From the viewpoint of many large corporations this has always been a great disadvantage: it can create a shortage of shortages. It is only logical, therefore, that corporate executives do everything possible to get into situations in which shortages are available. The established methods of doing this are (1) keeping production down, (2) restricting competition by other producers or substitute products, (3) using patent monopolies to keep out of production products or processes that would diminish the scarcity, and (4) throwing a tight mantle of secrecy over reserves that are kept off the market or out of production. In the case of many basic raw materials or food products—particularly uranium, tin, copper, coffee, wheat, sugar, milk, etc.—this is done through formally organized commodity agreements, marketing agreements, or cartels. In a still larger number of areas production is kept down and prices up by less formal arrangements. Under "price leadership," a dominant concern will set a certain pattern and the others will follow the leader. Over two hundred years ago Adam Smith described some of the informal ways of doing this: "People of the same trade seldom meet together, even for merriment or diversion, but the conversation ends in a conspiracy against the public, or in some contrivance to raise prices." Since then, conventions, conferences and clubs—all subsidized through tax deductions—provide much greater opportunities of this type. Trade associations make it possible for this kind of cooperation to be handled indirectly by experts who are not even on the direct payroll of the cooperating corporations. Hence it is that modern capitalism is moving toward a growing abundance of shortages.

These shortages appear in a huge variety of forms. Some come from the natural or historical disproportionality of productive forces. Soil, mineral, fuel, and climatic resources are distributed very unevenly among the countries of the world and within most countries. So are the technological and institutional capabilities of using these resources. Successful growth in any country invariably pushes it up to the limits of certain resources within its borders and makes it more dependent on imports. During the upward swing of the business cycle some sectors within any country hit the top of their capacity before others, thereby creating "bottleneck" shortages. Those who hold the neck of the bottle are seldom loath to take advantage of their opportunity; the result is inflationary price increases.

Some shortages stem from bad weather, droughts, earthquakes, or tidal waves. In 1972 and 1974 there were extensive droughts in many countries. One of these countries was the Soviet Union, which faced a serious shortage of feed stock for its farm animals and cattle. A massive Soviet purchase of American wheat sent the price of American grain skyrocketing. In a few weeks' time a handful of corporate traders (who were close to the Nixon administration) cashed in on advance information. "In those few weeks," according to Jim Hightower, "the grain oligopoly collected $300,000,000 in export payments from the taxpayers."[10] Although they did not share in this windfall at once, wheat farmers subsequently benefited from the high prices they were able to wrest from any other food-scarce countries. In what sense natural events are always "natural" is somewhat debatable. The extensive droughts in sub-Saharan North Africa have resulted in part from the pressure of fast-growing human and livestock population on food-producing ecosystems. "Denuding the semi-arid landscape by deforestation and overgrazing," two observers reported to the Club of Rome, "has enabled the desert to move southward, in some cases up to thirty miles a year, particularly in the years plagued by increasing droughts."[11]

Some shortages stem from conscious business decisions, usually supported by government action, to get higher prices by keeping the supply levels low. In periods of agricultural glut, this has often been done by destroying crops, pouring milk into the ground, and slaughtering livestock. The more modern tendency is toward keeping a lid on production —as has been done extensively in the United States—by maximum production quotas and by subsidies to farmers (usually in the name of conservation) for allowing fertile land to lie unused.

In energy, the maintenance of low supply levels has been an equally central—although less widely known—aspect of corporate policy. In the United States, as James Ridgeway reports "the Connally hot oil act, passed in the 1930s, first formally allowed the oil industry to set its own rate of production through creation of state 'conservation' agencies." [12] Under this legislation prices were kept at artificial levels by firm ceilings on domestic production. Later, as large amounts of oil became available in the Middle East, oil import quotas were set up to protect the American market from the threat of abundance. These were enforced by the co-operative relationships among the seven major Western companies: Exxon, Gulf, Texaco, Mobil, Socal, British Petroleum, and Shell. As revealed in the magisterial historical analyses by Robert Engler and John Blair, these companies have traditionally kept production down and prices up through price-fixing agreements, interlocking directorates, and banking ties.[13] The success of this Western cartel has led to its being referred to in the industry as the "Seven Sisters."

Early in the 1970s the Sisters were confronted by the fact that their junior partners in the major oil-exporting countries organized what they called "a cartel to confront the cartel," namely, the Organization of Oil Exporting Countries, or OPEC. Thus it was that the Western cartel suddenly had a new shortage thrust upon it. Its response to this opportunity has led to relations with OPEC that are best described in the remark of a rich Armenian oil speculator, Calouste Gulbenkian: "Oilmen are like cats; you can never tell from the sound of them whether they are fighting or making love." [14] Actually, it is the sound of making money. As OPEC has piled up petrodollars by continuously raising its prices while keeping output down, the Western oil cartel has made fabulous sums by operating as OPEC's distributors, raising the price of its non-OPEC petroleum toward OPEC levels and investing its huge profits in other energy sources (gas, coal, uranium, and solar energy). It has also achieved the semantic miracle of hiding its cooperative relationship with OPEC—which can be precisely described as a bilateral monopoly or duopoly—and creating the false impression that there is only one cartel, OPEC.

As prices rise, the Sisters and the Brothers are still faced by a short-range oil surplus that threatens prices and profits. They counter this threat with a combination of well-made shortages and expertly contrived warnings of imminent depletion. To support these warnings, they publicize oil-reserve figures that are limited to the "known recoverable" or "proven" reserves—in other words the inventories held underground. These artfully contrived statistics usually leave out or seriously underestimate the full amount of these inventories and the potentiality of newly discovered oil fields. Logically, therefore, one would expect that the companies would slow down the rate of new discovery, thereby reducing the burden of carrying overly large inventories and sharpening the illusion of impending doom. This is exactly what has happened: "The declining rate of oil discovery per year," Barry Commoner revealed in 1974, "is a result of company decisions to cut back on exploration efforts rather than of the depletion of accessible oil deposits. We are not so much running out of domestic oil as running out of the oil companies' interest in looking for it." [15]

As world oil prices have risen rapidly, there has been some recent increases in exploration, enough indeed to threaten the maintenance of well-designed shortages. Thus, in his first energy address to the nation, President Carter predicted a serious energy crunch in the 1980s. Since then, new oil fields in the North Sea, Alaska, Mexico, and many other countries have resulted in the oil industry itself now stating that no serious shortages are imminent until the 1990s. Even then, they maintain, if the price is right—that is, high enough—there will then be bountiful supplies. At the same time, however, they take vigorous action to prevent any tendency toward the expansions of supplies not under their control. In 1978, for example, the World Bank, reversing a long-standing policy, announced a plan to finance exploration by Third World countries. This plan was based on a study by the French Petroleum Institute, which reported that of seventy-one non-OPEC developing countries only ten had been adequately explored. Of these, as reported in *The New York Times*, twenty-three were "judged to have excellent prospects for finding oil or gas." At this point Exxon went to work on the U.S. Treasury Department and convinced it to force the World Bank not only to scale down its program but to put it in the hands of the Western oil companies rather than Third World public enterprises.[16]

In the case of almost all other minerals, known reserves are large and potential reserves still larger. But any individual country may face the prospect of imminent depletion of this or that resource. Hence a worldwide scramble for materials. The United States is extremely well situated, since its dependency on imports is limited mainly to cobalt, chromium, manganese, tin, bauxite, nickel, and zinc. In some of these fields, depletion of high-quality ores is just around the corner—and future needs could be met only by expanded imports, use of low-quality ores (which is expensive), or use of substitute materials. In any of these cases, depletion means substantial dislocation, as the populations of former mining areas are left stranded and the changeover costs of shifts to alternative sources are inflicted on the people in these areas and the general taxpayers.

Depletion of a specific resource—whether by destructive fishing methods, deforestation, soil depletion, or running down the supply of a given mineral—is indeed killing a goose that lays golden eggs. But goose killing is not necessarily bad for business. In the words of Daniel Fife and Barry Commoner, "the 'irresponsible' entrepreneur finds it profitable to kill the goose that lays the golden eggs, so long as the goose lives long enough to provide him with sufficient eggs to pay for the purchase of a new goose.[17] Ecological irresponsibility can pay—for the entrepreneur, but not for society as a whole." The fact must be faced, however, that ecological irresponsibility is the other side of the capitalist coin. The major responsibility of corporate executives, so long as they are not constrained by enforced law, is to maximize their long-term accumulation of capital and power no matter what the cost may be to geese, people, or physical resources.

MORE WASTE AND POLLUTION

Hatcheck Girl: Goodness, what beautiful diamonds!
Mae West: Goodness had nothing to do with it, dearie.

The Wit and Wisdom of Mae West

To those who marvel at the alleged efficiency of American technology under a so-called "free market" system, one may accurately reply in the style of Mae West. This kind of efficiency, dearie, has nothing to do with the proper allocation of resources. The free market's efficiency relates to the piling up of capital and power—and that kind of efficiency depends on profit calculations that do not take into account the vast liquid, gaseous, solid, and bacteriological wastes produced by the processes of production and consumption, and the costs these wastes may impose on others. The accounts of the corporation, even if purged of all the mystifications designed to conceal profit from tax collectors and mistakes from shareholders, can never reveal the "external costs," the damages inflicted on air, water, land, and people. Often, indeed, the expansion of these unpaid costs becomes a side effect—and sometimes a prerequisite—of drives toward greater corporate profitability. Thus, in the broadest sense, a larger GNP may be partly attained by the growth of waste and inefficiency. "It is a well-established fact," states a Club of Rome article, "that in the world's developed, industrialized regions materials consumption has reached proportions of preposterous waste."

The waste is obvious to even the most generous-minded visitor. The garbage pails of the First World—particularly in America—contain more food than the average diet in many Third World countries. Junk and litter pile up in huge trash heaps. An earlier estimate for the United States tells us that "the annual discard of 7 million cars, 100 million tires, 20 million tons of paper, 28 billion bottles and 48 billion cans is just the beginning." [18] Less obvious to the naked eye but much larger in quantity and pervasive in consequences are the residues from the processes of production, consumption, transportation, and energy conversion. Agriculture is made more productive by chemical pesticides that also impair plant and animal life, and by fertilizers that become pollutants as they are washed into the rivers, lakes, and oceans. Strip mining destroys vast areas of land. Factories and mines spew tons of arsenic, lead, mercury, sulphur oxides, asbestos, and other poisons into the water and the air. Industrial sewage emissions alone "account for 31 trillion gallons of waste, while all municipal emissions total 14 million gallons." [19] Automobiles emit not only carbon monoxide (a deadly gas at very low concentrations) but also sulphur oxides, nitrogen oxides, hydrocarbons, carbon dioxide, and particulates. The internal combustion engine—while a brilliant device for guzzling gasoline—turns out to be remarkably inefficient in converting fuel into power. "In oil-fired electric power generation and transmission," Herman Kahn reports, "about 70 percent of the energy in the fuel is lost before the user receives the power. Autos generally deliver, as motive power, only about 10 percent of the energy in the original petroleum." [20]

More broadly, in the production of energy from fossil fuels, huge amounts of potential energy are wasted through incomplete combustion, the production of waste heat, and losses in transmission. Instead of focusing merely on the energy content of the fuel, physicists have started to measure waste by relating the energy actually needed for a particular task (say, warming a building) to the energy actually provided. They have found that the energy technically needed for space heating, water heating, and refrigeration is only a small fraction of the energy actually provided. By this calculation the efficiency of an oil burner, which uses 60 percent of the energy in the oil, may be as low as 8 percent. In other words, while 40 percent of the fuel may be wasted, over 90 percent of the energy produced is also wasted.

What happens to all the wastes? "In one sense they are never lost; their constituent atoms are rearranged and eventually disbursed in a diluted and unusable form into the air, soil, and the waters of our planet. The natural ecological systems can absorb many of the effluents of human activity and reprocess them into substances that are usable by, or at least harmless to, other forms of life." [21]

But when effluents are released on a large enough scale, they saturate the natural absorptive mechanisms and exceed the limits of compatibility with healthful living, or even with some form of life itself.

The injurious effects of pollution are augmented by long sequences of interacting side effects. Radiation, fertilizers, pesticides, and industrial or municipal sewage may come back in the fish or fowl one eats, the water one drinks, or the air one breathes—and may be given to babies in mothers' milk. Through what may be called "pernicious synergy" two or more pollutants may combine to do more damage than the sum of the separate pollutants. This is the essence of the pollution problem—a man-made plague that threatens to increase exponentially.

Many well-intended "cures" may spread the pollution plague more widely. The high smokestack deposits pollutants into the upper-air currents, which may carry them far and wide. The electricity that is "clean" at the point of consumption may come from generating plants that pollute the air at distant spots. Air pollution is reduced by filtering the chimney emissions and then flushing the pollutants into the nearest sewer. For this purpose, the planet's streams, rivers, seas, and oceans serve as the largest sewers available to flush away the effluents of capitalism. In turn, water purification programs may make the water even worse. Since untreated sewage tends to deplete the oxygen supply of surface waters, it is often converted through treatment plants into inorganic effluents. But these, in turn, often support the growth of algae, which bloom furiously, soon die, and release organic matter that uses up the oxygen supply. Thus may a body of water "die," that is, lose the oxygen that supports aquatic life. To avoid this, the effluents are often filtered out of the water and then dumped onto the land or, through burning, shot into the air. The air pollution of thermal power plants may be cured by nuclear energy plants that, in providing "clean" electricity, also produce thermal pollution through the discharge of heated water in huge quantities and—much more dangerous—long-lived radioactive wastes and (as with breeder reactors) large amounts of plutonium, one of the most dangerous substances in the world.

Looking into the future, some observers fear that the protective layer of ozone that surrounds the earth may be depleted by the freon emitted from aerosol spray cans in many countries, and by the water vapor produced by high-altitude aircraft, both regular and supersonic. If this should happen, humankind's protection from ultraviolet solar radiation would be impaired. Others predict that present rates of energy conversion would, if continued to the year 2000, double the carbon dioxide content of the air. Even if the increase is smaller, the effect—according to Herman Kahn—would be "the trapping of long-wave infra-red radiation from the surface of the earth, which tends to increase the temperature of the atmosphere." [22] This additional heat would combine with the thermal pollution resulting directly from more energy conversion. The resulting "greenhouse effect," Robert Heilbroner writes, might even melt the Arctic and Antartic ice caps, raise the level of the oceans, and create tidal waves or permanent flooding in many areas that are now above water. The increased heat, itself, he feels, is a reason for "anticipating a fixed life span for capitalism." [23] Some observers combine these possibilities with the accidental or purposeful use of nuclear or bacteriological weapons, the blowing up of nuclear power plants, the escape into the atmosphere of laboratory-produced viruses, bacteria, genetic material, and other kinds of catastrophe. To dramatize the fact that such eventualities could be more destructive than old-time plagues of nature's own earthquakes, tidal waves and hurricanes, they use such terms as "biocide" or "ecocide." An easy scenario for eventual suicide is provided by imagining what would happen if the three fourths of mankind represented by underdeveloped countries were to squander natural resources at the same rate (in per capita terms) as, for example, the United States or the Western European countries. The answer of a Brazilian delegate at a United Nations conference on the environment: "There would be so much carbon, sulphur and nitrogen dioxide that mankind would be pushed toward extinction." [24]

In the meantime, the burdens of present pollution—as with the costs of unemployment and inflation—fall disproportionately upon the poor in all countries. For them there is rarely any escape to air-conditioned, water-filtered, soundproofed homes, or recreation areas of natural beauty and safety. For them, the ecocrises of filth in air, water, and land—often accompanied by congestion, noise, and insect and rodent infestation—are routinized parts of the environment to which they must try to adapt.

The most concentrated pollution, however, is felt in "modern" factories and mines. The Toxic Substances Strategy Committee, an interagency group set up by President Carter in 1977, reported in 1979 that "more than 100,000 workers were believed to die each year as a result of physical and chemical hazards at work and that the occupational exposure to cancer causing agents was a factor in an estimated 20 to 38 percent of all cancers." [25] In many cases, as with coal dust and asbestos, the physical cause of the trouble is well known to most people, but the companies involved have long succeeded in avoiding the extra costs—and diminished profits—involved in safety equipment. In other cases, where new chemical and other materials are introduced, little or no testing is done in advance and the first evidence of the damage done is the death of the workers. Thus the supermodern workplace may not only depress human energy and aspirations, as shown earlier in this chapter, but may also become a graveyard for the workers themselves.

MORE NUCLEAR POISON

> As a physician, I contend that nuclear technology threatens life on our planet with extinction. If present trends continue, the air we breathe, the food we eat, and the water we drink will soon be contaminated with enough radioactive pollutants to pose a potential health hazard far greater than any plague humanity has ever experienced.
>
> DR. HELEN CALDICOTT [26]

For the country as a whole nuclear radiation is the most poisonous pollutant.

It comes in three forms: *alpha particles,* which can penetrate only short distances into matter, but when coming into contact with a living body cell, can burst through the cell wall and do very serious damage; *beta particles,* which can penetrate much further than alphas; and *gamma particles,* which are like X rays and have very deep penetrating power. Any of these particles injures people by ionizing—that is, altering the electrical charge of the atoms and molecules in body cells. As at Hiroshima and Nagasaki, these particles can cause almost instant death. Even very small doses can produce cell changes that produce cancer after a latency period of twelve to forty years, or effect genetic mutations that may not be manifested for a few generations. But in recent decades this natural radiation has faded into insignificance in comparison with the flood levels brought about by so-called "advanced" technology.

A small amount of natural radiation reaches the earth in the form of ultraviolet rays from the sun and cosmic rays from outer space (most of which is filtered out by the outer atmosphere's ozone layer) and radioactive substances in some soils.

For a long time many people used to think that the only nuclear danger stemmed from atomic explosions, whether for testing purposes or actual war. From this viewpoint, there was no peril in the "peaceful uses of atomic energy." More recently, with growing popular education on the subject, it has become increasingly clear that in both the production of nuclear bombs and in the use of atomic energy to produce electricity, dangerous amounts of radiation are emitted at every stage:

1. *Mining.* The mining of uranium produces radioactive dust and radon, a still more dangerous radioactive gas.

2. *Milling.* The grinding, crushing, and chemical treatment of uranium ore produces waste ore called "tailings," which contain radioactive materials that last for thousands of years. In the last thirty years about 100 million tons have accumulated in the American Southwest alone.

3. *Enrichment.* To get fissionable uranium 235, enrichment plants must further refine the uranium ore. This also leaves radioactive tailings.

4. *Fuel fabrication.* The enriched uranium is then converted into small pellets, which are placed in long fuel rods. At this stage workers are exposed to gamma radiation from the enriched fuel.

5. *Nuclear reactors.* When operating properly, the reactors throw off large amounts of radioactive isotopes that may last thousands of years. Ordinary repairs subject workers to serious radiation dangers; for this purpose transient employees willing to expose themselves to high risks are customarily hired. Beyond ordinary repairs, major breakdowns have been frequent. The risks are so great that private companies in the United States refused to operate reactors until the government agreed to assume the major financial responsibilities for compensating people hurt by accidents.

6. *Nuclear waste.* Both nuclear reactors and the building of atomic bombs produce intensely radioactive spent fuels in liquid or solid form, in such "low level" wastes as contaminated articles of clothing, decommissioned plant components, and by-products given off through "routine emissions" of diluted liquids and gases. By 1979 there were 74

million gallons of high-level liquid wastes from military reactors in storage tanks. Many of these wastes boil spontaneously and continuously and will continue doing this for thousands of years. Leakages have already occurred in many places. No scientists, political leaders, or corporation executives have developed any foolproof plan for handling these indestructible wastes. I suspect it might be impossible to do so.

7. *Decommissioning.* After twenty to thirty years, every nuclear reactor becomes too radioactive to repair or maintain. It must then be "decommissioned" by disassembly, through remote control or burial under tons of earth or concrete to become a radioactive mausoleum for thousands of years.

Over the years, various government agencies interested in promoting nuclear power invented the idea of a "safe" level of radiation. But when investigations of low-dose ionizing radiation revealed that levels of radiation lower than those permitted were causing cancer, government agencies attempted to suppress the findings. Scientists are now coming to realize that there is no such thing as a "safe" level. One reason is that a single radioactive atom may initiate damage to a cell or gene. More important, *the effects of radiation are cumulative.* "If all Americans," observes two experts, "were annually exposed to the officially allowable dose of 170 millirems of radiation (the equivalent of about six chest X rays a year) over and above the background levels, there would be an increase of 32,000 to 300,000 deaths from cancer each year."[27] Indeed, the effects of any long series of exposures—whether from mining, milling, enrichment, fuel fabrication, nuclear reactors, nuclear waste, or decommissioning—can be the same as a very large dose all at once.

Then there is the military connection. In visiting India during the mid- and late 1970s, I learned that India's plans for nuclear energy plants were clearly based—despite official denials—on the fact that such plants would provide the Indian military with the materials for enlarging their nuclear bomb capability. The same motive, I found, inspired many other Third World countries to build nuclear energy plants, usually with equipment lacking many of the safety devices used in the First World countries of their origin. But at that time I failed to note the equally intimate connection in the United States between nuclear energy and the growing stockpile of atomic bombs. I operated on the impression that only "breeder reactors" produced the plutonium used in atomic bombs.

More recently, however, the American Electric Power Institute and Britain's Atomic Energy Authority have admitted for the first time that the spent fuel rods from the currently operating nuclear reactors are "plutonium mines."[28] This means that all the many countries building nuclear reactors can rather quickly follow India's example; and Pakistan seems to be already doing so. Even if not used for this purpose, plutonium is extremely deadly; if uniformly distributed, one pound could produce lung cancer in every person on earth. A by-product of plutonium is a still more deadly chemical with the strange name "americum," which is now used industrially in smoke detectors. If one of these is burned or, when defective, thrown on a dump, the radiation will quickly migrate into the air or the soil and enter human bodies through breath or food. When the new "fast breeder reactors" (now being planned in many countries) come into operation, the stockpiles of plutonium and americum will grow much larger.

The breakdown at Three Mile Island in 1979 gave the impression that the greatest threat in nuclear power plants is the possibility of a "meltdown" or "melt-through-to-China syndrome." Another equally terrifying possibility seems to have been overlooked—that *all reactors, both civilian and military, are potential neutron bombs.* To detonate any of them, terrorist groups or enemy agents would need nothing more than a conventional bomb. Thus, if there were a non-nuclear war in those parts of Western Europe now using nuclear-based electricity, the conventional bombing of power plants would release catastrophic nuclear devastation. As for the United States, it looks as though the Pentagon and the nuclear power industry together have built a veritable archipelago of potential enemy bases across the country.

As the antinuclear movement slows down the construction of nuclear power plants, the Establishment's reaction is to use such tactical defeats as an opportunity for forward marching on three fronts: getting huge Federal subsidies for a "synfuel" program for the 1980s, which itself would be a new source of large-scale pollution; shifting to coal for electricity generation on the condition that antipollution controls on coal burning and mining are relaxed; and sponsoring an Energy Mobilization Board which—in the words of Anthony Lewis—would have the power to "pre-empt the functions of local zoning or health or safety boards from Maine to Texas." [29] Such a board, of course, would be able to override local objections to new nuclear power plants and dumping grounds for radioactive waste. Thus, a friendly fascist federalism would come through new concentrations of regulatory (or de-regulatory) power as well as through the use of federal aid as a club.

MORE JUNK AND DISSERVICES

Since the GNP measures the total output of goods and services (and this terminology seems inescapable), one may be forgiven if he or she assumes that all goods are good and all services useful.

Nonetheless, a major side effect of capitalism's spectacular increase in the quantity of output has been a widespread degradation of quality that renders many goods into junk. The General Motors policy of "planned obsolescence" (also referred to as "dynamic," "progressive," "built-in" or "artificial" obsolescence) has been widely followed by the major manufacturers not only of automobiles but also of furniture, household equipment, housing, television, and radio. In their internal communications engineers and business people speak of "product death dates," the "time to failure" and "the point of required utility." [30] The overriding principle is to promote replacement markets by producing products designed for the junk heap. For one GM chairman, who calculated the profits obtained from this principle, planned obsolescence was "another word for progress." The other American motor companies, unfortunately, have been equally addicted to this type of progress.

Death-dating of products and their parts, unfortunately, is not the only form of quality degradation. Many household goods are fire hazards, shock hazards, or sources of dangerous radiation. Almost any automobile is an instrument of potential destruction, while many are death traps. The annual death toll from automobile accidents in the United States exceeds fifty thousand, while the number of people injured ranges between four and five million. Some of this carnage, of course, is due to bad driving, drunken driving, or sheer accident, if not even attempted suicide or homicide. Yet, much of this could be avoided through better braking systems, bumpers, body construction, and safety devices. The resulting economic loss, little of which hits the auto makers, was estimated at over $30 billion for 1974 alone.

Quality is also degraded by what modern market researchers call "psychological obsolescence"—that is, wearing the product out in the owner's mind. The pioneers in doing this have been the producers of women's clothes. It has become embedded in the industrial designing and redesigning of most automobiles, and the entire gamut of home furnishings, appliances, and communication equipment.

"Functional obsolescence" degrades existing products by producing new ones that do the same job differently, more quickly, or in a manner that appears to be better. Much of this appears to be genuine progress—as with safe, swift and quiet jet planes, easy-to-see television, high-fidelity recordings, and stereophonic equipment. Yet much of this is carried to excess—as in the case of supersonic civil aircraft, three-channel stereo, and kitchen equipment with huge control boards connecting to a variety of gadgets that are prone to breakdown and have doubtful utility. In the fields of producers' durable equipment and machinery, where performance standards and physical durability are strictly monitored by powerful producers' organizations, functional obsolescence is a major driving force. Indeed, according to Schumpeter and other economists, it provides the central dynamics of capitalism. It affords more profitability and productive capacity to boost the makers and users of the new equipment. The side effects are something else. In addition to shifting the balance between human labor and fossil fuels and contributing to the wastes of both, some of the new productive capacity is dangerous to life, limb, lung, eyes, and brain. This is particularly true not only of high-speed cutting and stamping equipment, but even more so of the toxic liquids, gases, and solids ushered in by the new technological revolution. A 1968 report by the U.S. Surgeon General revealed that 65 percent of industrial workers are exposed to toxic materials or harmful levels of noise or vibration. Only 25 percent of these workers were safeguarded in any way from these hazards.[31] Since 1968, with the uncontrolled introduction of new materials and machinery, the situation has not improved.

As durable goods have become more transient, such "non-durables" as meat, vegetables, and fruit have been made more durable by processing that gives them long "shelf life" in cans, bottles, jars, plastic wrappers, and freezers. "Even raw food products today are engineered commodities, designed to meet the steel grip of harvesting machinery or survive the long haul from Texas, California and Florida fields to eastern cities. Using genetics to harden fruits and vegetables, chemicals to ripen them artificially, and treated waxes and glosses to give them longer life in grocery bins, taste has been lost along the way." Dozens of natural varieties have disappeared from ordinary food stores, along with many natural nutrients that are not, or cannot be, replaced by injecting artificial nutrients. Food processors claim it is up to the consumers to prove that one or another of the many new chemical additives are dangerous. If the Food and Drug Administration had as much political courage as was exhibited by the Surgeon General on the health hazards of cigarette smoking, many food packages, and not only saccharin-saturated diet foods, would have to include a sentence: "The FDA warns that eating this stuff may be dangerous to your health." Jim Hightower, a political activist and campaigner against the food conglomerates, explains the situation this way: "Nutrition has not been deliberately trimmed by the food firms that dominate the market, but it has been advertently lost . . . It leaves you eating the image advertising, the synthetic nutrients, the chemical preservatives, the artificial flavors and the high price of manufactured foods—the inevitable results of oligopoly."[32]

In the pharmaceutical industry, FDA approval is required *before* many new drugs can be marketed. Yet such approval is often given on the basis of tests made by the manufacturers themselves or testing labs hired by them. Under these circumstances information on dangerous side effects may be suppressed. Thus in the case of MER/29, an anticholesterol drug, both laboratory tests and negative reports from doctors indicated such side effects as hair loss, cataracts, and blindness. Only after the drug had been in use for some time was it finally revealed that, under instructions from the company's vice-president, the laboratory directors had deliberately falsified the test results. One thing the drug companies also get away with is extensive manipulation of doctors. Dr. A. Dale Console, former medical director of E.R. Squibb and Sons, has testified that they do this through such promotional techniques as:

1. A "barrage of irrelevant facts [which the physician] has neither the time, inclination, nor frequently the expert knowledge to examine critically . . ."
2. The hard-sell tactics of detail men who follow the maxim "If you can't convince them, confuse them . . . "
3. Testimonials "used not only to give apparent substance to the advertising and promotion of apparently worthless products, but also to extend the indications of effective drugs beyond the range of their reality." [33]

These techniques succeed. In "serving" their patients, many doctors prescribe brand-name drugs that may cost ten to thirty times as much as identical drugs ordered by their chemical name. But medicine is only an outstanding case of private and public services where "more" may not be better—and may even be wasteful or dangerous. According to Dr. Richard Kunnes, at least one hundred thousand unnecessary hysterectomies (around 40 percent of the total) are performed every year.[34] Similar ratios have been estimated for tonsillectomies, mastectomies and thyroidectomies. In terms of genuine social accounting the unnecessary removal of a part of one's body is clearly a "disservice."

11

Subverting Democratic Machinery

> No truly sophisticated proponent of repression would be stupid enough to shatter the facade of democratic institutions.
>
> MURRAY B. LEVIN [1]

> It is the irony of democracy that the responsibility for the survival of liberal democratic values depends on elites, not masses.
>
> THOMAS R. DYE AND HARMON ZIEGLER [2]

IN *THE COMMUNIST MANIFESTO OF 1848* Karl Marx paid tribute to the "colossal productive forces" created by the industrial capitalists. He paid less attention to the greatest social invention of all time: the democratic machinery of constitutional government.

During the twentieth century, the improvement of democratic machinery has provided new opportunities for ordinary people to take part in the processes of government. Through democratic institutions people can hope to combat exploitation and discrimination, make government and business more responsive to popular interests, and win expanded, albeit grudging, recognition of human rights. In the United States, the largest and richest of the First World democracies, these institutions include:

A central government in which power is disbursed among three separate branches (President, Congress and Supreme Court)
A federal system of fifty separately elected state governments
Strong traditions of local government in over 80,000 cities, counties, and school boards
Competitive political parties
A Bill of Rights that protects freedoms of speech, press, assembly, and other civil liberties, together with legislation to recognize or enforce civil rights
Military and police forces subject to civilian control

In the constitutional democracies, capitalist establishments have tended to use the democratic machinery as a device for sidetracking opposition, incorporating serious opponents into the junior and contingent ranks, and providing the information—the "feedback"—on the trouble spots that required quick attention. As pressures were exerted from below, the leaders of these establishments consistently—in the words of Yvonne Karp's commentary on the British ruling elites—"allowed concessions to be wrung from them, ostensibly against their will but clearly in their own long term interests." Eleanor Marx, Karl Marx's youngest daughter, described their strategy (often opposed by the more backward corporate types) in these pungent words: "to give a little in order to gain a lot." [3] Throughout the First World the Ultra-Rich and the Corporate Overseers have been in a better position than anyone else to use the democratic machinery. They have the money that is required for electoral campaigns, legislative lobbying, and judicial suits. They have enormous technical expertise at their beck and call. They have staying power.

Hence it is that—as Dye, Ziegler, and a host of political scientists have demonstrated—that the upper-class elites of America have the greatest attachment to constitutional democracy. They are the abiding activists in the use of electoral, legislative, and judicial machinery at all levels of government. It is their baby. Ordinary people—called the masses by Dye and Ziegler—tend to share this perception. The democratic machinery belongs to them, "the powers that be," not to ordinary people. It is not their baby.

What will happen if more ordinary people should try to take over this baby and actually begin to make it their own? How would the elites respond if the masses began to ask the elites to give much more and gain much less—particularly when, under conditions of capitalist stagflation and shrinking world power, the elites have less to give. Some radical commentators claim that the powers that be would use their power to follow the example of the classic fascists and destroy the democratic machinery. I agree with Murray Levin that this would be stupid. I see it also as highly unlikely. No First World Establishment is going to shatter machinery that, with a certain amount of tinkering and a little bit of luck, can be profitably converted into a sophisticated instrument of repression.

Indeed, the tinkering has already started. Some of it is being undertaken by people for whom the Constitution is merely a scrap of paper, a set of judicial decisions, and a repository of rhetoric and precedents to be used by their high-paid lawyers and public relations people. Some of it is being perpetrated by presidents and others who have taken formal oaths to "preserve, protect and defend the Constitution of the United States." Sometimes knowingly, often unwittingly, both types of people will spare no pains in preserving those parts of the written or unwritten constitution that protect the rights of "corporate persons" while undermining, attacking, or perverting those parts of the Constitution that promote the welfare and liberties of the great majority of all other persons.

Some may call this the normal operations of modern capitalism. I call it subversion—and set forth the logic of this subversion in the following pages.

INTEGRATING THE SEPARATE BRANCHES

Integration of governmental agencies and coordination of authority may be called the keystone principle of fascist administration.
LAWRENCE DENNIS [4]

Although there have always been ups and downs in the relationship between the president, the Congress and the Supreme Court, the general tendency has been toward a strengthening of the presidential network. This is particularly true in foreign affairs.

Strangely, the first step toward greater domination of the Congress and the courts is to achieve greater mastery of the bureaucracy. This means tighter control of all appointments, including the review by White House staff of subordinate-level appointments in the various departments. It means tighter control of the federal budget, with traditional budgetary control expanded to include both policy review and efficiency analysis. In his effort to master the bureaucracy, President Nixon and his aides went very far in subjecting various officials to quasilegal wiretaps. President Carter broke new ground by having his economic advisers review the decisions of regulatory agencies that impose on corporations the small additional costs of environmental or consumer protection. Both presidents used their close associations with big-business lobbyists to bring recalcitrant bureaucrats into line and to see to it that they follow the "president's program" in dealing with the Congress or the courts.

Throughout American history wags have suggested that the U.S. Congress has been the best that money could buy. This joke expresses popular wisdom on how far big money can go in "owning" or "renting" members of the House and the Senate. In the present era of megabuck money, however, the old wisdom is out of date. With enough attention to "congressional reform" and the cost-effectiveness of campaign and lobbying expenditures, the top elites of the modern Establishment could buy a "much better" Congress.

Back during the New Deal and Fair Deal periods, a major impetus to congressional reform came from those who felt that a reorganized Congress would be more amenable to the leadership of a progressive

President. In those days and by those standards, congressional streamlining was seen as a major step toward more rational economic and social planning.

Today, the more prominent proposals for congressional streamlining are based on the bureaucratic principles of highly specialized division of labor and hierarchic control of the specialized units. Thus Professor Robert L. Peabody of Johns Hopkins University suggests that—like the Chase Manhattan Bank or General Motors—the committees of the House of Representatives be unified by a two-tiered structure. The top tier is to be shared by two special leadership committees, one on budget and one on agenda. Beneath them, on the second tier, there would be eight standing committees to take the place of twenty-one at present. And beneath these, there would be a maximum of fifty to seventy subcommittees—much less than the current 128. Above all, the work of each committee member would be more narrowly circumscribed than ever before, since no member would be allowed to serve on more than one committee and two subcommittees of that committee. With a structure of this type the party leadership of the House could become a more powerful force than ever before in subordinating the entire body to the interests of the Establishment's higher levels.[5] Indeed, the proposal is very close to the reorganization plan imposed by General deGaulle on the French Chamber of Deputies during the transition from the Fourth to the Fifth Republic.

A major part of the Peabody plan has already come into being. Some years ago President Nixon signed the Congressional Budget and Impoundment Control Act, which established a budget committee in both the House and the Senate and a joint House-Senate budget office. Setting up an assembly-line procedure on budgetary matters, the new law "tilts" the appropriations and revenue process toward more conservatively defined balanced budgets. The most significant aspect of the "reform"—although far from obvious to casual observers—was that it concentrated budgetary power in the hands of the members of Congress most sensitive to the needs and desires of the country's most powerful business interests. With such arrangements, presidential impounding of appropriations for social programs could be carried out with the prior approval of a cooperative Congress. More important, prior restraint on such appropriations could now be exercised through the instrumentality of a "budget ceiling" set forth in a concurrent resolution to be formulated by the budget committees of each house with the help of the Congressional Budget Office. Thus far budget ceilings have invariably been set at a level consistent with the maintenance of high official unemployment, thus squeezing many social programs that might otherwise have reduced unemployment and tilted toward higher wages and somewhat smaller profit margins.

But it is not the White House alone, however, that wields the rubber stamp or controls the transmission belt. Business interests may be equally important—particularly when they choose to operate directly, rather than through the Chief Executive Network. Indeed, the streamlined rubber-stamp machinery of Congress is susceptible to being used either to force certain actions on a reluctant White House (as occasionally happens with expanded military expenditures) or to unravel executive decisions regarded as insufficiently responsive to macrobusiness interests, as when congressional opposition was mobilized in the Senate to force the Nixon administration to back down on its earlier proposals for a guaranteed minimum income under Daniel P. Moynihan's Family Assistance Program. The extension of these tendencies as part of the processes of oligarchic integration certifies that the major gatekeepers of a more coordinated Congress may become important members of the Establishment in their own right.

But in neither corporation nor complex is a subordinate unit—whether subsidiary or regional office—expected to be merely a rubber stamp. Within certain flexible restraints, it is supposed to exercise initiative of its own. This is the kind of initiative that Albert Speer enjoyed—and promoted—as Hitler's minister of armaments and war production. Similarly, integration at the Establishment's higher levels requires a certain amount of free-wheeling initiative within the House and Senate. Every major group at the Establishment's highest levels already has *avant garde* representatives, proponents, and defenders among the members, committees and subcommittees of Congress. Thus at some date, earlier or later, we may expect new investigatory committees of Congress working closely with the major intelligence and police networks and handling their blacklists more professionally than those developed during the days of Joseph McCarthy.* We may expect special investigations of monopoly, transnational corporations, international trade, education, science and technology, civil liberties, and freedom of the press. But instead of being controlled by unreliable liberal reformers, they would be initiated and dominated by a new breed of professional "technopols" dedicated to the strengthening of oligarchic corporations, providing greater subsidization of the supranationals, strengthening the international capitalist market, filling "gaps" in military science and technology, extending the conformist aspects of the educational system, routinizing police-state restraints on civil liberties, and engineering the restraint of the press by judicial action. A small idea of what is involved here is provided by Professor Alexander Bickel's 1971 brief before the Supreme Court in the case of the Justice Department's effort to prevent publication of the

---

* See "Precision Purging" in "The Ladder of Terror" (chapter 14).

famous "Pentagon Papers." The Yale University law professor proposed the establishment of clear guidelines for prior restraint of the press by the executive branch. Here is a challenging task for imaginative lawyers —particularly if they work for strategically placed members of Congress eager to find a loophole in the old Constitutional proviso against the making of laws that abridge the freedom of the press.

In the winter of 1936, "the most liberal four members of the Supreme Court resigned and were replaced by surprisingly unknown lawyers who called President Windrip by his first name." This is part of how Sinclair Lewis—in his book *It Can't Happen Here*—projected his vision of how "it" *could* suddenly happen here.

Though a new "it" would happen more slowly, a decisive group of four or more justices can still be placed on the Court by sequential appointment during the slow trip down the road to serfdom. During this trip the black-robed defenders of the Constitution would promote the toughening of federal criminal law. They would offer judicial support for electronic surveillance, "no-knock entry," preventive detention, the suspension of *habeas corpus,* the validation of mass arrests, the protection of the country against "criminals and foreign agents," and the maintenance of "law and order." The Court would at first be activist, aggressively reversing previous Court decisions and legitimating vastly greater discretion by the expanding national police complex. Subsequently, it would probably revert to the older tradition of *stare decisis*—that is, standing by precedents. The result would be the elimination of opportunities for juridical self-defense by individuals and dissident organizations while maintaining orderly judicial review of major conflicts among components of the oligarchy and the technostructure.

If this slow process of subverting constitutional freedoms should engender protest, the Men in Black may well respond with judicial *jiujitsu.* The administrative reform and reorganization of the judicial system, for example, is needed to overcome backlogs of cases and provide speedier trials. It would require the consolidation of the judicial system, the development of merit systems for judicial employees, the raising of judicial salaries, and stricter standards for outlawing "objectionable" lawyers, all of which poses ample opportunity for undermining legal protection in the name of reform or efficiency.

Judicial approval of new functions for grand juries serves as another example. Historically, federal grand juries were created as a bulwark against the misuse of executive authority. The Fifth Amendment states that a person should not be tried for a serious crime without first being indicted by a grand jury. Thus, a prosecuting attorney's charges would not be sufficient—at least not until upheld by a specially selected jury operating in secret sessions. Historically, grand juries have been widely used to investigate charges of corruption in local government. More recently, they have been set up to investigate political cases under federal criminal laws dealing with subversion and the draft. There have been times when at least twelve federal grand juries were operating simultaneously and using their subpoena power vigorously. Collectively, these may be regarded as "trial runs" which a Supreme Court on the road to friendly fascism would perfect with decisions upholding the wide use of subpoena power by the grand juries and the denial of transcripts to witnesses.

The strong point of a friendly fascist grand jury system is the "Star Chamber" secrecy that could be made operational throughout the fifty states. But this should not obscure the contrapuntal value of a few highly publicized trials. A grand jury indictment can do more than merely set the stage for a showcase trial. It can sort out conflicting evidence in such a way as to induce a self-defeating defense. This can be much more effective than the elaborately contrived "confessions" developed by the Russian secret police in the many purges of Old Bolsheviks. Shrewd and technically expert legal strategies could crucify opponents without allowing them—dead or alive—to be converted into martyrs.

FRIENDLY FASCIST FEDERALISM

> In the name of fiscal survival the entire political base of this city [New York City] has been emasculated and constitutional privileges abridged. Conservative fiscal reform has a clear road.
>
> L. D. SOLOMON [6]

> The suspension of democratic rule in New York City was a fair price to pay for the good wishes of the investment community . . .
>
> ROGER ALCALY [7]

In the holy name of economy and efficiency, the separate existence of the states is ended. The whole country is divided into eight provinces with natural boundaries. One of the most logical of these is the "Metropolitan Province" including Greater New York, Westchester County up to Ossining; Long Island; the strip of Connecticut dependent on New York City; New Jersey, North Delaware, and Pennsylvania as far as Reading and Scranton. Each province is divided into districts, each district into counties and each county into cities and townships.

This is how Sinclair Lewis outlined the new structure of state and local government in *It Can't Happen Here.* In so doing he gave expression to some of the fondest dreams of American political scientists and public administration experts. In one bold stroke he provided both for metropolitan government on a truly large scale and a kind of state government that could facilitate rather than impede efficient federal administration. Doremus Jessup, Lewis's antifascist hero, living in the Vermont hills of District 3 in the Northeastern Province, looked upon all this and conceded that it was "a natural and homogeneous Division" of the country.

But this was before the era of federal aid, truly large-scale urban sprawl, and successive fashions in federalism. In the many decades since Lewis wrote his many novels on American life, the institutions of state and local government have changed substantially. At the same time, new techniques of decentralized administration have grown up as indisposable instruments of central control. In the corporations and the complex, the primary instrument is financial control through budgets, investments, and lines of credit. In the American government the primary instrument is federal aid, loans and guarantees, some given to state governments, some sidestepping the states and given directly to cities.

The new road to serfdom would unquestionably involve a strengthening of federal controls over state and local government. This would involve basic changes in the labyrinth of categorical federal aid programs which expanded during the "creative federalism" of Presidents Kennedy and Johnson. The very multiplicity of aid channels and strings tended to weaken the strength of any one string. The first steps toward overcoming this weakness were taken by the move toward block grants under the "new federalism" of President Nixon. Federal revenue sharing could go still further in this direction. If the federal government is to give a few huge sums to each state and to many cities, this would provide a stick-and-carrot of unprecedented political power. This new form of concentrated power would not be diminished by rhetoric concerning the return of "power to the people." It would probably be augmented by the inclusion in the new federalism of well-selected grants and contracts to private corporations for the conduct of local public functions.

Several institutional changes may also be expected. More vigorous councils of government in metropolitan areas, with greater power to approve aid to central cities, could help to repress any disturbing tendencies on the part of black-controlled central-city governments. Thus would the "white noose around the black ghetto," feared by many black leaders, be applied and tightened. Major federal agencies, moreover, would be expected to "get with it" by delegating greater authority to their regional and local offices. This kind of decentralization for Washington bureaus, already pioneered by the Internal Revenue Service and the Federal Aviation Administration, would provide stronger control at the local level. At the same time managerial logic would call for the expansion of the coordination councils already being set up by the president's Office of Management and Budget to bring together the top officials of federal agencies in each metropolitan area.

As a result of the impact of the 1974–76 recession on New York

City, an entirely new pattern emerged for the suspension of democratic rule at the local level. During the preceding decade or so, the New York City government had financed an expanding volume of local public works and social services by the large-scale flotation of city securities. In this effort, the elected city officials were encouraged and supported by the commercial banks and investment banking firms, which succeeded in steadily raising the interest rates they received on their tax-exempt securities. By 1975, with inflation pushing municipal costs upward and recession pushing munipical revenue downward, the city faced default on its current obligations. After a temporary period of uncertainty, the assets of the largest bondholders were saved by the State's creation of a Municipal Assistance Corporation ("Big Mac") to refinance the securities, and a Financial Emergency Control Board to seek balance in the city's budget through large-scale reductions in municipal services and employment. On the basis of these two steps, which in effect replaced local officials with top officials of the banking and business community, the Ford administration extended a three-year loan to the city under conditions that reinforced the bankers' insistence on an enforced policy of "hard times" for the middle and lower classes and possible prospects for higher profit rates for big business.

"If New York is able to offer reduced social services without disorder," observed a local publisher, L. D. Solomon, "it would prove that it can be done on the most difficult environment in the nation." [8] The "it," of course, is not merely the shifting of income from the majority of the people to a small minority, but the subversion of locally elected government: New York today; Boston, Chicago, Detroit, and Los Angeles a little later. The "later" may well arrive by the time that, with the next dip in the business cycle, federal guarantees are provided for municipal bonds on the basis of federally monitored state supervision of all major municipal activities. By that time the popularly elected mayors of America's major cities—many of them black—would be little more than figureheads, pawns, and "fall guys" for the faceless oligarchs controlling municipal finance.

Let it not be thought, however, that a new fascist federalism would be tightly organized. That would hamper the development of local initiative. We might expect, rather, that at the crabgrass roots of suburb-dominated state legislatures, many state governments would assume their old role of serving as laboratories for advanced ideas. One can see many home-grown Hitlers and mute, inglorious Mussolinis developing the arts of police state repression in California and Ohio, in Philadelphia, Minneapolis, and New Orleans. One can see some of the largest and most prestigious state-supported universities among the first victims. One can see state and local grand juries indicting the victims rather than the instigators of brutality and repression.

Walter Lippmann was recently asked whether he saw a danger of fascism in America. "There will be a danger," he responded. "I don't think there will be fascism on a national scale—the country's too big for national fascism. But I think there will be local fascism. In local communities, majorities or strong minorities will rise up if they think they're threatened. And they'll use violence ruthlessly." [9] It is clear that Lippmann was thinking of unfriendly fascism at the local level. This could serve as an important ingredient of *friendly* fascism for the country as a whole.

COMMUNITY CARNIVALS

The medieval carnival was a festivity before Lent when, with unrestrained dancing and gaiety, Catholic villagers said farewell to the eating of meat (in Latin: *carne vale*). In Brazil the minifascist militarists have exploited the carnival as an instrument of social control. All year long, the poor blacks in the *flavellas* surrounding Rio expend tremendous energies preparing their special costumes, songs, and dances. During carnival week they vie with each other for the honor of a few paltry prizes. The merchants and hotel owners cash in on the money spent by tourists who come to enjoy the splendid spectacle. In the ardors of festival preparation and then in the dancing itself, the poor people expend more energies than would be needed for a social revolution. This is the major benefit to the junta.

During the centuries of the Tokugawa *shogunate* in Japan all-year-round control of villagers was facilitated by five-man groups among the peasantry. Under Japanese fascism this system was restored in stronger form. Starting in 1930, a network of neighborhood groups enabled the central government to reach every household through a face-to-face hierarchy of command.[10]

During the 1960s the Democratic administration developed a unique combination of local participation and carnival. The avowed aim was to abolish poverty and raise the quality of life in slum and ghetto neighborhoods. The real objective, as Francis Fox Piven and Richard A. Cloward have shown, was to integrate into the Democratic party the large numbers of black people who had been streaming into the nation's central cities. This was accomplished by a new kind of pork barrel—a miscellaneous set of projects to be developed in poor communities "with the maximum feasible participation of residents of the areas and members of the groups served." Thousands of jobs were involved—a small number of high-paying jobs for "poverty professionals" and a larger number of low-paying jobs for the poor. The participation machinery led to neighborhood elections, advisory committees, frantic debate, demonstrations, confrontations.

As in the more traditional style of carnival, the frantic activity always bordered on violence—sometimes crossing the border. Unlike the traditional carnival, the festivities took place all year. And instead of preceding meatless months, they celebrated the ceaseless apportioning of federal pork.

For a truly successful friendly fascism, a revival of such programs would seem essential. Otherwise, the establishment would lack roots among the underclass. Aggressive organizers in the black ghettos might lead attacks on the faceless oligarchy itself. Better to invest some small change in neighborhood-uplift activities that will co-opt the more vigorous leaders of neighborhood organizations, divert the attention of their followers, and incidentally provide good jobs for certified professionals at the junior and contingent levels of the Establishment. The next round, however, could scarcely repeat the "war against poverty" in accordance with the model of the 1960s. More likely, it would come in the form of picayune public employment programs established under the banner of "full employment" but designed, rather, to take the edge off sustained unemployment in the central cities.

CONTRAPUNTAL PARTY HARMONY

> If a nation wishes, it can have both free elections and slavery.
>
> GARRY WILLS [11]

> The average American is just like the child in the family.
>
> PRESIDENT RICHARD M. NIXON [12]

If friendly fascism arrives in America, the faceless oligarchy would have little or nothing to gain from a single-party system. Neither an elitist party along Bolshevik lines nor a larger mass party like the Nazis would be necessary. With certain adjustments the existing "two party plus" system could be adapted to perform the necessary functions.

The first function would be to legitimate the new system. With all increases in domestic repression, no matter how slow or indirect, reassurance would be needed for both middle classes and masses. Even in the past, national elections have provided what Murray Edelman has described as "symbolic reassurance." According to Edelman, elections serve to "quiet resentments and doubts about particular political acts, reaffirm belief in the fundamental rationality and democratic character of the system, and thus fix conforming habits of future behavior." [13]

Second, political-party competition would serve as a buffer protecting faceless oligarchs from direct attack. This would not merely be a matter of politics—as when the slogan of "ballots not bullets" is used to encourage the alienated to take part in electoral processes. It would be a question of objectives. The more that people are encouraged to "throw the rascals out," the more their attention is diverted from other rascals that are not up for election: the leaders of macrobusiness, the ultra-rich, and the industrial-military-police-communications-health-welfare complex. Protests channeled completely into electoral processes tend to be narrowed down, filtered, sterilized, and simplified so that they challenge neither empire nor oligarchy.

Last but not least, the competing political parties would play a distinctive role in the complex processes of policy formulation by the ruling elites. The old-fashioned radical or Marxist is apt to say that the Republican and Democratic parties have always been the same. Under fascism, by this line of reasoning, if they are not liquidated altogether they would survive as Tweedledom and Tweedledee, with no difference between them.

This viewpoint, however, misjudges the nature of large-scale oligarchy and the necessity for creative policymaking. As I see it, competing parties that are *really* different *in certain respects* are essential for both the transition to a friendly fascist regime and the maintenance of its power. This goes beyond the provision of symbolic reassurance and a buffer zone, the two points already covered. It goes right to the heart of oligarchic policymaking.

According to Ferdinand Lundberg, the United States has a single party, the Property Party, with two subdivisions, the Republicans and the Democrats.[14] Picking this idea up, G. William Domhoff declares that "a Property Party with two branches is one of the neatest devices ever stumbled upon by rich men determined to stay on top." This view underestimates the factionalism within the "two branches." It also ignores the smaller discords created by minor parties and by nonparty political movements.

There have been many long-standing differences between the Republicans and the Democrats. The Republican party has long been the favorite party of big business; the Democratic party the haven of millionaires without full acceptance in the "upper crust." The farmer's appeal has been stronger among the large numbers of small-town, old-style businessmen and get-rich-quick professionals. The latter has provided more leadership opportunities for activists among ethnic and religious minorities, trade unions, and the lowest income groups. Each has enjoyed substantial sectional monopolies—the former in certain rock-ribbed Republican sectors of the Midwest and New England, the latter in the formerly "Solid South" and equally solid central-city districts. In terms of specific policies, there have been discernible (although partially blurred) tendencies toward these kinds of policy differences:

Republicans	Democrats
Higher interest rates and "tight" money	Lower interest rates and "loose" money
Protectionism and commodity agreements in foreign trade	Freer trade and commodity agreements
Higher levels of tolerated unemployment	Lower levels of tolerated unemployment
Less expansion in economic policy	More expansion policies of economic growth
Slow growth of welfare state	More rapid growth of welfare state
Modulated military expenditures	Larger military expenditures

The blurring of these tendencies is largely due to the power of the subdivisions or branches *within* each party. The Republicans have traditionally been the home of the so-called "northeastern corporate liberals," who join with liberal Democrats in developing policies of corporate state planning and welfare expansion. The Democrats have been the home of conservative Southerners who join with Republican conservative in holding up welfare-state reforms, and with Democratic and Republican liberals in advancing internationalist foreign policies. Republicans in the White House concentrate on trying to unify their own party. Because of Southern recalcitrance on racial issues, Democrats in the White House have a harder task in doing this: they go further in developing bipartisan foreign policies.

Despite these complex blurrings, the basic underlying difference relates to *the overhead costs of maintaining state-supported capitalism.* The Republicans express more clearly the views of business interests that see no reason to have the state assume greater obligations than those that are gradually forced upon it. The Democrats give better expression to the farsighted minority of businessmen who favor more rapid increases in welfare, military expenditures, and imperial commitments. The Republicans can be stubbornly stingy, because they know they can rely on the Democrats to pull them forward more rapidly. The latter can make more expansive gestures because they know they can rely on the former to modulate the pace of expansion.

During the early period of transition from national to international capitalism, Democratic leadership built up the "free world empire" and conducted two Asiatic wars. In turn, Republican leadership withdrew American troops from both Korea and Vietnam, cooled down the cold war and organized the politics-and-business-based détente and rapprochment with the Soviet Union and China. This alternation has expressed a clear political logic: neither party could have performed so well the task undertaken by the other. By the same token, the logic of the new authoritarianism points to a new role for a Democratic White House during much of the 1980s: leadership in rebuilding the "Free World" through closer cooperation with the socialist parties of Western Europe and Japan and the creation of an American-led complex with many junior and senior partners in the Third World. The crises and traumas of this transition period can be surmounted only through more stringent national and international controls than most Republican leaders by themselves are likely to negotiate, and higher overhead costs of system maintenance than the more old-fashioned Republicans may willingly accept. Thus, in their international achievements the Nixon and Ford administrations left behind a void that has beckoned invitingly to Democratic successors. On the other hand, absorbing stable communist regimes into the world capitalist economy may require the kind of "doing business with the communists" and business-based détente that might be more feasible under a Republican return to power.

In this strange dialectic of discord, minor political movements also have roles to play. The political supporters of George Wallace of Alabama—whether operating as a minority within the Democratic party or moving outside into third-party status—forced both parties to pay more attention to alienated white workers and the lower-middle classes. Ironically, they also served to counterbalance the more progressive forces within the democratic party and force stricter conformity with big-business interests. A still more pungent irony is provided by the role of left-wing splinter parties. As in the past, they provide feedback on mass discontents and formulate reforms and *avant garde* proposals that will be picked up in modified form by the Democrats. This function, in turn, can be fulfilled only if there are enough protests and resistance movements, like the peace movement of the late 1960s, or popular demonstrations, like the black riots and the welfare-rights agitations, to convince the Establishment of the political wisdom in paying slightly higher overhead costs for system maintenance.

UNION-BUSTING AND THE SLOW MELTDOWN

I believe leaders of the business community, with few exceptions, have chosen to wage a one-sided class war today in this country.

DOUGLAS FRASER [15]

Gone are the not-so-good days of blackjack and machine guns . . . Enter the slick smiling lawyer, armed with the latest strategies to subvert workers' legal rights to collective bargaining.

NANCY STIEFEL [16]

In their march to power in Germany, Italy, and Japan, the classic fascists were not stupid enough to concentrate on subverting democratic machinery alone. They aimed their main attack, rather, against the non-government organizations most active in using and improving that machinery; namely, the labor movement and the political parties rooted in it. In Germany, where these organizations seemed immensely powerful, many German leaders thought that even with Adolf Hitler as chancellor, fascism could make little headway. They underestimated the Nazis and their Big Business backers. "All at once," observed Karl Polanyi, the historian, "the tremendous industrial and political organizations of labor and other devoted upholders of constitutional freedom would melt away, and minute fascist forces would brush aside what seemed until then the overwhelming strength of democratic governments, parties and trade unions." [17]

In most First World democracies a slow meltdown has already started. As I pointed out in "The Take-Off toward a New Corporate Society" (chapter 2), conglomerate or transnational corporations expand beyond the scope of any labor unions yet invented. In the more narrow spheres where labor organization is well established, the unions have usually been absorbed into the Establishment's junior and contingent levels, often becoming instruments for disciplining workers. As the work force has become more educated, sophisticated, and professionalized, many labor leaders have become stuffy bureaucrats, unable to communicate with their members, and terrified at the thought of widespread worker participation in the conduct of union affairs. Some of them have been open practitioners of racism, sexism, and ageism. The media have done their bit by exaggerating the power of organized labor and the extent of labor union racketeering and corruption. The new class of conservative intellectuals, in turn, has launched devastating attacks on labor unions as interferences with the "free market" and as the real villains behind high prices and low productivity. All these factors have contributed to a major loosening of the ties between organized labor and the intellectuals, ties that are quickly replaced by grants, contracts, and favors from foundations and government agencies.

In the Third World countries of dependent fascism, antilabor activity has become much more blatant. There the response to trade unions is vigorous resort to the old-time methods used in Western Europe and America during the nineteenth century: armed union-busters, police and military intervention, machine guns, large-scale arrests, torture, even assassination. In countries like Argentina, Chile, Brazil, South Korea, Taiwan, the Philippines, Zaire, and many others, these measures have proved decisive in attracting transnational investment and keeping wages down. They have also helped beat back the forces of socialism and communism in these countries.

Although First World establishments have generally supported (and often braintrusted) this kind of action in the Third World, I do not foresee them resorting to the same strategies at home. The logic of friendly fascism calls, rather, for a slow and gradual melting away of organized labor and its political influence.

At the outset of the 1980s, major steps in this direction are already under way in the United States. They are being worked out by an impressive array of in-house labor relations staffs in the larger corporations and of out-house consulting firms made up of superslick lawyers, personnel psychologists, and specialists in the conduct of anti-union campaigns. The efforts of these groups are backed up by sectoral, regional, and national trade associations, the U.S. Chamber of Commerce, the National Association of Manufacturers, the Business Roundtable, and a long series of "objective" studies commissioned either by these groups or the new "think tanks" of the Radical Right.[18]

The heat for the meltdown is applied on four major fronts. First, the union-busters operate on the principle of containing labor organization to those places where unions already exist. This requires strenuous efforts to preserve a "union-free environment" in the South, in small towns, and among white-collar, technical, and migratory workers. When efforts are made to extend unionism into one of these areas, the union-busters come in to help the managers conduct psychological warfare. Often, the core of such a campaign is "the mobilization of supervisors as an anti-union organizing committee." Each supervisor may be asked to report back to a consultant, often daily, about the reactions of employees. There may be as many as twenty to twenty-five meetings with each employee during a union campaign. In one successful campaign at Saint Elizabeth's hospital outside of Boston, according to Debra Hauser, the methods used included the discriminatory suspension or firing of five union activists; surveillance, isolation, interrogation and harassment of other pro-union employees; and misrepresentation of the collective bargaining process by top management. "This resulted in the creation of an atmosphere of hysteria in the hospital." [19]

A second front is the dissolution of unions already in operation. Construction companies have found that this can be done by "double-breasting"—that is, by dividing into two parts, one operating under an existing union contract and the other part employing nonunion labor. The unions themselves can be dissolved through "decertification," a legal process whereby the workers can oust a union that already represents them. Under the National Labor Relations Law, management cannot directly initiate a decertification petition. But managers have learned how to circumvent the law and have such petitions filed "spontaneously" by employees. They have also learned how to set the stage for deunionization by forcing unions out on strikes that turn out to be destructively costly to both the unions and their members.[20]

The third front is labor legislation. In many states the business lobbies have obtained legislation which—under the label of "right-to-work" laws—make union shops or closed shops illegal. Nationally, they are trying to repeal the Davis-Bacon Act (which maintains prevailing union wage rates on government-sponsored construction) and impose greater restrictions on peaceful picketing.

Fourth, the most generalized heat is that which is applied by the austerity squeeze of general economic policies. This heat is hottest in the public employment area, particularly among teachers and other municipal or state workers where unionization has tended to increase during recent years.

As a result of all these measures, the labor movement in America has failed to keep up with population growth. Union membership in 1980 covered about 22 million employees. Although this figure is larger than that of any past year, it represents a 3 percent decline from 1970, when union members accounted for 25 percent of nonfarm employment.

This slow melting away of labor's organized force has not been a free lunch. It has cost money—lots of it.

But the consequences have also been large: a reduction in the relative power of organized labor vis-à-vis organized business. Anybody who thinks this reduction is felt only at the bargaining table would be making a serious error. Its consequences have been extremely widespread.

For one thing, the morale, crusading spirit, and reformist fervor has itself tended to dissipate within many, if not most, branches of the labor movement. Dedication toward the extension of democracy has often been replaced by cynical inactivism. This has been felt by all the many agencies of government that have traditionally looked to labor for support in the extension and improvement of government services in health, education, welfare, housing, environmental protection, and mass transporation. It has been felt by all candidates for public office, for whom labor support now means much less than in previous years. Above all, the weakening of the labor movement has been one of the many factors in the sharp conservative drift within the Democratic party. This drift reinforces the widespread idea that there is little likelihood of serious disagreement on major issues of policy between the two major parties. The continuation of this drift would be one of the most important factors in brushing aside what might still seem to some as the overwhelming strength of America's democratic machinery.

LESSONS OF THE WATERGATE CONSPIRACY

Watergate shows what comes from using cheap help.

JOHN SHAHEEN,
businessman [21]

One popular "lesson" of the Watergate conspiracy under the Nixon administration was that America had escaped by just a hair's breadth from becoming a police state. Had it not been for the taped lock discovered at the Democratic party's headquarters, had it not been for Judge John J. Sirica's persistent toughness, had it not been for James W. McCord's belated confession concerning the break-in at the Democratic headquarters, and so on . . . Another was that the uncovering of the White House's attempted cover-up proved the strength and resilience of both the courts and the Congress, thereby affirming the future viability of constitutional democracy. A more piquant "lesson," offered by Irving Kristol, is that "Watergate has endowed the businessman-in-politics with an aura of corruption and irresponsibility." As a result, laments Kristol, "this [the business] sector is now much feebler and more vulnerable than it was." A common element in many of these "lessons" is a neglect of the growing strength of big-business networks both inside and outside the formal structure of national government, both during and after the Watergate period.

But all lessons imply the existence of people trying to learn how to do something better. In this case, I suggest that the most active students have been the same people who, during the quarter century after World War II, learned how to unify the "Free World" and bring about the economic miracles of the postwar period. If, as I fear, the logic of large-scale organization, capital accumulation, and the need to cope with current crises and side effects presses toward an American *Gleichschaltung*, these are the lessons I believe they have learned from the failures and successes of the Watergate conspirators.

For Presidents and the key members of the Chief Executive network:

1. Don't let political amateurs like H.R. Haldeman and John Erlichman into top positions in the White House; provide a larger piece of action for cooperative members of Congress.
2. Where nonpolitical personnel are given top positions, use true experts with proven flair and flexibility, individuals like Henry Kissinger, Daniel Patrick Moynihan, Peter Flanagan, George Schultz, and Arthur Burns.
3. Be much more effective and unscrupulous in "plugging the leaks"

in all parts of the Chief Executive Network and critical agencies of government.

4. Make fuller use of established bureaucracies (like the FBI and CIA) rather than running the risks of alienating them by setting up parallel "plumbers' groups."
5. Don't ever get caught—prepare two or three layers of cover ahead of time, so that "cover-ups" will not have to be improvised on the spot. Naturally this requires periodic housecleanings and cover-building for both the CIA and the FBI.
6. Be prepared with a reserve supply of plausible diversions to divert attention from major scandals that may possibly touch the White House—including White House leadership of attacks on state, local, and business corruption. The Nixon administration's sacrifice of Vice-President Agnew, while temporarily distracting attention and deflating the dump-Nixon approach of some Agnew supporters, was far less effective than it would have been to bring indictments against a number of Democratic senators, governors, and mayors.

And for the Ultra-Rich and the Corporate Overlords, I believe the lessons have been these:

1. For the "cowboys" or roughneck billionaires who have just arrived: Pick up some of the finesse of the old-timers and learn the grand arts of smoother manipulation.
2. For the managers of "old wealth": Bring more of the defense-space-reality *arrivistes* into the charmed inner circles.
3. Take your time both abroad and at home, as with the slow, careful, meticulous, and highly secret groundwork that led to the military-police coup of September 1973 against the Allende government of Chile.
4. Be much more circumspect and indirect in the manner of providing support for election campaigns.
5. Pay more attention to ideological justifications for concentrated power.
6. Be prepared with the alternatives that make it possible to throw any president or vice-president to the dogs.
7. Don't rely on cheap help.

UNHINGING AN ANTI-ESTABLISHMENT WHITE HOUSE

Suppose that despite everything a truly anti-Establishment president is elected and installed in office. Further suppose that, like Senator George McGovern or former Senator Fred Harris, his program is not only to provide greater opportunities for women, racial minorities, and young people, but also to reverse the trend toward concentrated income, wealth, and power. Unlike McGovern and Harris, he succeeds in winning a huge popular following including blue-collar workers, white ethnics, lower and middle classes, scientists, artists, professionals, rebellious establishment technicians, and maverick millionaires. Finally, suppose that in the course of the campaign his program becomes more militant and coherent and that he sweeps into office a resounding majority in both houses of Congress. In his inaugural address, he pledges to cut the military budget, restore détente, strengthen the United Nations, recognize Cuba and Vietnam, impose price controls on the largest corporations, provide jobs at fair wages for everyone able and willing to work, conserve energy through a massive expansion of mass transport, set up one federal corporation to develop the government's oil reserves and another to break up the alliance between OPEC and the Seven Sisters by monopolizing the importation of petroleum.

To subvert such a government, some people might think that some kind of coup d'etat might be needed. Although this could conceivably happen, it need not. The prerogatives of the Corporate Overseers and the Ultra-Rich could be protected by a combination of legal means so effective that within a few years' time the president would be thoroughly discredited and the trend toward integrated oligarchy and imperial reconstruction could be resumed by the time of—or even before—the next presidential election.

There are at least three reasons why I believe that indirect methods of subversion could do the job.

First of all, the very strength of the new president would be a source of weakness. Willy-nilly, his successful campaign would raise hopes and expectations beyond the possibility of immediate fulfillment. (This was true even in the case of Jimmy Carter's anti-Establishment rhetoric throughout the 1976 presidential campaign year, rhetoric which was quickly reversed in his Inaugural Address and first State of the Union Message.) His broad, multihued coalition of supporters would include many elements that can more easily be unraveled than held together. Senator George McGovern's activities in 1972 clearly demonstrated the profound difference between a movement capable of winning the Democratic nomination and one capable of winning a presidential election. The very first months of a populist "McGovernment" would reveal the still greater difference between winning a presidential election and affecting the direction of change in American institutions.

Second, the American Establishment—divided though it is—has tremendous resources, staying power, and resiliency. The mere election of a popular populist as president would not by itself undo its institutionalized strength. Years of experience in constitutional manipulation and the orchestration of contrapuntal party harmony would provide a solid foundation for the Establishment's confrontation with a populist president.

Third, the thoroughgoing unhinging of an anti-Establishment White House would not require a tightly planned conspiracy. It would develop, rather, through the normal establishment processes of "rolling consensus." Many disparate elements at the higher and middle levels of the Establishment would "do their own thing" to disrupt the new regime from within, shatter its coalition of supporters, and create unsettling conditions in the country.

To present any specific scenario on how this might be accomplished would be to oversimplify the immense number of possible permutations and the linkage of any very specific situation with the events immediately preceding it. Nonetheless, since the processes of internal disruption are not very mysterious, a few major possibilities may be mentioned.

It may be presumed that even from the beginning of the drive to electoral victory, some of the president's closest supporters were Establishment figures who did not take seriously his anti-Establishment pledges. Some of them will automatically move into critical positions in the Chief Executive Network. To these must be added enough old-time "new blood" to make a critical mass. This would be supplied by members of the "liberal" wing of Big Business who extend a warm hand of cooperation to the new president—an offer that no new president can refuse, for even if he suspects that their strategy is to "divide and conquer," his own strategy is to do the same. Thus he would bring into critical positions of his administration (in the departments of Defense, Treasury, and State as well as the White House staff, the Office of Management and Budget, and other executive office agencies) a whole string of "double agents." In short order this would lead to a chain reaction of internecine squabbles, slowdowns, and explosions on every basic policy issue—and inevitable resignations, firings, and reorganizations. The president's closest supporters would be personally attacked as incompetent, parochial, corrupt, sinister, socialistic, or communistic. In due course, after his coalition starts to fall apart and the conditions in the country become unsettled, the processes of character assassination would reach the president himself. He would be pilloried (in some sequential order that cannot be predicted in advance) as a snob, a loner, a novice, a fool, an incompetent, and a moral degenerate who vacillates between recklessness and inability to make decisions.

A big step toward breaking up the president's coalition might be taken by trade-union allies demanding major wage increases. Pleas for patience and moderation would go unheeded, and he would finally give his support in a grudging manner that would lose him part of their support. In some sectors the immediate results would be wage increases that business leaders compensate for by both price increases and unemployment. This would move the burden onto the shoulders of lower- and middle-class consumers. It would also enrage the leaders of black, Hispanic, and Native American minorities, who would demand an immediate end to discriminatory employment barriers imposed by white ethnic and Protestant union leaders. To prevent new outbreaks of interracial and interethnic conflict, the president would move rapidly on public-job creation. But his emergency employment agencies themselves would become a battleground among minority activists fiercely competing for larger slices of an overly small pie. The pie would be kept small by old-line members of Congress dominating the budget committees of the House and the Senate and soon reconstructing the old two-party conservative coalition in Congress. In these efforts they would be directly helped by holdover conservatives in the federal bureaucracy, many of who oppose the new president from much deeper convictions than the earlier opposition to President Nixon by holdover liberals. The president's congressional opponents would be indirectly helped by the president's appointees in the emergency job program, many of them not only offensive to powerful members of Congress but given to emphasizing quick results rather than the niceties of financial control, civil service regulations, and other legal procedures. The Controller General's staff and a growing number of congressional committees would undertake detailed evaluations and investigations of executive incompetence, wastefulness, malfeasance, and misfeasance. Under the banner of restoring the usurped prerogatives of the Congress, these activities would broaden to cover every aspect of the administration's activities; by the end of the president's first year in office, a thorough logjam would obstruct all the president's legislative proposals. This logjam could be broken only by his acceptance of emasculating amendments—or by the conversion of his proposals into measures that restore, or even improve upon, the old tradition of promoting more extensive and intensive exploitation by the Corporate Overseers and the Ultra-Rich.

Finally, the breakup of the president's team and coalition would be facilitated by the still broader processes of economic disruption. As already shown, these would include business decisions to raise prices and curtail employment. As in previous historical periods, the business community would be divided on price-wage controls. But once they are used by the new president, these divisions would fade. Businessmen would manipulate the control system to keep wages lagging behind prices and establish price ceilings that either place an umbrella over the highest-cost producers or force weaker competitors out of business. Both large and small business concerns would cash in on the inevitable opportunities, created by controls themselves, for lush profits through speculation, hoarding, and black marketeering. Still larger speculative activities would be initiated by the largest transnational corporations, which can shift massive amounts of capital abroad, provoking seemingly anarchic fluctuations of both the dollar and stock-market prices. Every presidential effort to counteract this situation would be doomed to failure—with the single exception of moves dictated to him by the leadership of the banking community. But these, in turn, would help demoralize his administration, divide his coalition, and finally present the image of a president uncertain of whether he is coming or going. This image would be reinforced by his administration's declining prestige in other countries and the humiliating snubs of the president himself by leaders of Western, Communist and Third World countries.

Thus, at low overhead costs to themselves and perhaps even with huge financial gains, the top leaders of the American Establishment could convert the populist president's promises into worthless rhetoric and render the president's closest supporters and the president himself helpless, discredited, disillusioned, and pathetic fragments of political junk to be easily swept aside by the next administration.

COUP D'ETAT AMERICAN STYLE

> If the new military elite is anything like the old one, it would, in any great crisis, tend to side with the Old Order and defend the *status quo,* if necessary, by force. In the words of the standard police bulletin known to all radio listeners, "These men are armed —and they may be dangerous."
>
> FERDINAND LUNDBERG [22]

> A coup consists of the infiltration of a small but critical segment of the state apparatus, which is then used to displace the government from its control of the remainder.
>
> EDWARD LUTTWAK [23]

Capitalist democracy has often been described as a poker game in which the wealthiest players usually win most of the pots and the poor players pick up some occasional spare change. The assumption underlying the preceding pages of this chapter is that this cruel game will continue for quite a while in the United States.

But suppose the losers find out that the deck has been "stacked" and the rules manipulated against them. Suppose they organize enough power to offset totally any effort to unhinge their regime by peaceful means.

Under such conditions, many of the old dealers might well consider calling off the game. As in many Third World countries, might they not unseat their opponents through military force and rule through some kind of junta until they create the conditions for restoring constitutionalism in more well-behaved form?

I think this highly unlikely. Nonetheless, people close to Presidents

Kennedy, Johnson, and Nixon have occasionally voiced fears of military-CIA reprisals against sudden changes in presidential foreign policies. And in any case, I think it worthwhile to consider exactly how such a coup might be undertaken.

One view of this possibility was vividly presented some years ago by Fletcher Knebel and Charles W. Bailey II in their novel *Seven Days in May*. An unpopular president, according to their story, negotiates a disarmament treaty with the Russians over the vehement opposition of the Joint Chiefs of Staff. The chairman of the Joint Chiefs responds to this presidential "betrayal" by organizing ECOMCON, a secret assault force to take over the White House. He has the support of a powerful Senate committee chairman and an influential TV newscaster. But before the coup can be attempted, it is exposed by a loyal marine colonel in the Joint Chiefs' office. Although the moral is not spelled out by the authors, it is rather obvious: A much broader basis of support is needed (particularly among top Corporate Overseers), and that the organizers of a replacement coup must plan in advance to immobilize or liquidate any possible source of opposition within the armed or para-military forces.

Moreover, a first principle of any replacement coup in the First World is that the replacers operate in the name of "law and order" and appear as the defenders of the Constitution against others eager to use force against it. Something along these lines happened in Japan back in 1936 when a section of the army staged a short-lived revolt against the "old ruling cliques." The defeat of this "fascism from below," as Japanese historian Masao Maruyama points out, facilitated "fascism from above," respectable fascism on the part of the old ruling cliques. In modern America, much more than in Japan of the 1930s, the cloak of respectability is indispensable. Thus a "feint" coup by Know Nothing rightists or a wild outburst of violence by left-wing extremists could be effectively countered by the military establishment itself, which, in defending the Constitution, could take the White House itself under protective custody.

A preventive coup is more sophisticated; it avoids the replacement coup's inherent difficulties by keeping an undesirable regime—after it has been elected—from taking power. Edward Luttwak, author of the first general handbook on how to carry out a coup, has himself published an excruciatingly specific application: "Scenario for a Military Coup d'Etat in the United States." He portrays a seven-year period—1970 through 1976—in which as a result of mounting fragmentation and alienation, America's middle classes become increasingly indifferent to the preservation of the formal Constitution. Under these circumstances two new organizations for restoring order are formed. With blue-ribbon financial support, the Council for an Honorable Peace (CHOP) forms branches in every state. The Urban Security Command (USECO) is set up in the Pentagon. CHOP prepares two nationwide plans: Hard Surface, to organize right-wing extremists, and Plan R for Reconstruction, based on the principle that "within the present rules of the political game, *no* solution to the country's predicament can be found." Then, during the 1976 election campaign the Republican candidate is exposed by a former employee as having used his previous senatorial position for personal gain. With a very low turnout at the polls, the Democratic candidate easily wins. Thus "an essentially right-of-center country is now about to acquire a basically left-of-center administration." Immediately after election day, CHOP and USECO put into effect Plan Yellow, the military side of Plan R. By January 4, 1977, the new regime is in power.

A still more sophisticated form of preventive coup would be one designed to prevent the formal election of a left-of-center administration. In the event that the normal nominating processes fail to do this, any number of scenarios are possible before election day: character defamation, sickness, accidental injury, assassination. If none of these are feasible, the election itself can be constitutionally prevented. Urban riots in a few large central cities such as New York, Newark, and Detroit could lead to patrolling of these areas by the National Guard and Army. Under conditions of martial law and curfews during the last week of October and the first week of November large numbers of black voters would be sure to be kept from the polls. With this prospect before them many black leaders, liberals, and Democratic officials would ask for a temporary postponement of elections in order to protect the constitutional right to vote. Since there is no constitutional requirement that voting in national elections be held on the same day throughout the country, there might well be a temporary postponement in New York, New Jersey, and Michigan. The political leaders of these states, in fact, would soon see that postponement puts them in a remarkably influential bargaining position. After voting results are already in from all other states, the voting in their states would probably determine the election's outcome. Party leaders in Illinois and California would then seek postponement also. To restore equilibrium, elections could then be postponed in many other states, perhaps all of them. Tremendous confusion would thus be created, with many appeals in both state and federal courts—and various appeals to the Supreme Court anticipated. In short order Article II, Section 3 of the Constitution would come into effect. Under this provision the Congress itself declares "who shall then act as President" until new provisions for election are worked out by the Congress. If major differences prevent the Congress from making all these decisions, the stage is then set for the kind of regime described by Luttwak under a name such as The Emergency Administration for Constitutional Health (TEACH). In treating Americans like children in the family, the "Teachers" would not spoil the child by sparing the rod.

The best form of prevention, however, is a consolidation coup, using illegal and unconstitutional means of strengthening oligarchic control of society. This is the essence of the nightmares in *The Iron Heel* and *It*

Can't Happen Here. Both Jack London's Oligarchy and Sinclair Lewis's President Windrip, after reaching power through constitutional procedures, used unconstitutional means in consolidating their power. This is rather close to the successful scenarios followed by both Mussolini and Hitler.

If something like this should happen under—or on the road to—friendly fascism, I think it would be much slower. The subversion of constitutional democracy is more likely to occur not through violent and sudden usurpation but rather through the gradual and silent encroachments that would accustom the American people to the destruction of their freedoms.

12

Managing Information and Minds

There is no subjugation so perfect as that which keeps the appearance of freedom, for in that way one captures volition itself.
JEAN-JACQUES ROUSSEAU,
Emile

INFORMATION HAS ALWAYS BEEN a strategic source of power. From time immemorial the Teacher, the Priest, the Censor, and the Spy have helped despots control subject populations. Under the old-fashioned fascist dictatorships, the Party Propagandist replaced the Priest, and the control of minds through managed information became as important as terrorism, torture, and concentration camps.

With the maturing of a modern capitalism, the managing of information has become a fine art and advancing science. More powerful institutions use world-spanning technologies to collect, store, process, and disseminate information. Some analysts see a countervailing equilibrium among these institutions. While computerized science and technology produce shattering changes, it is felt that the schools and the media tend to preserve the status quo. Actually, all these institutions have been involved in changing the world. Each has played a major role in easing the difficult transition from national to transnational capitalism by winning greater acceptance of manipulation or exploitation—even as it becomes more extensive and intensive—by those subjected to them. Only through managed information can volition itself be captured and, as Rousseau recognized, can minds be so perfectly subjugated as to keep "the appearance of freedom."

Indeed, friendly fascism in the United States is unthinkable without the thorough integration of knowledge, information, and communication complexes into the Establishment. At that point, however, the faceless oligarchy could enjoy unprecedented power over the minds, beliefs, personalities, and behavior of men, women, and children in America and elsewhere. The information overlords, intellectuals, and technicians —sometimes unwillingly, more often unwittingly—would be invaluable change agents in subverting (without any law of Congress doing it openly) the constitutional freedoms of speech and press.

So much "progress" has already been made in the management of minds that it is hard to distinguish between current accomplishments and future possibilities. The difficulty is compounded by the fact that the best critics of the information industry (like the best analysis of the American power structure) have often exaggerated the damage already done. This is a risk that I too must run, although I should prefer, rather, to understate what has already occurred and—for the sake of warning—overstate the greater terrors that may lie ahead.

INFORMATION AS THE MARCH

The content and forms of American communications—the myths and the means of transmitting them—are devoted to manipulation. When successfully employed, as they invariably are, the result is individual passivity, a state of inertia that precludes action.

HERBERT SCHILLER [1]

For Hitler, according to Hermann Rauschning, marching was a technique of mobilizing people in order to immobilize them. Apart from the manifest purpose of any specific march (whether to attack domestic enemies or occupy other countries) Hitler's marchers became passive, powerless, non-thinking, non-individuals. The entire information complex—which includes education, research, information services, and information machines as well as communications—has the potential of becoming the functional equivalent of Hitler's march. As I reflect on Hermann Rauschning's analysis of Hitler's use of marching as a means of diverting or killing thought, I feel that it would be no great exaggeration to rewrite one of these sentences with the word "TV" replacing "marching." That gives us this: "TV is the indispensable magic stroke performed in order to accustom the people to a mechanical, quasi-ritualistic activity until it becomes second nature." *

As a technique of immobilizing people, marching requires organization and, apart from the outlay costs involved, organized groups are a potential danger. They might march to a different drum or in the wrong direction . . . TV is more effective. It captures many more people than would ever fill the streets by marching—and without interfering with automobile traffic. It includes the very young and the very old, the sick

* In "The Rise and Fall of Classic Fascism," chapter 1.

and the insomniac. Above all, while marching brings people together, TV tends to separate them. Even if sitting together in front of the TV, the viewers take part in no cooperative activity. Entirely apart from the content of the messages transmitted, TV tends to fragment still further an already fragmented population. Its hypnotic effect accustoms "the people to a mechanical, quasi-ritualistic activity until it becomes second nature." And TV training may start as early as toilet training.

Unlike marching, TV viewing can fill huge numbers of hours during both day and night. According to the *Statistical Abstract*, the average TV set in America is turned on, and viewed, for more than six hours a day, which amounts to over forty-two hours a week. This is much more than the average work week of less than thirty-six hours and still more than the hours anyone spends in school classrooms. Among women, blacks, and poor people generally, the average figure rises to over fifty-five hours a week. Televised sports events attract huge numbers of spectators. Widely touted educational programs for children help "hook" children at an early age, thereby legitimating their grooming to become passive viewers all their lives. But it should not be assumed that the more adult, educated, and privileged elements in the population are immune to TV narcosis. The extension of educational TV in general—like "public interest" or "alternative" radio—caters mainly to elite viewers. If this trend continues, even intellectuals and scientists, as pointed out to me by Oliver Gray, a former Hunter College student, may well be trapped into hours upon hours of viewing the cultural heritages of the past, both artistic and scientific.

Many parts of the information complex also serve a custodial function that separate people from the rest of society. This is a form of immobilization that goes far beyond the march.

The hypnotizing effect of TV, both mass and elite, can also be augmented by allied developments in modern information processing and dissemination. For example, the fuller use of cable and satellite technology could do much more than bring TV to areas outside the reach of ordinary broadcasting facilities. It could also provide for a much larger number of channels and a larger variety of programming. This could facilitate the kind of sophisticated, pluralistic programming which appeals to every group in the population. The danger is that an additional layer of "cultural ghettoization" might then be superimposed on residential ghettoization. With extensive control "banks" of TV tapes that can be reached by home dialing and with widespread facilities for taping in the home, almost every individual would get a personalized sequence of information injections at any time of the day or night.

TV fixes people in front of the tube in their own houses, without a marginal cent of additional social overhead to cover the cost of special buildings. The young people who walk the streets with transistor radios in their hands, or even with earphones on their heads, are imprisoned in their own bodies. During the 1967–74 period of the Greek junta, the number of TV receivers and viewers in Greece steadily rose—much more rapidly than the number of people released from jails in recurring amnesties. By the time the junta was replaced by a conservative civilian government and all the political prisoners were let free, TV sets were already being installed in the bars of Athens and the coffee houses of village Greece. In America meanwhile TV sets have been installed, as a reinforcement of the custodial functions, not only in jails and hospitals but also in nursing homes for the aged. One of the reasons why nursing homes are an important growth industry for the 1980s is the fact that TV, radio, and tapes provide the "indispensable magic stroke" needed to accustom older people to acceptance of life in a segregated warehouse.

According to Arthur R. Miller, TV teaching programs, entirely apart from their content, "anesthetize the sensitivity and awareness" of students, no matter what their age. This paraphrase of Arthur Miller's comment on electronic teaching devices is particularly relevant when techniques are provided for audience reaction. With teaching machines, the programmed students are given the feeling of particpation by their having to provide answers to carefully administered questions. "Students often seem dominated by the machines," reports Miller. "They don't seem to realize that they are boss and can push a button, turn the thing off and walk away." [2]

With the participatory cable-TV programs of the future, as illustrated in the MINERVA project studied by Professor Amitai Etzioni of Columbia University, the members of the audience could immediately "vote" their choice and a well-controlled local or national plebiscite could readily be staged. A trial run along these lines was conducted by the New York Regional Plan Association in 1973. Six one-hour films purporting to define *the* issues in housing, transportation, the environment, poverty, urban growth, and government—in that order—were shown on practically all of the TV stations in the tri-state (New York, New Jersey, and Connecticut) metropolitan area of New York City. The visual presentation of issues was backed up by a paperback modestly titled *How to Save Urban America*.[3] Through church, civic, and business organizations, a few hundred thousand viewers were gathered in small groups to watch the films and "vote" on the issues by responding to the multiple-choice questions formulated by the staff. Their "ballots" were then processed by George Gallup's National Institute of Public Opinion, which promptly reported how "the people had voted." The functional significance of this $1.5 million experiment (whose prime corporate sponsors were Chase Manhattan, the Bell System, IBM, and Coca-Cola) is that it provided valuable experience in the combined arts of official issue-definition, collective TV viewing, and illusionary particpation by TV viewers. Many similar experiments may be expected in the future, as a prelude to larger-scale and more firmly controlled operations.

THE SYMBOLIC ENVIRONMENT

> Through clever and constant application of propaganda, people can be made to see paradise as hell, and also the other way around to consider the most wretched sort of life as paradise.
>
> ADOLF HITLER [4]

"You may fool all of the people some of the time; you can even fool some of the people all of the time," said Abraham Lincoln, "but you can't fool all of the people all of the time." Yet Lincoln's famous statement antedates the modern-day information complex and its potentialities for service to modern capitalism. Hitler's boast about what he could do with "the clever and constant application of propaganda" is also outdated—so too, his more quoted statements that big lies are more easily believed than small ones. Improvements in the art of lying have kept up with advances in communication hardware. The mass-consumption economy of transnational capitalism requires the ingenious invention of impressively (sometimes even artistically) presented myths to disguise the realities of capitalist exploitation. In the misleading advertisements of consumers goods the arts of professional lying are technically referred to as "puffery . . . the dramatic extension of a claim area." With the rapid extension of puffery to include all aspects of politics and institutional advertising, it is not too hard to visualize the faceless oligarchs as managing to fool most of the people (including some of themselves and more of their professional aides) most of the time.

The size of lies varies immensely with the directness or indirectness of propaganda. Thus advertising in the mass media deals mainly with small lies projected into the minds of millions of viewers, listeners, and readers. The truly big lies are those that create the myths of what George Gerbner calls the "symbolic environment." [5] These myths penetrate the innermost recesses of consciousness and effect the basic values, attitudes, and beliefs—and eventually volition and action themselves—of viewers, listeners, and readers. Herbert Schiller analyzes five of the myths, which in his judgment have represented the media's greatest manipulative triumphs of the past: (1) the myth of individualism and personal choice; (2) the myth that key social institutions are neutral instead of serving concentrated wealth and power; (3) the myth that human nature does not change, despite the mythmakers' successes in helping to change it; (4) the myth of the absence of serious social conflict; and (5) the myth of media pluralism.[6]

Of making myths there is no end. In an era of friendly fascist "triple-speak," as I pointed out in chapter 9, the imagery of major myths must constantly be updated, and one obvious technique in both mass and elite media is "take over the symbols of all opposition groups." Peace, equality, black power, women's rights, the Constitution, for example, may become prominent in the sloganry justifying increased armament, oligarchic wealth, institutionalized white and male supremacy, and the subversion of constitutional rights. The thin veneer of Charles Reich's Consciousness Three could become a useful facade to adorn the evolution of his Consciousness Two into a more highly developed technocratic ideology. Under friendly fascism, one could expect the shameless acceptance of a principle already cynically tolerated in advertising: "Exploit the most basic symbols of human needs, human kindness, and human feeling." For those hardened to such appeals, there would be a complementary principle: "Make plentiful use of scientific and technical jargon."

Of course, not even the most skillful of media messengers can juggle their imagery so as to avoid all credibility gaps. In this sense, Lincoln was right: at least some of the people some of the time will be aware that someone is trying—very hard—to fool them. But it is wishful thinking to assume that these failures in mind management will necessarily have a positive outcome. Unfortunately even credibility gaps can be functional in the maintenance of a nondemocratic system. They may deepen the sense of cynicism, hopelessness, and alienation. A barrage of mythmaking can create a world of both passive acquiescence and of little real belief or trust. In such a world, serious opponents of friendly fascism would have but a slight chance of winning a hearing or keeping anyone's allegiance.

IMAGE AS THE REALITY

> Hitler's vast propaganda successes were accomplished with little more than the radio and loudspeaker, and without TV and tape and video recording . . . Today the art of mind control is in the process of becoming a science.
>
> ALDOUS HUXLEY [7]

In looking back on his previous writings on science-based totalitarianism, Aldous Huxley in 1958 maintained that since Hitler's day vast progress had been made in applied psychology and neurology, fields which he regarded as the special province of "the propagandist, the indoctrinator and the brainwasher." But even Huxley failed to appreciate the tremendous progress since Hitler's day in advertising and the other mind-managing arts of the information complex.

References to Hitler and Mussolini are unfortunate, however, if they give the impression that mind control under friendly fascism would be characterized by the wild demagogy and frantic emotionalism of old-fashioned fascism. The logic of the emerging corporate society and the new informational institutions themselves point toward more modulated and sophisticated approaches.

No totalitarian regime is possible without censorship. But in the age of the modern information complex there is much less of a role for the old-fashioned censor as an outsider who clamps down on the mass and elite media against their will. Today, far more information is available than can be possibly used by the mass media in their present form. The filtering-out process by itself represents suppression on a mammoth scale. The editors of *The New York Times,* for example, confront a world in which "all the news that's fit to print" probably comes to about 100 million words a day, a very small proportion of all potential news. About one tenth of this—or 10 million words—gets written up every day. But of all the news that is actually written there is never space to print more than 10 percent. Thus, the printed news is probably no more than 1 percent of the available possibilities. It is the editors of course, who select what in their best judgment is "fit to print," just as in the preparation of a movie, most shots may end up on the cutting-room floor. TV and radio newscasting is still more selective. Occasionally, the nature of this selectivity comes to the public attention, as when Fred Friendly quit his job as head of CBS news because he was not allowed to cover the Senate's Vietnam War hearings complete and alive. In terms that relate to newspaper and magazines as well as TV and radio, Friendly pointed out that CBS was in business to make money and that informing the public was secondary to keeping on good terms with advertisers. "I must confess that in my almost two years as the head of CBS News I tempered my news judgment and tailored my conscience more than once." [8]

In a certain sense, events exist only if they are recorded or reported by the media. Thus, every month there are many scores of detailed congressional hearings that are recorded only in the recondite and largely unread committee hearings, most of which are not even accorded the honor of being listed in the publications of the Government Printing Office on in library catalogues. "When people exercise their constitutional right to petition Congress," Theodore J. Gross has suggested, "the members of Congress then petition the media for attention. But most of their petitions are turned down. For this, there is no redress." [9] Thus can the bulk of congressional hearings become "non-events." When a petition is granted, certain unwritten conditions may be imposed—namely, that the event be staged in order to be titillatingly "newsworthy" or that none of the content be directly offensive to major advertisers or other powerful interests. There thus originates what Daniel Boorstin has called the "pseudo-event," [10] something that has been "planned, planted, or incited." A special kind of pseudo-event is the "actuality," a tape-recorded pronouncement or interview available to any radio station that dials the correct number. The tapes of televised actualities may, like old-fashioned press releases, be mailed to TV stations.

In George Orwell's *1984* Winston Smith and his fellow bureaucrats in the Ministry of Truth labored diligently to rewrite past history. Under friendly fascism, in contrast, skillful technicians and artists at scattered points in the information complex will create current history through highly selective and slanted reporting of current events. Like self-regulation of business, self-censorship is the first line of defense. "Prior restraint" is more effective when part of volition itself, rather than when imposed by courts or other outside agencies.

Under friendly fascism the biggest secrets would no longer be in the thriller-story areas of old-fashioned espionage, military technology, and battle plans. Nor would there be little if any censorship—even among America's more prudish partners in the dependent fascist regimes of Brazil, Chile, Pakistan or Indonesia—of visual or written portrayals of frontal nudity and sexual intercourse. The primary blackout would be on any frontal scrutiny of the faceless oligarchs themselves and their exploitative intercourse with the rest of the world. It would not be enough to divert attention toward celebrities, scandals, and exposés at lower and middle levels of power, or new theories exaggerating the influence of knowledge elites, technicians, labor unions, and other minor pressure groups. Neither scholars, reporters, congressional committees, nor government statisticians would be allowed access to the internal accounts of conglomerates and transnationals. Whenever such information would be compiled, it would be done on the basis of misleading definitions that underestimate wealth, profit, and all the intricate operations necessary for serious capital accumulation. As already indicated, "straight talk" must never be recorded in any form, and, if recorded, must be promptly destroyed. Recurring clampdowns by "plumbers' groups" would also enforce established procedures for official leaks to favorite reporters or scholars. At present, information on corporate corruption at the higher levels is played down in both the mass and elite media. Under friendly fascism, while the same activities would take place on a larger scale, they would be protected by double cover—on the one hand, their legalization by a more acquiescent and cooperative state, and, on the other hand, the suppression of news on any such operations that have not yet been legalized.

The whole process would be facilitated by the integration of the media into the broader structure of big business. Thanks to the recurrent shake-ups, quasi-independent newspapers and publishing houses would become parts of transnational conglomerates, a trend already well under way. To make a little more money by exposing how the system works, bringing its secrets to light, or criticizing basic policies (as in the case of this book's publication) would no longer be tolerated. Dissident commentators would be eased out, kicked upstairs, or channeled into harmless activities. "Prior restraint" would be exercised through the mutual adjustments among executives who know how to "go along and get along."

Although "actualities" have thus far been used mainly in political campaigns, it seems likely that in the transition to a new corporate society they will become a standard means of making current history.

Whenever necessary, moreover, residual use would be made of direct, old-fashioned censorship: some matters cannot be left to decentralized judgment. Thus, where official violence leads to shooting people down in jails, hospitals or factories, or on the street or campus, there would be a blackout on bloodshed. If a My Lai should occur in Muncie, Indiana, the news would simply not be transmited by the media. A combination of legal restraints, justified by "national security" or "responsibility," would assure that the episode would simply be a non-event.

NARROWING THE SCOPE OF CONTROVERSY

While the Constitution is what the judges say it is, a public issue is something that Walter Cronkite or John Chancellor recognizes as such. The media by themselves do not make the decisions, but on behalf of themselves and larger interests they certify what is or is not on the nation's agenda.

LARRY P. GROSS [11]

A problem usually becomes a "public issue," as pointed out in an earlier chapter, when open disputes break out within the Establishment. But even then, there is a selection process. Many vital disputes—particularly those among financial groups—are never aired at all. Sometimes the airing is only in the elite media—business publications, academic journals, or the liberal or radical press. Those who seek to create a "public issue" must often first submit their petitions to the elite media, hoping that they may then break through to the mass media. Issues that are finally "certified" by a Walter Cronkite or John Chancellor are, in the words of Larry P. Gross, thereby placed on the "nation's agenda." But this privileged position cannot last any longer than a popular song on the "hit parade." Civil rights, busing, women's lib, pollution, energy shortages—such issues are quickly created and then unceremoniously even cast into the shadows of the elite media. Under such circumstances, the time available in the hit parade of vital issues is not enough for serious presentation, let alone sustained analysis, of alternative views. This kind of issue creation helps nourish the drift toward a new corporate society in which the range of public issues would be narrowed much more rigorously and the nation's agenda rendered much more remote from the real decision making behind the curtains of a more integrated establishment.

In *Don't Blame the People,* a well-documented study of bias in the mass media, Robert Cirino shows in detail how "money buys and operates the media" and how this fact "works to the advantage of those with conservative viewpoints," namely, the radical right, the solid conservatives, and the moderate conservatives. The radical left and the solid liberals are outside the limits, thus leaving the moderate liberals to "compete alone against the combined mass media power of the conservative camp."

But to have their petitions recognized by the mass media, the moderate liberals usually have to accept or operate within the unwritten rules of the game. Thus their tendency, I would argue, is increasingly to press upon moderate conservatives the kind of reforms which, although usually opposed by solid conservatives, are required to strengthen Establishment conservatism. Similarly, the tendency is among the solid liberals and the radical left to win some slight hearing for their own voices by accepting as a fact of life (what choice is there?) the agenda as certified by the media. The middle ground is moved still further to the right as conservative or moderate-liberal money subsidizes the radical left and the more militant liberals.

Such shifts are supported by the growth of highly sophisticated conservatism, as illustrated by the *National Review, Commentary,* and *The Public Interest.* Within these elite circles the spirit of conservative controversy flourishes, both dominating the agendas of nonconservatives and giving the appearance of broader freedom. How much further a friendly fascist regime would go in narrowing still further the limits of elite opinion among solid liberals and the radical left is impossible to predict. The important point is that the basic trends in the information complex could render dissenting or critical opinions increasingly isolated and impotent.

MANUFACTURING OPINION BY POLLING

> The poll, though a scientifically shaped instrument, cannot be a neutral construct . . . The (opinion) survey is invariably a mechanism of manipulative control.
>
> HERBERT SCHILLER [12]

Many social scientists have dreamed wistfully of opinion polls that might provide a truly unbiased reflection of what various groups of people are really thinking. But the requirements for translating this dream into reality are many. They include efforts to estimate the intensity and salience of opinions as well as their direction. They include depth interviews that get beyond the rigid limitations of getting brief responses to a fixed set of prefabricated questions. And since any set of questions implies some bias in the very selection and presentation of the subject matter, another requirement would be the conduct of opinion surveys by a wide variety of different groups, including those that reject the basic premises and value orientations of the more powerful elements in society. The hope of some day living up to such requirements has nourished the belief that opinion polls, by conveying the people's will more pointedly and frequently than elections, might lead at last to the attainment of true citizen sovereignty.

But the basic thrust of opinion measurement has been to assist in the manipulation of opinion by large corporations, government agencies, and well-financed political candidates. A major part of the corporate effort has been in market research. With the growth of advertising on radio, and then on TV, audience surveys became the analogue of the statistics on the circulation of newspapers and magazines. There was no other way to estimate the size of the audience. The surveyors went further: they provided information not only on audience size but also on audience make-up reaction and preferences. This information is particularly useful to business when it is tied in with specific marketing and public relations efforts. Probably the largest and stablest flow of funds to opinion research companies comes from executives in search of help on changes in products, packaging, or advertising techniques. Some of these companies have been brilliantly successful in helping public relations men project fountain pens as body images, automobiles as wives, mistresses, or mothers, cigarettes as symbols of masculinity and sexual potency, and ladies' underwear as reassurance of femininity to working women who have taken over functions traditionally limited to men. In all such cases, the more scientifically valid the survey, the more it can do to help manipulate consumer opinion and guide consumer behavior.

The same principle applies to opinion polling by government agencies and political candidates. The highly professional survey can be immensely helpful in packaging either a policy or a candidate. The impact on political campaigns is particularly powerful when, as with selling soap or cigarettes, polling is combined with image creation through TV. "The real combined effects of polls and television," write two observers, "have been to make obsolete the traditional style of American politics, and to substitute a 'cool' corporate-executive style. This is the 'new politics' as it actually is today—purposefully analytic, empirically opportunistic, and administratively manipulative." [13] In this new politics, as in the most advanced market-research surveys, polling rises to the realm of "straight talk" and by that token is highly confidential. Only through leaks or exposés do we learn of studies like the Semantic Differential Test conducted by John Maddox as preparation for the creation of Nixon's TV image in the 1968 campaign. By asking people all over the country what qualities the best possible chief executive should have, Maddox created an Ideal President Curve and uncovered a Personality Gap—particularly on the "cold-warm continuum"—between Nixon and Humphrey. "If the real personality warmth of Mr. Nixon could be more adequately exposed, it would release a flood of other inhibitions about him—and make him more tangible as a person to large numbers of Humphrey leaners." [14] The term "real personality warmth," to describe Nixon was, of course, a departure from the frankness of pure straight talk, but nevertheless conveyed the message to Nixon's campaign managers: their task was to wrap a cold candidate in a package of apparent warmth.

On the other hand, instead of being a confidential guide to mind managers, opinion polls and surveys can themselves be constructed for direct propagandistic purposes. For example, when the TV industry was being criticized for gulling little boys and girls into the bliss of mass consumption (wthout reference to the quality of the products sold), the Television Information Office (the public relations unit of the National Association of Broadcasters) commissioned the Roper Organization to conduct a poll. In due course they were able to issue a press release to the effect that "seventy four per cent of adult Americans approve the principle of commercial sponsorship and support of children's television programs." But the questions asked by Roper were cleverly slanted. Thus: "How do you feel—that there should be no commercials on any children's program or that it is all right to have them if they don't take advantage of children?" The editors of *Transaction* made this comment: "The saving beauty of that last clause!" [15] A poll-taker's masterpieces may be found regularly in the many polls on current policy issues and in those political polls designed to celebrate the virtues of the candidate financing the poll. In 1972, one of the Nixon campaign organizations put this question to the voters: "Do you think President Nixon has gone far enough in combating crime or should he go still further?" This is a clever variant of the old question "Have you stopped beating your wife?" Any answer forces the respondent to accept the premise behind the question.

In the past few years, Herbert Schiller points out, "the best-known polling companies have either become weighty economic units in their own right, or have been incorporated into business conglomerate empires." Louis Harris and Associates, Yankelovich, Daniel Starch, the Roper Organization, and at least sixteen others have all been bought up by big business. This trend to consolidation is associated with the transnational extension of the larger polling companies and their intimate working relationships with the transnational public relations firms. These trends seem likely to continue. If they do, whatever looseness that now exists between polling practices and the needs of the powerful is bound to diminish. The truly scientific polls would become confidential aids to manipulation and the trickier polls (which themselves may be prepared on scientific lines) increasingly used in the managing of minds and the packaging of consciousness. With TV and education as a new form of lockstep, the image as reality and monitoring as the message, the final touches could be added to the new realities of citizen, consumer, and employee serfdom.

THE ELECTRONIC THRONE

The White House is now essentially a TV performance.
EDMUND CARPENTER [16]

No mighty king, no ambitious emperor, no pope, or prophet ever dreamt of such an awesome pulpit, so potent a magic wand.
FRED W. FRIENDLY [17]

In capitalist countries the business of all the private mass media is making money from advertising revenue. Their product is the seeing, listening, or reading audience—or more specifically the opportunity to influence the audience. Although the members of the TV and radio audience seem to be getting something for nothing, in reality they pay for the nominally free service through the prices they pay for advertised products. The larger the estimated audience, the more money the media receive from advertisers.

The biggest exception is the provision of free time—usually prime time—to the chief executive. In return, the media feel they maintain the goodwill of a government which has granted them without any substantial charge the highly profitable right to use the airwaves. This indirect cash nexus is customarily smothered in a thick gravy of rhetoric about "public service." But no equivalent services are provided for the chief executive's political opposition, or for lesser politicians. And in the United States, as distinct from some other capitalist countries, the media extort enormous fees from all candidates for political office, a practice that heightens the dependence of all elected officeholders (including the president) upon financial contributions from more or less the same corporations who give the media their advertising revenue.

Friendly fascism in the United States would not need a charismatic, apparently all-powerful leader such as Mussolini or Hitler—so I have argued throughout this book. The chief executive, rather, becomes the nominal head of a network that not only serves as a linchpin to help hold the Establishment together but also provides it with a sanctimonious aura of legitimacy through the imagery of the presidential person, his family, his associates, and their doings. The chief executive is already a TV performer, and his official residence is indeed "an awesome pulpit" from which he and his entire production staff can wield a potent "magic wand."

If historical analogies to old-fashioned fascism are needed, then the Japanese Emperor is a little closer than Hitler or Mussolini. The further integration of the Establishment's top levels would not remove power from the chief executive, but it would accentuate the need for at least one fully presented face, to help counterbalance the facelessness of the oligarchy and legitimate the regime as a whole. What is more, liberal commentators can be relied upon to exaggerate the power of the throne, thereby distracting attention from the powers operating behind and through it. This phenomenon itself is vivid testimony to the power of presidential imagery as a substitute for reality.

MONITORING AS THE MESSAGE

No one shall feel alone, ignored
As unrecorded blanks,
Take heart, your vital selves are stored,
In giant data banks.

Author's adaptation from
FELICIA LAMPERT [18]

Although all the novelists of totalitarian futures foresaw monitoring by despotic rulers, they generally failed to appreciate the potentialities of advanced technology. The Oligarchs of Jack London's *The Iron Heel* and the Minute Men in Sinclair Lewis's *It Can't Happen Here* rely on spies. In Eugene Zamyatin's *We* everyone lives in apartments with transparent glass walls (with permission curtains can be pulled down during sexual intercourse) and an agent of the Well-Doer checking entrances and exits. Modern monitoring methods appear only in George Orwell's *1984,* Big Brother's spies watch people through two-way TV screens and listen to them through microphones. In the Garrison State of political scientist Harold Lasswell, the Elites do not even get this far. Their use of modern technology is limited to coercion, propaganda, and drugs.

This collective underestimation has special meaning. If farsighted people in earlier decades could go wrong at a time when informational technologies were moving along very slowly, estimates prepared in the 1970s and 1980s, when these technologies are progressing at startling speed, might be even more off base.

Nonetheless, my own guess is that in the new era of international capitalism societal monitoring has important consequences entirely apart from the content or quality of the information obtained. To revert to McLuhan's style of discourse, the message is that "they" are watching.

Although Big Brothers of friendly fascism in the United States might not use two-way screens, their instruments of personal surveillance would be highly advanced. On the basis of present technologies alone, we may assume the availability of the following options:

1. The tapping of any telephone wires or cables
2. The use of any wires in the "wired society" as listening devices, even when the receiver is on the hook or the dial at "off"
3. The tapping of computer tapes and computer communication lines
4. Listening in through remote auditory devices independent of wires or plants
5. The major extension of visual surveillance and optical scanning through TV monitoring and taping in public places, work places, and (with telescopic TV operating through windows) homes
6. Recording individual peculiarities through fingerprints, voiceprints, and polygraphs (sometimes called "lie detectors")
7. Checking on human movement and activity through remote sensing devices such as infrared cameras and heat-radiation detectors
8. The extension of "mail cover" techniques, which record the names and addresses of senders and receivers, to include scanning of contents
9. Sensing and reporting devices embodied in credit cards and automobile tags
10. Transponders (miniature electronic devices) implanted in the brains of arrestees released on bail, criminals on parole or probation, and patients leaving mental institutions [19]

Rather than replacing old-fashioned undercover agents, the new techniques would require more and better trained personnel. During the 1970s an estimated two hundred thousand people were working for America's foreign intelligence apparatus. While some of these were involved in the surveillance of people involved at home in antiwar and ecology movements, the full growth of high-technology, professionalized domestic monitoring would probably require another two hundred thousand positions. With this kind of staffing it would no longer be necessary for policemen to masquerade as newspapermen at demonstrations and press conferences. Qualified newspapermen—along with editors and administrative personnel—would handle the task more efficiently through a form of "on-the-job moonlighting." Students with special scholarships would be able to record professors' lectures and classroom discussions. Both medical personnel and actual patients would monitor confessions on the psychoanalyst's couch and uninhibited activities at encounter groups. A large professional core, moreover, would be able to handle a still larger number of volunteers. Thus the use of Boy Scouts as informers, as initiated some years ago by the FBI in Rochester, suggests untold opportunities for similar use of school children, 4-H clubs, and other youth groups. Under Operation SAFE (Scout Awareness for Emergencies) Boy Scouts were instructed among other things to report on unusual activity or lack of activity in neighbors' homes.

Covert monitoring, however, would probably be dwarfed by the overt collection of information from acquiescent respondents. The decennial census, as required by the Constitution, would become a ceaseless census—with occasional head-counting supplemented by annual, quarterly, monthly, weekly, and, at times even daily reports and sample surveys. Market surveys and opinion polling would cover the entire population—and special target areas—more thoroughly than ever before. Sophisticated research projects and evaluation studies would multiply, with priority given to actual or potential disaffection. Educational institutions and large employers would explore new frontiers in the testing of intelligence, skills, emotional stability, and personal values.

In foreign intelligence activities, the justification for collecting mountains of data has traditionally been the resulting molehill of secret information on military capabilities, intentions, or movements. In corporate espionage the object has been to uncover technological or marketing secrets. Under friendly fascism, however, surveillance would have a broader objective: the promotion of conformist behavior. The details of monitored behavior might be less important than the influence on behavior of the fear that one's words or actions are being recorded.

It must not be thought, however, that personal privacy would be entirely destroyed. Rather, it would become a special privilege enjoyed by the highest level of the Establishment and its organizations. This privilege would not be costless. It would require protective work by experts in uncovering or jamming all monitoring devices, in responding evasively to all official questionnaires, in keeping serious researchers busy on other projects, and in feeding "inside dopesters" with titillating information on the middle levels of decision making.

WOMB-TO-TOMB DOSSIERS

All monitoring, no matter what the primary purpose may be, provides informaton that can be used in compiling dossiers on individuals. As a Rand Corporation computer expert has put it, "You can extract intelligence information from a statistical system and get statistics from an intelligence system." [20]

But to extract high-grade intelligence on individuals, three requirements must be met.

The first is the recording of all information received. With the expanding use of electronic recording devices, this requirement is already being met.

The second is the pooling of all available information. At first, it seemed that the way to do this was through a Federal Data Center to collect and computerize all machine readable data from all federal agencies. In the name of better statistical information, this was first proposed in 1965 by a committee of the Social Science Research Council, headed by Richard Ruggles, a Yale economist. The idea was further articulated and defended in reports by Edgar S. Dunn, Jr., of Resources of the Future, and Carl Kaysen, head of Princeton's Institute for Advanced Study. The proposal was publicly attacked by a few members of Congress as a threat to individual privacy. Less publicly, it was criticized as a naive and old-fashioned form of overcentralization ill-suited to modern organizational forms. In its place there developed the more advanced concept of a data complex—that is, a network of specialized data banks. Parts of this network are already in operation: the new National Crime Information Bureau; the files of the various civilian and military agencies; the millions of personal files held by the Social Security Administration, Internal Revenue Service, Department of Defense, Veterans Administration, Civil Service Commission, Passport Office, National Science Foundation, Census Bureau, and the revived Selective Service System; the new statistical data banks being set up in the fields of education, health, and mental health; and the more than 100 million personal files in the hands of credit-rating bureaus and banks. Major progress is being made in the facilitating of data interchange through standardization of coding, remote access facilities, and procedures for the release of presumably confidential information. As of early in 1980 detailed plans were worked out to register the country's young people without their knowing through what is known as "passive" or "faceless" registration. This would be done by compiling a computerized list of names and addresses by assembling the information from school records, the Internal Revenue Service, the Social Security systems, and state driver's license bureaus.

The third requirement is the capability to sift or synthesize available raw data. A complete womb-to-tomb dossier on any individual—even if expressed in wholly intelligible English—would be a series of volumes more difficult to comprehend than James Joyce's *Finnegan's Wake*. To be useful, a dossier must represent refined—that is, highly filtered—data, not raw indigestible data bits. This requirement is also being met through a combination of computerized scanning facilities and the growth of personal expertise in data selection.

The most significant factors, however, are the uses to which dossiers may be put. Under friendly fascism, I suggest, these uses would be a combination of the well known and the novel.

The most well-known use would be witch-hunting. This would come in slow stages, and could include: the updating (or revival) of the Attorney General's list of subversive organizations, already attempted by former President Nixon; [21] new legislation and Supreme Court decisions to remove what former Assistant Attorney General Robert C. Mardian called "the recent tidal wave of legalisms which has clouded all personal security programs"; [22] the extension of witch hunts and blacklists to all government contractors and enterprises, such as TV stations, operating under government franchise; the broadening of grounds for dismissal (or refusal to hire) from loyalty and security to simple efficiency. The old principle of guilt by association, developed by Senator Joseph McCarthy during the late 1940s and early 1950s would be more powerful, inasmuch as with modern monitoring and retrieval much more information would be more powerful, inasmuch as with modern monitoring and retrieval much more would be known about any person's associations. "Second order associations," that is, the associations of a person's relatives and direct associates would also be tracked down. "I have in my hand a computer printout proving that . . ." etc., could be the classic opening statement of the new Grand Inquisitors. But this would rarely be done—as in the McCarthy era—by a lone wolf on the floor of the Congress. Rather, it would be done by faceless men behind the closed doors of bureaucratic committees or grand juries.

A similar use would be direct character assassination and defamation. Here the womb-to-tomb dossier can be invaluable. On the one hand, it can reveal embarrassing personal facts on practically everyone. Seen in context, these facts may indeed demonstrate past personal wrongdoing or even proclivities for future behavior of the same sort. On the other hand, if the dossier is complete enough, it can provide the basis for pulling facts out of context and holding them over a person's head as a weapon against him. For many years J. Edgar Hoover, as head of the Federal Bureau of Investigation, provided such a serivce to presidents. With the new technologies, this service could be supplied as a matter of course to all top members of the oligarchy.

In the McCarthy era Senator Millard Tydings of Maryland was publicly pilloried through use of a photograph showing him in close conversation with Earl Browder, the then Communist leader in the United States. The photograph was a phony one—prepared by putting two unrelated photographs together. The creative assembly of unrelated sounds is now possible through electronic means. A person's words, as recorded on electronic tape, may now be easily edited by dropping out key words. If enough care is exercised, nobody can detect the elision. Beyond that, if the vocal part of a person's dossier is large and varied enough, the phonemes—separate sounds—can be completely rearranged. Thus through "tape-recoding," a person's own voice may be used to say anything that the tape recorders want him to say. With much greater difficulty the same principle is applicable to the editing of film and video tapes. Here the problem is one of whether the visual record is large enough. If so, the use of new RAVE methods (Random Access Video Editing) would allow preparation of the Tydings-Browder type of picture in cinematic form. There would be few limitations other than the imagination or the conscience of the editors.

A more novel, and widespread, use would be the application to people—called personnel or "human resources"—of the inventory-control methods developed during the 1960s with respect to goods and machinery. The first problem in inventory control has always been that of managing huge amounts of records. With computerization, this task has at long last become manageable. In the personnel field, however, even such simple tasks as compiling rosters of scientific and technological personnel have been bungled. With the growth of a computerized dossier network, however, and enough R & D investment in its perfection, it will be possible to keep up-to-date inventories on all employees in America. As with industrial inventory management, this new system will facilitate efforts to find the right people for specific slots and arrange for whatever retooling might be necessary for a smooth fit.

Here also *jiujitsu* techniques could be used, by seizing the attackers of the dossier system and using their arguments in strengthening it. Outcries against misinformation in the files could be met by procedures for providing fuller information. Protests against military surveillance of civilians could be met by extended civilian surveillance. Complaints against duplicating and uncoordinated work by monitoring agencies could be met by more coordination and cooperative interchange. The central thrust of those demanding protection of individual rights to privacy and due process could be deflected by developing complicated devices for the purging or destruction of incriminating files—devices that the oligarchs themselves could easily utilize for their own protection and that of their most trustworthy managerial and technical aides.

ECONOMIC AND SOCIAL VINDICATORS

The tacit messages of personal surveillance and dossier compiling are: "*They* are watching you," and "*They* know all about you." Whether or not they really watch and know much about you may be less important than the fear created by the very existence of surveillance and dossier activities.

The monitoring of economic and social trends, in contrast, tends to counteract any fear that *They* don't know what is going on in the world.

In economic and social intelligence the tacit message is: "*They* are getting all the best information needed to guide the ship of state." Confidence in this message is built up by an accelerating expansion of far-flung data collection. The Census Bureau and other government agencies operate expanding archives of economic, social, environmental, and political information. Monitoring is done through an increasingly sophisticated battery of instruments—from the direct head-count and comprehensively administered questionaire to the sample survey and satellite scanning. The largest corporations are increasingly active in the design of these instruments, through which they obtain essential data for market research and business analysis in general.

Within the government sphere of the establishment, public programs are increasingly subject to a bewildering variety of cost-benefit analyses, evaluation surveys, and economic-impact or environmental-impact studies. The technical support for this immense activity comes from a "statistocracy" of experts in archival collection, a network of professional analysts who convert the raw data into presumably objective analyses, and from many thousands of experts who make their living—whether in universities, research institutions, or consulting firms—by processing the data and the analyses. Much of the processed data flows through narrow channels, officially or unofficially removed from public scrutiny. The portions that are made public are ever more complex, adding considerably to the information overload on the knowledge elites. But the very existence of this rising flood of data tends to give the impression that the leaders of government have the best possible information at their fingertips. This impression is reinforced by the elaborate rituals of ceremonial meetings with experts and advisers. It is strengthened still further by the technocratic promise that improved economic and social intelligence will provide the data base for better policymaking or, in Kenyon B. DeGreene's more explicit words, the improved "management of society".[23]

Some decades ago public reporting of economic and social information by corporations and governments was seen as an instrument of democratic accountability, of rendering an open accounting to the public. There were two weaknesses in this view. First, the assembly and initial interpretation of the information was left entirely to the reporting agency. In the case of corporate financial accounting, it is the corporation itself that hires the certified public accountants and—as Professor Abraham Briloff has demonstrated—calls the tune.[24] In the case of government, it is the agency head or Chief Executive Network that organizes the information. In both cases, the reports are mainly designed to show a favorable record. Second, both corporations and governments usually enjoy enough of a privileged position in the information complex to prevent or swamp any countervailing interpretations by others. There is little doubt that the officials of a friendly fascism could go much further in suppressing unfavorable data, shaping its interpretations, or generally turning statistical sows' ears into silk purses. A number of current practices and recent episodes illustrate the pattern, which friendly fascism would surely intensify.

- During the Nixon administration, as the official statistics on unemployment, prices, and crime became rather unpleasant, the president's men often took the task of releasing such data away from the professional statisticians. The impact of "bad news" was eased by having it released by higher officials who invariably gave it a more favorable interpretation.
- Professional statisticians themselves may police the definitions and concepts used in the basic-data collection, so that the product gives the "appropriate" impression without the intervening services of a fancy interpretation. Definitions worked out in past periods are frozen, thus keeping hidden unemployment out of official employment data, hidden price rises out of price indices, hidden profits out of reported profits, corporate crime out of reported crime statistics. The justification for this hardening of the statistical categories is the need to make present data comparable with past data. This justification can readily be forgotten, however, when—without reference to comparability with the past—conceptual reformation is needed to give a more favorable picture. With unemployment, the basis for such reformulations is already being developed. A few years ago the Council of Economic Advisers concocted "variable unemployment," a new definition that succeeded in cutting the official unemployment figure by at least a million. A prominent economist has gone still further in this direction by inventing an "unemployment severity index," which reduces the perceived volume of unemployment still more. Others concentrate on male household heads out of work for a long period of time. By excluding the hardships of many others, including women, unmarried males, and male household heads not included in the narrow "labor force" concept, they almost define unemployment out of existence.
- The older rhetoric of democratic accountability through public reporting can reinforce the armor of establishment power. We can expect many more public reports on the state of the city, metropolis, state, and union, and the social achievements of large corporations. One of the most ambitious efforts in this direction is the spadework now being done on the so-called "periodic social audit of the corporation." [25] This idea originated with the American Institute of Certified Public Accountants, some of whose members saw a new "product line" that could help their corporate customers ward off attacks by "Nader's Raiders" and other corporate critics. By the late 1970s trial runs on this new form of corporate audit were completed and big business was able to drape its activities with the help of better tailored data than ever before available.

While the certified public accountants have not yet solved the technical problem of how to best present public reports on the social achievements of their corporate clients, the national-income economists have done much better. Strongly attacked during the 1960s on the ground that GNP is not an adequate all-purpose indicator of welfare or utility, they have moved forward creatively to fabricate such an all-purpose indicator by making a few adjustments in GNP. William Nordhaus and James Tobin have added to GNP various estimates on the value of leisure, unpaid household work, and the services provided by consumers' durable equipment. Then they have subtracted the estimated costs of pollution and other "disamenities and urbanization."[26] They baptized the resulting figure MEW, a "measure of economic welfare," modestly claiming that it allows for "the more obvious discrepancies between GNP and economic welfare." Professor Paul Samuelson proceeded to pick up the Nordhaus-Tobin MEW, rename it NEW (meaning "net economic welfare") and formally present it—minus most of the Nordhaus-Tobin qualifications—in the next edition (the ninth) of his widely used introductory textbook, *Economics*.[27]

But what about the essential inappropriateness of regarding *any* measure of output quantity (no matter how much adjusted or refined) as an indicator of social welfare? Raising this point in 1966, I proposed a system of social or societal accounting to provide an ordered array of not only economic data but also "cultural, technological, biophysical, institutional and political information," much of which would be qualitative instead of quantitative and, if quantitative, noncommersurable and nonaggregative.[28] I developed these proposals during a period of overexuberant acceptance of President Johnson's "Great Society" rhetoric for shifting national policy goals from the quantity of output to the "quality of life." But as President Johnson vastly expanded U.S. involvement in the Vietnam War, the enthusiasm of social scientists for such an approach rapidly waned. The economists were the only social scientists who did not allow the horrors of U.S. military activities in Southeast Asia to distract them from buckling down to serious work. In response to charges like mine of "economic philistinism," they developed, as already shown, the more subtle economic philistinism of GNP in NEW clothes. But NEW also is due for multisided attack—particularly by all those who look beyond the scrubbed-up Samuelson version and take seriously the limitations more frankly stated by Nordhaus and Tobin. And in response to these, a broader "social philistinism" is being developed through composite statistical aggregates that presume to rank cities or nations in accordance with their so-called "quality of life." When these are increasingly criticized for leaving out "cultural, technological, biophysical, institutional, and political information," flexible technicians are sure to come up with broader-gauged measures. It is virtually inevitable that most of these indicators will help vindicate the goals and exploits of an increasingly powerful Establishment, thus becoming social vindicators more than indicators. Indeed, my own proposals could be misused in this fashion. This potentiality is inherent not so much in the nature of the proposals themselves as in the fact that any truly multidimensional effort to develop a systematic array of qualitative and quantitative information on the "state of the nation" is an immense undertaking. Like the uses of atomic energy for peaceful purposes, it requires a vast commitment of resources that only the Establishment itself can provide.

EDUCATIONAL AUTHORITARIANISM

> Students are carefully channeled, processed, manipulated, tested, inspected, indoctrinated, programmed and eventually packaged. . . .
>
> RICHARD GREEMAN [29]

To find powerful instruments for managing minds, however, one need not look only to fancy new technologies. The entire educational system itself may be seen as a mammoth set of disciplined activities that—irrespective of any specific indoctrination of knowledge or programming of skills—can help produce docile, accepting personalities.

Almost every component of America's mammoth school system serves as a training ground in the submission to authoritative rules and procedures. By being given meaningless assignments and subjected to large-scale, uniform testing, students are trained in the acceptance of meaningless work, mindless rules and mind-numbing orders from superiors. Rebellion itself often leads to little more than different forms of passivity —the passivity of those who drop out completely, of those who idly go through the motions, or of those who, by trying to "beat the system," tacitly accept the system as the springboard or framework of thought and action. Whenever student rebellion erupts more violently, a typical reaction is to pacify the rebels and their supporters by trotting out some new variation of "student government," thereby sidetracking the energy of activists and paving the way for a quick return to passivity. When rebellion is directed against restrictive entry to the sytem, the system's doors may be opened a little more (to women and to minorities, for example), so that new groups may have "equal opportunities" for personal pacification. This, in turn, tends not only to enlarge the system as a whole but also promotes more sophisticated stratification. At the level of so-called "higher education" the clear tendency is toward a sharp ranking along such lines as these:

The elite schools	For future elites at the Establishment's higher levels
The small bohemian colleges	For activist dissenters
The State (and city) colleges and universities	For middle level white-collar workers and middle-class professionals and technicians
The junior and community colleges	For the sons and daughters of lower class people

It is hard to think of a new corporate authoritarianism in America without an increase in the student population at the bottom level and without still sharper stratfication within the entire structure.

It would be a mistake, however, to think of passivity as a consequence manifested only at the lower levels. College undergraduates tend to be more docile than high school students, graduate students more "processed" than undergraduates, the recipients of higher degrees more channeled and packaged. At all levels teachers themselves are rendered passive by the pacifying operations they perform on others. It is their volition also which is captured, even though they may openly scoff at bureaucratic rules and themselves exhibit the appearance of freedom.

This appearance is usually most impressive among those who are most fully captured—namely, the most trusted processors and channelers in the professoriat of the Ivy League and other elite schools. From these home bases come the scientists, consultants and advisers who roam the corridors of the Establishment's middle and higher levels. In a certain sense their freedom is real—but just so long as they passively accept the Establishment's basic values and strategic policy orientation.

Within these confines, they—and their lower-caste brethren in the State universities and private research institutions—are inordinately active. Those who are less successful may be constrained by the rules of modern positivism, which channel creative thought and research toward technical questions subject to presumably "valuefree" empirical or semi-empirical testing. The furious controversies that may rage within these limits distract attention from the systemic processes that provide the real-life framework for the technical debates. No better examples can be found than the current controversies concerning energy and inflation. Many fine scientific minds are doing impressive work on energy conservation and—what is more interesting to physical scientists—atomic fusion, solar energy and other sources of energy that escape over-reliance on fossil fuels. Often, the missing element is the connection between these proposals and the profit-power position of the energy cartels and conglomerates. This subject verges on "straight talk" and must be left for the privacy of the corporate boardrooms. Similarly, the debates on double digit inflation swing mindlessly back and forth between "cost push" or "demand pull," indirect controls or direct controls, monetary policy or fiscal policy, and political courage or political cowardice. Although these debates lead nowhere, they are well reported by the media. But "profit grabs" are outside the pale of polite discourse and anyone who mentions the role of transnational corporations in raising capital by "taxing" consumers is *ipso facto* unsound. He or she may be tolerated as an instructor who befuddles the minds of young students in nonelite colleges—but serious debate on an issue of this type will not be joined, nor will such undocile thoughts be given serious attention in the elite media of learned journals.

CUSTODIAL FUNCTIONS

Many parts of the information complex also serve a custodial function that separates people from the rest of society. This is a form of immobilization that goes far beyond the march.

With such closed institutions as prisons and asylums, the custodial function is clear, albeit often hidden under the facade of manifest functions: rehabilitation or therapy. In schools, colleges, universities and research institutions, there is more reality to the manifest functions of providing certified knowledge, skills and values. But the custodial function always lurks in the background—usually unmentioned, always highly prized. Nurseries, kindergartens and elementary schools are a form of collectively-organized daytime baby sitting. High schools keep the "kids" off the streets, out of the home and apart from the labor market. The vast expansion of higher education has proved an indispensable part of modern capitalism's answer to the problem of how to enjoy a large supply of unemployed labor without the embarrassment of a large increase in open unemployment. Undergraduate and graduate "make work" seems less costly than the expansion of public service employment at fair wages. Research assistants and doctoral candidates accept minor pittances for their labors, grateful that they are protected from the horrors of the primary, secondary and tertiary job markets and hopeful for the day they may be vouchsafed entrance into the elite job categories. Overwhelmed by the information overload, thousands upon thousands of professionals and scientists are confined in libraries or behind ever higher piles of books, journals and reprints, immobilized by the no-win, sure-fail urge to "keep up." Many of the most intelligent, creative and brilliant people of the country are imprisoned within the walls of the narrowly defined discipline, laboratory or professorial chair, amply rewarded by respect and emoluments so long as they never (or rarely) venture forth beyond the imprisoning walls into the undisciplined area of genuine controversy. "Shoemaker, stick to your last," is the unwritten rule, "or you may not last . . ."

13

Incentives for System Acceptance

> It should be possible to design a world in which behavior likely to be punished seldom or never occurs. We try to design such a world for those who cannot solve the problems of punishment for themselves, such as babies, retardates and psychotics, and if it could be done for everyone, much time and energy would be saved . . .
>
> B. F. SKINNER [1]

> "And that," put in the Director sententiously, "that is the secret of happiness and virtue—liking what you've *got* to do. All conditioning aims at that: making people like their unescapable social destiny."
>
> ALDOUS HUXLEY [2]

THE OPEN BRUTALITY of the old-fashioned fascist regimes has misled many observers into equating fascism with official violence—as though official violence were something new under the sun. This oversimplified equation of fascism with brutality obscures the very real and widespread "positive reinforcements" that the German, Italian, and Japanese fascists provided for large parts of their populations through somewhat better living standards—at least until the tides of war engulfed and substantially destroyed these valued rewards.

This brings us up against one of the difficulties in understanding tendencies toward friendly fascism in the First World. On the one hand, the emerging logic of corporate authoritarianism requires a complex blend of rewards and punishments. On the other hand, the myths of old-style fascism lead many observers to look for overt terror and neglect positive incentives that result in "liking what you've got to do." Or else, appreciating the present power of positive incentives, they may—like Reimut Reiche, the West German Marxist—feel that "the techniques of manipulative rule used today are a necessary condition for the functioning of the capitalist system without fascism."[3] Having one-sided images of old-fashioned fascism in the back of their minds, people like Reiche fail to see the expanded use of these manipulative techniques as a necessary condition of the capitalist system *with friendly fascism.* Or else, overly influenced by Orwell's nightmare, they are unprepared for a strange new blend of Huxley's *Brave New World* with Orwell's *1984.* One of the many achievements in the new era of more perfect capitalism has been the proliferation of widespread incentives far more meaningful than any older forms of bread and circuses. While some people may have to be "knocked off" in the slow processes of integrating the Establishment's top levels, consolidating empire, and subverting constitutional machinery, it is cheaper to maintain control by a large amount of small but carefully distributed payoffs.

EXTENDED PROFESSIONALISM

To understand the growth of professionalism, we must think of the employers' need not only for skills but also for docility. With the emergence of a more educated and highly trained population, there are many rough challenges to the corporate elites. Trade unions can engage in more sophisticated bargaining, capitalizing on informal slowdowns, wildcat strikes, and expert knowledge of corporate and bureaucratic operations. Among unorganized workers, incentives for loyal and efficient work decline. Blacks, other minorities, and women demand larger proportions of high-level positions. Some experts and technicians "blow the whistle" by leaking inside information or linking themselves with outside groups trying to attack their organizations. And bubbling upward from all levels are aspirations for fulfilling employment disconnected from consumer exploitation, environment degradation, or militarism.

Control of this situation could not be won by any return to old-fashioned methods: not the iron law of subsistence wages, nor union-busting, nor bread-and-butter trade unions, nor the simple replacement of troublesome workers by machinery. The logic of oligarchic management, rather, requires an employee reward system that helps buttress market demand without interfering with the increased concentration of wealth, gives all workers unmistakable stakes in the regime, and contributes to the future fragmentation of both masses and technicians. This can best be done by a vast extension of bureaucratized professionalism to all kinds of work. The governing principle would be controlled mobility through many levels of conditional satisfactions.

Many elements of such a system are already at hand. Finely graded positions and ladders of advancement are provided by civil service arrangements. The advanced techniques of personnel management provide for job specification, job analysis, performance rating, seniority, within-grade increases, promotions, and career counseling. Mechanization and new technology require a wide variety of specialized positions, some linked closely to the machinery, others invloved in functions not worth assigning to machines. People become "personnel," a special form of "materiel." As "human resources" or "human capital," they can be as valuable and as manipulable as money in building wealth and power.

In a loose but immensely impressive manner, social scientists, personnel managers, and assorted experts in investment of human capital are working assiduously to achieve one of the conditions that Aldous Huxley (writing his 1947 foreword to *Brave New World*) felt essential if people are to be induced to love their servitude: "a fully developed science of human differences, enabling government managers to assign any given individual to his or her proper place in the social and economic hierarchy." [4]

Many critics of present-day America—including William H. Whyte, Lewis Mumford, and Charles Reich—have bewailed these elements. But by concentrating on the present and often exaggerating their case in order to attract necessary attention to hidden evils, they have tended to obscure the greater dangers that lie ahead. If America is already dominated by Whyte's Organization Man, Reich's Corporate State and Mumford's Megamachine, what could be worse?

My answer is another version of the distinction between cold water and ice. Under friendly fascism, the water would be much colder. The chunks of ice, now floating around conspicuously, would disappear as separate phenomena. With everything frozen, the change would be qualitative. The vast hierarchy of professionalized roles would extend in all directions. Sideways, it would cover every field of employment. Upwards, it would provide special status, emoluments, and rituals governing the life of the full professionals—and some superprofessionals or stars—among managers, militarists, scientists, writers, and entertainers. Downwards, it would provide niches, if not careers, for sub-, para- and quasi-professionals. There would even be sub-professional roles (and informal training facilities) for deviants, dropouts, dole-receivers, criminals, and resisters, with higher status groups serving as professional pacifiers for each of these categories. In Huxley's *Brave New World,* where all people are born in test tubes, everyone belonged to one of five groups, ranging down from Alpha and Beta at the top to Gamma, Delta, and Epsilon. Although less advanced in eugenic control, the United States would be more advanced in personnel policy. Its status graduations would run from Alpha to Omega, with many fine subdivisions among the Alphans and Omegans. And the ever-present incentive of rising a little higher would serve as a major force for systemic stability within the many corridors of the new Tower of Babel.

JOB, PROMETHEUS, FAUST

In this vast Tower of Babel, people would not be herded together like sheep. Rather, every woman and man would be separated from everyone else, each with her or his own personal niche, number, and furnishings. While growing like Topsy in confused response to crisis and demands, this labyrinthine social structure would, in function, be exquisitely designed—like the natural-habitat zoos with unpassable ditches instead of bars—to give the illusion of freedom. Within the system's constraints, there would also be options. With seniority, sweat, or manipulation, people can get a better cell. With good behavior, indentured experts can move from the boredom of routinized work into a sunny prison courtyard where they may enjoy expense accounts, professional mobility and mutual back-scratching, and select their own forms of dehumanized and dehumanizing labor. While rewards are distributed in accordance with each one's power and service to the system, the illusion of meritocratic justice is provided by computerized rating systems that, by purporting to report on intelligence and effort, strongly suggest the stupidity and immorality of the weak.

In this new form of status slavery, there can be no single style of servitude. The life-styles of Modern Man and Woman in Captivity under the United State would, despite their newness, be little more than updated forms of ancient legends expressing mankind's deepest fears. Thus, some would be Job, some Prometheus, some Faust.

The average worker would be the Job of the future. Suffering from boredom, apathy, alienation, and the erosion of any earlier dreams of rising in the world, he is prepared to hibernate forever. He takes out his aggressions on others, particularly those beneath him. With harmless words, unlike the Job of the Bible, he curses his gods, his family and the "powers that be." But, in action, he goes along passively and accepts his fate.

The Prometheus of the future would be the technician who brings to the system the essential fires of technological or scientific skill. But he is bound by a narrow and specialized role that prevents him from using this skill for the liberation of humankind. No eagle, but his own unending doubts gnaw at his liver. He feeds on others also and, by his example, teaches them to consume themselves.

The Faust of the future sells his soul in exchange for the opportunity to engage in an endless rat race for ephemeral satisfactions. By an updated version of Parkinson's Law, his work expands to take over all his time, even his dreams, leaving little if any available for anything else. He soars high and frantic, tasting prestige here and power there, condemned to constant movement. If he slows down, he may be destroyed.

His pact with today's devil is very close to the "brutal bargain" brilliantly described in Norman Podhoretz's biographical account of how he rose from the Brooklyn slums: "It appalls me to think of what an immense transformation I had to work on myself in order to become what I have become; if I had known what I was doing I would surely not have been able to do it . . . In matters having to do with "art" and "culture" (the "life of the mind," as I learned to call it at Columbia), I was being offered the very same brutal bargain and accepting it with the wildest enthusiasm." [5]

The neo-Faustian bargain, as Podhoretz describes it, is that in matters of dress, speech, and social contacts he had to "transform" himself. Only by accepting the superiority of the intellectual class he was entering and the inferiority of those among whom he had been born and raised was he able to become a successful editor and conspicuous member of the New York intellectual establishment. "That was the bargain—take it or leave it." Whether or not there was some fine print in the Podhoretz bargain, whether or not there were other and less explicit "brutal bargains" that he accepted later in order to continue "making it," is a question that might take another decade or two for Podhoretz—penetrating self-analyst though he is—to explore. In my own upward movement through both government and academia, I have made many bargains covering "the life of the mind," although I invariably tended to enter into them willingly without being aware at the time of any hidden "brutality." Thus it is easy for me to understand how most of the Faust-like intellectuals, scientists, and artists of United State would eagerly accept the superiority of the system that provides their opportunities for service, if not the ultimate benevolence of the higher powers they serve.

For all three—Job, Prometheus, and Faust—anxiety runs deep concerning the security they do not really believe in, the rewards that come ever so slowly, the decline of bodily and sexual powers. At times, family and friends may be a refuge. But increasingly they are things to be used—and then, when they lose their usefulness, to be thrown away like toilet paper or no-return bottles.

This anxiety is sharpened by both unemployment and inflation. Hidden unemployment at all levels, while unreflected in official statistics, is nonetheless widely sensed by the employed. The unemployment of the underclass, while never large enough to threaten the system, is large enough to enhance the lower and middle-income employees' appreciation of their own stake in the system. The unemployment of technicians results in employed technicans tightening their grip on their own positions. The recurring rise and fall in the job outlook hones the fine edge of anxiety. It is sharpened still further by the hidden taxes levied through creeping or walking inflation. Neither one's current income nor one's savings can be relied upon any more for security. The system itself becomes one's rock and one's deliverance; the chains of servitude, one's salvation.

As yet the educational system does not go nearly as far as it might in conditioning people to accept Alpha-to-Omega professionalism. Basic education "for its own sake"—whether called "liberal," "academic," or "general"—is still a valued objective in some parts of the educational complex. Vocational education to prepare people for specific slots is still only *a part* of the system. Under the Nixon, Ford, and Carter administrations, however, with the active participation of many experts who never regarded themselves as Nixon, Ford, or Carter admirers, "career education" was developed as a new doctrine to expand old-time vocational education until it permeates and tends to dominate the entire educational system.

FOR CONSUMERS: KIDNAPPER CANDY

Now megatechnics offers, in return for its unquestioning acceptance, the gift of an effortless life: a plethora of prefabricated goods, achieved with a minimum of physical activity . . . life on the installment plan, as it were, yet with an unlimited credit card, and with the final reckoning—existential nausea and despair—readable only in fine print . . . The "Big Bribe" turns out to be little better than kidnapper's candy.

LEWIS MUMFORD [G]

Oh Lord, won't you buy me a color TV?
I'll wait for delivery each day until three.

JANIS JOPLIN,
"Mercedes Benz"

Extended professionalism, of course, implies accelerated consumption. On the one hand, money (along with status) is the major payoff to everyone from Alpha to Omega and the major source of psychic income. This money, and the increments obtainable through credit, is useful only if it can be spent on consumers' goods and services. On the other hand the output of every stratified complex—particularly with new technologies—is an ever larger volume of goods or services. The investment of part of this output increases capabilities of producing for consumption. Neither foreign markets nor expanded militarism can go far enough, by themselves, in absorbing the enlarged output. To keep the system going, everyone must be induced to absorb more and more goods and services.

At first blush, accelerating consumption might appear as a redeeming—or at least unobjectionable—feature of friendly fascism. Isn't consumption the ultimate goal of economic activity? If underconsumption was one of the evils of older-style capitalism, wouldn't ever-rising consumption be a constant virtue? Wasn't Aldous Huxley going a little too far in lampooning the compulsion upon the citizens of his *Brave New World* to consume so much a year? If poverty means too few goods and services, would not of even higher levels of consumption be the long-sought realization of one of mankind's oldest dreams, the elimination of poverty?

Then there are the interrelated questions of product debasement and the neglect of public services. Here again, by emphasizing current evils, social critics have tended to give the impression that the situation could not become worse and—in accordance with the tacit assumption of inevitable progress—will probably improve. If consumers have been defrauded by misleading advertising, bad merchandise, and price-gouging, cannot substantial reforms be expected? If the public sector has been unduly constrained (leading to what Galbraith describes as the contrast between private opulence and public squalor) can we not expect an expansion of the public sector? The optimism in such rhetorical questions is supportable by two unquestionable trends—the relentless rise in public-service expenditures and the inclusion within the public-service sphere of new or expanded forms of consumer protection and consumer advisory services.

On the other hand, I foresee the possibility of exploitative abundance—abundance which enslaves consumers through a destructive combination of genuine and pseudo-satisfactions. There are already many tendencies in this direction, tendencies that could be accelerated during the transition from semi-oligarchy to full oligarchy.

One of these—the tendency toward more throwaways—is regarded as inevitable by Alvin Toffler. In *Future Shock* he predicts that the well-oiled machinery for the creation and diffusion of fads—now entrenched in automobiles and clothing—will be adopted throughout the economy. In this new economy of impermanence we will "face a rising flood of throwaway items, impermanent architecture, mobile and modular products, rented goods and commodities designed for almost instant death." [7] Toffler hints that in the throwaway society, consumption might really be designed to meet human needs. But he fails to stress that these would be less the needs of consumers, more those of businessmen seeking additional capital and power. Toward these ends, much more could be accomplished than in the past—particularly with the new pinpoint propaganda capabilities of cable TV—in educating consumers to seek sexual surrogates, higher status, and ego inflation by overeating, overreducing, and building up stocks of short-lived, wasteful, unused, or time-consuming durables. After more than a decade of soaps, deodorants, and washes to overcome odors of mouth, armpits, feet, navel, or vagina, we can look forward to the promotion of new perfumes to bring back "that good old natural body odor" with higher-price sprays hailed as "body bouquet" or "sex scent." A new industry of psychogratification, staffed with artists and environmental entrepreneurs, would provide people with both simulated and real experiences.

They would go much further than the orgies and "feelies" of *Brave New World*, using electronic stimulation of the brain, mixed-media assaults on the senses, and efficiently staged group therapy and communal massage experiences. Past achievements in the creation of fictitious consumer needs may be as nothing in comparison with Toffler's titillating future.

SERVITUDE'S SERVICES

One of the many illusions of the modern world has been that economic growth gives people more leisure or free time. And this despite the encroachment of work and work's anxieties far beyond the hours of recorded physical presence at the workplace! But, as Swedish economist Staffan B. Linder has pointed out, high-level consumption also eats up time. The choice among varied goods and products takes times. Rational procurement becomes so time consuming that it is more rational—according to Linder—to save time by buying wastefully.[8] The goods you buy require valuable maintenance or repair time—services decreasingly available on the market. If they are not thrown away, that may be because of the lack of time to throw them away. The services you are expected to want consume so much time that time-efficiency methods must be applied: either do a lot of things simultaneously or cut down on the time for each. Eating, lovemaking, exercising, meditation, reading, contemplation, relaxation—all are compressed into ever-shorter quantities of time. Under the accelerated consumption of techno-urban fascism, this trend would be accentuated. Charlie Chaplin's *Modern Times* would be reenacted in new form, with Charlie spending less time at the conveyor belt and much more of his time in high speed, semiautomated running through the enlarged spectrum of required consumption. If *Readers' Digest* was one of the great commercial successes of the mid-twentieth century, I can see a still greater future for quick-eating food, quick-scanning drills to replace quick-reading courses, a two-year Bachelor of Arts degree, a twelve-minute version of *Hamlet* for cable TV and Beethoven's Ninth Symphony on a six-minute cassette. As for completely free time, the only genuine form of leisure, the Job of the future would have little, Prometheus less, and Faust none.

During the decades since the end of World War II, as John K. Galbraith has pointed out, the growth of mass consumption has imposed vast burdens on women.[9] Far more than men, they have had to spend large amounts of time in both shopping for consumer goods and managing household equipment. During the next decade or so, it may be expected that some of this burden will be shifted onto male shoulders. If this by itself be female liberation, it is the kind of liberation that allows more women to escape from the frying pan of accelerated consumption to the fire of extended professionalism. For men, this means more equality in sharing the burdens of servitude. For the purveyors of goods and services, both private and public, it means a broader and more secure base for consumer exploitation.

Much has been made of the transition from a goods to a service economy. Yet a growing part of the services rendered by professionals may turn out to be "disservices," as I have suggested in "The Side Effects of Success" (chapter 4). Most of the professionalized service systems assume that service is a unilateral process, like waiting on tables. According to John McKnight of Northwestern University, these systems tend to communicate three propositions:

> You are deficient.
> You have a problem.
> You have a collection of problems.

The professionals, in turn, are the "loving" or "caring" problem solvers, who use these deficiencies of their clients to feather their own nests. Thus, McKnight suggests, people are "prepared for anti-democratic leaders who can capitalize upon the dependencies created by unilateral, expert, professionalized helpers who teach people that 'they will be better helped because I know better.' "

CONDITIONAL BENEFACTIONS

For people who earn their own income, consumer control through accelerated consumption is indirect. For those receiving an open dole from the state—in welfare payments, food stamps, or rent subsidies—it is much more direct. As Piven and Cloward have repeatedly pointed out, these payments serve as cyclical instruments for "regulating the poor." [10] On the upswing they reinforce the system by allaying social discontent. On the downswing, actual or threatened withdrawal forces people into low-wage humiliating work. Another function (only touched on by Piven and Cloward) is to supplement emerging tendencies toward both extended professionalism and accelerated consumption. In addition to building up many cadres of relief-giving professionals, the relief system tends to encourage demands for paraprofessional opportunities. On the consumption side, the recipients—like Pavlov's dogs—are kept salivating in sustained hunger for both necessities and luxuries. In any transition to friendly fascism, these salivary anxieties would be exacerbated by the conversion of any rights won in the past into conditional benefactions. Thus relief would be given, maintained, or withdrawn on the basis of individual tests—an open means test and various hidden tests concerning loyalty, dissent, and political activity. Indeed, new forms of "conditionalism"—essential to the use of benefactions as positive reinforcements—would be developed for last-resort public employment, scholarship aid, health insurance, pensions, and other expanding forms of welfare state "goodies."

The accelerated use of computers to record and investigate the "character" or "good behavior" of recipients gives "conditional benefaction" the potential of becoming a much more precise operation.

The process may also be extended beyond what is normally considered the welfare population. Under mature oligarchy, a somewhat larger proportion of employees enjoy limited benefits of job tenure and pensions. These rights—to use the words of William H. Whyte *The Organization Man*—imprison the thus-honored employees in the beneficence of the organization. They create in addition a barrier of hostility between the beneficiaries and the larger number of workers who envy these petty privileges. All lower-income workers may be drawn further into "conditionalism" by the imposition of user charges on services that had previously been available gratis. In the case of publicly supported community colleges, for example, tuition fees replace previous rights to free education, with the result that lower-income students, if not eliminated altogether, are offered scholarships or partial tuition waivers on the basis of means tests and attestation of their worthiness for public largesse.

RATIONED PAYOFFS

It has long been thought that networks of upward mobility might democratize a power structure and that higher levels of consumption might equalize wealth and income. The exploits of modern capitalism have proved that "it ain't necessarily so." The expansion of bureaucratic careerism, while providing new opportunities for many people of lower birth, has been perfectly consistent with semi-oligarchic deveolpments. Mass consumption has come about through a huge enlargement of the total pie, with no redistribution of shares in favor of the poor. Only by keeping these points in mind can one appreciate the much greater change that would take place under friendly fascism: a much larger concentration of wealth, income, and all the other attributes of power.

There is a sense in which a little wealth tends to produce large wealth, large wealth much greater wealth, and great wealth immense wealth. In the monetary world, this is the inexorable law of compound interest. A similar law applies to power. Large concentrations of power tend to grow still larger through an integration and compounding of the many sources of power. This can provide continuing incentives for the wealthy and powerful to keep up the effort and "get themselves together." With sustained thrusts of economic growthmanship, it is possible for top-power holders to ride the modified business cycle and accumulate more money and power during recessions, inflationary splurges, and prolonged stagflation. More important, they can ride recurring cycles of dissent and consensus, enhancing their wealth during each. The technological growthmanship of the Golden International provides much larger shares of income, wealth, and power for the faceless oligarchs themselves—a process facilitated by the selective rationing of income, consumption, and departmentalized privilege throughout the Establishment's middle levels.

The name of the game is "incentive," the long-hallowed term used by economists to describe the positive reinforcements that government provides for private business. The transition to a new corporate society requires new bursts of innovation in providing more "tax expenditures" for business, more subsidies for banks and transnational corporations, more extensive use of private contractors to handle public functions, and more of all the other aids to business reviewed in "Big Welfare for Big Business" (chapter 2).

New vistas are available through the development of public and mixed-public enterprises. Still greater vistas are possible through the proliferation of direct federal controls over wages and prices. These can provide government agencies and private interest with powerful new instruments for directing the flow of income. Politically, these can be used to bring recalcitrant enterprises into line and encourage the channeling of political funds and influence in desired directions. Automatically, without any conscious effort, they penalize smaller or more rambunctious enterprises and promote an integration of orientation and effort, if not of formal consolidation.

All of these devices, it may be noted, can readily be formulated as "solutions" to pressing economic and social problems, even though increased concentraiton of income and wealth is seen as part of the problem to be solved. Yet no one has ever come up with money incentives for reducing the inequities in income and wealth distribution. The essence of business incentive systems—even those which purport to help "small" business—is to socialize the risk in business risk-taking and reward the wealthy for success in becoming wealthier.

From the viewpoint of the population at large, this is an extension of the filtering-down philosophy expressed in the motto: "The way to feed pigeons is to give hay to horses." The weakness of this motto is that it ignores pigeon droppings. In the managed society, these would be assiduously mopped up and filtered down to lower species.

In the other direction, I foresee an equally powerful extractive process that would siphon income, wealth, and power upward. Established instruments for doing this are tax devices that place the greatest burden of government services upon the lowest income groups. Some of these—such as sales, excise and value-added taxes—are openly regressive.

Others, like taxes on personal income and corporate profits, may be nominally progressive but—when conditions allow them to be passed on to the bulk of consumers—are little more than sophisticated ways of siphoning income away from the majority of the population. Cleverly administered price and wage regulations can help create such conditions. The extensions of metropolitan operations may have a similar effect, as the central-city poor are taxed to subsidize services for middle-level elites in the more affluent suburbs. In the case of cable TV, this can happen merely by a uniform installation charge, with ghetto residents—where installations are cheaper—paying the same fee as high-income suburbanites with huge distances and much more expensive wiring between dwelling units.

Similarly, most—but not necessarily all—reform measures provide a means of siphoning up political power. Where they involve new benefactions or new regulations, this can happen whenever their provision involves the setting up of a new or stronger bureaucracy. Any concrete benefits for people at the middle and lower levels of the social pyramid are balanced off by additional power or prestige at the top. This is why many reforms that may indeed be great victories for the organizers of the poorer or weaker elements of society may turn out also to be a form of payola. Under German and Italian fascism the top industrialist and miiltarists "paid off" in a rather uncontrolled manner to the semi-gangster types in the fascist parties. Under friendly fascism the payoffs would be more orderly and better distributed among political and technical functionaries, without the Ultra-Rich, the Corporate Overseers, or their executive managers running the risk of building up unreliable political forces.

Moreover, both the filtering-down and siphoning-up processes would probably be handled with fastidious care for legality or ex post facto legalization. Naturally, this would necessitate considerable changes in the legal structure. A model for this exists in the many tax loopholes developed in past decades, most of which convert (illegal) tax evasion into (within the law) avoidance. On the road to friendly fascism there would be massive changes of this type—through both statutes and judicial decisions—in the various laws governing taxation, foundations, banking, industry, utilities, public contracts, pollution, consumer protection, and natural resources. In purely legal—as distinguished from moral—terms, the blatant "corporate crime" or "crime in the suites" exposed by the muckrakers would diminish. Under friendly fascism, with the faceless oligarchs fully in charge of and above the law, they might even vanish.

Even under such a regime, however, there would be work for muckrakers. At the middle levels of the various hierarchies and complexes, the expansion of welfare-state benefactions and regulations opens up the doors for a new Age of Corruption. A new generation of business bribers, small-time land speculators, urban hustlers, and mafiosi-type racketeers (with multi-ethnic backgrounds) crowds through these doors, viciously clawing at one another. For them, law avoidance is less available, law evasion more normal. Recurring anticorruption campaigns and crack-downs serve valuable functions. At times, they lead to "reform legislation" strengthening oligarchic controls. More generally, as sophisticated forms of dramatic circus, they distract attention from the more legalized corruption at higher levels.

THE EFFULGENT AURA

While the greater concentration of both power and wealth would be largely hidden, let us not think it would be totally invisible. Although Kafka's K could never understand what was really going on in the Castle, he could nevertheless see it in the distance—even through the heavy snows. Similarly, many castles of the modern Establishment are visible from the distance. No matter how much the Rich and the Super-Rich may shun conspicuous consumption, glimmering of hidden oppulence—in the form of manorial estates, lordly offices, *haute cuisine* executive dining rooms, art treasures, jewelry, dog and horse shows, and sea and air yachts—would undoubtedly filter through public relations screening. Tidbits of baronial caprice and whimsy, of superprivleged gratifications, would find their way downward through the labyrinthine mazes of every complex, thereby testifying to the power of "They." The word would probably get around that "They"—more than anybody else in society—have availed themselves of the latest advances in geriatrics and gerontology. In *Future Shock*, Toffler suggests that "advanced fusions of man and machine—called 'Cyborgs'—are closer than most people suggest." Dr. Leon R. Kass of the National Academy of Sciences has already warned that "an extended life span, made possible by such techniques of modern medicine as organ transplants and artificial pacemakers for the heart, would become a privilege of the rich." [11] In a new corporate authoritarianism we may expect that after sufficient experimentation on lower-status people the faceless oligarchs will go further than anyone else in availing themselves of the heart pacemakers, artificial organs, and other mechanical extensions that will prolong their life span at high levels of activity and gratification.

Would such perceptions of "Life in the Castle" breed resentment? Undoubtedly. But hardly to the extent of threatening the regime.

Under extended professionalism, there would be a sense of justice concerning the distribution of rewards. With accelerated consumerism, the immediately perceived face of a person's increased consumption could counterbalance any vague sense of relative deprivation in contrast with the dimly perceived living standards of distant oligarchs.

Above all, great aggregations of wealth and power, as always, would emanate an effulgent and magnetic aura. They would attract thousands upon thousands of seekers after patronage, favors, tidbits, legacies, grants, contracts, access, or even benign glances. Under friendly fascism in the United States, the aggregate efforts of all such camp followers—from university presidents, middle-level businessmen, and foundation executives to free-floating writers, scholars, artists, and technocrats—would go much further in accelerating and justifying the processes of more exploitative accumulation.

14

The Ladder of Terror

The very first essential for success is a perpetually constant and regular employment of violence.

ADOLF HITLER, *Mein Kampf*

America has always been a relatively violent nation.

National Commision on the Causes and Prevention of Violence.[1]

THERE IS NOTHING DISTINCTIVELY FASCISTIC about violence and brutality. Force, fraud and violence, "have always been features of organized government." To recognize that "America has always been a violent nation" is to correct a false self-image among many Americans and to identify a characteristic that helps make the whole world kin. It does not put the finger on the essence of the drift toward friendly fascism. Indeed, the apparent ebbing of overt domestic violence after the 1970 outbursts has coincided with the slow but steady processes of integration at the highest levels of the Establishment and of more effective manipulation of government machinery by big business, increased management of information and minds, and more extensive use of incentives for system acceptance.

Punishments by themselves can never be a sufficient method of control. As B. F. Skinner has repeatedly insisted, they are essentially negative in character; they condition people *not* to do certain things without training them for what *should* be done. Even Hitler, with all his frankness about the use of violence, supplemented violence with a perpetually constant and regular employment of mind management and positive incentives. Moreover, the withholding or withdrawal of positive rewards can itself be a positive form of terror. This is particularly true of the deep fears spread by inflation, unemployment, job insecurity, career anxieties, and conditional benefactions. For at least half the population, the inexorable operations of the business cycle keep these fears alive in the back (or front) of the mind.

On the other hand, there are serious weaknesses in control through positive reinforcements alone. Positive rewards are expensive, even when carefully rationed. If enough resources ar used to reward the middle-level elites, then there are less resources available for the rest of the population. To keep the lower-level masses under control—in effect, to keep them from demanding the same incentives that the higher elites require—aversive sanctions are required. A new corporate society could not be managed by velvet gloves alone.

THE RUNGS OF VIOLENCE

> Force is never more operative than when it is known to exist but is not brandished.
>
> ALFRED THAYER MAHAN [2]

> Thought in many of its aspects this visible world seems formed in love, the invisible spheres were formed in fright.
>
> HERMAN MELVILLE,
> *Moby Dick*

Some years ago Herman Kahn bewailed the existence of "two traditionally American biases" toward the use of force in international affairs. On the one hand, there was "an unwillingness to initiate the use of moderate levels of force for limited objectives" and, on the other hand, "a too great willingness, once committed, to use extravagant and uncontrolled force." To promote a more deliberate approach to the use of force, he set forth an "Escalation Ladder" with forty-four rungs, leading from low-level international crises met by threats and ultimata through the use of conventional weapons up to various kinds of nuclear war, and finally all the way up to "spasm or insensate war—all the buttons are pressed and the decision-makers and their staffs go home—if they still have homes . . ." [3]

Kahn's analysis is also applicable, with certain variations, to the Establishment's use of force at home. Police operations during the 1960s and early 1970s often swung between "too little" and "too much." Since then, the military and paramilitary services have worked together intensively, with the support of various academic research institutions, to develop professional capabilities to make the punishment fit the perceived situation.

To help bring into the open some of the tacit premises underlying the more advanced planning, training, and practice by military and police professionals, I have prepared the table "The Ladder of Domestic Violence." As with Kahn's Escalation Ladder, this table helps explain the

THE LADDER OF DOMESTIC VIOLENCE
Available for Use by . . .

	Establishment	Both Sides	Opposition	
	14. Counterrevolution	14. Civil War	14. Revolution	
		13. Coup d'Etat		
	12. Counterinsurgency		12. Insurgency	
			Rebellion	
			Mutiny	
H		11. Execution		H
I		Mass, group, individual		I
G	10. Pacification Sabotage		10. Disruptive Sabotage	G
H		9. Personal Injury		H
		Mutilation, drugging, torture,		
		rape, assault, incapacitation		
		8. Riot		
		Looting, physical destruction		
		Injury Threshold		
	7. Legal Confinement		7. Kidnapping	
	Concentration camp			
M	Cordon sanitaire, curfew			M
E	Jails, hospitals, etc.			E
D	Exile			D
I	House confinement			I
U	6. Court Trial		6. Citizens' Tribunal	U
M	5. Arrest		5. Sit-Down or Sit-In	M
	Mass			
	Individual			

Forceful Confrontation Threshold

4. Job Action
   - Purge, blacklists
   - Reorganization
   - Isolation

L
O
W

2. Dossier-building

1. Surveillance

3. Harassment
   - Threats
   - Invective

4. Strike
   - General or partial
   - Regular or wildcat
   - Slowdown, "working to rule

L
O
W

2. Peaceful demonstrations, hunger strikes, suicides, marches, assemblies
1. Noncooperation
   - Law evasion or avoidance, withdrawal, nonfraternization

unfolding logic with respect to the use of domestic force. Naturally, in any specific situation, a combination of various modes may be used at one and the same time—such as harassment, arrests, and assaults, with the relative proportions of the various modes determined by the nature of a particular crisis and the interaction among competing control agencies.

As in Kahn's analysis, the primary emphasis is on the development of capabilities to operate at any or all levels depending on the specifics of any situation. To be credible, most of these capabilities must be used from time to time, or at least displayed to be fully effective. At the same time, as Mahan has advised, the more forceful measures should not be overly used or explicitly threatened. An atmosphere of fear is itself a powerful force. Present fears, to recall Macbeth's words, are even "less than horrible imaginings." With but slight expenditures of force, an all-pervasive sense of fright may be produced in the "invisible spheres" of life. An ounce of actual violence can yield a pound of terror.

PRECISION PURGING

> We're faced with an unprecedented problem. Not only are revolutionary terrorists finding it easier to infiltrate the bureaucracy but we're getting more people in government who feel they should be ruled by a sense of conscience. . . .
>
> ROBERT MARDIAN [4]

Since surveillance and dossier building have already been discussed in "Managing Information and Minds" (chapter 12), we may now proceed up the ladder to "job actions." To be sure, unemployment and job insecurity are the most pervasive forms of job action: in an environment of genuine full employment, more precisely punitive job actions would not be very threatening; one could always walk away from one position and find another, perhaps better, one elsewhere. This is one of the many reasons for Establishment opposition to genuine full employment—particularly at a time when the bonds of ideology seem weak and purges are needed to help purify the Establishment's middle and lower ranks.

During the "nightmare decade" of the 1950s, congressional hearings and long, tortuous "loyalty" and "security" investigations became the tools of a modern-day Inquisition. Under the whiplash of the House Un-American Activities Committee, Senator Joseph McCarthy, J. Edgar Hoover, and various right-wing extremist groups, purges and blacklisting hampered dissent in general, stifled liberal or radical ideas in government, academia, and the media, and promoted the large-scale conversion of dissenters into loyal establishment supporters.

Many of those who fear a return to old-style "McCarthyism" probably are due for a double surprise, one pleasant, one unpleasant. The pleasant surprise is that old-time red-baiting—particularly the kind that identifies opponents as the conscious or unconscious agents of Moscow or Peking—may prove difficult to bring back in full-blooded form. It is not easy to attack American radicals as recipients of Russian or Chinese financial aid at a time when government subsidies are given to large capitalist enterprises doing business with this or that Communist regime.

In contrast, the unpleasant surprise would be the emergence of a new-style McCarthyism, rooted in the Establishment's inner core rather than its extremist fringes and operating much more subtly, not against "reds" and "pinkoes" alone, but rather against people on the ground of mental instability, technical unfitness (as determined by allegedly objective tests), or unemployability. New methods of doing this are being developed. Various congressmen have already proposed legislation requiring full field investigations of the one million or more persons who apply for U.S. jobs each year. Administrative officers are devising new "probationary periods" after which any employee may be terminated on efficiency grounds. This form of "preventive purge" avoids any costly appeal procedures that may be invoked when a probationary employee is stigmatized as disloyal or a security risk.

Older employees, in contrast, may be subjected to the "silent purge" sanctions of reorganization. The logic is clear. Whenever reorganization occurs, opportunities are created for terminating unfavored personnel by abolishing various divisions and units, while at the same time creating new positions for favored individuals through new divisions and units. In the drift toward friendly fascism, reorganizations of this type are inevitable at all levels. A continuous rhetoric of attack against "deadwood" facilitates the replacement of organizational dissenters or freethinkers by individuals whose loyalty to the system is greater than their personal sense of conscience.

Those dissenters who remain—or suddenly crop up—may be given assignments that isolate them from the organization or force them either to make their peace or resign. This might be called the "Herbert treatment," after Colonel Anthony B. Herbert, who exposed war crimes against civilians in South Vietnam and was promptly sent back home to take charge of kitchens and laundries in an army training camp. In the ITT merger case, something similar seems to have happened with the lawyers in the Justice Department's Antitrust Division, while the head of the division, Richard McLaren, was "kicked upstairs" by an appointment to the bench. In reporting on such cases in private business, the *Wall Street Journal* ran this headline: "Spilling the Beans: Disclosing Misdeeds of Corporations Can Backfire on Tattler—Whistle Blowers Lose Jobs, Face Ostracism, Threats." [5]

During the period of the first Watergate exposures, many middle-level employees were encouraged to "blow the whistle" on wrongdoing in the corporations for which they worked. One of the longer-term effects of these disclosures, as revealed by Joann S. Lublin, staff reporter for the *Wall Street Journal*, was to establish object lessons on what may happen to individuals who uncover and publicly reveal "fraudulent, harmful or wasteful activities on the part of their employers." Ronald Secrist, the man who "spilled the beans" about bogus insurance policies written by the Equity Funding Corporation, came to the conclusion that his years of work in the insurance industry "gained me nothing but the option of being crooked to survive." After informing the Securities and Exchange Commission about inventory mistatements and inflated sales in Cenco's financial reports, Thomas M. Howard was turned down by about 150 firms when looking for his next job. Henry Durham, an ex-marine who informed a Senate committee about mismanagement, false documentation, and waste in the Lockheed Company's production of military aircraft, was "ostracized, fired, criticized and virtually abandoned [by former friends]." Although it is impossible to assess the extent to which such sanctions are currently being used in either business or government, it is clear that every such action has resonant reverberations among other employees who hear about it.[6]

FORCEFUL CONFRONTATION

Above the "Forceful Confrontation Threshold," the next three rungs in the escalation ladder consist of arrest, trial, and confinement. In using these sanctions, police and military forces may also escalate beyond the "injury threshold" by assaulting people while arresting them, torturing them in preparation for trial, and mutilating them while in confinement. There have been enough examples of such behavior in the United States —particularly with the arrest of blacks, Hispanics, Native Americans, and poor people generally—to give the impression that a more repressive America would provide more of the same.

This impression is at least partly buttressed by some of the plans developed by military and police authorities on the use of domestic force. Thus, the following table "Riot Control Pyramid Phasing System" summarizes materials from an FBI police instructor's bulletin. Bulletins of this type suggest rather quick escalation from the use of local police to a complete takeover by federal troops.

In my judgment, this is a false impression. The major thrust of police professionalism in a new corporate society is to overcome what Herman Kahn referred to in the international arena as "an unwillingness to initiate the use of moderate levels of force for limited objectives." Negatively, this means giving up the use of immoderate force that might, by arousing too great a reaction or even radicalizing middle-of-the-roaders,

RIOT CONTROL PYRAMID PHASING SYSTEM *
TABLE 19

	Phase	What Events Occur	Who Keeps Order?	Who is Notified	Who Decides to move to Next Phase
	IV	Disturbance continues to spread, serious domestic violence is in progress	Federal troops		
MAY	III		National Guard County and state forces Whole police department	Federal troops alerted	The Governor
BE					
	II	More arrests are made Arrests are made	Sniper squad Helicopters	Local and state intelligence officers; through Military Intelligence, the Pentagon	The Mayor
BYPASSED			Additional on-duty police	Local emergency headquarters	
	I	A peaceful demonstration involving any number of people	The police who are on duty	FBI Mayor Fire Chief Police Chief	The police commander on duty

* FBI Police Instructor's Bulletin, as published by National Association for Research in Military-Industrial Complex (NARMIC), May 1971.

prove counterproductive. Positively, this means the development of more subtle methods of—in Brigadier Frank Kilson's phrase—"divorcing extremist elements from the population which they are trying to subvert." Some of the available methods are listed in "Innovative Police Action." All of these have already been used—with moderate amounts of accompanying personal injury—in various parts of the United States. A good part of the experimentation has developed in the District of Columbia, with its unusually large proportion of black residents, under an "anti-crime" law enacted during the early years of the Nixon administration.

INNOVATIVE POLICE ACTIONS

1. No-knock police entry on private premises.
2. Preventive detention.
3. Arrest on illegal or unconstitutional grounds.
4. Large-scale arrest with "field arrest forms." *
5. Mass arrest without "field arrest forms."
6. Denial of bail, or setting of bail beyond reach.
7. Failure to inform arrested people of their Constitutional rights.
8. Denial of access to lawyers.
9. Harassment of civil liberties lawyers.
10. Trumped-up charges, often through falsified arrest records.
11. Replacement of total immunity rights by "use immunity." **
12. Optimal show trials.
13. Extra-heavy sentencing, particularly of "multiple offenders."
14. Punitive forms of jail confinement.
15. Restrictive controls over people released on probation.

In reviewing the flowering of these various methods in the past, Richard Harris points up an interesting paradox. On the one hand, the popular justification for these measures has been to maintain law and order by punitive action against criminals and dissidents. In doing so, on the other hand, officials of the Justice Department themselves flagrantly violated many laws of due process. The paradox may be resolved, Harris points out, by retroactive legalization of the illegal: "The danger today is not only that the Constitution will continue to be violated by the Government, as it has been repeatedly in the past couple of years, but that the present Administration will rewrite the essential protections contained in

---

* Field arrest forms may provide for a Polaroid photograph of arrested person with arresting officer together with the officer's statement on the circumstances of arrest.

** Older federal immunity laws under the Fifth Amendment provide that no person may be compelled to testify against himself unless granted *total* immunity. Under *use* immunity, such a person may be prosecuted on the basis of other evidence.

that document, with the consent of the governed, and the agreement of Congress and the Supreme Court, in the name of private and public security." [7]

PERSONAL INJURY

> If it takes a bloodbath . . . let's get it over with.
>
> RONALD REAGAN,
> *when governor of California* [8]

> Research is under way on non-lethal weapons [for the National Guard]: wooden or rubber projectiles that could temporarily immobilize; high-pressure water streams; piercing noises; blinding lights.
>
> ALAN L. OTEN [9]

Above the personal injury level the more obvious punishments that come to mind are assault, torture, mutilation, and murder (or "executive action" in the strange language of the CIA). None of these measures are unknown in present-day America, whether in the isolated form of police brutality behind prison walls, the alleged murder of Fred Hampton by the Chicago police, the killings by STRESS police units in Detroit and other cities, or larger-scale, more publicized form of assassinations as at Kent State, Jackson State, and Attica prison. None of these measures would be foreseen under friendly fascism. Indeed, with the war in Vietnam over, the well-developed capabilities of the "eliminating with prejudice" or "wasting" have been transferred to the domestic scene. *If* a bloodbath is needed, the paramilitary and military forces are prepared to act on Macbeth's maxim: "If it were done when 'tis done, then 'twere well it were done quickly."

A lot hangs, however, on how the wielders of deadly force decide whether or not "it takes a bloodbath." Too many criminals or corpses can create widespread resentment or disillusionment, perhaps even within the paramilitary forces themselves. To be thoroughly effective, one of two things are needed: convincing justification or a thorough blackout on what actually happens. In the absence of these conditions, it may be doubtful that bloodshed is really needed if other fearful, but less deadly, sanctions are available.

An early approach to this problem was the equipping of police forces with tear gas and rubber truncheons. The more advanced approaches include many varieties of chemical gases, blinding lights, deafening noises, and drug pellets or darts that can be shot from guns. These methods require greater restraint in the use of traditional firearms. Thus the pattern of the Attica massacre could be avoided; in future prison riots, prisoners could be incapacitated through the use of drug-tipped darts from the kind of guns now used on grizzly or polar bears. Vigorous crowd dispersal need not be handled in the style of the killings at Kent State. The more probable example to be followed is the style of the Chicago "police riot" during the 1968 Democratic National Convention. Considering the provocations the Chicago police regarded themselves as subjected to, and considering the police force's potential for greater destructiveness, this "riot" was a model of modulated self-control: hundreds of beatings without a single death. A facilitating circumstance was the fact that most of the demonstrators were white middle-class students. To achieve similar restraint in the handling of lower-class blacks, Puerto Ricans, or Chicanos, (who tend to fight back more vigorously), considerable training will be required. This will necessarily involve greater emphasis on rifle and revolver marksmanship, so that "shoot to disable" may compete with "shoot to kill."

Another advanced method of punishment is commitment to a mental institution. Nominally, this is merely a form of legal confinement that sidetracks most of the procedural restraints on incarceration in jails. Actually, it is often a brutal form of degradation and incapacitation. The purely physical injuries often inflicted on mental patients—straitjacketing, beatings, withdrawal of the simplest amenities—are often much less damaging than the psychological injuries. The person stigmatized as "mentally ill," "insane" or "mad" is automatically defined as someone who is "less than human" and no longer entitled to human rights of constitutional protection. Some people accept this definition, thereby relinquishing their humanity. If one disputes this definition, a new version of the "Catch 22" principle comes into being. If an alleged madman insists that he is not sick and that he wants to leave, as Dr. Thomas Szasz has charged, "his inability to recognize that he is, is regarded as a hallmark of his illness." [10]

The Soviet Union has led the way in employing psychiatric authority and commitment to asylums as a means of disciplining dissenting intellectuals. In the United States, where asylums have long been dumping grounds for the poor, the helpless, and the aged as well as the genuinely insane, new legal limitations have been put on the more arbitrary forms of commitment, and the rights of the mentally ill have been at least theoretically affirmed in a number of court decisions. The right climate of opinion, however, or a determined effort by the Establishment could easily reverse this direction. The weapon of "normality," wielded by the prestigious discipline of psychiatry, could be an extremely powerful one for friendly fascism.

Exactly how powerful is demonstrated by the history of lobotomy, an operation that involves a surgical incision into the frontal lobe of the brain. After more than fifty thousand people were lobotomized in the 1940s and 1950s, most of them in mental institutions and women and old people in particular, the technique was abandoned. As the U.S. Public Health Service said in 1948, lobotomized people tended to "lose their values, their interest in everyday life and their feelings for themselves and others." Lobotomy was rejected only partially because of questions about its effectiveness, its consequences on the personality, and its potential for abuse. In fact, a better treatment had been developed—doctors turned to massive use of tranquilizers, and hundreds of thousands of people on drug therapy were released from institutions. More recently lobotomy has started a major comeback—but in far more modern form. It is now called psychosurgery. Instead of relying on the knife alone, psychosurgeons now use ultrasonic waves and irradiation. The various areas of the brain and their functions have been mapped far more extensively. Simple incisions and separations can be supplemented by planting electrodes in the brain for the administration of electric stimulus. Complicated control mechanisms, using the panoply of computer technology, are in the offing. For a short period, vast claims were being advanced for these new techniques, and in a few cases they may have actually been tried out on experimental subjects like children and prisoners.

Reports of psychosurgery, indeed of lobotomy before it, have frequently been exaggerated. Even without exaggeration, the public is apt to be squeamish enough about intervention in the brain to react negatively. Nonetheless, it is testimony to psychiatry's power, its clients' powerlessness, and public acquiescence that lobotomies were so widely employed without sufficient investigation or safeguards. The new psychosurgery has likewise been slowed by hostile publicity, but the limitations placed on its application largely derive from its unknown or uncertain effects. What will happen when these techniques are in fact perfected, and unpleasant side effects better controlled? When will it become far more effective to put the jail inside the deviant's head rather than put the deviant inside the jail? When, instead of an eerie, emotionless "zombie" the result of these procedures is a cheerful, lively, hard-working, but docile "good citizen"?

COVERT ACTION

> A society in which people are already isolated and atomized, divided by suspicions and destructive rivalry, would support a system of terror better than a society without much chronic antagonism.
>
> EUGENE V. WALKER [11]

Covert action is the most obvious form of indirect punishment. Its widespread use abroad by the CIA has helped develop the personnel and methodology for domestic application. It has also provoked hot rivalry (as well as tense cooperation) between the CIA and other agencies involved in clandestine operations: the FBI, the various arms of the Department of Defense, the Secret Service and the larger state and local police departments. Among those secret activities already partially revealed to the public have been the following:

Operation CHAOS	CIA
COINTELPRO	FBI
GARDENPLOT	Department of Defense
SWAT (Strategic Weapons And Tactics) teams	Police Departments

In addition, as reported by R. Harris Smith, scores of large transnational corporations "have their own covert branches and very often recruit out of the CIA." [12] Recent congressional investigations in this area have concentrated on the CIA and the FBI, giving very little attention to other agencies of the federal government, and none to the covert operations of state and local police forces or large corporations. Even within this narrow focus, the investigators could not penetrate very far. Members of the investigatorical committees had reason to fear that if they went too far, they themselves—as objects of covert surveillance—would be subjected to retaliation. CIA and FBI officials, as "loyal Americans," eager to protect their patriotic activities from prying politicians, lied like troopers to congressional interrogators, with no danger of ever being charged with perjury. Miles Copeland, a former CIA official, reports on the views of his former colleagues this way: "Almost all the [CIA] people I talked to assured me unashamedly, almost proudly, 'Of *course,* we are going to lie to the congressional committees.' They felt that as loyal Americans they cannot do otherwise." [13] Looking back on his own behavior, Walter Sullivan, former deputy director of the FBI, has been still franker: "Never once did I hear anybody, including myself, raise the question: is this course of action which we have agreed on lawful . . . We were just naturally pragmatic." [14]

Nonetheless, a few interesting tidbits have been brought to light. Thus the FBI's COINTELPRO program included:

- Anonymously attacking the political beliefs of targets in order to induce their employers to fire them.
- Anonymously mailing letters to the spouses of intelligence targets for the purpose of destroying their marriages.
- Falsely and anonymously labeling as government informants members of groups known to be violent, thereby exposing the falsely labeled member to expulsion or physical attack.
- Sending an anonymous letter to the leader of a Chicago street gang . . . saying that the Black Panthers were supposed to have "a hit for

you." The letter was suggested because it may "intensify . . . animosity" and cause the street gang leader to "take retaliatory action." [15]

Although COINTELPRO was alleged to have been discontinued in 1971, in 1975 a former FBI operative, Joseph A. Burton, publicly revealed the continuation of the same kind of tricks, in subsequent years.[16] Other former agents have disclosed how, under instructions from the FBI, they operated as provocateurs, suggesting illegal activities to antiwar groups, in one case even supplying them with explosives.[17]

All these tidbits, however, merely illustrate the logic of Walter Sullivan's pungent comment about being "naturally pragmatic." The pragmatics of covert action require more effective cover, better coordination among federal, state, local, and private operations, and—above all—a higher level of professionalism. One can envision an informal civil service network, with CIA and Green Beret types of various nationalities moving back and forth throughout the United States and the entire "Free World," with promotions and family security benefits based on professional skill in covert action. Under these circumstances one can look forward to improved capabilities not only for harassment but also for the use of deadlier force through induced heart failure, deep lobotomy (surgical, electrical, or pharmaceutical), induced suicide (as attempted with Dr. Martin Luther King), and "accidental" automobile fatalities. One may expect much greater ingenuity in providing the kind of advice and material with which supermilitant opponents of the Establishment may act out revolutionary fantasies by moving upward on the ladder of terror, thereby providing police agencies with the justification needed for the application of overt force.

CONFLICT AMONG THE "SLOBS"

I can hire one half of the working class to kill the other half.

JAY GOULD,
In reference to Knights of Labor strike, 1886

Jay Gould's boast that he could hire half the working class to kill the other half should be regarded less as a report on his employment practices than as an affirmation of confidence in the strategy of indirect violence. The mere act of bringing different ethnic groups to the same city or factory was often far more effective than extra expenses for hiring strikebreakers or financing the political campaigns of officials who sent the police or National Guard in to break heads.

After World War II, largely as an unforeseen consequence of the mechanization of Southern agriculture, millions of black people from the rural South moved into America's central cities. Here they came into many forms of conflict with other ethnic groups who had "made it" on the lower or middle range of the social ladder. In turn, blacks were followed by people from Puerto Rico, Mexico, Central America, and the Caribbean.

For the higher powerholders, still predominantly White Anglo-Saxon Protestant (WASP), this passage of hatred has been a godsend—what people of French ancestry in Louisiana call *lagniappe,* an unexpected dividend. The "slobs" could be expected to fight among themselves almost endlessly—for jobs, for admission into unions or civil service positions, for entry into this or that neighborhood, for acceptance into higher status schools, even colleges and universities.

During the 1960s and the early 1970s, conflicts among the "slobs" (much more vulnerable than others to business downturns) were fanned by a wide variety of factors. In New York City, as Nathan Glazer and Daniel Patrick Moynihan have pointed out, "The Protestants and better-off Jews determined that the Negroes and Puerto Ricans were deserving and in need and, on these grounds, further determined that these needs would be met by concessions of various kinds from the Italians and the Irish (or, generally speaking, from the Catholics[s] . . . and worse-off Jews."[18]

Blacks themselves were caught between two conflicting tendencies: assimilation (or integration) and separatism. The assimilationists asked for acceptance on equal terms by white employers, neighbors, landlords, and trade unions. Their demands, often based on the self-demeaning assumption that black students could not get a proper education unless sitting alongside whites in a classroom, often met with stubborn resistance and sometimes with a condescending acquiesence that offered quick "plums" to token blacks. The separatists and nationalists, in turn, sometimes sought to unify their followers by raising the level of ethnic invective against "Whitey" and occasionally descending to the level of countering white racism with black racism and anti-Semitism. This conflict was exacerbated by deep tensions between upwardly mobile black professionals, business people, technicians and the majority of stable working-class elements, and the members of the highly unstable "underclass."

With the stagflation of the late 1970s, the potentials for more acute group conflicts have grown. More and more people compete with each other for fewer and fewer job opportunities. Moreover, so-called "affirmative action" programs, which sought to provide more openings for black and Latin job-seekers have been converted into what Representative Augustus Hawkins once called "negative action"—namely, the firing of a large proportion of minority people (and women) who previously benefited from preferential hiring. Ghetto crime increases. In the public schools, there are more beatings, thefts, rapes, riots, and murders. In white communities the result is fear—deep fear of the "Black Terror" that may strike in the streets (unless properly cordoned and patrolled), in their homes (unless properly guarded or armed), and in the public schools (unless segregated). This is what Andrew Hacker had in mind in his analysis of white fears some years ago when the unemployment-inflation outlook was less foreboding: "Those who preoccupy themselves with the immortality and irresponsibility found in slum society would do well to turn their attention to the new generations of youngsters being spawned in our ghettoes at this very moment . . . In the process of creation right now are rioters and rapists, murderers and marauders, who will despoil society's landscape before this country has run its course . . . Violence will mark relations between the races. Whites will live in increasing fear of a depredations against their persons and property . . . If a single word characterizes white attitudes, it is *fear*." [19]

By the end of the 1970s and the beginning of the 1980s this fear was exacerbated by new outbreaks of cross-burnings in front of the homes of black families in the North and hate-ridden attacks on blacks moving into formerly lily-white suburbs. Nazi-style swastikas have been painted on synagogues and on the graves in Jewish cemeteries. Jay Gould would clap his hands in glee at the coming prospect of new waves of conflict among ethnic and religious minorities.

A VIOLENCE-VIGILANTE CULTURE

Well, what is a vigilante man?
Tell me, what is a vigilante man?
Has he got a gun and a club in his han'?
Is that a vigilante man? . . .
Would he shoot his brother and sister down?

WOODIE GUTHRIE

Under "advanced" capitalism, Woodie Guthrie's old question might be asked again—not to probe the motives of someone who might "shoot his brother and sister down" but to establish his identity. One answer to the question is given by Kanti C. Kotecha and James L. Walker in their article "Police Vigilantes": "Police vigilantism can be defined as acts or threats by police which are intended to protect the established socio-political order from subversion, but which violate some generally perceived norms for police behavior." [20] Unlawful police violence is usually covert. Beatings and torture may be hidden by the doors of the police van or jailhouse. The police may form off-duty groups—like the terrorist "death squads" in Brazil or "The Band" in the Dominican Republic—that dispense with legal formalities in "disposing" of dissenters or petty criminals who fail to buy protection. Another answer leads straight to the door of the chief executive, whose personal network usually includes various groups of illegal operators. In this way, in Alan Wolfe's pungent words, "vigilantism may be turned on its head: instead of a private group using illegal violence for public ends, a public group uses illegal violence for private ends." [21] Also, as in the case of President Ford's indirect encouragement of the antibusing rioters in Boston, a chief "law enforcer" may promote conflict among the "slobs" by condoning illegal violence by private groups.

But the central domain of terror continues to be the "symbolic environment." While the myths and fantasies of popular culture are replete with opiate-like images of virtue or cleverness rewarded, boy-getting-girl, girl-getting riches, and everyone getting pie in Pollyanna's sky, more "realistic" imagery is used to sell movies to audiences and TV audiences to advertisers. Symbolic violence gets and keeps attention. And despite sporadic gestures toward "cooling it," the long-term tendency seems to be toward escalation. "The world of television drama is, above all, a violent one," report George Gerbner and Larry P. Gross, the two most assiduous monitors of American TV. "More than half of all characters are involved in some violence, at least one tenth in some killing, and three fourths of prime time hours contain some violence." [22] The net effect of this tendency, as Gerbner and Gross point out, may be "a demonstration of power and an instrument of social serving, on the whole, to reinforce and preserve the existing social order." Although their emphasis is on the preservation of the status quo, their analysis clearly suggests that an increase in symbolic violence could help usher in a new serfdom of fear, anxiety, and simultaneous identification with the unconstrained and violent forces of "law."

15

Sex, Drugs, Madness, Cults

HOW DOES A SOCIETY blow off steam: Where are the escape valves that offer relief from tension and anxiety?

A powerful head of steam is an inescapable by-product of trends toward friendly fascism. The rewards of extended professionalism, accelerated consumerism, and elite power work *if*—and *only if*—they create anxiety. Much of this anxiety (and even terror) is free floating and, like explosive gases, might be touched off by stray sparks—unless dissipated by channeling into available escape valves.

Four of these escape valves—sex, drugs, mental illness, and cults—merit special attention. Although each is usually seen from entirely different perspectives, in each we find a phenomenon already uncovered in other spheres—that actions hailed as hallmarks of progress may turn out to be major steps down the new roads to serfdom. As I shall now proceed to suggest, friendly fascism, American style, might well be described as a sex-driven, drugged, mad (or Therapeutic), and cult-ridden society.

SEX: THROUGH LIBERATION TO REPRESSION

Since World War II the so-called "sexual revolution" has started to demolish old-fashioned sexual repression. This has evidenced itself in a significant lifting of taboos on premarital sexual intercourse, marital infidelity, male and female homosexuality, masturbation, prostitution, and even incest. Explicit representation of nude bodies and a wide variety of sex acts are now much more acceptable not only in "how-to-do-it" sex manuals but also on TV and the stage, and in movies, dance, poetry, and novels.

If Wilhelm Reich were alive today (and should stick by his guns), he would probably hail the sexual revolution as destroying the basis of any future fascism. Indeed, he said just about that back in 1933: "The biologic rigidity of the present generation can no longer be eliminated

. . . However new human beings are born every day, and in the course of thirty years the human race will have been biologically renewed; it will come into the world without any trace of fascist distortion." Liberation from sexual repression, Reich insisted, would bring human freedom. And Reich hammered this point home with the assertion that "Sexually awakened women, affirmed and recognized as such, would mean the complete collapse of the authoritarian ideology." [1] Although Reich died in jail in 1957 (after being convicted for fraud in the sale of his "orgone box"), his spirit has carried on. For more than a decade after his death, many "counterculture" enthusiasts thought that the possibility of political repression would somehow or other be destroyed by the lifting of sexual repression. This, indeed, is part of Charles Reich's optimistic prediction that liberated lifestyles will undermine the Corporate State. Others have seen the sexual revolution as freeing both men and women from the commercialization of sex and as opening up new horizons of freedom and equality.

Yet, there are at least three elements in the sexual revolution that might contribue to, rather than reverse, present trends toward technology-based authoritarianism.

First of all, the sexual revolution has helped make more women available to more men on easier terms. A "liberated" woman, as Anselma Dell' Olio has put it, is often regarded as one who "puts out" sexually at the drop of a suggestive command, doesn't demand marriage, and "takes care of herself" with contraceptives. This type of liberation has little to do with the kind of love that is based on the two-way communication and respect and that only exists between equals. It has little to do with the changing of sex roles in family, school, workplace, or economic politics. In her "The Sexual Revolution Wasn't Our War" in *Ms.* magazine, Dell' Olio has put it this way: "We have come to see that the so-called Sexual Revolution is merely a link in the chain of abuse laid on women through patriarchal history. While purporting to restructure the unequal basis for sexual relationships between men and women, our beneficent male liberators werc in fact continuing their control of feminine sexuality." [2]

Second, there seem to be growing tendencies toward engineered routinization of sex. A new "sex technology"—backed up by expanded R & D—propagates techniques not only of birth control and abortion but also of body massages, foreplay, intercourse, and afterplay. As with other forms of social engineering, the sex technologists suggest a technical solution for almost every sexual probelm. Over the short run, emotions remain in the picture—because their excitement contributes to the consumer expenditures essential for the income and profits of *Playboy-Penthouse-Hustler*-style magazines, more explicit pornography, rent-a-girl enterprises, and the new corporate brothels. Over the longer run, to the extent that sex drives are more thoroughly separated from truly deep emotions and warm interpersonal relations among mutually respecting individuals, the emotional content could be largely drained out. This is the friendly fascist perspective: sex as a quick impersonal activity that contributes to individual alienation and social fragmentation. "As political and economic freedom diminishes," Aldous Huxley once wrote in an introduction to his *Brave New World,* "sexual freedom tends compensatingly to increase." It helps reconcile people to "the servitude which is their fate."

Finally, the sexual revolution could possibly have a dual effect on human energies. For the majority of people, it could drain off, along with violent sports, alcohol, and drugs, energies from any dedicated efforts to oppose oligarchy, empire, and the subversion of formal democracy. This would be classic escapism—well garbed, perfumed, self-induced, and beefed up with smooth commercialism and technological gadgetry. For the oligarchs and their professional aides in the technostructure, however, it could build up a new form of manipulative *machismo.* Their difficulties in coping with the fathomless bafflements of the Establishment, their frustrations at not receiving respect and honor from subordinates, associates, mates, and children, their self-doubts concerning the meaning of the rat race and rewards of manipulative power—all these can be compensated for by the synthetic potency of orgasm-cum-flattery bought cheap and worth every dollar on the corporate expense account. With this kind of bedroom support, the banker, executive, general, admiral, and professional can go back to the fray with renewed energies.

DRUGS: RELIGION OF SOME PEOPLE

In today's First World, oppression takes many different forms. It is rooted in the frustration of rising aspirations, in the anguish of old crises in new forms, in the new environmental crises, and in the erosion of authority. Above all, the impact of tendencies toward extended professionalism is to accentuate fragmentation, anxiety, and alienation. The by-products of accelerated consumption are boredom, apathy, and tension. The slow growth of concentrated elite power builds up repressed aggressiveness and despair at all levels. Throughout the population, including the top elites, an eagerness for escape could lead to a Drug Age in which—in the words of Harrison Pope, Jr., "drug use ranges from simple fun—a transient relief from boredom—to an entire way of life, an identity which buffers against apathy." Hallucination, he adds, "can become a means for a psychological or philosophical quest, a search for meaning in a society perceived as unloving, lonely, and meaningless." [3]

The power of drug relief is the huge range of demands fulfillable by modern industrialism's expanding pharmacopeia. A. E. Housman referred only to traditional alcoholic drinks when he wrote his famous lines to the effect that ". . . malt does more than Milton can/To justify God's ways to man." Conviviality and good cheer can be promoted by marijuana, hashish, and amphetamines. LSD and its many rivals can open up new vistas of fanciful and other-worldly sensation. Some of these provide indescribable heights of pleasure. As Dr. Marshall Dumont puts it, the "abdominal orgasm that follows the 'opiate flash' is better than sex." "Uppers" provide temporary *fun,* or relief from boredom, apathy, or alienation. They may be followed by "downers" that may "ease the crash" and put one at blissful ease or into a light or deep slumber. Both uppers and downers allow people to sidestep the pressures of competition, aggression, and loneliness.[4]

Market demand for these various forms of drug relief is already far more widespread than indicated by public distress about "junkies" among black and Puerto Rican minorities. Heroin and methadone are increasingly used among the rat racers in the technostructure and the upper elites. As for age, the great majority of the "pillheads" are to be found among the adult population. The 25–64 age group outnumbers the 14–24 group by more than 2 to 1. It also has much more money to back up its demands. This is where the future market potential lies. If you are lonely, nervous, unattractive, overweight or underweight, if you have difficulty in sleeping or waking up, if you have upset this or clogged that, mass advertising tells you that the answer is a pill or a drink. But telling you is only half the story. The most strategic messages are found in these drug company advertisements in psychiatric and medical journals: [5]

> WHAT MAKES A WOMAN CRY? A man? Another woman? Three kids? No kids at all? Wrinkles? You name it . . . if she is depressed, consider Portofane.
>
> SCHOOL, THE DARK, SEPARATION, DENTAL VISITS, MONSTERS—THE EVERYDAY ANXIETY OF CHILDREN SOMETIMES GETS OUT OF HAND. A child can usually deal with his anxieties. But sometimes the anxieties overpower the child. Then he needs your help. Your help may include Vistaril.

The aim of the drug industry seems to be much more than getting people to define human and social problems as open to medical remedies; it includes enrolling all levels of so-called "health personnel" as pushers. Already, the mass use of tranquilizers is spreading from mental institutions and hospitals to out-patient clinics and treatment in doctors' offices.

Other professions are getting into the swim. "Well-adjusted" behavior can also be produced in the classroom—without any changes in the apathetic or stultifying, often implicitly racist atmosphere of many schools—by administering Ritalin to "hyperactive" children. "Two hundred thousand children in the United States, it has been estimated, are now being given amphetamine and stimulant therapy, with probably another hundred thousand receiving tranquilizers and antidepressants." [6] Looking into the future, two professors of education have hopefully seen this number rising into the many millions: Biochemical and psychological mediation of learning is likely to increase," they assert; "new dramas will play on the educational stage as drugs are introduced experimentally to improve in the learner such qualities as personality, concentration and memory."

Some psychologists envision still greater dramas in other stages. In his presidential address at the American Psychological Assocation, Professor Kenneth Clark announced that, as a result of "many provocative and suggestive findings from neurophysiological, biochemical and psychopharmacological research . . . it is now possible—indeed imperative—to reduce human anxieties, tensions, hostilities, violence, cruelty and the destructive power irrationalities of man, which are the basis of wars." [7] He then made a formal proposal: "Given these contemporary facts, it would seem logical that a requirement imposed upon all power-controlling leaders and those who aspire to such leadership would be that they accept and use the earliest perfected form of psychotechnical, biochemical intervention which would assure their positive use of power and reduce or block the possibility of their using power destructively . . ." [8]

It is in the sphere of direct rehabilitation that drug relief is most vigorously spread by alleged cures. The most heavily financed rehabilitation efforts, instead of dealing primarily with a person's need and demand for drugs, involve counter-drugs. Thus, back in the 1890s, many physicians joined with Dr. J. R. Black when, in a medical journal article, he concluded that "I would urge morphine instead of alcohol for all to whom such a craving is an incurable propensity." [9] Heroin, in turn, was originally invented and introduced by physicians as a cure for morphine addiction. Methadone—also addictive and capable of producing a "high"—is now used to block heroin addiction. In rehabilitation circles, major hopes are being placed on even newer counter-drugs: cyclazone, naloxone, M5050, and many others.

The inner logic of all these tendencies, I suspect, is to produce eventually a qualitative change in public controls: the removal of the major legal restrictions not only on marijuana but also on heroin and amphetamines. Under such conditions the repressive controls on addicts would be lifted. Mainliners would be as free to induce their own tastes as winos, alcoholics and "pill heads." As in England, where low-cost heroin has been widely available under the National Health Service, robbery and larceny would no longer be necessary to support a hundred-dollar-a-day habit. With less costs imposed on others, more people would be free to injure themselves. If and when such a reform comes, it would be presented as a triumph for more humanism in the handling of lower-class addiction. In a broader sense, however, it could be a major step toward friendly fascism.

"Each one of us," mused the Controller in *Brave New World,* "goes through life in a bottle. But if we happen to be Alphas, our bottles are, relatively speaking, enormous. We should suffer acutely if we were confined in a narrower space." Under friendly fascism also, each person would live in his or her own bottle, and everyone—even the Alphas—would complain about the confinement. But in this fully Bottled Society, everyone, instead of being limited to a dose of standardized *soma,* would be able to win relief from frustrations through the intake of pills, drinks, injections, and sniffs from an enormous variety of smaller bottles.

MADNESS: ESCAPE FROM MADNESS

Would not the diagnosis be justified that many systems of civilization—or epochs of it—possibly even the whole of humanity—have become "neurotic" under the pressure of the civilizing trends?

SIGMUND FREUD [10]

The old-fashioned madhouse—often referred to as "Bedlam," "looney bin" or simply "insane asylum"—was one of the earlier blights of civilization. An element of progress may be found in its replacement by modern practices of psychiatry, psychoanalysis, psychiatric social work, and similar forms of social engineering. On the other hand, the usual criticism of modern psychotherapy is that there is still too much of the filth, ignorance, degradation, and cruelty of Bedlam in the present-day asylum. In practically every state of the union, any crusading journalist for a TV station or newspaper can make instant headlines by exposing shocking conditions in the nearest public institutions to which the "mentally ill" are committed. The immediate impact was previously to suggest the need for larger budgets and more professional care; more recently, "deinstitutionalization" became the common goal of reformers, civil liberatarians, and budget cutters. Only slowly do the other defects of modern psychiatric care emerge as starkly as those of asylum.

One of these is the tendency of modern psychotheraphy to become a new instrument of direct repression. This is most evident, as Dr. Thomas Szasz has pointed out in a long series of powerfully argued books, in "institutional psychiatry." Rather than dedicating themselves to a confidential and unique relation with each client, institutional psychiatrists tend to become agents of the state and, in that capacity, are responsible for certifying various people as mad (by a variety of unbelievably elastic quasidiagnostic terms) and thereby commiting them to incarceration. Whether they want it or not, those who are thus imprisoned escape from the stresses and strains of the "real world" outside the locked doors and barred windows of the mental hospital. Instead of the harsh competition, fragmentation, and materialism of the outside world, they enter a strange new world of dull and (for some) soothing routines, of the constrained anxieties relating to the small rewards and punishments administered by staff and other inmates, and of unrestricted opportunities for illusions and delusions. For some—perhaps the majority—the real delusion is that they are essentially different from the staff, the physicians, and the nondeviants in the outside world.

"Because the concept of mental illness is infinitely elastic," argues Dr. Szasz, "almost any moral, political or social problem can be cast into a psychiatric mold." He then drives his point home by discussing the possibility of a new fascism: "Unlike political fascism, which sought its justification in the value of the "good of the state," and subordinated everything else to it, the moral fascism we have been cultivating subordinates all to the value of the 'Welfare of the people.' " [11]

A far more widespread tendency, however, is the authentication by most forms of psychotherapy of widespread escape from the anxieties of the real world. As opposed to the over two million in-patients and outpatients receiving formal "mental health" treatment in 1976, one may estimate that there were four to five times as many—from eight to ten million people—rather fully involved in various forms of more informal varieties of "therapy." These forms, and the labels affixed thereto, vary from traditional psychoanalysis to group therapy, encounter groups, marathon groups, family therapy, and behavioral therapy. Some are intimately associated with drug therapy or even with psychotherapy.

Like drugs, this kind of help can become powerfully addictive; the people who are hooked experience painful withdrawal systems. But unlike drug addicts, the people "in treatment" can readily switch from one form to another. This leads to considerable shopping around. Only rarely do therapists allow attention to be focused on the many sources of anxiety and misery that lie in the political, economic, and social sphere. To do so would require not only dealing with social fragmentation and exploitation but encouraging the kind of resistance and counterattack that could only be handled by a political movement that may not yet exist. So willy-nilly the therapists, sometimes consciously and with the immediate interests of their individual patients at heart, accept the realities of a mad society—and provide the escape valves required for its acceptance by their patients.

This is a consumer-service area of considerable potential. Dr. Gerald Klerman, professor of psychiatry at Harvard University, estimates that one out of eight Americans—about 28 million people—"can expect to experience depression during his life." [12] In a report for the National

Institute of Mental Health, Dr. David Rosenthal projects a larger market: "possibly 60 million Americans are borderline schizophrenics or exhibit other deviant mental behavior in the schizophrenic category." If friendly-fascist tendencies continue, the number of people getting "help" could well be somewhere between Dr. Klerman's 28 million and Dr. Rosenthal's 60 million.

For this expansion to take place, two technical conditions will probably have to be met: (1) a large expansion of subprofessional helpers and (2) tacit assurance that most of the "helpees," so long as they behave themselves according to dominant values, will face little risk of compulsory commitment.

The social sciences have never been lacking in delusions. Delusions are nourished by grant applications that exaggerate the results to be attained, by grants and contracts that legitimate these ebullient claims, and by recognition from political leaders desperately in need of the legitimation obtainable only from recognized "authorities." Each social science discipline seems to produce its specialized delusions—the economist's vision of an econometric model guiding the behavior of oligarchic capitalists, Carl Kaysen's "corporation with a soul," Daniel Bell's university as the central institution of modern capitalism, or B. F. Skinner's world of autonomous B. F. Skinners administering the postive reinforcements that will bring people "beyond freedom and disunity" to beneficial adjustment. Oddly enough, the psychiatrist—the self-avowed specialists in diagnosing and treating the delusions of others—seem most susceptible to delusions of grandeur. Few others have gone as far as Dr. Howard P. Rome in calling the entire world their "catchment area." Dr. G. Brock Chisholm has gone still further by urging that psychiatrists "must now decide what is to be the immediate future of the human race. No one else can. And this is the prime responsibility of psychiatry." [14]

CULTS: BELONGING THROUGH SUBMISSION

As we have seen already, greater cohesion at the peak of a capitalist establishment is perfectly consistent with social fragmentation among the population at large. Accordingly, there comes into being a huge and desperate demand for something to belong to and believe in.

Such a demand could be met in the 1980s by a popular anti-establishment movement. One could visualize large numbers of lower- and middle-income people working together to transform capitalist society into a democratic, pluralistic socialism or a truly humanistic capitalism. In the struggles of such a movement, people could find not only a new spirit of community but a new or restored faith in the future of family, community, and country. They could find the best possible protection against environmental degradation, unemployment and inflation, and the ever-present dangers of limited or unlimited warfare. If such a movement came into being, of course, it would face the danger of being shattered into pieces by a combination of minor concessions, the co-opting of key leaders, penetration, provocation, and direct repression. The possibility that such a movement might come into being and overcome this danger is one of the reasons why friendly fascism is not inevitable.

More probable, however, is the absorption of many potential leaders or devoted followers of such a movement into one or another religious or quasi-religious cult. In 1976, according to *U.S. News & World Report,* anywhere from one to three million Americans, mostly in their twenties or late teens, are active in hundreds of these new cults.[15] One of these is the Unification Church, led by Sun Myung Moon, the millionaire Korean industrialist. The Moon church offers thousands of young Americans the security of perennial childhood. "To lonely young people drifting through cold, impersonal cities and schools," one observer reports "it offers instant friendship and communion . . . a life of love, joy and inner peace, with no hassles, no doubts and no decisions." [16] Other young people are absorbed into the Divine Light Mission led by the young Indian, Guru Maharaj Ji; the International Society for Krishna Consciousness, whose flowing robed "Krishna chanters" may be seen dancing on the streets of many American cities; the Church of Scientology; Jews for Jesus; and the Children of God, sometimes called "Jesus freaks." In turn, EST (Erhard Seminars Training), like most of its competitors in the packaging of encounter groups and group therapy, appeals mainly to people in their late twenties, thirties, and early forties. Erhard's message is simple but powerful: "There is nothing out there. No one cares. Do you get it? You can change nothing. Accept what is." [17]

And for those who are older, have already "made it," and fear that they have "had it," there are the beginnings of a new fundamentalism made up of "evangelicals" who, by the late 1970s, according to Carey McWilliams, attracted up to 40 million followers in the mainline Protestant denominations alone.[18] Others may turn to astrology, transcendental meditation, or belief in extrasensory perception.

Although some of the going enterprises in this area have already become financially successful, I do not see many elements of this sector being absorbed into the capital-rich world of the transnational conglomerate. The outlook, rather, is for a highly competitive market in which a few cults may remain and many will disappear to be replaced by new ones. Some will stress retreat from the world, while others will seek to bring God back into the classroom. Some will offer personal salvation by getting in touch with one's body or inner self, while others will offer it by closer contact with God or the universe as a whole.

Underlying all this diversity, however, I see two common elements: acceptance of the existing social structure and the submission to an authoritarian doctrine or leader. The satisfaction thereby provided can go far in narcotizing the dissatisfactions of those who feel they are being "ripped off" by a heartless world. On the road to friendly fascism, the new cults can provide exploited people not only with a sigh (to use Karl Marx's old phrase) but with those "uppers" and "downers" that channel tensions into harmless activities and thereby promote submission to the growing powers of the faceless oligarchy and the Golden International.

16

The Adaptive Hydra

If we want things to stay as they are, things will have to change. Do you know?

GIUSEPPE DI LAMPEDUSA,
The Leopard

THE MYTHICAL HYDRA of Greek antiquity was a remarkable animal. If an attacker cut off one of its many heads, it would function through the others. And then a new head would sprout to replace the lost one.

The modern complex outdoes the ancient Hydra. It has many more heads, and each of them enjoys less visibility. It has greater regenerative powers; for each head springs from a managerial reservoir full of upwardly mobile men (and a few women), breathlessly awaiting more room at the top. This modern Hyrda is also *adaptive*—both in the passive sense of responding to change and in the active sense of anticipating or guiding it.

During the period between the years 1984 and 2000, the generations coming into the Establishment's positions of higher power will be those born during World War II and the decade thereafter. Of these, the oldest will be those who were of college age at the time of the various "rebellions" of the 1960s. They will be people who, while probably passive onlookers at that time, nonetheless jumped into the counterculture by the time it became respectable. They will probably still maintain longish hair and mod clothes, and inhale or ingest whatever drug becomes the latest fad. Just as Charles Reich's corporate planners were more sophisticated than the Consciousness One individualists, the faceless oligarchs of the Berkeley-Columbia generation would probably be far more advanced than the corporate-military planners of today. Some of them may indeed be former militants—like Eldridge Cleaver—who have "got religion" and changed their spots. "One who pays some attention to history," Noam Chomsky warns, "will not be surprised if those who cry most loudly that we must smash and destroy are later found among the administrators of some new system of repression." In any case, having already adapted themselves to changing conditions and opportunities, these new leaders will probably show remarkable adaptivity in facing up to changing challenges to the Establishment's power.

FRYING PAN–FIRE CONFLICTS

Many years ago Frank Stockton wrote a short story about a semi-barbaric king who used to try accused criminals in a public arena. The defendant was forced to open one of a pair of doors in the arena wall. Behind one there was usually a hungry tiger. If the man chose that door, he was killed immediately and declared guilty. Behind the other door was supposed to be a slave girl who, if that door was opened, became his wife as a reward for his innocence. When the king's daughter took a lover from the peasant class, the king decided to punish the man by placing him in the arena. After asking her father which door was which, the princess signaled her lover to choose the right-hand door. He did so. At this point Stockton ends the story: "And so I leave it with all of you: Which came out of the opened door—the lady or the tiger?"

When I first heard this story discussed in a high school class, the question seemed to be one of female psychology. Did the princess direct her lover to the tiger, sparing herself the pain of seeing him married to another? Or rather, being unable to face the spectacle of seeing him torn to pieces, did she direct him to the lady?

Even in high school, I was never able to accept the question entirely as it was put. Knowing already that everything a father says is not necessarily so, I wondered whether perhaps in this very special case, the king had placed a tiger behind *each* door. More recently, reflecting on the behavior of leaders who preserved their power for long periods, it has occurred to me that the king probably put a tiger behind one door and a pack of wolves behind the other. In either case the daughter did not really know what the options were and her lover faced a classic choice between a frying pan and a fire.

As I peer down the road to friendly fascism, I see many choices of this type. From the viewpoint of the Establishment, the logic is absurdly simple: any grievance that ordinary people suffer may be cured by measures that consolidate the repressive power of the Big Business-Big Government partnership. Nor is this an entirely new logic; rather, it is merely the fruition of a long sequence of reforms—often first articulated by socialists or communists—that have strengthened the structure of concentrated power. Debates over these reforms have usually included few if any references to the power elites that would ultimately run them or benefit from them. Indeed, as is often the case with welfare-state reforms, the most vocal opposition has sometimes come from conservatives or reactionaries who were not prescient enough to know on which side their bread was buttered.

If one looks quickly back at the preceding eight chapters, he or she will find copious examples of such system-strengthening reforms. Among them are centralized economic planning, executive agency reorganization, streamlining Congress, more integrated data collection, and, above all, government control of prices and wages. Any one of these can be hailed in advance as a forward step toward a more humanist, enlightened, egalitarian, or democratic society—and have often so been hailed by liberal or radical reformers. Yet any one could turn out to be another step down one of the many roads to serfdom.

A crucial example is the debate over the mode of recruiting people into the American army: voluntary enlistment or a return to conscription. As formulated within the Establishment's higher circles, the issue has been *how* to maintain or enlarge an already huge war force. When Presidents Nixon and Ford liquidated the draft, their purpose was to reduce the opposition to American intervention in Vietnam. The shift to a volunteer army helped achieve this purpose. It also tied in with a reduction in the size of the war force and a massive expansion in weapons that needed very little manpower for their use. In 1979 and 1980 the campaign to register American youth for a subsequent draft has been part of resurgent militarism based on a rapid expansion in both missile systems and armed forces. In this context, the most important question is not voluntary recruitment versus registration for a draft; it is the pace of the arms race, the future of detente, and the preparations for "new Vietnams." If these larger issues are obscured, then the method of recruiting people into the army is a frying-pan-versus-fire question. Militarism can be remolded either way. There are dozens of false micro-alternatives of this type. These are crossroads where either road can lead in the direction of friendly fascism. On the macro-level there are such broader issues as deflationary stagnation or inflationary recession, polarization versus consensus, standardized liberalism versus conservatism—each pair of which may be nothing other than alternative roads to serfdom.

Actually, none of these alternatives turns out to be a simple pair. In the real world, there are more ways to be killed than suggested by the limited options of being fried in a pan, being directly burned, or being attacked by tigers or wolves. When I was very young—even before reading Stockton's "The Lady or the Tiger"—the nice, well-behaved boys on my block used to propound a difficult question: How would you prefer to be killed—by being shot, poisoned, drowned, hung, stabbed through the heart, or thrown off a roof? Today, the scientists, "security managers," and military contractors offer a still more bewildering variety of destructive options: at least a dozen different varieties each of new intercontinental missiles, large or small submarines, manned or unmanned aircraft, and chemical and bacteriological warfare. Less frank than the boys on my block, however, they usually fail to indicate that in any future war in which some of these options are chosen the senders as well as the receivers may also be annihilated.

If all these bright ideas were to originate in one spot, the spectrum of choice would be much more narrow. But adaptivity on the road to friendly fascism depends on "oligarchic democracy" within an establishment's top and middle levels. In his own rather limited way, Albert Speer recognized the necessity of working this way as Hitler's minister of armaments and war production. Instead of sending out authoritarian orders from his office, he tried to develop a spirit of so-called "parliamentarianism" in accordance with which arguments and counter-arguments were heard on all sides before decisions were made. He preferred "uncomfortable associates to compliant tools." [2] He thus exploited the creative energies and spontaneity of many technocrats who, lacking or stifling all moral scruples, dedicated themselves to solving the technical problems assigned to them or originated by them. What Speer nurtured in the context of the more rigid bureaucracies of Germany has already been fully developed in the modern Establishments of the First World. Coordination already takes place in accordance with what Charles E. Lindblom of Yale University once called "partisan mutual adjustment." Without stating it directly, Lindblom put his finger on the nature of system strengthening in a power structure undergoing transformation into Super-America, Inc.

If this kind of power structure is to come into being and maintain itself, redundancy is essential. Errors made at one point can thus be corrected at other points. Naturally, in the process of eliminating some internal conflicts, the Establishment's leaders knowingly or unwittingly create others. As the partnership between Big Business and Big Government becomes much closer, personal infighting becomes more intense. Some plutocrats remain wedded to the old order, preferring the established ways and fearing the leap into global operations. Tactical conflicts arise about who gets how much of the pie and, more broadly, about the shape of empire; the pace of oligarchic integration; the timing of constitutional subversion; the degree of informational management; the delicate balance between positive reinforcements and the use of violences; the uses of sex, drugs, madness, and cults; and the scope of system-strengthening reforms and adaptation.

On all these points, the oligarchs need conflicting proposals and pressures from executive managers and junior-contingent members. From time to time, indeed, the intensity of such conflicts might stymie the processes of mutual-adjustment decision making, or even threaten the oligarchy's viability. Yet, its internal tensions would be much less fierce than those that raged violently in fascist Germany, Japan, and Italy. There, the business oligarchs often found themselves uncomfortably pressed by the political leaders and military overlords, or both. In contrast, the Corporate Overseers and Ultra-Rich of the United States would enjoy a much larger degree of hegemony and the possibility of enlarged empire without the unsettling horrors of openly initiating a large-scale war to extend their frontiers—an option never available to Hitler, Mussolini, or the Japanese leaders.

The price of oligarchic democracy is sustained controversy in the executive suites—mostly behind closed doors, some spilling over into arenas of more public visibility. The minimum benefit is the prevention of top-level stagnation. The optimum outcome—from the viewpoint of the friendly fascists—is an oligarchy capable of creative dynamism.

MULTILEVEL CO-OPTATION

Just for a handful of silver he left us,
Just for a riband to stick in his coat.

ROBERT BROWNING,
The Lost Leader

Co-optation, according to Phillip Selznick in a study of organizational behavior, is "the process of absorbing new elements into the leadership or policymaking structure of an organization as a means of averting threats to its stability or existence." [3] From the viewpoint of a country's establishment, co-optation has historically gone far beyond averting threats; it has served the more positive function of strengthening the system. In some cases co-optation has been associated with system-strengthening reforms. Michael Harrington points out that in adopting various welfare-state programs that originated in the German socialist movement, "it was the Junker Bismarck who came up with the truly bold scheme: he proposed to co-opt socialism itself." [4] But a system can also be strengthened by absorbing elements into minor roles far below the leadership or policy-making level. Some of these roles may be purely symbolic, some technical, some administrative. When William Wordsworth "left us" (in Robert Browning's words) to become poet laureate, he did not enter the inner councils of the expanding British empire. When Daniel P. Moynihan spent the first two years of the Nixon administration as counsellor to the president, his role was both symbolic and technical. As a former high Democratic official and an officer of the left-liberal Americans for Democratic Action, he was a living symbol of the Nixon administration's adaptability. He also did a superb technical job in formulating Nixon's welfare reforms. The late Chapman James, the Air Force's top-ranking black general, performed all three functions. It was he whom the Secretary of Defense Melvin Laird, according to Mary McGrory, always sent out to prove to dissenters that the military, like the war in Vietnam, was not racist.[5]

In most cases, the "handful of silver" is far less generous and the "riband" smaller than in the cases of Wordsworth, Moynihan, or James. In Robert Browning's poem, "They with the gold to give, doled him out silver/So much was theirs who so little allowed." The key word in Browning's poem is "doled." By being short-changed on the silver, by receiving more copper pennies and "ribands," the salivary glands of actual and would-be co-optees are kept working more energetically. In return, high benefits may be received by the Establishment: the weakening of opposing groups, administrative linkages with such groups, symbolic substitutes for reform, or the rhetorical trappings for reform proposals not meant to be acted upon. Less obvious, but probably just as significant, is what might be called "preventive co-optation"—namely, keeping internal dissidents working within the system instead of openly expressing their opposition.

At times, it is very difficult to tell the difference between co-optees, on the one hand, and those who see themselves as "boring from within," that is, as activists who seek to improve the system by working within it. The person who does this, to use Joseph S. Clark's phrase "gets along by going along." [6] But the more he goes along, the more the hope of being an effective-change agent may fade into the background and become little more than a personal rationalization for being a full-fledged co-optee.

The processes of moving toward friendly fascism in America would rather automatically—without any conscious planning—provide thousands of lower-level plums for dissidents and rebels demanding "a piece of the action." Some of these would go in advance preemptively to those showing exceptional promise; others would be held out as prizes. In either case, choices would be available. Positions close to the leadership or policy-making structure, however, would probably be available only after considerable effort and intrasystem coalition-building and politicking. Often, entire organizations or subsystems might be co-opted. In what could be called "subsystem co-optation," liberal and purportedly radical organizations could be used to provide young people with opportunities to "work off their steam" harmlessly or to provide the backdrop for the system's normal compromising in the resolution of routine conflicts. Conspicuous advisory or public relations positions could probably be provided for oppositionists, including former left-wingers of a previous generation.

Multi-ethnic co-optation can also be taken for granted. Particularly conspicuous roles would undoubtedly be assigned to both blacks and Jews. According to Samuel F. Yette, the selection of black appointees to administrative posts in government has already shown the way toward attaining three goals: "(1) to provide color credibility wherever such credibility was crucial to selling an otherwise invalid product; (2) to neutralize such talent by taking it from potentially radical stations (the hiring off of militants) and placing it officially on the side of the establishment . . . ; and (3) to have a black person in position to take responsibility for antiblack policies and decisions, usually made exclusively by whites—without the black appointee's knowledge, consent or ability." [7] These practices can be used in foreign-policy areas also. Alphonso Pinkney, the Hunter college sociologist, sees the possibility of "American troops, with many Black soldiers, airlifted to South Africa to help the White government conduct an anti-insurgency operation against the rebellious African majority." [8] In early 1976, with the help of Floyd McKissick, something similar—but limited to black mercenaries—was briefly attempted in Angola.

While a much smaller minority of the population than blacks, Jews have been conspicuous in the past for their progressive and liberal tendencies. As some Jewish businessmen and professionals have shifted to conservatism, major opportunities naturally develop for a minority of Jews to achieve strategic positions at the establishment's upper levels, particularly in the Chief Executive Network. Before the Nixon-Ford-Carter administrations there were occasional Jewish members of both the Supreme Court and cabinet, and a small sprinkling of Jews in the White House staff and in Executive Office positions. Under Nixon, Ford, and Carter an unprecedented number of Jews reached significant positions at the highest levels of government—namely, secretaries of state, defense, and treasury, chairman of the Federal Reserve Board and members of the Council of Economic Advisers. In American society, personnel actions of this type, which represent considered political judgments, are entirely consistent with the development of an authoritarian oligarchy, although starkly inconsistent with historic Jewish ideals and the progressive tendencies of most Jewish Americans.

No matter which way America goes during the remainder of this century, more women will undoubtedly reach positions of higher prestige and visibility. Whether or not we get a woman president eventually, the time is not far off when there will be a woman Supreme Court justice, women astronauts, and more women as corporation executives, generals, police officers, legislators, politicians, professionals, and middle- and top-level bureaucrats. Such a development is not at all inconsistent with the crystalization of a full-fledged oligarchy. Indeed, it could help. By bringing more women into well-established masculine roles, it could undermine system-transforming tendencies in the women's liberation movement and maintain, if not strengthen, the manipulatory *machismo* that seems inherent in many of the tendencies toward friendly fascism.

CREATIVE COUNTERRESISTANCE

In general, there are two kinds of counter-resistence: one is *reactive,* the other *preventive.*

EUGENE V. WALTER [9]

Many of the previous chapters deal with the counterresistance operations of genuine capitalism. These operations—both preventive and reactive, both suave and rough—have been so successful in preventing a revolutionary movement in America that the very use of the term "counter-revolution" instead of "counterresistance" is little more than obeisance to the fantasy-life of radical idealists nursing memories of revolutionary glories in other countries or a bygone era. Their continued use in the years that lie ahead—particularly in manipulating democratic machinery, managing information, and providing incentives, punishments, and escape valves—could pave the way to friendly fascism. The adaptive use of system-strengthening reforms and multilevel co-optation could stave off the kind of reforms that might weaken or transform the system.

But beyond the subjects already discussed there are at least three other types of creative counterresistance that might be anticipated.

Under the ancient Hebrew kings there were always cities of refuge, sanctuaries to which people could flee. In other cultures this often became the function of religious buildings. Under the fascist and communist dictatorships of the past, according to Carl J. Friedrich and Zbigniew Brzezinski, the church, the family, the universities, and the military forces themselves often provided "islands of separateness" in which individuals could withdraw from the regime's oppressiveness and nurse hopes for a better day.[10] What Friedrich and Brzezinski fail to point out is the possibility that these islands of separateness may also serve to strengthen the regime by providing dissidents with a mechanism for withdrawal. In 1961, Paul Goodman spelled out this possibility in an imaginative essay entitled *1984:*

> There were two main movements toward rural reconstruction in the early '70's. The first was the social decision to stop harassing the radical young, and rather to treat them kindly like Indians and underwrite their reservations . . . The second wave of ruralism was the amazing multiplication of hermits and monks who began to set up places in the depopulated areas for their meditations and services to mankind.[11]

What Goodman leaves out is the likelihood of such reservations in urban ghettoes and in various suburban communities—and not only for youth, but also dissidents from all age, ethnic, and income groups. Many of these could be financed by benevolent foundations, if not by police and intelligence agencies themselves.

The second type of creative counterresistance goes a step beyond the islands of separateness: the direct sponsorship of indirectly controlled opposition. There are many precedents for this style of actions. In the early 1960s the technocrats in the French planning office got some of the socialist leaders to propose a more liberal "Counter-Plan." This style of opposition helped make the official plan more acceptable. In similar fashion the dominant Mexican political party has often subsidized opposition parties merely to liven up the rather fully controlled electoral process and thereby strengthen its own position. In the Soviet Union, according to Leopold Tyrmand, the Stalinist Establishment often showed greater ingenuity. It gave certain conspicuous positions to two categories of recognized dissent: professional non-Party people and professional oppositionists. The division of labor was significant. On the one hand, the non-Party person—often one with established prestige in the arts or sciences—conspicuously followed the Party's position. He thereby demonstrated its broad appeal. On the other hand, the professional oppositionist made a big to-do about disagreeing with the Party on inconsequential matters. This dramatized the Party's broadmindedness.[12]

The third type of creative counterresistance is entrapment. Islands of separateness and controlled oppositions can do more than sidetrack energies into harmless channels. They can also bring potentially dangerous people together into situations in which they can be decisively handled. The most obvious methods are co-optation, reform, or a combination of the two. The more these methods are used the easier it would be, in a minority of cases, to use brutal suppression. This ties up, of course, with the ever-present potentialities for using agents provocateurs—amply supplied with funds, equipment, and technical know-how—to provoke acts of violence that can be used as a triggering mechanism for a bloodbath.

INNOVATIVE APATHETICS

> The tyranny of a prince in an oligarchy is not so dangerous to public welfare as the apathy of a citizen in a democracy.
>
> BARON DE MONTESQUIEU,
> *The Spirit of the Laws*

"Apathetics," the nourishment of apathy, is more a by-product of semi-oligarchic and oligarchic power than a conscious pursuit. Apathy is fostered by both the triumphs of the System and the labyrinthine complexity that protects individuals and groups from accountability for its failures. It is promoted by the information, rewards, and escape valves that make the system tolerable, and by the direct or indirect punishments that make serious opposition intolerable. It is deepened by the perception that reforms may strengthen the System, reformers be co-opted, and resistance be prevented, sanitized, or suppressed.

The present processes of transition from capitalism to friendly fascism almost automatically produce additional attitudes that accelerate these tendencies. On the one hand, there are those who predict that a more repressive society (whether or not defined terms of fascism) is inevitable. On the other hand, there are those who assert that such a contingency is impossible. But all of these contradictory views—impossibility, inevitability, irreversibility—have one element in common: They rationalize or promote the apathetic stance.

It would be a great mistake to think of apathy strictly in terms of inaction. Doing so would focus on action—as distinct from analysis—as the only alternative to apathy. There is also such a phenomenon as *intellectual apathy*. In part, this is already being promoted by channeling off intellectual actvities into relatively harmless areas, remote from the System's power structure, by the subtle anti-intellectualism of vocational training and career-oriented education, and still more by the way in which the mass media, particularly TV, determine the shifting agenda of "public issues." There is a widespread anti-intellectualism among the Etablishment's opponents. This is what Herbert Marcuse once called "a handout to the establishment, one of the fifth columns of the establishment in the new left." An obvious by-product of disillusionment with the kind of absurd intellectualism embodied in traditional liberalism and dogmatic Marxism, this kind of intellectual apathy can protect incipient friendly fascism against the kind of serious analysis that might help lay the basis for preventive or remedial action.

17

The Myths of Determinism

"Nonsense! Nonsense!" snorted Tasbrough. "That couldn't happen here in America, not possibly! We're a country of freedom."

SINCLAIR LEWIS,
It Can't Happen Here

"It cannot happen here" is always wrong: a dictatorship can happen anywhere.

KARL POPPER [1]

IMPOSSIBILITY: IT COULDN'T HAPPEN

THE THOUGHT that some form of new fascism might possibly—or even probably—emerge in America is more than unpleasant. For many people in other countries, it is profoundly disturbing; for Americans, it is a source of stabbing anguish. For those who still see America as a source of inspiration or leadership, it would mean the destruction of the last best hope on earth. Even for those who regard America as the center of world reaction, it suggests that things can become still worse than they are.

An immediate—and all too human—reaction among Americans, and friends of America, is to deny the possibility. In other countries it might happen—but not here. In the Communist world, dictatorships of the proletariat or the Party . . . Military juntas in Argentina, Brazil, Chile, Nigeria, and many other places . . . Other dictatorial styles in India, Pakistan, Iran, Saudi Arabia, and the Philippines . . . But nothing like this in the prosperous, enlightened nations of Western civilization and the Judeo-Christian tradition. Above all, not in the United States of America, not in the land of the free and the home of the brave . . .

But why not? Why is it impossible?

Many of the arguments purporting to demonstrate impossibility actually demonstrate little more than an unwillingness to "think the unthinkable." Some people try to protect their sensibilities behind a tangle of terminological disputation. The word "fascism," they say, is an emotion-laden term of abuse, as though the brutal, inhuman realities behind other terms—whether "manipulatory authoritarianism," "bureaucratic collectivism," or "military junta"—do not also evoke deep human emotions. Some people argue that the future threat in America is socialist collectivism, not fascism, implying that those who detect a fascist danger are spreading leftist propaganda for the purpose of bringing on a different form of despotism. Others merely react to exaggerated claims that fascism is already here or is inevitable.

Nonetheless, there are at least three serious arguments used by those who think that it could not happen here.

One of the most subtle arguments is *"American capitalism does not need fascism."*

On this point, let me quote from Corliss Lamont, who grew up as a member of one of the families most closely associated with the Morgans and other titans of American banking:

> The capitalist class in the United States does not need a fascist regime in order to maintain its dominance. The radical and revolutionary movements are weak and disunited. A large majority of the trade unions are conservative, and are actually part of the establishment . . . I do not see in the offing any constellation of forces that could put fascism across here.[2]

To buttress his case, Lamont points out that the threat to American civil liberties was much greater during the periods of notorious Palmer raids after World War I and of McCarthyism after World War II. He also cites various judicial victories in recent civil liberties cases. Unfortunately, he does not deal directly with the structure of the "capitalist class" and the Establishment, nor with any of the domestic and international challenges to American capitalism. Moreover, his thesis on the weakness of "radical and revolutionary movements" and the conservatism of trade unions is a double-edged argument. True, these factors are no serious challenge to capitalist dominance. By the same token, they could not be regarded as serious obstacles to creeping fascism. On this matter, Lamont leaves himself an escape clause to the effect that he does not see the necessary constellation of forces "in the offing."

A similar escape clause has been carved out by Theodore Draper. In a scholarly critique of an earlier article of mine on the subject, he added as an afterthought that he did not intend to give "assurances that we will not follow the German pattern of history into some form of fascism." And then he added that although the Republic is not *"im-*

mediately" (my italics) in danger, "If worse comes to worse, we may yet get some form of fascism."

A more widespread argument is *"American democracy is too strong."*

It is true, of course, that old-fashioned fascism never took root in a country with a solid tradition and history of constitutional democracy. The kind of democracy that grew up in both England and the United States was too much of a barrier to the Oswald Mosleys, the Huey Longs, and Father Coughlins of a past generation. Even in France, the rise of the French fascists under Pétain occurred only after military conquest by the Nazis.

But this kind of argument boils down to nothing less than the identification of obstacles. It provides no evidence to suggest that these obstacles are immovable objects that cannot be overcome or circumvented in the future.

In the early 1970s this argument took a more exhilirating—albeit occasionally flatulent—form. *The democratic forces are becoming stronger.*

In *The Greening of America,* Charles Reich predicted a "revolution of the new generation." He saw in the counterculture of youth a movement that would break through the metal and plastic forms of the Corporate State (which he held was already here) and bring forth a new flowering of the human spirit. This optimistic spirit was repeated in global terms by Jean Francois Revel a year later. In *Without Marx and Jesus,* Revel pointed out that dissent has always thrived in America and that the new dissenters are building not merely a counterculture but a countersociety that rejects nationalism, inequality, racial and sexual discrimination, and all forms of authoritarianism. As the first and best hope of the world, America will soon produce "a *homo novus,* a new man very different from other men." [3]

I have never laughed at these salvationist predictions. They are based on an honest perception of many of the things that are not merely good, but wonderful, in my country. In fact, as I demonstrate in "The Democratic Logic in Action" (chapter 20), neither Reich nor Revel, nor other celebrants of America's potentialities have done sufficient justice to the variety of these hopeful currents. But they have tended to exaggerate their strength, perhaps on the theory that a strongly presented prophecy might be self-fulfilling.

I think it imperative to articulate more fully hopeful visions and to ground them on the more hopeful parts of the present. But in doing so, it would be highly misleading to ignore the fact that the new democratic currents represent a threat to all those elements in the Establishment that look forward to a more integrated power structure. This means conflicts whose outcomes cannot be predicted. Revel himself writes that America is "composed of two antagonistic camps of equal size—the dissenters and the conservatives." Writing before the rise of the new Radical Right, he then hazarded the guess that "the odds are in favor of the dissenters." Nonetheless, he accepted the possibility of the authoritarian suppression, sidetracking, or co-opting of the dissenters. I think he would agree with me today that if this should happen there would be many subspecies of the new man—and new woman—faceless oligarchs, humanoid technocrats, and comatose addists of loveless sex, drugs, madness, and cults.

A third argument is that *"While possible, a new form of fascism is too unlikely to be taken seriously."*

I see this view as a tribute that blindness pays to vision. It is merely a sophisticated way of conceding possibility while justifying inaction. The outside chance, after all, rarely deserves to be a focus of continuing attention. In terms of its implications, therefore, "unlikely" may be the equivalent of either "impossible" or "so what?"

In daily life, of course, people and groups do take precautionary action to protect themselves or others against some unlikely events. This is the basis of the vast insurance industry in the capitalist world, which provides protection for some people against some of the monetary losses resulting from ill health, accidents, theft, fires, earthquakes, or floods. In all these cases of unlikely "bads," not insurance but prevention is the best protection. In the case of friendly fascism, it is the only protection.

Yet prevention is always difficult and requires entry into many fields. The prevention of disease and the prolongation of life go far beyond mere medical services; they involve nutrition, exercise, housing, peace of mind, and the control of pollution. The prevention of theft and corruption goes far beyond anything that can be done by police, courts, and jailers; it involves employment opportunities, working conditions, the reduction of discrimination and alienation, and a cleaning of higher-level corruption. The record is also discouraging in the case of all the unlikely major calamities of the modern age: power blackouts, the disposal of radioactive wastes from nuclear power plants, the control of plutonium from fast-breeder reactors, the spread of nuclear weapons, and the escalation in ever-deadlier forms of nuclear, chemical, and bacteriological overkill. Here preventive action spreads into other fields, going far beyond anything that can be done by "fail-safe" mechanisms. It involves nothing less than alternative forms of energy, human as well as solar, and the destruction of the deadliest weapons, if not the elimination of war itself as a mode of resolving conflicts.

There are two natural reactions in the face of the difficulties of prevention. One is to push the possibility into the background by mathematically based arguments that the statistical probability is very low. The other is to exaggerate both the horror and the probability of the calamities to be avoided, justifying such exaggeration on the grounds that it alone can move people to action.

I cannot accept either. As in the following chapters, I prefer to deal with preventive action directly. I do so because in my considered judgment, the coming of some new form of fascism in the United States—and other First World countries—is not only more likely than the extreme catastrophe, but it would also contribute to conditions under which most of the others would become less unlikely. At times, I find myself saying that friendly fascism is a a two-to-one probability well before the end of the century. Then I stop and remind myself that in diagnosing broad historical trends no quantitative calculus is really possible. A more balanced statement is that friendly—or even unfriendly—fascism is *a truly significant, not an insignificant, possibility.* Perhaps it is even highly probable.

INEVITABILITY: IT WILL HAPPEN

When Herbert Marcuse writes about "incipient fascism," when Kenneth Lamott used "para-fascism" to describe California as the "distant warning system for the rest of the United States," when Michael Parenti talks about "creeping fascism," the main purpose is to identify present tendencies and future dangers. Similar use might be made of "proto-fascism" or—better yet—"pre-fascism." These are unwhispered words of warning, often engulfed by the vast silences on such subjects by the mass and elite media.

But the ambiguity of these words is often a weakness, one not to be overcome by stridency. They are wide open to anyone's interpretation that what creeps down the road will necessarily get to the road's end, that the latent must become full-blown. The "womb of history" metaphor used so vigorously by Marx tends to suggest that a little fascism is like a little pregnancy. With a strange innocence concerning the possibility of miscarriage or abortion, it can then be assumed that the pre- and the para- must eventually become the real thing itself.

But even without the use of such words I have found that any strong argument on the possibility of neofascism in America leads many people to conclude that it is inevitable. For some, both the logical case and the empirical evidence in present-day tendencies appear overwhelming. The fact that friendly fascism may come in a variety of forms and circumstances—rather than in some single guise and scenario—strengthens the sense of high probability. For others, perhaps, the judgment of inevitability heightens whatever masochistic pleasure people may get from premonitions of doom, or provides justification for personal escapism from any form of political activism or commitment. For still others, I suspect, the sense of inevitability is intensified by disenchantment with liberalism, socialism, and communism. Many of the very people who in previous periods were attacked as agents of "creeping socialism" or "creeping communism" now feel that if either were to arrive in America—unlikely though this possibility may be—the result might not be too much different from the fruition of "creeping fascism." Indeed the possible convergence of neofascist state-supported capitalism and high-technology state socialism tends to give the impression that there are few alternatives to some form of repressive collectivism as the profile of man's fate by the end of this century.

The power of modern determinism lies in its "if-then" formulation: "If one does A, then B will result." In truly scientific terms the "will result" is generally a probability statement. But in the real world of political or managerial control, there is always a strong tendency to let the probabilistic tone fade into the background and to exploit the propagandistic potentialities of a more deterministic mood. In the work of many self-styled Marxists, this has led to an interesting contradiction. On the one hand, the collapse of capitalism under the battering ram of a proletarian revolution is often seen as inevitable. On the other hand, the leaders of the working class must not merely ride the waves of an inevitable future. Rather, they must work strenuously to bring the inevitable into being. Expressing the essence of a long stream of philosophic thought from Kant through and past Hegel, Engels put this powerfully in his cryptic thesis that "freedom is the recognition of necessity." While anti-Marxists are always eager to attack the alleged determinism of Karl Marx, they are rarely unloath to voice their own form of determinism. Thus Friedrich Hayek vigorously argues that (1) it was the socialist trends in Germany that led to German fascism, (2) a little bit of socialism leads inevitably to large-scale collectivism, and (3) socialism inevitably leads to fascism.[5] In other words: "If s, then f."

Finally, in modern science there is a large strain of hope and faith in the eventual discovery and elucidation of deterministic laws of social control. B. F. Skinner has expressed this hope and faith more frankly than most of his colleagues in psychology and other disciplines. His critics have argued cogently that his views have a totalitarian bent—and I have already suggested how Skinnerian reinforcements could be used to help economize on terror and develop what Stephen Spender once called "fascism without tears." Another critical comment is in order, however. The very idea of deterministic control tends to spread inner feelings concerning the inevitability of some repressive form of collectivism—whether Skinner's type or some other. In turn, the sense of inevitability tends to undermine any serious efforts to develop alternatives or fight. The prediction that "It must happen"—particularly if the subjective feeling is more powerful than the rationalistic qualifications and "ifs" that most self-respecting intellectuals will automatically tack on to it—can contribute to a sense of hopelessness and the apathetic acceptance of the unfolding logic. It thus holds forth the potentiality of possibly—not inevitably—becoming a self-confirming prophecy.

IRREVERSIBILITY: ETERNAL SERVITUDE OR HOLOCAUST

Not mine own fears, nor the prophetic soul
Of the wide world dreaming on things to come
Can yet the lease of my true love control,
Suppos'd as forfeit to a confin'd doom.

WILLIAM SHAKESPEARE,
Sonnet 107

To shake people out of apathy toward some future danger, the self-destroying prophecy is often attempted. Its essence is the confident prediction of doom, either confined or unconfined. Thus the coming of neofascism to the United States may be seen as the maturation of an invincible oligarchy, or even as prelude to the global holocaust of all-out nuclear warfare.

I am peculiarly sensitive to this temptation. When a few of my students argued a decade ago that fascism would shake Americans from torpor and prepare the way for a more humanist society, I countered one irrationality with another by arguing that the "improbability of any effective internal resistance" to neofascism would doom all hopes of a humanist future. I drew an exaggerated parallel with the past by pointing out that after all serious internal resistance had been liquidated by the German, Japanese, and Italian fascists, "the only effective anti-fascism was defeat by external powers." Since the "only war that could defeat a neofascist America would be a nuclear war, a holocaust from which no anti-fascist victors would emerge," I concluded with the prophecy: "Once neofascism arrives, the only choice would be *fascist or dead.*" [6]

My phrasing at that time was an echo of Franklin D. Roosevelt's wartime rhetoric: "We, and all others who believe as deeply as we do, would rather die on our feet than live on our knees." [7]—itself borrowed from the exhortation of the communist leader, Dolores Ibarruri ("La Pasionaria") in rallying the Loyalist forces against the Franco uprising in Spain. It was an effort to suggest "better dead than fascist." The aim in each case, of course, was to stress the urgency of vigorous and dedicated opposition to tyranny—indeed, to give up one's life, if necessary, to prevent the victory of tyranny.

Today, while still agreeing with Roosevelt that there are things worth dying for, I would rephrase the ancient rhetoric this way: "Better alive and fighting tyranny in any form than dead and unable to fight." If neofascism should come to America, people may have to learn how to fight on their knees. The guiding rhetoric should be Churchill's statement that "We shall fight in the fields and in the streets; we shall fight in the hills; we shall never surrender." [8] To paraphrase: "We shall face the faceless oligarchs inside and outside the Establishment; we shall fight them openly when possible, secretly when necessary; we shall fight them legally and illegally; like the people of all oppressed countries from time immemorial, we shall fight on our feet, on our knees, on our bellies, on our backs; we shall never surrender."

Such an attitude is not mere bravado. The "Thousand Year Reich" lasted for only twelve years. More recently, the long-lived fascist or proto-fascist regimes of Franco in Spain and Salazar in Portugal were replaced by constitutional democracies. The junta of the Greek colonels, despite strong NATO support, proved to be rather short lived. The awesome power of the Shah's dictatorship in Iran was overthrown by a multiclass revolutionary uprising. One need not sing paeans of praise to the new regimes of Spain, Portugal, Greece, or Iran to realize that they have all been—at the very least—much lesser evils than the greater evils preceding them.

Similarly, I cannot conceive of a neofascist America—in the context of either a "Free World" remodeling or a "Fortress America"—as an immortal phenomenon. There is a limit to the destructiveness of any engine of exploitation and the further modern capitalism may move toward the perfection of exploitation, the more severe will become the internal conflicts among the oligarchs themselves, the more divisive the conflicts within various levels of the Establishment, and the less quiescent and more rebellious the large masses of exploited employees, consumers, taxpayers, and voters.

But what about a nuclear holocaust? Would not a neofascist America inevitably lead to a nuclear *Götterdämerung* that would destroy all of modern civilization, perhaps even all of human life on the planet?

Not necessarily. First of all, the nuclear dangers—as I have already shown—exist already. This sword of Damocles has long been hanging over our heads and, I am afraid, the threat will become greater in any event.

But just as nuclear war has been avoided in recent years, it might be avoided under neofascism also—whether the "Free World" empire shrinks or expands, whether it breaks up into quarreling blocs or, whatever its geographical coverage, it is held together under more mature American leadership. Big Capital knows one thing about Big War, namely, that another one would mean another giant forward step for communism and another historical contraction for capitalism, perhaps even capitalism's long-predicted demise.

In short, the terrors of neofascism—no matter what the balance between "friendly" rewards and "unfriendly" punishments—are so real that an effective warning does not require predictions of total and irreversible doom. The modern Paul Revere may not get his messages across if, when telling people that friendly fascism may be coming, he also suggests that the end of the world is around the corner.

THREE

True Democracy

The utterance of democracy is a way of saying *no* to inequality, injustice and coercion.

GIOVANNI SARTORI

It is better to allow our lives to speak for us than our words.

MAHATMA GANDHI

Even an ant can harm an elephant.

AFRICAN PROVERB

18

It Hasn't Happened Yet

> The Communist Party characterized Bruening's regime as already fascist, then Papen's regime, then Schleicher's regime, so that when the fascist Hitler came to power, theoretically, it was not prepared for the difference in political *quality* which the difference in political *degree* had brought about.
>
> SIDNEY HOOK [1]

FROM THE PRECEEDING CHAPTERS some readers may have received the false impression that friendly fascism has already arrived in the United States.

If so, I believe they may have read something into the text that is not really there. I cannot prevent anyone with obsessions about America from projecting his or her beliefs into my pages. Nor can I prevent people who disagree with my analysis from caricaturing it in the effort to make a point.

At the same time there are real difficulties in distinguishing between the small changes of degree that may occur in the future. Cold water is rather similar to ice, particularly if some chunks of ice may be floating in it.

In any case, to say that a new fascism is already here could cut the ground from under serious efforts to consider "What is to be done?" It could be as dangerous as any of the myths of determinism.

As a brief preliminary to discussing preventive action, therefore, I feel obliged to attack the illusion that "it" has already happened, as well as to suggest the reasons that it has not.

THE USA TODAY VS. FRIENDLY FASCISM, USA

If friendly fascism had already arrived in the United States, a book like this could not be published—unless previously edited to make repression seem more acceptable and its reversal impossible. And if the dark age were just around the corner, the pressure from the typical be to give the impression that the wave of the future is either impossible or desirable. In the latter case the message would be "Get with it . . ."

Under today's conditions of greater freedom, some cry "Fascism!" to voice anguished protest against current evils. For anyone who has been painfully and continuously repressed or persecuted, repression and persecution are *his* or *her* reality. This has not happened to most white people. But it has happened to many blacks, Hispanics, and Native Americans. This should be kept in mind when recalling that the president of a black college a few years ago charged that America has "come to embrace Hitlerism," or when one hears the term "fascist pigs" in attacks on racists and police brutality. Indeed, I could almost go along with the idea that neofascism will have arrived in America whenever most white people are subjected to the kind of treatment to which many black people have long become accustomed. But then I stop short. America has *not* embraced Hitlerism—nothing like it. To look only at police brutality in urban ghettoes, the murders at Jackson State, Kent State, and Attica prison, and the almost-genocidal war waged against the people of Indochina for over ten years, and *not* at the rest of American life, would be an exercise in obsessional perception. It would also mean a tragic underestimate of the length, breadth, and depth of the destructiveness of a new fascism in America. Thus to all those—black, white, Hispanic, Native Americans, or others—properly indignant against present evils, I am inclined to say, "Buddy, you ain't seen nothing yet."

Some people shout "Fascism!" or "Totalitarianism!" to arouse an apathetic public. This accords with a time-honored practice in American politics. Old-style businessmen and politicos lambasted Franklin D. Roosevelt's New Deal with the prediction that "grass will grow in the streets." They branded Harry S Truman's Fair Deal as "creeping socialism." When Richard Nixon imposed wage-price controls, Murray Rothbard, America's leading libertarian economist, proclaimed that "On August 15, 1971, fascism came to America." During that same year, when radical students tried to break up one of his public addresses, Daniel Moynihan cried out "I am a political scientist and I smell fascism." Without the help of Moynihan's nose, many liberals and radicals have also smelled fascism just around the corner. To cry "Wolf! Wolf!" when wolves are on the prowl, however, is not as misleading as it was for

Aesop's shepherd to cry "Wolf!" just to see if his friends would come. In today's jungles there *are* wolves. But to imply that they can take over in one apocalyptic descent on the fold is to sow distrust. After too many calls of this type, few will respond.

Something like this happened during Hitler's rise to power in Germany. As I have shown in "The Rise and Fall of Classic Fascism" (chapter 1), while the Socialists welcomed Hitler's predecessors as "lesser evils," the Communists attacked them as fascists and branded the Socialists "social fascist." This stance has persisted in a form of perverted Marxism, which states that modern capitalism is merely a *masked* form of dictatorship. "Imperialism under challenge," writes Felix Greene," will drop the mask of 'liberalism,' of 'democracy,' and will openly identify itself with the violence and the repressive forces on which its power rests." [2] As another version of the "fig leaf" myth discussed in chapter 1, this imagery suggests that the power structure behind the mask does not really have to be consolidated; so steps toward strengthening need not be fought. It suggests that bourgeois democracy is of little or no consequence, perhaps not even worthy of trying to defend or extend.

Although it is easy to set aside the mask–fig-leaf imagery, it is much harder to compare the United States of today with some future friendly fascism. The present is a period in which change is rapid, multi-dimensional, and confusing; much of it is shrouded in mystery. A friendly fascist future could materialize in a variety of forms.

The present, moreover, is a mixture of Good and Evil, of some of the Best and some of the Worst in mankind's history. To glorify it as heaven on earth would be a ridiculous caricature, as it would also be to depict a neofascist future as a living hell for everyone. Even under Hitler, as Richard Grunberger has pointed out, "most Germans never knew the constant fear of the early-morning knock on the door." [3] Indeed, up to the outbreak of World War II, except for the increased prosperity brought on by public works and the arms boom, "Most people retained the impression that within their own four walls life remained appreciably unchanged." The imagery of water changing to ice can be preserved only by thinking of a vast stream in which some parts are frozen over sooner and other parts much later.

The most direct way to look at the freezing process is to contrast the realities of social control in the United States today with those to be expected in a friendly fascist future. In "The Unfolding Logic" (chapter 7) I used an abbreviated summarization to compare a future friendly fascism with classic fascism. Let us now use similar shorthand to compare it with present-day America:

USA, Early 1980s	Friendly Fascism, USA
"Free World" empire in process of slow shrinkage and confused adjustment to changing conditions	Drive to maintain unity of "Free World" empire, contain or absorb communist or socialist regimes, and perhaps retreat to "Fortress America"
A divided, semi-oligarchic Establishment facing deep difficulties in responding to changing crises	A more integrated Big-Business–Government power structure, backed up by remolded militarism, new technocratic ideologies, and more advanced arts of ruling and fooling the public
An economy oriented toward subsidizing concentrated profitability, despite the social and economic consequences	A more unbalanced economy, rooted in extended stagflation, manipulated shortages, more junk, and environmental degradation
Growing power of Chief Executive Network, together with chaotic conflicts at all levels of government	Subtle subversion, through manipulative use and control of democratic machinery, parties, and human rights
Semi-unified information management with beginnings of scientific monitoring and dossier-keeping	Informational offensives, backed up by high-technology monitoring, to manage minds of elites and immobilize masses
Major trends towards rewards based on credentialized professionalism, mass consumption, and elite power	Rationed rewards of power and money for elites, extended professionalism, accelerated consumerism for some, and social services conditional or recipients' good behavior
Tendencies toward both professional and unprofessional use of domestic violence, with outbursts of ethnic conflict and scapegoatery	Direct terror applied through low-level violence and professionalized, low-cost escalation, with indirect terror through ethnic conflicts, multiple scapegoats, and organized disorder
Anxiety relief through such traditional escape mechanisms as alcohol, gambling and sports, and ultra-violent drama	More varied and extensive anxiety relief through not only traditional escape mechanisms but also through sex, drugs, madness, and cults

USA, Early 1980s	Friendly Fascism, USA
With immature oligarchic control, little decisiveness and insufficient adaptability in coping with crises	Internal viability grounded on system-strengthening reforms, multilevel co-optation, creative counterresistance, and innovative apathetics

If the contrast between these two columns is not sharp enough, one reason is that "in today already walks tomorrow." In human affairs, as distinguished from the world of physics and chemistry, differences of both degree and quality are hard to judge. Let me now start to redress the balance.

First of all, the processes of imperial consolidation are moving slowly and tortuously. Open interventionism is more talked about than practiced. Judged by the size of the armed forces (as distinguished from the growth of overkill), militarism has not returned to its Vietnam levels.

Second, despite erosion of democratic machinery, the level of democratic openness and opportunity in the United States is still high, particularly in comparison with many other constitutional democracies. Although threatened, personal privacy exists. The thick clouds of government secrecy are often pierced. Civil liberties and civil rights are alive (although not in the best of health) and can be fought for openly. Labor unions can organize and strike. If "it" had already happened, these freedoms would be cherished memories or fraudulent facades.

WHY IT HAS NOT YET HAPPENED

In considering the rise of classic fascism during the 1930s, I hope that historians will some day explain the failure of the fascist movements in the United States and England. Consideration of the reasons why it did not happen either here or there *then,* may throw some light on the obstacles that have thus far kept any new fascism from dominating either country *now.*

In "The Rise and Fall of Classic Fascism," (chapter 1) I have already shown that the old fascist movements rose to power mainly in the "second place" countries whose dominant elites were eager to replace the "major powers." Also, Italy, Germany, and Japan were countries in which democratic institutions were relatively recent and had never taken root. In each, industrial cartelization was widespread and militaristic traditions—particularly in Germany and Japan—deeply embedded in history and culture.

Among the major powers, in contrast, and particularly in England and the United States, there was no similar dynamism aimed at winning more; they already had plenty. Democratic institutions and traditions were probably the strongest in the world. The liberties that existed had been fought for and slowly won for more than a century. Business life was much more competitive. Militarism was reserved for colonial expeditions or gunboat diplomacy; it was never a major force at home. The native fascists were extremists. Although they enjoyed some support from higher Establishment levels, their behavior (as well as the color of some of their shirts) suggested suspicious resemblances to political movements in adversary countries. And in the United States, where the Great Depression of 1929–39 was probably more of a shock than in Europe, the leadership of Franklin D. Roosevelt's New Deal inspired widespread hope for democratic solutions to the economic crisis.

In the early 1980s, I see various reasons why friendly fascism, while a serious threat and perhaps even a probability, has not yet arrived.

The first is that the combination of domestic and foreign crises has not yet become so serious that the unfolding logic completely unfolds. The United States is still the richest country in the world. If the belt of austerity is tightening, the girth is still large. The "Free World" is still led by the United States, even though in faltering fashion; it still encompasses the majority of the world's population. In other words, while it would be dangerous to project into the future Corliss Lamont's statement that American capitalism does not need fascism, his statement explains the faltering nature of those steps in that direction that were taken in the 1960s and the 1970s.

The second reason is that despite substantial erosion in constitutional democracy, there are still many people and groups who insist on using the freedoms and opportunities that are available. I am not referring only to the electoral, legislative, and judicial machinery of representative government. I am referring to union organization, neighborhood organization, and a host of spontaneous or only semi-organized movements of self-help or defense against resurgent militarism or corporate aggression. Although some people still seem to subscribe to the old adage that liberty is too precious to be used, its use helps explain its survival.

Equally important is the fact that the unfolding logic of oligarchic integration tends to intensify the confusions among the few at the Establishment's pinnacle. This is the practical—although immensely difficult—lesson to be learned from the concentration of oligarchic power in the classic fascism of Germany, Italy, and Japan: the tensions among the oligarchs become more intense. In the face of mounting challenges, the outcome can be either inaction or, as in the case of the Axis, overextension.

The ability to respond successfully to crisis may also be undermined by the very strategies of information management that help maintain the power of the Establishment. Expanding systems of economic, social, and political intelligence tend to flood Establishment leaders with more information than they can absorb. Additionally, "hard" statistics, usually based on concepts and premises of an earlier time, give greatly distorted images of reality, while "soft" facts are often concocted to please higher-ups and help the technical interpreters climb the ladder of career advancement. Also, emerging triplespeak, as discussed in chapter 9, serves to narrow the circles in which straight talk is practiced. Neither side can bring itself to openly discuss—or even have its experts seriously attempt to analyze—the basic contradictions involved in accumulating, capital through enhanced profitability, which reduces mass purchasing power, and chronic inflation, which reduces the value of the money made. Both sides are loath to alert the middle levels of the Establishment to the inseparable connection between First World profitability and the conflicts with the Second and Third Worlds. No group or leader will take the risk of authorizing the extensive technical analyses needed to develop and carry out the policy of exploiting the conflicts between China and the Soviet Union, and of trying to absorb established communist regimes into the world of transnational capitalism; to do so would let too many people in on the realities of straight talk. The result is a swirling fog of jargon and myth which, while helpful in mystifying other educated people, may also addle the heads of the jargon experts, the mythmakers, and the economic and political overlords themselves.

There is another self-defeating aspect of advanced capitalism's unfolding logic: the production of an enormous potential for anti-Establishment action. In the world of pure physics, action provokes reaction; in the nineteenth-century world of Marx, capitalism was to produce its own gravediggers, the proletarians. In the last decades of the twentieth century, the reaction to the growth of the corporate-government complex defies any simple formulation. *But it is there:* embodied partly in alienation, anxiety, apathy, and self-hatred, expressed partly in free-floating discontent and resentment, and often taking the form of scattered acts of protest and resistance. The fact of concentrated power tends to promote an interest in deconcentration. Its excesses may enlarge that interest. By promoting false participation in decision making, the processes of concentration may have the unintended consequence of nurturing demands for genuine participation. To put it in a nutshell, the dominant logic tends to create a counter-logic that is more than a counter-logic: an alternative logic of true democracy, which is positive rather than merely reactive, and which transcends old distinctions between capitalism and socialism.

Before proceeding to the logic of democracy, a word on circular response. On the one hand, far-flung anti-Establishment action might tend to dispel the confusions within the Establishment's higher level and bring about the very unity whose absence Richard Nixon once bewailed.

On the other hand, the democratic logic itself—if more effectively practiced—would have the effect of splitting away from the Establishment many of its leaders and advisers who have lost faith in the marketplace as a legitimate entitlement to power, privilege, and property. This could mean great opportunities for those who use the alternative logic as a guide to social reconstruction.

19

The Long-Term Logic of Democracy

> Democracy is a process, not a static condition. It is becoming, rather than being. It can easily be lost, but is never fully won. Its essence is eternal struggle.
>
> WILLIAM H. HASTIE [1]

SOME PEOPLE RESPOND TO FEARS of creeping despotism with utopian visions of a delightful future—that is, with wish lists of all the good things they would like to see in America. The bad, in contrast, is waved into the shadows or wished out of existence.

But the top-down logic of transnational capitalism and the Golden International cannot be countered by mere wish lists. Inspiring visions of a truly civilized civilization in the West, although a tonic for their creators, are no antidote for creeping barbarism. Any serious opposition must be based on a logic of its own. Without an alternative logic, rooted in the changing conditions of life, there would be little hope of animating and bringing together the many forces needed to counter the power of oligarchy, empire, and manipulative repression. Friendly fascism might indeed be the inevitable wave of the future.

Fortunately, there is an alternative logic.

It is a logic grounded in humankind's long history of resistance to unjustified privilege. It is the logic which eventually led—after centuries of struggle and defeat—to the virtual end of slavery, serfdom, and colonial empire. It is the logic of all those who seek freedom from ripoffs, manipulation, and the other evils of concentrated power, of all those who seek true individualism through the kind of cooperative commitment that provides meaning and purpose throughout the life cycle. It is the logic of seeking *the opportunity for all persons to take part—directly and indirectly, both in large and small measure—in the decisions that affect themselves, others, and the larger communities of which they are a part.* It is the logic of true democracy.

Properly understood, this logic is rooted in the recognition that human beings will always be both good and evil. It is based on the premise that all future societies, like those in the past, will contain varying combinations of the two. In the past, however, the logic of democracy has always been shrouded in mystification, and all victories have been partial, with every democratic advance counterbalanced by some new form of concentrated power.

THE DEMOCRATIC MYSTIQUE

> The words men fight and die for are the coins of politics, where by much usage they are soiled and by much manipulation debased. That has evidently been the fate of the word "democracy." It has come to mean whatever anyone wants it to mean.
>
> BERNARD SMITH [2]

> For the first time in the history of the world . . . practical politicians and political theorists agree in stressing the democratic element in the institutions they defend and in the theories they advocate.
>
> United Nations Educational and Scientific Organization [3]

Since the destruction of Axis fascism in World War II, "democracy" has become an honorific label oratorically affixed to almost every national system in the world. Gone are the days when American conservatives parroted James Madison's contention that the Constitution established American government as a republic, not a democracy. We seldom hear any more that the only kind of democracy is direct democracy confined, in Madison's words, "to a small spot." There are still those who believe in their hearts that any moves toward more democracy would be a descent into the inferno of mobocracy, loutishness, vulgarity, ingnorance, inefficiency, anarchic breakdown, or despotic rule by swinish (and, in central cities, dark-skinned) multitudes. But the whisper of their hearts is rarely spoken aloud. Even the new conservatives, wracked by doubts and reservations, approach the subject as though walking on eggshells, content to preach hierarchy, meritocracy, and technocracy while avoiding a direct confrontation with democracy. In suggesting less democracy, the pundits of the Trilateral Commission take the position that they are saving it. Meanwhile, communist movements pledge allegiance to democracy. For them, a proletarian dictatorship is a democratic dictatorship, representing the majority of the people. It is merely a transitional stage to prevent the restoration of capitalism and prepare the way toward an eventual classless society in which the dictatorial state will have withered away.

"Sure, we'll have fascism, but it will come disguised as Americanism." This famous statement has been attributed in many forms to Senator Huey P. Long, the Louisiana populist with an affinity for the demagogues of classic European fascism. If he were alive today, I am positive he would add the words "and democracy." Indeed, to understand the difficulties facing the logic of true democracy, one must realize that the unfolding logic of friendly fascism leads directly to democratic disguises.

Nonetheless, many elements of true democracy have often existed—and exist today. But like traces of a precious metal scattered through vast ore deposits, they are not easy to find. Some are mixed with a "fool's gold" that glitters deceptively. Besides, as though in some great compression of geological time, the rock formations are constantly in flux and occasionally in upheaval. No simple task to bring together—even in one's mind—the many elements for a viable alternative to a system of concentrated power.

DEMOCRATIC STRUGGLES

Often, the logic of democracy is revealed simply in some reaction (other than flight or apathy) to concentrated power. If this reaction is merely one of saying "no" to inequality, injustice, or coercion, it is nonetheless positive. While "no-sayers" may be gagged, imprisoned, or murdered and their ties with each other shattered, the history of humankind is full of resounding "noes" and recurring efforts—spontaneous or planned—to win some freedoms.

Some of the more memorable efforts occurred in ancient times when despotic tribal chiefs or city-state tyrants were overthrown and replaced by assemblies of adult males (with the exception of slaves). Something similar developed a century or so ago in Swiss cantons and New England town meetings. These were all cases of so-called government *by* the people, self-government, or *direct* democracy. Qualified adult males all had a chance to take part in the processes of decision making—whether through majority vote or consensus. They were not representatives; they were the rulers themselves. However, the women, children and slaves, were not represented; they were ruled.

More frequently, though, a single tyrant shares powers with a few others; or as a few more burst (or are brought) into the select circle, a limited democracy comes into being. The barons at Runnymeade wrest a Magna Carta from a king. A council of elders, a more varied assembly, or a number of "estates" is set up to advise the ruler, share in rule, or choose the ruler. Among themselves, the aristocrats learn to treat each other as "peers," that is, as equals. Despite differences and conflicts among them each must get the respect, courtesy, information, and time required for participation in decision making. And each must give the same—at least formally—to others. This is the meaning of "noblesse oblige" (nobility obliges), which among peers is equivalent of "égalité oblige" (equality obliges).

With the industrial revolution, as the older aristocracy of the landed nobility merged with the new aristocracy of business and finance, the scope of this limited democracy was enlarged. It was broadened still more as this or that group of Establishment leaders sought to advance their own interests through alliances with tradesmen, artisans, laborers, and peasants. There thus came into being a *representative* democracy in which all men of property or substance could help choose representatives in government, have access to an array of specialized courts, and enjoy many personal rights. To protect themselves against a majority that might infringe on these rights, restraints were often provided in written or unwritten constitutions. This gave us *constitutional* democracy. Eventually, as suffrage was extended, representative constitutional democracy was extended still more until, like a pancake being almost infinitely flattened, it became all but transparently thin. As large corporations became "persons" before the law (and thereby entitled to personal rights), they tended to displace or diminish many direct personal relations among real people. They looked on most real people as atomized units with roles in mass production, mass consumption, mass education, mass communication, and mass culture. There thus came into being *mass* democracy, under which increasingly powerless people were given through voting a chance to exercise—in the words of Giovanni Sartori—"a powerless fraction of power." Paradoxically, the largest number of voters appear at the polls under *plebiscitary* or *totalitarian* democracy, where the function of voting is to elect a candidate who has no opposition, or to legitimate some other decision already made. In less extreme cases, despite a huge component of false democracy, mass democracy may contain some true elements of civil and political liberties and self-organization. But the relative proportions of false and true do not change very much if the "ins" show "compassion" for the masses by doing a little more for them, if former "outs" replace the "ins," or if either group reduces somewhat the height of the Establishment's pyramid. A larger proportion of true democracy is provided to the extent that there is a reduction of status distances and exclusionary barriers based on sex, color, race, religion, national origin, or age. Yet this kind of *social* democracy may also develop—to a certain extent—as a means of recruiting a few leaders from oppressed groups into a more representative oligarchy.

Nor can mass democracy suddenly become true democracy when a "dictatorship of the proletariat" provides *economic* (or *socialist* or *people's*) democracy by guaranteeing full employment, free medical care and education, low-cost housing, and more broadly available welfare-state services. In taking control of the major means of production, the dictatorship also abolishes basic civil and political liberties and concentrates enormous power in the hands of party leaders. One of the reasons there has as yet been no socialist takeover of corporate power in any First World country is the deep attachment that people have to the civil and political liberties that have always been sacrificed under Second World socialism. This attachment is among the reasons why, as I have pointed out in "Subverting Democratic Machinery" (chapter 11), friendly fascism would preserve most democratic formalisms.

The giant scale of modern organization is another reason for concentrated power in all parts of today's world. Persons, families, and neighborhood or village groups are pygmies (and labor unions and most political parties nothing but somewhat larger lightweights) in comparison with the huge private and public bureaucracies and the globe-spanning clusters, constellations, complexes, and establishments that dominate most of the planet. Here too there is a tendency for limited democracy to broaden, but too often in a manner that promotes a greater concentration of power. The manager of a large system can be successful only by becoming part of a management team. The system itself can become colossal only by administrative decentralization—that is, by delegating mountains of detailed decisions to area and functional specialists, and keeping for the few at the top the most critical functions of central guidance. This requires far-flung hierarchies of management teams. It is *managerial* democracy. Similarly, First World leaders can guide the policies of former colonies more efficiently through economic and political manipulation rather than by the more direct and costlier techniques of old colonialism. This is *imperial* democracy—sometimes referred to as neocolonialism, noncolonial empire, or indirect imperialism. In the United Nations almost all the countries of the world are represented; and in its General Assembly each nation has one vote. This is a limited *international* democracy.

Often, the logic of reaction to limited democracy is some form of broadening. To counter the power wielded over them by employers, workers form unions. This has often been called *industrial* democracy. Industrial democracy goes much further when workers participate in management at one or more levels of the managerial hierarchy, and workers' self-government or participatory management develops. Similarly, representatives of consumers, "the public," or government may sit on top management boards. But any form of broadened democracy can, in fact, become a facade for legitimating the narrowing of control. This happens when labor leaders become instruments of control by corporate overseers, racketeers, or the two together, or when consumer or public representatives on a board are manipulated by top financial interests. A still more flagrant facade is *marketplace* democracy. Government restriction or intervention is reduced in favor of the "impersonal" forces of the so-called "free market." But "free market" is mainly a euphemism for free-wheeling by faceless oligarchs whose invisible hands dominate most markets. A simliar facade is *chamber of commerce* democracy, under which national or state functions of government are turned over —under the banner of *grass roots* democracy—to local cabals of corrupting contractors, land speculators and corruptible officials. Another facade has at times been provided by *functional* democracy, under which business, labor, professions, and many other interests are formally organized in guilds, chambers, or corporations that exercise governmental powers. As I have pointed out in chapter 1, this was one of the myths that classic fascism employed to conceal repressive control by Big Business-Big Government partnerships. Today, as new-style partnerships develop in most First World societies, a new corporatism is emerging, a corporatism described by some observers—with sublime indifference to the implications for personal liberties—as *corporatist* (or *consociational*) democracy.[4] This brings us back to friendly fascism coming in the guise of democracy or even—if its savants are clever enough—of "true" democracy.

Despite the mystifications, the elements of true democracy are strewn throughout the world. How many? I cannot count them. The chemistry of society provides no fixed table of elements. Old ones change their form and news ones—invented as well as discovered—burst into being. In each country of the world the old and the new combine in unique and changing patterns. There is no country without "fool's gold" and the coarser elements of open despotism and manipulative tyranny. But there is no country without some portion (even if only minute traces) of those truly democratic elements that may be symbolized by such adjectives as direct, representative, constitutional, political, economic, social, or industrial. One or more of these may be crushed into dust and apparently obliterated. But, somehow or other they always rise again. Indeed, the false rhetoric of the oligarchs often encourages those who attempt inroads into the structure of concentrated power.

The nature of these inroads—currently weak though they may be—is the subject of the next chapter.

20

The Democratic Logic in Action

O this is not Spring but in the air
There is a murmuring of new things.
This is the time of dark winter in the heart
but in me are green traitors.
KAY BOYLE

SOME YEARS AGO the turmoil of dramatic movements in America—civil rights, antiwar, students, woman's liberation—rang like shots around the world. From Yugoslavia in the early 1970s Vladimir Dedijer wrote to *The New York Times* that "The future of the world depends so much on the American New Left . . . Therefore it [America] is the greatest country in the world." [1]

By the end of the 1970s many observers had already jumped to the other extreme. The New Left had vanished, it was said. Many of its former leaders—having passed the magic age of thirty—had settled down to middle-class placidity or been co-opted into Establishment rat races. The counterculture had become a commodity sold at record stores and health-food counters. The euphoria faded, abroad and at home.

For those who still pose the question of where all the flowers have gone, and want to listen, there is an answer: Now, in the early 1980s, there are more flowers than there were a decade earlier. However, instead of being bunched together, they are widely scattered. True, there is now a New Left committed to varied forms (and labels) of socialism. But far beyond this, there are new currents and undercurrents of change swirling through all the strata of First World society. In part, these currents are responses to the crises of social disorganization, global disorder, stagflation, and environmental degradation. In part, they express evolving human needs for participation and commitment, needs that are not suppressed—but indeed are sometimes nurtured—by material deprivation or material accumulation. In either case they represent the long-term logic of democracy as expressed in a new awareness of human potentialities, in scattered action on a thousand fronts, and in challenging questions concerning positive alternatives to every aspect of concentrated power.

These currents are much more than knee-jerk reactions to stimulus; they also express the long-term historic human urge for truly democratic mixtures of freedom and responsibility. I see in these currents the possible beginnings of a new bottom and a new middle that may already, for all anyone knows, comprise a new—although largely silent and lamentably weak—majority. If so, it is a silent majority that has thus far spoken through minority actions only. Also, these actions are sporadic as well as scattered. Sometimes little or no ground is gained. Often, small Pyrrhic victories are followed by the disappearance of the victorious groups once a battle has been won. Often, victory is followed by the co-optation of successful leaders. Indeed, some of the most promising public-interest movements are financed by banks, corporations, and Establishment foundations as a way of "keeping their finger" on movements that might go too far if not subjected to the delicate controls of upper-class budgeting.

Thus, where a thousand buds may have blossomed, some are frozen before flowering or wilt prematurely after a brief opening. But still they appear and reappear.

A GOOD NEIGHBOR IN A NEW WORLD ORDER

> We are not wholly patriotic when we are working with all our heart for America merely; we are truly patriotic only when we are working also that America may take her place worthily and helpfully in the world of nations . . . Interdependence is the keynote of the relations of nations as it is the keynote of the relations of individuals within nations.
>
> MARY PARKER FOLLETT [2]

When confronted with the choice between Fortress America and a more mature Trilateral Empire, the democratic response begins with Mercutio's "A plague o' both your houses!" It continues with a search for the avenues leading toward a more civilized world.

Here, the logic of democracy (as on all other points) provides no detailed plan or formula. Like the unfolding logic of friendly fascism, it merely suggests broad objectives. The rest is left to necessary, indeed endless, debates on both "what?" and "how?"

As these debates develop, I see a few promising moves. Third World regimes push for a new international *economic order,* defined mainly as improved patterns of trade with, and investment in, the First World. In turn, this demand has led to similar calls for a new *information* order, to free Third World countries from domination by First World media, and a new *technological* order, to provide them with better access to the technologies for their appropriate development. Others add *cultural,* to recognize the rich values of diversity in national traditions and styles of life. If we then add *political,* the idea becomes so broad that limiting adjectives may as well be dropped. While the American Establishment may demur, those Americans who are more conscious of the interdependence among peoples and less addicted to superpower posturing are increasingly willing, I believe, to move toward a new order in general. Here, the difficulty is that many of the worst things in the world are new: more destructive weapons systems, new escalations of the same arms race, and new forms of domination by transnational corporations and cartels.

What kind of world order would be *both* new and more civilized?

One sign of progress in America, I believe, is declining attachment to the idea that—by grace of manifest destiny, innate superiority, or economic and military superiority—the American government and its close allies must answer this question by themselves. A modest coming of age, but not to be sneered at. Moreover, it is associated with a growing ability by many Americans to work with people from First, Second, and Third World countries in a spirit of interdependence rather than domination. At a time when Establishment leaders have skuttled the détente which Nixon and Brezhnev initiated in 1972, I see signs of hope in opposition to the new militarism and in support of some improved form of détente. It would be comforting to find some easy method of strengthening these positive currents and converting the American government from bully to good neighbor. All I can do at this point is insist that the logic of democracy requires much more open debate—and more straight talk—on such controversial issues as these:

1. *Should not preparations be made for a Detente II to replace Detente I?* As a cooling-off to the cold war, Detente I was a vague bilateral argreement expressing the mutual interest of the United States and the Soviet Union in avoiding any direct confrontation that might result in nuclear war. Neither NATO nor the Warsaw Pact countries were party to the agreement. Excluding the Third World as well, it left the door open to warmer, or even hot war by either party in most parts of the Third World. Is it not imperative to prepare for Detente II which would produce clearer, more multilateral bases for arms control and disarmament?
2. *Should the U.S. government more fully accept socialist measures or regimes in other countries?* In 1938, when Mexico expropriated

American oil companies, President Roosevelt turned his back on pressures from the companies and on U.S. traditions of military intervention in Mexico. A financial settlement (very favorable to Mexico) was eventually negotiated. This was one of the high points of Roosevelt's Good Neighbor Policy. Today, in a "world of neighbors" (to use a phrase from Roosevelt's first inaugural address), would not similar responses to socialist measures or regimes be more civilized than the repetition of old efforts at subversion or destabilization? More specifically, would not the international atmosphere be better if the U.S. government should extend more promptly to Cuba and Vietnam the same diplomatic and trading relations belatedly worked out with the Soviet Union and China?

3. *Are the vital interests of American corporations abroad identical with the vital interests of the American people?* The essence of rational public relations by any large corporation is to win acceptance of such an identity by the power centers of government. Thus, when Prime Minister Mossadegh of Iran nationalized British and American oil companies in 1953, the British and American governments organized a coup to overthrow Mossadegh and get agreement on the division of oil profits. This was quite different from the handling of the Mexican oil crisis some years earlier. Now, almost thirty later, with not only Iran but the entire Persian gulf facing a succession of crises, the issue is much broader. High American officials define the flow of Persian Gulf oil, distributed by Western companies, as so vital to the American people that any interference would justify U.S. use of military force. Representative Jim Weaver (D., Ore.) is not so sure. "We must all ask ourselves," he argued in March 1979, "if we believe it worthwhile to send our sons to die in the Persian Gulf so that we can continue to fuel our Winnebagoes. Is it worthwhile to go to war so that we don't have to wait in line at the gas station to buy gas we fritter away?" [3]

4. *How useful in world affairs is the use or threat of military force by the United States?* To the leaders of the military-industrial complex the value of military spending and stockpiling is clear; it is their special form of welfare handout from government. It also has the advantage of promoting the idea that force can be used to settle economic, social, and moral conflicts, thereby accelerating spending on instruments of force. But if conventional weapons were truly powerful, the British would still be ruling India, Somoza would still be in power in Nicaragua, the Shah of Iran would still sit astride his peacock throne and American preparations to use force in the Persian Gulf would tend to reduce—

rather than build—tensions in that area. As for nuclear weapons, what trust can one place in national leaders, military or civilian, who would take seriously the use of methods that would guarantee the death of most Americans in an effort to "defend" America?

DEMOCRATIZING THE ESTABLISHMENT

The vulgar charge that the tendency of democracies is to levelling, meaning to drag all down to the level of the lowest, is singularly untrue; its real tendency being to elevate the depressed to a condition not unworthy of their manhood.

JAMES FENIMORE COOPER [4]

We can have democracy in this country or we can have great wealth in a few hands, but we can't have both.

LOUIS D. BRANDEIS [5]

From the viewpoint of the Powers That Be, the democratic currents running throughout America are unquestionably disagreeable. Both Big Business and Big Government are increasingly unpopular. If their decisions tend to stick, this is not because of active consent by the majority of Americans; it is the product, rather, of passive acquiescence under conditions of felt helplessness. The consequence is increasingly widespread feelings that THEY are not to be trusted. At times, these feelings are expressed in open opposition to Establishment programs—particularly to the expansion of nuclear energy, the restoration of the draft, and preparations for renewed military intervention in Third World countries. They are articulated in citizen activism that runs the gamut of the entire political spectrum. They are expressed in the new vigor of minority political movements by both libertarians and radicals.

Moreover, as Robert L. Heilbroner has observed, America is "in the midst of an extraordinary outpouring of literature on, about, into, out of, and by Marx." [6] In the wake of the example set by the Union for Radical Political Economy, every discipline in the social sciences now has a Marxist, neo-Marxist, or anti-Establishment caucus with a regular publication. The number of openly socialist authors has grown still more rapidly. In 1975, under the auspices of the Democratic Socialist Organizing Committee (DSOC), seven Nobel Prize winners joined in a statement questioning the economic systems of "advanced industrial democracies," and calling for "the exploration of alternative economic systems." At least two dozen left-wing political oragnizations—many of them dividing, subdividing, submerging, and merging in intricate philosophical dance steps that even the FBI must have difficulty in following—are in open operation. Some of these are strict, down-the-line adherents of official (albeit often switching) party lines. Others are more open to, and may even welcome, internal discussion and dissent. Many have gone far beyond the old tradition of regarding Marx, Engels, Lenin, or Mao as gospel givers, often using Marx's methods to dissect the evils of concentrated bureaucratic power. I suspect that in no other capitalist country at any other time in history has there been such a varied, large, and growing literature challenging basic principles of its governing Establishment.

Disagreeable though they have been, the Establishment's many opponents have still not gone very far in discussing, as James Russell Lowell has characterized them, The Powers That Ought To Be. Some hope that the Establishment can be forced or cajoled into being more responsive, "compassionate," or "humanitarian." Some may think that they themselves, if only given the chance, would be much better than the present THEY. Others oppose in principle almost any form of power, authority, of leadership—less because of any utopian anarchism, more from sheer skepticism concerning the possibility of power, authority, and responsibility that are truly—rather than rhetorically—democratic. Although I too have some skepticism on this matter, I believe that the majority of the American people would welcome any progress in democratizing the American Establishment. But any such progress requires democratic controversy on all the difficult questions raised in this chapter. At this point I shall touch only on those that bear directly on the problem of concentrated power.

1. *Should not limits be set on the concentration of private wealth and income?* The owners and controllers of huge private fortunes have always had something in common with true democrats: they both have recognized the incompatibility of true democracy and "great wealth in a few hands." The long-term purpose of inheritance taxes and progressive income taxes, of course, was to put a reasonable ceiling on both wealth and income. To go back to this original purpose would require a reform of the tax laws that would remove the loopholes and tax shelters specially created for the Ultra-Rich. This need not bring their living levels down to "the level of the lowest." Indeed, even the most fervent egalitarians, I suspect, would be willing to allow people to accumulate as much as a few million dollars of assets (in 1980 currency) and keep, a few hundred thousand in income. This would be far from "levelling." All it would mean would be a reduction in a few thousand people's addiction to the thrills of irresponsible power and perpetual self-indulgence, and in their ability to bribe politicians and escape prosecution for violations of civil and criminal

law. Like many drunkards, they will resist any cure. But once cured, their lives might even be happier.

2. *Should not public control of the larger corporations be expanded?* Corporations are in business to make money; this involves getting and keeping whatever power is needed to maintain profitability and stay in business. As Milton Friedman has often pointed out, to expect them to exercise social responsibility entirely on their own is nonsense. Unfortunately, efforts to cope with this situation have usually been limited to single remedies. The two oldest remedies have been the break-up of giants into smaller (and presumably more competitive) organizations and the imposition of public interest standards by presumably "independent" regulatory agencies. In Western Europe and Scandinavia, much more use has been made of four other methods: public ownership at the national or local level; mixed public-private ownership; public or workers' representatives on boards of directors; and workers' ownership. Experience has tended to show that neither competition nor regulation can be very effective without a credible threat of some form of public or worker ownership. In the United States would not a combination of all six approaches be desirable?
3. *Should not government be both decentralized and deconcentrated?* Much progress made in the public control of private corporations —whether through regulation, breakup or public ownership—holds forth the danger of overly concentrated government power. This is one of the great contradictions of true democracy. It cannot be resolved merely by efforts to make government more responsible. It is also essential to decentralize government. This principle should be applied to the operations of almost all government agencies, just so long as it does not open the back door to takeovers by narrow vested interests. Also, much of the necessary public-sector expansion—in medicine and electricity generation as in public education—should take place locally and regionally.
4. *What about the alleged inefficiencies of public-sector activities?* Not the private, the public, or the nonprofit sector has a monopoly on inefficiency. It is nonsense to contend that one is necessarily more inefficient or efficient than the other. The major difference is that corporate inefficiencies (particularly the huge social costs they push onto others) are more hidden from view. The inefficiencies of public agencies are more open to public exposure. In any case, is not full exposure and accountability needed for all three sectors?

BALANCING THE ECONOMY

What I wish to emphasize is the *duality* of the human requirement when it comes to the question of size: there is no *single* answer. Man for his different purposes needs many different structures, both small ones and large ones, some exclusive and some comprehensive.

E. F. SCHUMACHER [7]

Among economists I see some awareness that economics has, in John Kenneth Galbraith's words, "an instrumental function—instrumental in they are rather weak—hence the general recognition that few econo-system but the goals of those who have power in the system." [8] But I am not sure that even those who share Galbraith's views on this matter have much faith in the possibility that economists will take the lead in evaluating alternative structures of economic power. They are more likely, I suggest, to follow in the wake of democratic currents.

Fortunately, there are such currents. Insofar as theory is concerned, they are rather weak—hence the general recognition that few economists have any useful answers to economic questions. Some people even blame economists for inflation, high taxes, unemployment, shortages, waste, pollution, junk, and other aspects of an unbalanced economy. This, of course, is unfair; economists merely serve the vested interests whose activities have these consequences. Insofar as economic statistics are concerned, most people take them with a huge grain of salt. Many have unlearned the false lesson, taught them over the first decade after World War II, that growth in the GNP is a touchstone of economic progress. Insofar as citizen action is concerned, the positive currents are somewhat stronger. This may be found in the organization of cooperatives, in self-help movements, and in the many neighborhood groups that have been developing what Karl Hess calls "community technology." The popularity of E. F. Schumacher's *Small Is Beautiful* attests to the existence of a widespread urge to create labor-intensive forms of production as a counterbalance to whatever giant, capital-intensive operations may be truly necessary. Above all, by the end of the 1970s progressives of all stripes belatedly realized that fighting inflation could not be left to the bankers and conservatives who try to send unemployment up as a way to keep prices down. Progressives now seek *both* full employment and price stability, rejecting the tradeoff argument that attaining either one requires sacrifice of the other.

But any further progress along these lines will be beset by enormous difficulties—and at least four key questions.

1. *How can stagflation best be fought?* Any serious fight against

stagflation involves nothing less than an effort to manage the capitalist business cycle in its latest form. This can be seriously attempted only by staking out a positive program aimed at price stability and guaranteed jobs (part-time as well as full-time) for all who are able, willing, and wanting to work for pay. The former objective requires not only certain fiscal and monetary policies but also government price controls and antispeculation measures; the latter, last-resort government job opportunities at good wages. If these two approaches are combined with major reductions in war spending, the conversion of military facilities to peacetime activities, and the development of soft energy resources, America could move from a situation of manipulated scarcity to one of planned abundance. Even with an expansion of labor-intensive work, it would be possible to shorten the official work week and provide more leisure time for those who want it.

2. *How can decentralized planning best be organized?* Many of those who grew to maturity during the period of the New Deal, Fair Deal, or Great Society think of planning in overcentralized terms. Fortunately, one of the encouraging aspects of American life in the 1980s is that many old-timers and new-timers are beginning to think of planning from the very bottom up—from neighborhoods, workplaces, towns, and regions. Only for a few doctrinaire sects does this mean the complete lack of national effort at integrating local plans. Besides, there are some operations—such as the reconstruction of a railroad network—that must be conceived in national or even transnational terms to provide a framework for local planning. The one thing I am sure of is that decentralized planning cannot be left to dedicated civil servants and professional advisers, no matter how locally rooted they may be. Active participation by citizens' movements outside the formal channels of government is also essential. How to go about this is one of the great challenges of the 1980s.
3. *What about profits?* This is one of the hush-hush subjects in American debates on economic policy. Yet the Corporate Overseers oppose planning for guaranteed jobs and price stability mainly because they know that if effective, such planning would not only curb windfall gains from shortages but also tend to reduce the rate of profit on invested capital. I wish they would say so more openly; they are correct on both scores. But such planning would not destroy capitalism. In certain ways it might strengthen—as well as humanize—it. The controls involved in price stability would curtail paper profits. Guaranteed jobs, while tending to raise wage rates, would also provide the larger purchasing power needed for sustained profitability. In return for losing some of their freedom over the use of profits, the larger corpora-

tions might gain—as in Sweden—the opportunity to increase their aggregate profits.

4. *What about small business?* Both recessions and inflation are deadly enemies of small enterprises. Yet the controls involved in planning for price stability and guaranteed job could injure small business unless planners at all levels recognize this danger. They must also recognize that giant corporations invariably try to use small companies—subsidiaries, suppliers, or distributors—as pawns on the economic chessboard. Plans at all levels should aim at providing more opportunities for small ventures; this involves generous capital assistance, technical assistance and training. Any guaranteed-job program should include—as did the early versions of the Humphrey-Hawkins full employment legislation—planning for self-employment. Could not serious and continuing support of this type for small business promote a vital counterbalance against the dominant tendency toward corporate concentration?

DEMOCRATIZING THE SOCIAL BASE

Democracy is not brute numbers; it is a genuine union of true individuals . . . . I am an individual not as far as I am apart from, but as far as I am a part of other men. . . . Thus the essence of democracy is creating. The technique of democracy is group organization.

MARY PARKER FOLLETT [9]

The neighborhood movement potentially forms a vital strand of an emerging force for democratic change.

HARRY BOYTE [10]

I swear to the Lord
  I still can't see
Why Democracy means
  Everybody but me.

LANGSTON HUGHES,
The Black Man Speaks

If one focuses on the formal machinery of democratic government, it is hard to find democratic currents that provide much hope for the future. The picture is much less bleak, however, when one looks at the many social groupings that are bringing people together both to do things for themselves and use and protect the machinery of democracy.

The American labor movement, for example, although still representing a minority of the gainfully employed and would-be employed, is experiencing unique alterations. Within the old-line craft unions of the building and trucking industries—long-ridden by money-grubbing bureaucracies, corruption, and company-supported racketeering—a new generation of union leaders is rising. Industrial unionists have taken the leadership in forms of collective bargaining that try to protect the full range of wages, hours, and working conditions. New successes in unionization drives are occuring in the low-wage, anti-union bastions of the South, Midwest, and small-town America. The most successful trade union expansion is taking place among white collar workers—with government employees (including police and fire people) and teachers (including college professors) taking the lead. Important beginnings are under way among technicians, office workers, retail employees, custodial staffs, household workers, and migratory farm labor. All this holds forth the promise of a more democratic, more discrimination-free, more humanistically oriented, more intellectually alert, and more influential labor movement.

With partial support from labor unions, there has also been an important development unprecedented in the history of America or any other country: a huge proliferation of public-interest citizen groups. Some of these have huge attention spans. Among these are the long-lived Americans for Democratic Action, the Council on Economic Priorities, Common Cause, the Public Interest Economics Foundation, and the Exploratory Project on Economic Alternatives. "Ralph Nader's initial concern with automobile safety," Hazel Henderson reports, "has grown into a million-dollar conglomerate enterprise funded by small, individual contributions, which covers a range of systemic concerns from the drive to control corporate behavior by federal chartering, to battling for tax and regulatory reform and funding citizen and student-activist groups across the country." [11] Much of Nader's work has involved class-action law suits on behalf of people never before able to initiate court proceedings to defend their common interests.

Within each established religion, there are those—some militantly active, some timidly restrained—who go far beyond the rituals of prayer, preaching, and charity in opposing war, bias, poverty or pollution. Many scientists have brought support for such activities into their professional as well as their personal lives. This is evidenced by the work of such groups as the Federation of American Scientists, the Center for Science in the Public Interest, the Scientists' Institute for Public Information, and the Union of Concerned Scientists. Each of these covers a remarkably broad range of public interests. Public-interests groups have also been organized among college students at all levels including the professional school of social work, urban planning, architecture, law, and medicine. Even some professional groups heretofore most conspicuous for self-serving myopia and political passivity have been touched by these currents. Hence the formation of such groups as the Committee for Social

Responsibility in Engineering, the National Association of Accountants in the Public Interest and—lo and behold!—the National Affiliation of Concerned Business Students. And it was an employee from a Madison Avenue advertising firm who coined the slogan (for use against corporate advertising of the "free enterprise" system): "If You Think the System Is Working, Ask Someone Who Isn't."

Perhaps even more important than the above activities has been—to quote from a 1979 report by Frank Riessman—"a tremendous proliferation of local community groups, block associations (10,000 in New York City alone), tenants groups, housing self-management groups, neighborhood revitalization groups, and other community-based groups. . . . ACORN (Association of Community Groups for Reform Now) was operating in five states two years ago and is now in 13 states. . . . Massachusetts Fair Share in 1976 had eight affiliated groups around Boston with 600 members and now has 25 groups across the state with over 13,000 members." [12] More broadly, the Alliance for Volunteerism estimates 6 million voluntary associations; a study by ACTION indicates 37 million volunteers. In middle-class neighborhoods many of these groups are active in fighting blockbusting, red-lining, rent increases, condominium conversions, and supermarket ripoffs. In lower-class neighborhoods they fight on similar issues, but with more attention to planned shrinkage, welfare cuts, inadequate health and education; they set up rape crisis centers and battered womens' shelters. Broadly, as Riessman points out in the same report, they "are anti-bureaucracy, anti-big, anti-waste, anti-elite, pro-participation, pro-accountability, and pro-productivity on the part of government."

If it were not for the impressive growth in citizen activism of all types—neighborhood organizations, public-interest groups and labor unions—I would be much more hesitant in talking about decentralized planning. History is full of too many cases in which sweet talk about bottom-up planning has been a facade for top-down domination. Besides, the smartest people among the Corporate Overseers are not only planners par excellence; they are well versed in the arts of decentralizing some things in order to build larger and more manageable empires. The best protection against these oligarchic arts is a thorough honeycombing of society through a wide variety of interelated organizations that can at least resist top-down domination and at best countervail and substantially reduce the concentrated power of transnational corporations and the Chief Executive Network.

For the present, however, the processes of bottom-up honeycombing are far too weak. If they are to be strengthened, some tough questions must be faced. I shall simply list two of the most baffling questions:

- How can people's organizations be extended and strengthened?
- How can they avoid becoming bureaucratized or co-opted?

In addition, I shall briefly discuss these questions:

1. *What can be done to eliminate discriminatory barriers to participation?* Legal remedies against racism, sexism, ageism, and other forms of discrimination are important; and they must be used wherever necessary, not only against the dominant institutions of society but also against any people's organizations guilty of these sins. But legal remedies can be brought into being, enforced, or improved only through organization and agitation by those who have been victimized by discrimination. This means sustained and dedicated action by every group.
2. *What can be done to bring together the scattered fragments of citizen activism?* Single-purpose organizations are often self-defeating; they may reproduce at the lower levels of society the same fragmentation and particularism that are the side effects of large-scale bureaucratization. The remedy is the aggregation of diverse and mutually supporting interests through networks, coalitions, and joint or parallel operations. Often, this means taking part in partisan or "nonpartisan" politics. Is it possible to have a political party not dependent on financing by big corporations and the rich?
3. *What about improvements in the formal machinery of democracy?* The oligarchs of society are always involved in reorganizing democratic machinery to make it more responsive to their needs. That is why, in the absence of bottom-up honeycombing, I am suspicious of electoral, legislative, and judicial reforms. From the viewpoint of true democracy, however, the agenda for reform or reconstruction is staggering; it involves a reconsideration of almost every element of governmental machinery at all levels: the electoral system, the judiciary, legislatures, organizational structures and management methods.
4. *What about the protection of civil liberties?* Bottom-up honeycombing and use of democratic machinery, however, depend on the protection of civil liberties—both the older liberties of speech, assembly, and organization and the newer liberties of personal privacy, the right to know, and sexual rights. This, too, requires organization. I dread thinking of what the state of civil liberties in America would be today without the valiant efforts over many years by the American Civil Liberties Union, the National Emergency Committee on Civil Liberties, and the National Lawyers Guild. These organizations have defended thousands of people whose civil liberties were abridged; in so doing, they have made life more worthwhile for millions of others who have never known to whom they owed certain freedoms. Much more is needed in the days ahead—not only to defend the best elements in the status quo but to mount a positive offensive for the strengthening and extension of civil liberties, civil rights, and other human rights, both economic and political.

INFORMATION FOR HUMAN LIBERATION

Perseus wore a magic cap that the monsters he hunted might not see him. We draw the magic cap down over our eyes and ears as make-believe that there are no monsters.

KARL MARX[13]

Tell the truth and run.

YUGOSLAV PROVERB

During the 1960s the people of the civil rights and antiwar movements initiated a process of revelation more far-reaching than that of the so-called "muckrakers" of earlier years. By demanding that American society live up to its highest promises, they revealed the yawning gap between ideals and realities. As their early militancy subsided, many others joined their ranks. Consumer advocates, tax analysts, and environmentalists are now bringing to light the latest tricks in the exploitation of consumers, taxpayers, and the environment. Labor leaders are revealing how large corporations have depressed the level of real wages and the power of labor movements by price hikes, capital flight, and the building up of a large pool of surplus labor. Many others are identifying the tacit racism, sexism, and ageism built into the society's dominant values and institutions. Civil liberties groups have been doing more than ever before to bring to light the dirty linen of the Establishment's repressive actions in both past and present. They are sounding the warning bell repeatedly against recurrent assaults on the Bill of Rights. Critics of America's military and imperial operations have been repeatedly exposing this corruption and wastefulness of the Pentagon, the dirty tricks of the CIA and its allies, and the subversive activities here and abroad of many First World transnational corporations.

These efforts have invariably been helped by those whom Ralph Nader calls "whistle blowers." These are the private and public employees, who, in Nader's words, protest publicly against any evil—"from pollution to poverty to income erosion to privacy invasion"—perpetrated by their employers.[14] Their efforts have helped ease the work of investigative journalists, against-the-stream legislative investigators at all levels of government, and against-the-stream academics. Indeed, all the recent "books of revelation," including legislative hearings and reports, would easily fill a thirty-foot bookshelf. If more people around the world could read them, they would learn that America is much more the stuff that dreams are made of than CIA agents, Coca-Cola, neutron bombs, and TV addiction. If more Americans could read them, or better yet, if their messages were handled fairly by the mass media, the Establishment's ideologies and myths would be much less capable of hiding the monsters of the world.

But questions remain.

1. *Is more muckraking needed?* According to Murray B. Levin, revolutionary exposés have an unintended consequence: "Muckrakers receive wide publicity while attacking specific evils and specific companies (occasionally an entire industry) but they do not attack the patterns of property ownership. . . . Such attacks siphon emotions away from broader critique, hinder the development of critical theory, and create the belief that when the specific evil is remedied, all will be well."[15] Levin might have added that they may also serve to deepen feelings of apathy and helplessness. Nonetheless, I think America needs much more, and better publicized, revelationary activity. Levin's critique suggests the need for exposés that *do* attack basic patterns of control, direct emotions *toward* broader critiques, and nurture an awarness of the *limitations* of any specific remedy. I would go further. While the Establishment is the central source of muck, it enjoys no total monopoly. Corruption, deception, and error are found elsewhere also—even among the activists in people's organizations. They too should be exposed without fear or favor.
2. *What about better information on the state of the nation?* Abstractly, I am still attracted by the idea of some system of social accounting that would provide an ordered array of information—qualitative as well as quantitative—on the changing state of American life. Yet Establishment moves in this direction—as I have pointed out in "Managing Information and Minds" (chapter 12)—have tended willy-nilly to provide as many vindicators as indicators. Moreover, even the most sacrosanct of government statistics often turn out to be totally misleading, particularly when based on definitional categories frozen many years ago and never adjusted to meet the changing conditions of life. Therefore, I agree completely with S. M. Miller's view that "it would be wise to encourage counter-indicators and counter-analysis."[16]
3. *Could the new communication technologies be used to advance true democracy?* With cable television, the number of TV channels could be increased immensely and two-way communication could be provided between senders and receivers. Also, by turning a dial or pushing buttons one could plug into a great variety of previously-taped educational or cultural programs. Some people wax enthusiastic over these possibilities. I view them skeptically. Unless the control of these systems is radically changed, they would probably turn out to be new forms of mind management.

In the meantime, the most important advance would be for the winning of better access to the media by artistic groups, labor unions, schools, neighborhood groups, and health centers.

RELEASING HUMANISTIC VALUES

The God who saves us will not descend from the machine; he will arise once more in the human heart.

LEWIS MUMFORD[17]

Many people have entered the Eighties with new commitments to moral and esthetic values. Late in the 1970s, a Harris poll revealed a significant value shift. People were asked basic questions concerning the stress they would place on alternative approaches to values, rewards, interpersonal relations, and living standards. Majority and minority opinions were reported as follows:

The Majority	The Minority
Learning to appreciate human values more than material values: 63%	Finding ways to create more jobs for producing more goods: 29%
Finding more inner and personal rewards from work: 64%	Increasing the productivity of the work force: 26%
Spending more time getting to know people better on a person-to-person basis: 77%	Improving and speeding up our ability to communicate with each other through better technology: 15%
Teaching people how to live with basic essentials: 79%	Reaching a higher standard of living: 17%

As in most opinion polls, a certain amount of distortion was created by the phrasing of the questions. Thus, appreciation of human values was falsely contrasted with job creation, a distinction hardly to be appreciated by those suffering from the inhumanity of unemployment and job insecurity. Other opinion polls have shown that 75 to 90 percent of respondents favor last-resort government jobs as a response to unemployment. Better-balanced questions, therefore, would have probably increased the majority in the left-hand column. Other surveys tend to suggest marked progress in appreciating—although not yet overcoming—

the deep-rooted nature of racism, sexism, and ageism in American society. I think there has also been some progress in efforts to escape the *machismo* that undermines the well-being of many American families and the role of the United States in the family of nations.

1. *How can more democratic values be nurtured?* The usual response is to proclaim the decisive roles of childhood learning from early infancy, and of subsequent education in school. But this begs the question; it is in homes and schools that nondemocratic values are customarily instilled. How can the values of parents and teachers be improved? I see no serious answer in the assumption that more humanistic values will automatically "arise once more in the human heart" in response to concentrated power, as a result of brilliant preaching or as a natural evolution once survival needs are met. Like happiness, the values of true democracy emerge—I suspect—not by direct design, but rather as a by-product of things people do. Perhaps they arise as people learn from each other.
2. *What are the potentialities for nonviolent action in America?* In opposing nuclear energy, some environmentalists have revived the nonviolent methods of social action developed by Mahatma Gandhi in India and adapted to American circumstances by Martin Luther King and other civil rights activists. Without suggesting nonviolence as an all-purpose alternative to every oppressive act on the "ladder of terror" (discussed in chapter 14), I still think its potentialities are enormous. Americans need a substitute for William James's quasi-militaristic motto that we need "a moral equivalent of war." That substitute can be found in nonmilitary forms of moral action. From this viewpoint, more might be learned from the examples of Gandhi and King than from the therapies of Keynes and Freud, let alone the cults of escapism and submission.
3. *How can deep anxieties be alleviated at their roots?* Like my comments on the previous two questions, my answer to this one cannot take the form of a prescription. If anxiety relief is sought through madness, the cults of submission, and the misuse of sex and drugs, little help is provided by efforts to stop the symptoms. Rather, people can help each other in trying to deal with the causes of alienation, helplessness, and the loss of meaning in life. Ralph Nader's whistle blowers, when confronted with wrongdoing within their organizations, look for allies within and outside the organization and then act in accordance with principles of morality higher than mere bureaucratic loyalty. They may "suffer the consequences" personally; in return, they can retain—or regain—their self-respect. Perhaps whistle-blowing can be thought of in broader terms. For example, are there not ways in

which the long-term unemployed—consigned to the degradation of public assistance, the street hustle, and ghetto-life indignities—can also blow the whistle?

TRUTH AND RATIONALITY

There are no whole truths; all truths are half-truths. It is trying to treat them as whole truths that plays the devil.

ALFRED NORTH WHITEHEAD [18]

The true problems of living—in politics, economics, education, marriage, etc.—are always problems of overcoming opposites.

E. S. SCHUMACHER [19]

An encouraging aspect of college teaching is the skepticism with which students react to any "whole truths" that professors may try to pump into their heads. To get the grades that may help them get financial aid or jobs, students may memorize ideological tidbits and half-baked facts while keeping their skepticism under tight control and abstaining from expression (or clarification) of their own views. But this adaptation to the rigors of "higher" education does not mean genuine acceptance of the "value-free" posturing of those social scientists who throw trivial data into computers or pretend that oracular truths may be deduced from mathematical models. More broadly, I see resistance to technocratic orientations that would limit rationality to means alone, leaving ends and side effects out of consideration. Some law students and lawyers have been bringing the Bar before the bar of moral judgment or public opinion. Some medical students and physicians have been laying the medical profession out on the operating table. Some physical scientists have been examining the internal politics of science's formal pressure groups, informal control networks, and ties to the military-industrial complex. Some management students and managers are beginning to think in terms of basic morality. And beyond the halls of academe, larger numbers of people are searching for more ethical ways of living. Whether they find it in orangized religion, in personal worship, in meditation, or even in cults, one thing is clear: They are not exactly willing to separate means from ends, rationality from morality, or the True from the Good and the Beautiful.

None of this quite conforms to the adaptive rationality of the Hydra-headed Establishment, or to the unfolding logic of friendly fascism. Yet all of this is insufficient. The logic of true democracy involves *learning through doing*. "The essence of democracy is creating," writes Mary Parker Follett. When I showed these words to a high official in a mammoth bureaucracy, his eyes glazed over. "What does that mean?" he demanded. His reaction illustrated another part-truth, again from Follett: "Concepts can never be presented to me merely; they must be knitted into the structure of my being, and this can be done only through my own activity." [20] My activity and the structure of my being tell me a few part-truths that cannot be simply presented to others but that many others, I know, have learned from their own experience: that the real world is enormously complex; that unsought consequences may prove more important than central intentions; that democratic life involves the integration of opposites; that problems are attacked more than solved; [21] that wholes cannot be understood by trying to add up their parts; that good analysis (which divides things into pieces) requires imaginative synthesis (to bring pieces together); that many truths (in George Bernard Shaw's words) "enter the world as blasphemies"; that the deepest interests of most people are hard to fathom; that eternal values are eternally changing; that narrow rationality can lead to MAD and other forms of madness; that the rationality of democracy is one that brings new values into being; and that the logic of democracy requires the formulation of questions that have no quick, easy, or simple answers.

Two questions have lived with me for over four decades:

1. *What about democratic management in human affairs?* I worked for many years in developing some concepts of democratic management and planning.[22] In retrospect, I have learned that much of this has been absorbed into the rhetoric of nondemocratic elitism, the practice of co-optation, and the arts of protecting or expanding concentrated power. But still the question burns in my mind. Could not the best elements of so-called "scientific management"—perhaps blended with the "scientific workmanship" hinted at by Harry Braverman [23]—be used in the unending struggle for true democracy? And to quote an almost blasphemous truth by the author of *Small Is Beautiful* (a truth most of his followers have ignored): "Large-scale organization is here to stay." From his long experience on Britain's National Coal Board, Schumacher then goes on to suggest some principles that might help combine "the orderliness of *order* and the disorderliness of creative *freedom*." He concludes by asserting that any such principles must be developed by going to the practical people, learning from them, synthesizing their experience into theories, and then returning to the practical people who must put these principles into practice.[24] Any people who do this illustrate Follett's words on the essence of democracy.
2. *Is a truly humanistic capitalism possible in America?* Any answer to this question depends on how one defines "humanistic." For some, humanism is the compassion of the Ultra-Rich as they take money from the middle classes and throw crumbs to the poor; it

is the largesse of dictators who declare recurrent amnesties for some of those who have survived torture; it is the smile on the face of any friendly despotism. For me, a humanistic capitalism has always been one in which a choice of productive and fulfilling job opportunities is always available for those able and willing to work for pay, inflation is prevented, and a guaranteed minimum income is provided for anyone. Barrington Moore goes further in envisioning capitalism-with-a-difference. He suggests far-reaching social changes: major reductions in military expenditures, an end to the tragic human waste of urban and rural poverty, stronger protections against arbitrary authority, "a wholesale redirection of scientific efforts toward human ends . . . an end to compulsive and socially wasteful forms of consumption and a very large increase in the services and amenities provided by the public sector." [25] Ideals of this type appeal strongly to all those seeking basic reforms in America—including the stronger liberals in the Democratic party. American reformers—including the stronger liberals in the Democratic party—have long worked·to develop such ideals and translate them into action. Many have done this with the feeling that, in effect, they were trying to save capitalism. In return, they have continuously been branded "eggheads," "pinkos," or "crypto-socialists." For moving cautiously on even lesser reforms, President Franklin Roosevelt himself was branded "traitor to his class" and died as the most hated as well as the best loved of all presidents. The branders of today—in company with the more sectarian Marxists—consistently maintain that stability, guaranteed jobs, and guaranteed minimum income are inconsistent with capitalism.

Barrington Moore himself lugubriously concludes that his style of reformed capitalism is "extraordinarily unlikely." Its clientele would be too small and weak, and the resistance to it enormous. The bulk of the reforms would be bitterly opposed by those with vested interests in military production, in other forms of wasteful production and consumption, and in high differentials in prestige, income, and wealth. Popular support could easily be mobilized on behalf of these interests, particularly if serious foreign threats are found to exist or are created. The Establishment's leaders are more apt to consider concessions if they themselves have considerable leeway—and the existence of this leeway depends on "world hegemony and continued exploitation." [26] If the capitalist world continues to shrink, such leeway may also diminish.

Back in 1945 an old friend and colleague told a story to explain his belief that genuine full employment without inflation or militarism might be possible in America. A grandfather was explaining to his grandson how a frog tried to escape an alligator. The frog jumped from a log into the river, swam through the river and hopped on into the land—

as the alligator came closer and closer. The alligator finally cornered the frog under a tree and opened his mouth to swallow the frog. "But the frog looked up," the grandfather said, "and just as the 'gator's jaws were clamping down, the frog flew up into the tree." "But, Grandpa," said the little boy, "frogs can't fly." "Indeed, they can't, my grandson, indeed they can't," was the answer, "but this frog flew—*he had to*."[27]

Sweden is one country where capitalism *had to* change. Supported by an enormously powerful labor movement, the Swedish socialists could long ago have nationalized the largest sectors of Swedish capital. Instead, they used their power to obtain "concessions"—mainly, public participation in the use of profits and very high levels of welfare-state services—that the large capitalists have benefitted from enormously, but which they would never have conceded if they had not feared nationalization. So with less nationalization than any other West European (or Scandinavian) country, Sweden has a unique combination of relative price stability and high levels of both employment and profitability. Perhaps the reason is that, in Sweden, countervailing power based on local and national organizations does more countering than veiling. Or is it perhaps that a credible threat of socialism is necessary to make captialism work more effectively for both the capitalists and the majority of the people?

It is also important to note that in Sweden Big Business and Big Government work very closely together. The result, according to Roland Huntford, is that the Swedes have become "the new totalitarians."[28] What Huntford misses is the fact that Sweden—like Norway and Denmark—is one of the most open societies in the world; there are long-standing guarantees of the public's right to know. Above all, the Scandinavian countries enjoy what Eric Einhorn of the University of Massachusetts calls "a participant political culture."[29] According to Dankwort Rustow of City University of New York, the essence of democracy in these countries is "the habit of dissension and conciliation over ever-changing issues and amidst ever-changing alignments."[30] This habit is rooted in a democratized social base, with widespread democratic participation in even the smallest of local decisions. This leads me to a question, the very asking of which makes me uncomfortable. If the base of American society were much more democratized—along such lines as I have briefly touched upon earlier in this chapter—would it be possible for the growing partnership between Big Business and Big Government to be counterbalanced and humanized? On such a fulcrum, would it be possible to nudge the United States toward becoming more of a good neighbor in a new world order? Would it be possible to move toward a democratized Establishment, a more balanced economy, the use of information for human liberation, the emergence of more humanistic values, and the development of a more rational rationality?

All I can say is that everything depends on what people do—which brings me to the next and final chapter of this book.

21

What Can You Do?

> As life is action and passion, it is required of a man that he should share the passion and action of his time, at peril of being judged not to have lived.
>
> OLIVER WENDELL HOLMES, JR. [1]

TODAY, POSING THE QUESTION "What is to be done?" is often a facile cover-up for doing nothing or passing the buck to others. Nor are matters clarified making the verb active and adding a vague or totally unidentified *"one, we,* or *you."*

"What can one (or we or you) do?" is usually a glib way of avoiding the multiplicity of ones, of actors, in the real world. It is emptier than a performance of *Hamlet* without the Prince of Denmark; it is like a play without any actors at all.

Or else it is a way of discussing what *they* should do. "What should public policy—or the public policy maker—do about stagflation? Or the draft? Or the MX missile? Or nuclear power?" asks the traditional teacher of so-called public policy. The de-animated *public policy* and the unnamed *policy maker* become fetishistic masks behind which usually stand the Corporate Overseers, the Ultra-Rich, the political leaders, or whichever technocratic experts may be "in" at the moment.

But when the question is seriously asked and seriously answered, specifics are needed as to just *who* is to do what, when, and how. In this spirit, let me raise the question "What can *you* do?"

YES, YOU . . .

In the early days of the Vietnam War, while my students were beginning to protest against American intervention, I was full of ideas about what *they* should or should not do. Many more thousands of Vietnamese and Americans were killed before I began to ask what *I* should do.

I have tried to learn something from that experience. Now, when someone asks what can *we* or *one* do, I answer that it all depends on which we or one is discussed. When someone asks "What can you do?" I accept the question as referring to me specifically. I answer by telling what I have been doing as teacher, writer, and sometime political activist. Reviewing the choices I see ahead of me, I ask what they think I *should* do. This helps bring the discussion down from the make-believe world of action without actors to the real word of identifiable doers. The question then becomes "What might *you* in your own capacity do now or later—here, there, or somewhere else?"

In this real world of specific doers, of course, it is usually *they* who do the more important things. The myths of citizen and consumer sovereignty hide the crude realities of semi-oligarchic or oligarchic power. Conventional technocratic wisdom escapes this impasse by hailing the vanguard role of the knowledge elites. Conventional radical wisdom, in turn, idealizes the vanguard role of the working class—with major disputes as to which part of the working class (old, new, or "under") may be the critical sector. Then there are those who, in the light of the 1960s and the early 1970s, still look for leadership to the blacks, young people, or women—any group that has suffered most conspicuously at the hands of the establishment. Alan Gartner and Frank Riessman, somewhat skeptical of these groups, suggest that as consumers are increasingly exploited a "consumer vanguard" may emerge. Interestingly, they see any vanguard as a group that serves to unite all the other progressive forces. This view is widely shared by those who look to broad liberal-radical coalitions as a major force in the defense and expansion of human freedom.

This line of thought goes very far to modifying, if not destroying, old premises, whether embodied in establishment ideology or in classic Marxist dogma, concerning the vanguard role of any narrowly defined group or class. In the sphere of socialist thought James Weinstein has commented on the absence of any one sector whose immediate needs are seen as a key to uniting all others. "At different times particular sectors of the working class will play a leading role in the movement—as students and blacks did in different ways during the 1960s and industrial workers did in the 1930s—no one sector is a strategic short-cut to convincing the majority of Americans about the need for socialism and a socialist party to take power."[2] Similarly, John and Barbara Ehrenreich, after discussing the fragmentation of work under modern capitalism, suggest that "there is no longer any reason, other than a romantic one, to insist on the unique centrality of the workshop as the locale for the development of class consciousness in the United States."[3] In the context of their discussion it should be understood that "class consciousness" refers to an awareness of common interests on the part of all people who are (or want to be) engaged in paid employment. This is an enormously heterogeneous set of persons and groups that make up at least 75 percent of the adult population. In the light of this heterogeneity, it becomes rather difficult to make a priori judgments as to the source of the most significant initiatives. May not anyone—whether follower or leader, no matter how humble or previously inactive, no matter where he or she is located in the social structure—exercise useful initiatives?

ANYONE ANYWHERE, REALLY?

> Anyone, anywhere can make a beginning; this is an arena where one person can count, as Rosa Parks counted in the civil rights movement . . .
>
> STAUGHTON LYND [4]

On December 1, 1955, after a hard day's work, Rosa Parks, a forty-three-year-old black seamstress of Montgomery, Alabama, was returning home in a crowded bus. She was sitting in the front part of the black section, directly behind the white section, which was fully occupied. When more whites entered the bus, the driver told all the blacks to move further back. This was an established custom, and the other blacks complied. Rosa Parks refused. The driver called a policeman, who arrested her at once. A few days later the Montgomery Improvement Association, led by Martin Luther King, Jr., organized a black boycott of all city buses. Within a few years' time, civil rights boycotts and demonstrations—usually with white participants—were being staged in hundreds of cities throughout the South.[5]

Did Rosa Parks really make this beginning? The mythology of all the civil rights movements answers "yes." But the real answer is "no." Many black persons throughout the South had earlier been arrested for having been "uppity" in a bus. In the same city of Montgomery a few years earlier Vernon Jones, a black preacher, had refused to vacate his seat under similar circumstances—and had gotten away with it.[6] Also, the boycott led by Martin Luther King had had its origins in the responses of other lesser-known—and now unremembered—blacks who felt that something must be done *this* time. In turn, King's vigorous leadership of the boycott goes back to the wave of hope that swept over the South after May 31, 1954, when the Supreme Court, responding to many years of pressure by the National Association for the Advancement of Colored People, ordered school desegregation "with all deliberate speed." It was also rooted in decades of black admiration of the boycotts and civil disobedience campaigns led by Mohandas K. Gandhi against British domination of India. And it was far back in 1893 when Gandhi, sitting in a South African railroad car, was asked to move to make way for whites. Like Rosa Parks many decades later, he refused and was forcibly ejected. By the next morning, under the shock of this event, "Gandhi had evolved from a private citizen to a political actor."[7] Thus, Rosa Park's refusal was a culmination of thousands of beginnings, some of which were recorded, most of which were forgotten, over many years; here was an unpredictable outcome of thousands of sparks that flickered briefly and at the time seemed to have no consequence.

Can *any* individual reaction to exploitation or manipulation have consequences?

Of course it can.

The first consequence is on one's self. Any protest or resistance is better than the narcissistic "retreat to personal satisfaction" described by Christopher Lash,[8] or the self-absorption therapies which, according to Edwin Schur, treat the "individual (together with a few partners in direct interaction) as some kind of closed system."[9] I say this even though some personal plunges into activism may be little more than the working out in public of arrogant fantasies of personal omnipotence. In full-employment campaigns I have seen more than one activist who, in the words of Peter Marin, "excludes from consideration all felt sense of solidarity, community or the power of collective labor or responsibility."[10]

Another consequence is learning—or the unlearning that is often necessary before new things can be learned. One can learn a lot from errors and failures as well as successes. This is attested to by my experiences in two grueling campaigns for genuine full employment. Social learning can also take place. During the movement against the Vietnam War many people learned new modes of personal satisfaction through modest actions in cooperation with others. In neighborhood programs today many people are learning that they can be truly effective only if *enough* single individuals make important "beginnings" by refusing to take part in the retreat into narcissism.

Can ants really harm mighty elephants? At first thought, it seems unlikely. Elephants are customarily surrounded my myriads of insects of all types, none of which can penetrate the thick elephantine hide. Also, elephants snuff out the life of countless ants whenever, without even knowing it, they step on ant hills. Yet elephant trainers are eager to explain the wisdom behind the African proverb: a single ant will drive an elephant mad . . . *if* it crawls into the elephant's trunk. This is unlikely if there is only one ant in the neighborhood.

Any part of a modern establishment has many more vulnerable apertures than an elephant. These can be penetrated and exposed by all sorts of people—from disaffected executives, wives, and husbands to disillusioned scientists, professionals, and technicians; from blue-collar workers to shop stewards and higher union officials; from Girl Fridays and Man Fridays to the floor and window cleaners; from those who until now have had little reason for hope to those who, despite repeated failures, are everlasting wellsprings of long-range optimism. Wherever you may be, there are opportunities for action.

"I have four columns marching on Madrid," boasted General Francisco Franco back in 1937, "and one inside the city." With the help of this fifth column, he finally overthrew the republican government in Madrid. In today's First World establishments the difference between inside and outside is not so clear. Many outsiders work inside the walls. Some of the insiders, as I pointed out in "The Adaptive Hydra" (chapter 16), see themselves as ousiders boring from within. If this be a personal rationalization for those seeking a "handful of silver," it also sugggests that under conditions of more acute crisis, many co-optees will change colors again. Indeed, it is hard to see how any capitalist establishment could be fundamentally reformed or replaced without help from insiders. No matter how many columns may move from outside, four or five "fifth columns" could make all the difference.

HIGH ASPIRATIONS, REALISTIC EXPECTATIONS

No one person can do very much. This is why broad networks, coalitions, and movements are important. It is also why the question "What can *you* do?" must be realistically faced in terms of exactly where and what you are, what your capabilities might be, and who and what you might want to become.

The range of possible action is enormous. It is only barely hinted at in the agenda questions posed in the previous chapter, "The Long-Term Logic of Democracy." Indeed, the opportunities for small victories—particularly in the United States—are enormous. Here, a blatantly neofascist legislative effort or judicial decision can be held up or diverted. There, improvements in public services can be won. Here, an environmental monstrosity can be stopped in its tracks. There, some conspicuous victims of injustice can be saved, freed, or retroactively rehabilitated. Here, an entire neighborhood can be mobilized to improve run-down buildings, establish or improve a health clinic, or upgrade a local school. Here, an entire classroom can be raised to the level where formal learning becomes a wondrous excitement. There, a careful research study can rip aside the shrouds of mystification and false consciousness. Here, people can learn how to work together on behalf of interests broader than, but including, their own. Here, there, and almost everywhere some people can find some portion (in Walter Lippmann's words) of "the kind of purpose and effort that gives to life its flavor and meaning."

But you should also be realistic. On the path to any victory, the organizers—including *you*—may themselves be co-opted into the Establishment. At the moment of victory, the motive power animating your associates—and *you*—may be dissipated. As psychologists have long pointed out, a gratified need is no longer a motivator. And any success itself may strengthen the Establishment by demonstrating its presumed perfectibility.

Realism has another dimension. People will tell you that if you use new ideas, nobody will understand you. If you do, you will be isolated. People will tell you not to aim too high. If you do, you are doomed to disappointment. This problem of expectations will confront you in any sphere of action—whether the organization of workers or neighborhoods, the elimination of discrimination, or campaigns against war, the arms race, unemployment, and inflation. It even arises in the field of civil liberties. Do you really expect that the FBI can soon be returned to its original task of fighting crime? Do you really expect that in this age of competing intelligence forces, covert operations, and computerized dossiers, your personal privacy can long be protected against the menace of monitoring? If you do, this is as unrealistic as to expect quick conversion of TV and radio networks into instruments of democratic, rather than oligarchic, communication. Anyone who expects such Monday morning miracles is doomed to quick frustration and apathetic withdrawal. Only with a realistic expectation schedule can one keep on going the rest of the week—or month, year, or decade . . .

Let me put the question still more frontally. Should the defenders of America's Bill of Rights stand foursquare for all civil liberties for everyone, even though this would place an intolerable burden on the existing system of courts, legal defense, and mass media? Should the advocates of capitalism-with-a-difference commit themselves wholeheartedly to reforms that are unlikely? Should Establishment response to crisis be countered by alternative responses that may be doomed to failure? Should valuable time be spent popularizing an alternative vision that is truly visionary? In short, is it reasonable to ask the opponents of friendly fascism to make the kind of demands that create unrealistic aspirations?

My answer to these questions is "Yes, *if* . . ."

The *if* relates to the vital distinction—usually ignored—between expectations and aspirations.

It would be a deception of one's self and others to foster expectations of the impossible. But whether you are engaged in passive defense, counterattack, or positive initiatives, it is essential to combine realistic expectations with high—sometimes rising—aspirations. You will, in fact, get more of what people really need if your actions start with an orientation toward those needs rather than being "realistically" trimmed in advance to what conventional wisdom says they can readily get. To be an effective actor instead of merely a reactor, you must help raise aspirations far beyond the level of current expectations.

The shrewdest heads in the Establishment understand this distinction very well. That is why they level furious attacks against high aspirations in general, and personal attacks against anyone who tries to articulate them specifically. If articulated aspirations are broad enough to include the needs of the great majority of the people, it may be more difficult to carry out divide-and-rule, the old strategies. Instead of trying to get what they need and want, the reasoning goes, people should be brainwashed into wanting what they get. More apathy by the masses, they seem convinced, is the prerequisite for preserving democratic machinery.

Realistically, I see an increase in the height and scope of popular aspirations as vital to resolving the inescapable contradiction of any effort to expand human freedom. Only if the aspiration level is high enough can minor victories serve to increase rather than diminish motivations. Only thus can leaders be strengthened by minor victories rather than being led down the primrose path to co-optation. Indeed, if aspirations are high enough, there is less need to wait until things get worse before anything is done. If they are broad enough to include the needs of people everywhere, it may be easier to tolerate whatever reductions in First World living standards might result from contractions in foreign military operations and military spending at home. The more perfect accumulation of capital and power requires more acceptance and less resistance by those who are weakened in the process. If more people hope for more power over their own lives, they are less apt to be satisfied with reforms that enhance the power of faceless oligarchs. So long as expectations are realistic, the daily frustrations resulting from high aspirations may serve to fuel the patient anger and the impatient, long-range hopes that must animate all action against friendly fascism.

Many decades ago, in trying to bring straight talk into movements against classic fascism, Antonio Gramsci dealt with this distinction indirectly. "Pessimism of the intelligence," he advocated, but "optimism of the will." Today, extending Gramsci's remark, I suggest that optimism and pessimism have to be woven into *both* intelligence and will. Will must recognize the huge difficulties in the immediate future. Intelligence must be oriented toward the more hopeful possibilities at any time—particularly in the long run.

MY COUNTRY RIGHT AND WRONG

For me patriotism is the same as humanity. I am patriotic because I am human and humane. It is not exclusive. I will not hurt England or Germany to serve India . . . My patriotism is inclusive and admits of no enmity or ill-will.

MAHATMA GANDHI

Guard against the impostures of pretended patriotism.
GEORGE WASHINGTON,
Farewell Address

In Gertrude Stein's opera *The Mother Of Us All,* Susan B. Anthony, the women's rights pioneer, declares, "I am not puzzled; but it is very puzzling." In fact, she was deeply puzzled; that was Gertrude Stein's point. Similarly, one who applies intelligence and will in discovering and developing the logic of democracy must expect to face puzzlements. Anyone who tries to demystify or displace the Kafkaesque castles of power in the modern world creates another mystery if he or she pretends to know what exactly will happen next. Confronting the Golden International, the Ultra-Rich, and the Corporate Overseers, or even their smallest underlings is no tea party, picnic, or mere intellectual game. Any such effort involves uncertain opportunities and personal risks. No one who persists in attacking the Establishment and resists co-optation can expect to be rewarded by it on earth—although after death official tribute may be paid to his or her memory. The most immediate reward is to have not only one's competence but one's patriotism called into question.

This brings us to a deep puzzlement: what is patriotism really? I am not satisfied with Samuel Johnson's definition of 1775 "Patriotism is the last refuge of a scoundrel." And I can only partly accept Ambrose Bierce's re-statement in *The Devil's Dictionary:* "I beg to submit that it is the first." Rather, I favor George Washington's implied distinction between genuine and pretended patriotism. This is like the difference between true and "fool's gold" democracy. But it is a much more puzzling distinction. The rhetoric of false democracy has beclouded the atmosphere for only a few decades. The rhetoric of false patriotism is older than the nation itself. It was always used by the classic fascists. It is a favorite artifice of friendly fascism today.

I can easily understand why George Washington warned against pretended patriotism. The Declaration of Independence held forth the promise of more democracy than any country had ever yet attempted. But, in the words of Earl Robinson's "Ballad for Americans," "Nobody who was anybody believed it. Everybody who was anybody—they doubted it." The more conspicuous doubters, in the words of Tom Paine, were the "sunshine patriots" who shrank from the service of their country in time of crisis. Equally dangerous were the many speculators who made fortunes by charging extortionate prices for the arms, food, and clothing used by Washington's soldiers. During the entire struggle for independence, moreover, the social life of the new nation's cities was dominated by the rich "anybodies" still loyal to King George and the blessings of imperial monarchy. After the war, when Jefferson served as ambassador in Paris, he reported back on his difficulites with rich Americans: "Merchants are the least virtuous of citizens and possess the least of *amor patriae*."[11] After serving two terms as president, Jefferson explained this phenomenon: "Merchants have no country. The mere spot they stand on does not constitute so strong an attachment as that from which they draw their gains."[12]

I think I understand the kinds and roots of false patriotism today. Some years ago Francis W. Coker of Yale University put his finger on the divisive and exclusive patriots who "insist that the country must always be set above the rest of the world" and "in the name of patriotism conduct a virulent propaganda against economic and political measures of which they disapprove," including the admission of "undesirable" foreigners but also the free expression of dissident views in schools, churches or the media.[13] In his *Militarism, USA,* a sober critique based on years of experience in the U.S. Marine Corps, Colonel James A. Donovan identifies the dangerous patriot: "the one who drifts into chauvinism and exhibits blind enthusiasm for military actions. He is a defender of militarism and its ideals of war and glory. Chauvinism is a proud and bellicose form of patriotism . . . which identifies numerous enemies who can only be dealt with through military power and which equates the national honor with military victory." With an insider's gift for telling detail, he relates this kind of dangerous patriotism to the vested interests of the "vast, expensive, and burgeoning military-industrial-scientific-political combine which dominates the country."[14] In *The Reason for Democracy,* published after his death in 1976, Kalman Silvert of New York University provided another pungent description of false patriots: "People who wrap themselves in the flag and proclaim the sanctity of the nation are usually racists, contemptuous of the poor and dedicated to keeping the community of 'ins' small and pure of blood, spirit and mind."[15] The people described by Coker, Donovan, and Silvert are the kind of scoundrels Samuel Johnson and Ambrose Bierce were referring to—and anyone acting in the spirit of true democracy should be prepared for opposition from them.

But there is more to it than that. Throughout the Establishment there are "anybodies" who define patriotism as loyalty to themselves, their organization, or the regime, not to the Constitution, the country, or any higher principles of morality. To them, the Nuremberg principle was never enunciated. Their ideal subordinates are little Adolf Eichmanns who, not bothering about right or wrong, carry out any policies or orders given to them. Then there are the technocratic patriots who, fully accepting the dominant values of the Establishment, compete with each other in working out the details of the policies or orders. Unlike Eichmann's, their evil is not banal. Like the patriotism of Albert Speer's technicians in the Nazi war machine, it is creative, adaptive, and innovative—and totally divorced from any sense of moral responsibility. And at the Establishment's pinnacle, connecting it with other castles of power in the

Golden International, are the movers and shakers of the giant transnational conglomerates and complexes. Like the merchants described by Jefferson, they have no country and the least of *amor patriae*. If Jefferson were alive today, I think he would amend his statement to point out that while standing on and drawing their gains from many spots, they have real attachments to none.

I think I also understand the questionable patriotism of flag-waving "nobodies" in the lower and middle classes. At the beginning of the 1970s some "hard hats" in the building trades thought they were being patriotic by beating up youthful demonstrators against the Vietnam War. For those of them whose families had come to America to escape conscription, war, and oppression in Old War countries, this was a crude way of demonstrating their thankfulness for being able to live in the greater freedom of the New World. For those who had never been able to go to college, who suffered the insecurities of the highly irregular and seasonal construction industry, and who felt the humiliations of manual labor in an increasingly white-collar culture, this was an opportunity to demonstrate their physical superiority over the college kids. At the beginning of the 1980s, some white- and blue-collar workers joined in waving the American flag while burning Iranian flags and beating up Iranian students. What they demonstrated was a very human—although somewhat pathetic—desire to rally around a cause in which they could believe. Here was an obvious wrongdoing to oppose, and a brief chance to join with others in expressing a common national purpose.

But I am puzzled as to why true patriots seem to hide their love for America. Perhaps, as Kalman Silvert wrote after criticizing flag-waving racists, people who "like to think about embracing all their fellow citizens are ashamed to use the symbols of nationhood." These have been sullied by the posturing of false patriots. Perhaps true patriots feel that love of country should be stated by actions alone—even though this means yielding up the words and the symbols to the impostors. Perhaps, as they struggle against huge odds to amend the flaws in American life, their attachment to America recedes into the background. The awareness of this attachment can only be further diminished when the people in America's central-city ghettos hear the words of "America the Beautiful" telling them: "Thine alabaster cities gleam/Undimmed by human tears."

Nonetheless, I am puzzled. In 1948, Alan Paton, the South African writer, published a great novel, *Cry, the Beloved Country*. I remember wondering then what could be so beloved about that country, a land of bondage and fear, in comparison with my own country. I still wonder why so many of my own countrymen—particularly my students—are hesitant to express their love. Perhaps they must live in other countries long enough, as I have done, to appreciate the glories of America and learn that there is no other place where they can be at home. Perhaps they are put off by examples of blind patriotism. "Our country right or wrong," the famous toast by naval officer Stephen Decatur, seems to hail the closing of eyes to the wrongs committed by some Americans in the name of America.

To love America is not to cover up the misdeeds done by people of this country. A good parent is one who sees the faults of children as well as their beauties. He or she tries to understand those faults and, where possible, help correct them. This does not mean withdrawing love and giving it back depending on how the child behaves. For him or her, it is "My child right and wrong, but by child." True love is never blind.

In Germany today the true patriots are those who, among other things, are trying to come to grips with the essence of past Nazi horrors. In the Soviet Union the true patriots are those who try to understand the nature and roots of Stalinism and the Stalinist legacy, rather than simply uttering some words about "the cult of personality" and running away from the subject. In America the true patriots are those who face the fact that Americans have always been both right and wrong and, instead of trying to squelch criticism, calmly take the position "My country right *and* wrong." They are those who defend the good, the true, and the beautiful in American life. They are willing to take risks in attacking what is wrong. And as I have been pointing out in earlier chapters, there is much wrong in the making today.

I came to maturity hating the wrongdoers of classic fascism. They were truly hateful. I cannot say that I hate the racists, chauvinists, sexists, polluters, interventionists, price fixers, labor-haters, academic frauds, false patriots, and corporate criminals and corrupters who are taking us down the paths toward friendly fascism. Hatred is *their* game. They hate people at home and abroad, and I suspect that many of them hate themselves. They are as much the victims as the beneficiaries of a system that needs some reconstructing. They need compassion. They also need their comeuppance. They must be fought in the factories and the fields, in the offices and the supermarkets, in the courts and the legislatures, at the ballot boxes, in the classrooms, on the picket lines, in the press and on the air waves. They must be fought with every nonviolent and nonwarlike means that the ingenuity of man, woman, or child can devise.

These are no simple tasks. With so much to be done and undone, there is room—and need—for anyone anywhere. There are endless needs for uncovering exploitation and abuses wherever they may occur, whether intended or unintentional; and for demystifying the mysteries that obscure the workings of concentrated capital and power. It is necessary to act even while knowing that any line of action may have unintended consequences and prove to be myopic, perhaps even blind. It is essential to learn from mistakes and false starts, and to begin again in an endless struggle to make things better rather than sit idly by, waiting until they become worse. It does not matter so much whether one prefers defending the best in the status quo, seeking a truly reformed capitalism or preparing the way for democratic socialism. It does not matter what crisis one responds to, what aspect of the democratic vision one cherishes most, or which portion of the democratic logic one acts on and develops. What matters is that one finds companions in journeys that may not be brief but should be joyous.

In the course of these journeys the dominant logic of today may be totally submerged by a new wave of a democratic future that seems improbable at present. This is the hopeful challenge behind all the puzzling entanglements of "What is to be done and undone?"

O brave new world that has such challenge in it!

Notes

Introduction: A Patriotic Warning

1. Kenneth Dolbeare, "Alternatives to the New Fascism," paper delivered at the American Political Science Association, September 1976.
2. Alan Wolfe, "Waiting for Rightie," *The Review of Radical Political Economics*, Fall 1973.
3. Anne Morrow Lindbergh, *The Wave of the Future: A Confession of Faith* (New York: Harcourt Brace 1940).
4. For the term "blind anti-fascism," I am indebted to Arnold Beichman, who in referring to Robert Heilbroner's attacks on "blind anti-communism," complains that progressives may not recognize the existence of "blind anti-fascism" or "blind anti-racism" in *Nine Lies About America* (New York: The Library Press, 1972). If Beichman's point is that myopia, blind spots and blindness are to be found at all points on the political spectrum, I thankfully agree.
5. The argument that the Employment Act of 1946—apart from any of its framers' intentions—has laid the legal basis for the modern corporate state is presented forcefully by Arthur S. Miller in *The Modern Corporate State: Private Governments and the American Constitution* (Westport: Greenwood Press, 1976).
6. Gunther Anders, "Theses for the Atomic Age," *The Massachusetts Review*, Spring 1962.
7. Alvin Toffler, *Future Shock* (New York: Random House, 1970).
8. William L. Shirer's statement was made in a press interview appearing in the *Los Angeles Times* in 1972.
9. Marvin Harris, *Cannibals and Kings* (New York: Random House, 1979).
10. For the distinction between the ignorance of the wise and the wisdom of the ignorant I am indebted to Mary Parker Follett: "There is the ignorance of the ignorant and the ignorance of the wise; there is the wisdom of the wise and the wisdom of the ignorant. Both kinds of ignorance have to be overcome, one as much as the other; both kinds of wisdom have to prevail, one as much as the other." *The New State: Group Organization the Solution of Popular Government* (New York: Longman's Green, 1918; reissued Gloucester, Mass.: 1965).
11. *Nine Lies About America.*

Chapter 1: The Rise and Fall of Classic Fascism

1. Roland Sarti, *Fascism and Industrial Leadership in Italy, 1919–1940: A Study in the Expansion of Private Power under Fascism.* (Berkeley: University of California Press, 1971).
2. Edward R. Tannenbaum, *The Fascist Experience, Italian Society and Culture, 1922–1945.* (New York: Basic Books, 1972).
3. R. L. Carsten, *The Rise of Fascism* (Berkeley: University of California Press, 1967).
4. David Schoenbaum, *Hitler's Social Revolution* (New York: Anchor Books, 1967).

5. William Manchester, *The Arms of Krupp, 1587–1968* (New York: Bantam, 1970).
6. William Shirer, *The Rise and Fall of the Third Reich* (New York: Simon and Schuster, 1960).
7. Masao Maruyama, "The Ideology and Dynamics of Japanese Fascism," in Ivan Morris, ed., Masao Maruyama, *Thought and Behavior in Japanese Politics,* 1963 (New York: Oxford University Press, 1969).
8. "The Ideology and Dynamics of Japanese Fascism."
9. *Fascism and Industrial Leadership in Italy, 1919–1940.*
10. *Fascism and Industrial Leadership in Italy, 1919–1940.*
11. Robert A. Brady, *Business as a System of Power* (New York: Columbia University Press, 1943).
12. Speech to Nuremberg Congress, September 3, 1933.
13. Hermann Rauschning, *The Voice of Destruction* (New York: Putnam's, 1940).
14. *The Rise and Fall of the Third Reich.*
15. *The Rise and Fall of the Third Reich.*
16. Robert Payne, *The Life and Death of Adolph Hitler* (New York: Praeger, 1973).
17. *The Life and Death of Adolph Hitler.*
18. *The Rise and Fall of the Third Reich.*
19. *The Rise and Fall of the Third Reich.*
20. Albert Speer, *Inside the Third Reich* (New York: Macmillan, 1970).
21. Hermann Rauschning, *The Revolution of Nihilism* (New York: Longmans Green, 1930).
22. *The Rise and Fall of the Third Reich.*
23. *The Wave of the Future.*
24. Lawrence Dennis, *Operational Thinking for Survival* (Colorado Springs: Ralph Miles Publisher, 1969).
25. Hugh R. Trevor-Roper, *The Last Days of Hitler* (London: Macmillan, 1956).
26. Carl J. Freidrich and Zbigniew Brzezinski, *Totalitarian Dictatorship and Autocracy* (New York: Praeger, 1961).

Chapter 2: The Takeoff Toward a New Corporate Society

1. "The Internationalization of Capital," *Journal of Economic Issues,* March 1972.
2. Zbigniew Brzezinski, *Between Two Ages* (New York: Viking, 1970).
3. Daniel Fusfeld, "The Rise of the Corporate State in America," *Journal of Economic Issues,* March 1972.
4. Charles L. Mee, Jr. *Meeting at Potsdam* (New York: M. Evans, 1975).
5. Amaury de Riencourt, *The American Empire* (New York: Delta, 1968).
6. Andrew Shonfield, *Modern Capitalism* (New York: Oxford University Press, 1965).
7. V. I. Lenin, "Introduction," Nicolai Bukharin, *Imperialism and World Economy,* 1915 (New York: Monthly Review Press, 1973).
8. *Imperialism and World Economy.*
9. V. I. Lenin, *Imperialism, the Highest Stage of Capitalism* 1916 (Moscow: Progress Publishers, 1970).
10. Susanne Bodenheimer, "Dependency and Imperialism," in K. T. Fann and Donald C. Hodges, eds. *Readings in Imperialism* (Boston: Peter Sargent, 1971).
11. General Golbery do Couto e Silva, quoted by Eduardo Galeano, "Brazil and Uruguay: Euphoria and Agony," *Monthly Review,* February, 1972.
12. Sylvia Porter "The New Monetary System," *New York Post,* September 13, 1971.
13. "Western Policies the Topic at Meeting of Elite," *New York Times,* April 25, 1977.
14. *Between Two Ages.*
15. Anthony Eden, "Getting the Free World Together," *New York Times,* May 5, 1972.
16. *Newsweek,* June 16, 1975.
17. Ralph Nader, Introduction to Morton Mintz and Jerry S. Cohen, *America, Inc.* (New York: Dial Press, 1971).

18. James O'Connor, *Fiscal Crisis of the State* (New York: St. Martin's Press, 1973).
19. Alvin Toffler, *The Third Wave.*
20. Lord Ritchie Calder, quoted by Alvin Toffler, *The Third Wave.*
21. National Science Foundation, Experimental Research Program on Appropriate Technology, Division of Intergovernmental Science and Applied Technology, approved by the National Science Board, January 17, 1980.
22. I have provided a more detailed review of productivity and efficiency indicators in my *Organizations and Their Managing* (New York: Free Press, 1968).

Chapter 3: The Mysterious Establishment

1. Herbert Gans, *Deciding What's News: A Study of CBS Evening News, NBC Nightly News, Newsweek and Time* (New York: Pantheon, 1978).
2. The most significant general books on the American power structure are these: G. William Domhoff, *Who Rules America?* (Englewood Cliffs: Prentice-Hall, 1967); *Who Really Rules? New Haven and Community Power Re-Examined* (Santa Monica: Goodyear Publishing, 1978); *The Powers That Be: Processes of Ruling Class Domination in America* (New York: Vintage, 1979); Gabriel Kolko, *Wealth and Power in America* (New York: Praeger, 1962); Ferdinand Lundberg, *The Rich and the Super-Rich* (New York: Lyle Stuart, 1968); C. Wright Mills, *The Power Elite* (New York: Oxford University Press, 1956); Morton Mintz and Jerry S. Cohen, *America, Inc.* (New York: Dial Press, 1971), and *Power, Inc.* (New York: Viking, 1976). There are also other books that deal with important aspects of the subject: Richard J. Barber, *The American Corporation: Its Power, Its Money, Its Politics* (New York: Dutton, 1970); Richard J. Barnet and Ronald Muller, *Global Reach* (New York: Simon and Schuster, 1975); John Blair, *Economic Concentration: Structure, Behavior and Public Policy* (New York: Harcourt Brace Jovanovich, 1972); Andrew Hacker, *The Corporation Take-Over* (New York: Harper and Row, 1964); Stanislas Menshikov, *Millionaires and Managers: Structure of U.S. Financial Oligarchy* (Moscow: Progress Publishers, 1969); and Andreas K. Panandreou, *Paternalistic Capitalism* (Minneapolis: University of Minnesota Press, 1972).
3. Robert Townsend: Review of Robert Heilbroner, et al. "In the Name of Profit," *The New York Times Book Review,* April 30, 1972.
4. Leonard Silk, *Capitalism, The Moving Target* (New York: Quadrangle, 1974).
5. Paul Samuelson, *Economics,* 9th Ed. (New York: McGraw-Hill, 1973).
6. *The Rich and the Super-Rich.*
7. Arthur M. Louis, "America's Centimillionaires," *Fortune,* May 1968.
8. *Report on Millionaires:* report by U.S. Trust Company of New York, June 27, 1979.
9. Herman P. Miller, "Inequality, Poverty and Taxes," *Dissent,* Winter 1975.
10. Murray Rothbard Letter to the Editor, *New York Times,* March 1, 1972.
11. *The Power Elite.*
12. Richard J. Barber, *The American Corporation* (New York: E.P. Dutton, 1970).
13. Gerald Colby Zilg, *Behind the Nylon Curtain* (Englewood Cliffs: Prentice-Hall, 1974).
14. Robert Heilbroner, *The Limits of American Capitalism* (New York: Harper Torchbooks, 1966).
15. *The American Corporation.*
16. Senator Lee Metcalf, Congressional Record, June 24, 1971, cited in Richard May, *The Wall Street Game* (New York: Praeger, 1974).
17. Andrew Hacker, *The End of the American Era* (New York: Atheneum, 1970).
18. Bertram Gross, "The Secret Success of Jimmy Carter: Profits Without Honor," *The Nation,* June 2, 1979.
19. Marriner Eccles, *Fortune,* January, 1961.
20. The chart is borrowed from G. William Domhoff, *The Powers That Be* (New York: Random House, 1979). My only addition is the title.
21. This discussion is based largely on Domhoff's *The Powers That Be.*
22. For background in Greenbriar Conference: Domhoff, *The Powers That Be;*

Wesley McCune, *Who's Behind Our Farm Policy?* (New York: Praeger, 1956); James Deakin, *The Lobbyists* (Washington, D.C.: Public Affairs Press, 1966); and Donald R. Hall, *Cooperative Lobbying—The Power of Pressure* (University of Arizona Press, 1969).

23. Andreas Papandreou, *Paternalistic Capitalism* (Minneapolis: University of Minnesota Press, 1972).
24. Daniel Bell, *The Coming of Post-Industrial Society* (New York: Basic Books, 1973).
25. John K. Galbraith, *The New Industrial State* (New York: Mentor, 1968).
26. Daniel P. Moynihan, "The Professionalization of Reform," *The Public Interest*, Fall 1975.
27. *The Rich and the Super-Rich.*
28. D. F. Fleming, *The Cold War and Its Origins* (New York: Doubleday, 1961).
29. James MacGregor Burns, *Roosevelt: The Soldier of Freedom, 1940–1945* (New York: Harcourt Brace Jovanovich, 1970).
30. Ronald Radosh, *Prophets on the Right* (New York: Simon and Schuster, 1975).
31. Walter Goodman, *The Committee* (New York: Farrar, Straus and Giroux, 1968).
32. Irving Howe and Lewis Coser, *The American Communist Party* (New York: Praeger, 1963 edit.).
33. Frank Friedel, *America in the Twentieth Century* (New York: Knopf, 1965).
34. Colonel James A. Donovan, *Militarism, U.S.A.* (New York: Charles Scribner's Sons, 1970).
35. Francis X. Sutton, Seymour Harris, Carl Kaysen and James Tobin, *The American Business Creed,* 1956 (New York: Schocken, 1962).
36. Carl Kaysen, "The Social Significance of the Modern Corporation," *American Economic Review,* May 1957.
37. C. L. Sulzberger, "Should the Old Labels be Changed?" *New York Times,* July 1964. Quoted in Ayn Rand, *Capitalism: The Unknown Ideal* (New York: Signet, 1967).
38. *Capitalism: The Unknown Ideal.*
39. Arthur Burns, *Looking Forward,* 31st Annual Report of the National Bureau of Economic Research, 1951.
40. Seymour Martin Lipset, *Political Man* (New York: Doubleday, 1960).
41. Daniel Bell, *The End of Ideology* (Glencoe, Ill.: Free Press, 1960).
42. *The Coming of Post-Industrial Society.*
43. John K. Galbraith, *The New Industrial State* (Boston: Houghton Mifflin, 1967).
44. John K. Galbraith, *Economics and the Public Purpose* (Boston: Houghton Mifflin, 1973).
45. Amitai Etzioni and Richard Remp, "Technological 'Shortcuts' to Social Change," *Science,* January 7, 1972.

Chapter 4: The Side Effects of Success

1. *New York Times,* May 7, 1973.
2. Charles Reich, *The Greening of America* (New York: Random House, 1970).
3. Stanislas Andreski, "On the Likelihood of the Possibility of a Collapse of the Political System of the United States of America."
4. James Reston, "Who Speaks for America?" *New York Times,* April 16, 1972.
5. "The Dirty Work," *Wall Street Journal,* July 16, 1971.
6. Report of a Special Task Force to the Secretary of Health, Education and Welfare, *Work in America* (Cambridge: MIT Press, 1973).
7. Robert Dubin, "Workers," *International Encyclopedia of the Social Sciences,* vol. 16 (New York: Macmillan, 1968).
8. John and Barbara Ehrenreich, "Work and Consciousness," *Monthly Review,* July-August 1976.
9. Vance Packard, *A Nation of Strangers* (New York: McKay, 1972).
10. Richard Goodwin, *The American Condition* (Garden City: Doubleday, 1974).
11. Edward Shorter, *The Making of the Modern Family* (New York: Basic Books, 1975).

12 Suzanne Gordon, *Lonely in America* (New York: Simon and Schuster, 1976).
13. Hannah Arendt, *The Origins of Totalitarianism* (New York: Meridian, 1958).
14. *The American Condition.*
15. Hans Morgenthau, "Reflections on the End of the Republic," *New York Review of Books,* September 24, 1970.
16. George Charles Roche III, *The Bewildered Society* (New York: Arlington House, 1972).
17. HEW, *Work in America.*
18. Studs Terkel, *Working* (New York: Pantheon, 1974).
19. Abraham Briloff, *Unaccountable Accounting* (New York: Harper & Row, 1972).
20. *Lonely in America.*
21. Donald W. Tiffany, James R. Cowan and Phyllis M. Tiffany, *The Unemployed* (Englewood Cliffs: Prentice Hall, 1970).
22. Harvey Brenner, *Mental Illness and Economy* (Cambridge: Harvard University Press, 1973).
23. Edgar Z. Friedenberg, *Coming of Age in America* (New York: Random House, 1965).
24. Margaret Mead, *Culture and Commitment* (Garden City: Doubleday, 1970).
25. Clayton Fritchey, "Crime and Politics," *New York Post,* May 4, 1976.
26. Abraham Lass, "1+1=Terror," *New York Times,* November 20, 1971.
27. Quoted by Robert N. Winter-Berger, *The Washington Pay-Off* (New York: Dell, 1972).
28. Herbert Robinson, "Discount Group Hears a Prediction of Wave of Pay-Offs," *New York Times,* May 23, 1972.
29. "Federal Agencies Press Inquiry of Housing Frauds in Big Cities," *New York Times,* May 8, 1972.
30. David Durk, "Viva La Policia," *New York Times,* December 29, 1971.
31. Edwin H. Sutherland, *White Collar Crime,* 1949 (New York: Holt, Rinehart and Winston, 1961).
32. *White Collar Crime.*
33. *The Rich and the Super-Rich.*
34. Jack Anderson, with Les Whitten, "Haldeman On His Mind," *New York Post,* September 13, 1975.
35. Ralph Nader, Introduction, *America, Inc.*
36. Michael Tanzer, *The Sick Society* (New York: Holt, Rinehart and Winston, 1971).
37. Ward Just, *Military Men* (New York: Knopf, 1970).
38. Arthur H. Miller, Alden S. Raine and Thad A. Brown, "Integration and Estrangement," *Society,* July/August, 1976.

Chapter 5: The Challenge of a Shrinking Capitalist World

1. Daniel Bell, "The End of American Exceptionalism," *The Public Interest,* Fall 1975.
2. Michael Harrington, *Socialism* (New York: Saturday Review Press, 1972).
3. United Nation Declaration on the Establishment of a New International Economic Order, 1974.
4. "One could say that a state of cold war has marked the relations of the Soviet Union with the other leading powers ever since the cessation of open conflict between the new Bolshevik regime and the 'imperialists' in the early 1920s." Henry L. Roberts, "The Cold War," in John A. Garraty and Peter Gay, eds. *The Columbia History of the World* (New York: Harper and Row, 1972).
5. "A Conversation with George Kennan," interview with George Urban, *Encounter,* September 1976.
6. "Review of Current Trends in Business and Finance," based on a report by the secretariat of the Economic Commission for Europe. *Wall Street Journal,* August 18, 1975.
7. Mary Kaldor, *The Disintegrating West* (New York: Hill and Wang, 1978).

Chapter 6: Old Crises in New Forms

1. "Notes on the U.S. Situation at the End of 1972," *Monthly Review*, January 1973.
2. Paul Samuelson, *Economics* (New York: McGraw-Hill, 1973, Ninth Edition).
3. William Safire, "What Recession?" *New York Times*, October 10, 1974.
4. This is my own interpretation, in "Welcome to Stagflation," *The Nation*, August 1979.
5. Walter Grinder, *Business Week*, August 4, 1974.
6. Frank F. Furstenberg, Jr. and Charles A. Thrall, "Counting the Jobless: The Impact of Job Rationing on the Measurement of Unemployment," in Stanley Moses, ed. *Planning for Full Employment*, The Annals, March 1975.
7. Quoted in Bertram M. Gross, "Anti-Inflation for Progressives," *The Nation*, June 23, 1979.
8. Gene Koretz, "Global Inflation: A Disease in Search of a Cure," *Business Week*, March 1974.
9. Stated for first time in "Welcome to Stagflation."
10. Stephen Hymer, "The Internationalization of Capital."
11. *Business Week*, September 24, 1979.
12. Harry Braverman, *Labor and Monopoly Capital* (New York: Monthly Review Press, 1974).
13. *The Fiscal Crisis of the State.*
14. David Bazelon, *The Paper Economy* (New York: Random House, 1963).
15. *The Economic Impact of Disarmament* (Washington, D.C.: U.S. Government Printing Office, January 1962).
16. Captain David M. Saunders, U.S. Naval Institute Proceedings, September 1965.
17. Robert Tucker, "Israel and the United States," *Commentary*, November 1975.
18. Hasan Ozbekhan, "The Role of Goals and Planning in the Solution of the World Food Problem," in Robert Jungk and Johan Galtung (eds.), *Mankind 2000* (Boston: Universitetsforlaget, 1969).
19. Robert Clarke, *The Science of War and Peace* (New York: McGraw-Hill, 1972).
20. J. B. Phelps et al., *Accidental War: Some Dangers in the 1960's* (Ohio: Mershon National Security Program, Ohio State University, 1960).

Chapter 7: The Unfolding Logic

1. Walter Laqueur, "Fascism—the Second Coming," *Commentary*, February 1976.
2. John D. Rockefeller, *The Second American Revolution* (New York: Harper and Row, 1973).
3. Ronald Steel, "Interview with Walter Lippmann," *Washington Post*, March 25, 1973.
4. Robert Michels, *Political Parties*, 1915, Eden and Cedar Paul, tr., (Glencoe, Ill.: Free Press, 1949).
5. C. L. Sulzberger, "Heart of U.S. Darkness," *New York Times*, March 31, 1974.
6. Michel Crozier, Samuel Huntington, and Joji Watanuki, *The Crisis of Democracy* (New York; New York University, 1975). Michel Crozier has informed me that he never agreed with Huntington on this point, and in his new book *On Ne Change Pas La Societe Par Decret* (Paris, Bernard Grosset, 1979), Crozier urges more democracy, not less.
7. Alan Wolfe, "Capitalism Shows Its Face: Giving Up of Democracy," *The Nation*, November 29, 1975.
8. Donald Zoll, "Shall We Let America Die?" *National Review*, December 16, 1969.
9. Maxwell Taylor, *Swords and Ploughshares* (New York: Norton, 1972).
10. Speech at the Virginia Convention, June 16, 1788.
11. Editorial, "Subverting America," *New York Times*, June 17, 1973.
12. "Sumitomo: How the 'Keiretsu' Pulls to Keep Japan Strong," *Business Week*, March 31, 1975.
13. Richard Falk, "A New Paradigm for International Legal Studies," *Yale Law Journal*, April 1975.

14. "The Specter of Weimer," *Commentary,* December 1971. A similar point is made by Arnold Beichmann in *Nine Lies About America.*

Chapter 8: Trilateral Empire or Fortress America?

1. Felix Greene, *Imperial America* (Baltimore: John Hopkins, 1967).
2. Victor Zurza, "Soviet Nightmares," *Washington Post,* March 5, 1976.
3. Margarita Maximova, *Economic Aspects of Capitalist Integration* (Moscow: Progress Publishers, 1973).
4. Sankar Ray, "U.S. and European Multinationals: Intensified Contradictions," *The Economic Times,* New Delhi, January 16, 1976.
5. Gabriel Kolko, "Vietnam and the Future of U.S. Foreign Policy," *Liberation,* May 1973.
6. "Angola: What is Moscow Up To?" *National Review,* March 19, 1976.
7. Irving Kristol, "Kissinger at Dead End," *Wall Street Journal,* March 10, 1976.
8. Peter Berger, "The Greening of American Foreign Policy," *Commentary,* March 1976.
9. C. L. Sulzberger, "Our Haphazard Empire," *New York Times,* March 17, 1977.
10. George Liska, *Imperial America* (Baltimore: Johns Hopkins, 1967).
11. Robert Osgood, "The Nixon Doctrine and Strategy," in Robert E. Osgood, et al., *Retreat from Empire?* (Baltimore: Johns Hopkins, 1973).
12. Robert Tucker, "The American Outlook: Change and Continuity," in Osgood, *Retreat from Empire?*
13. *Between Two Ages.*
14. George Liska, *Beyond Kissinger: Ways of Conservative Statecraft* (Baltimore: Johns Hopkins, 1976).
15. *Between Two Ages.*
16. Henry Kissinger, "Defense of 'Grey Areas'", *Foreign Affairs,* April 1955.
17. David Binder, "A Modified Soviet Bloc in U.S. Policy," *New York Times,* April 6, 1976.
18. Robert Pfaltzgraff, Jr., "The United States and a Strategy for the West," *Strategic Review,* Summer 1977.

Chapter 9: The Friendly Fascist Establishment

1. Amaury de Riencourt, *The Coming Caesars* (New York: Capricorn, 1964.
2. Eugene J. Kaplan, *Japan, the Government Business Relationship* (Washington, D.C.: U.S. Government Printing Office, 1972).
3. Richard F. Jansen, *Wall Street Journal,* April 24, 1972.
4. "The New Banking," *Business Week,* September 15, 1973.
5. *Future Shock.*
6. Arthur S. Miller, *The Modern Corporate State: Private Governments and the American Constitution* (Westport: Greenwood Press, 1976).
7. Paul Dickson, *Think Tanks* (New York: Atheneum, 1971).
8. This is a slight expansion of the analysis by Michael Klare in *War Without End* (New York: Vintage, 1972).
9. Richard Falk, "Exporting Counterrevolution," *The Nation,* Special Issue on Intervention, June 9, 1979.
10. Quoted by Colonel James A. Donovan in his *Militarism, U.S.A.*
11. Richard A. Gabriel and Paul T. Savage, *Crisis in Command: Mismanagement in the Army* (New York: Hill and Wang, 1978).
12. William W. Turner, *Power on the Right* (Berkeley: Ramparts, 1971).
13. Sasha Lewis, "The Far Right Plan for 1980," *Seven Days,* August 14, 1979.
14. Joseph Trento and Joseph Spear, "How Nazi Nut Power Has Invaded Capitol Hill," *True,* November 1969.
15. Falangist Party of America, *Prospectus,* Box 5, Crystal Bay, Minnesota, 1979.
16. This is discussed in Bertram Gross, "Anti-Inflation for Progressives," *The Nation.*
17. Americans for Democratic Action, *A Citizen's Guide to the Right Wing,* Washington, D.C., 1978.

18. Quoted by Steve Manning, "'New Right' Forces Expect to Win," *Guardian,* October 3, 1979.
19. Arno Mayer, *Dynamics of Counter-Revolution in Europe, 1870–1956* (New York: Harper Torchbooks, 1971).
20. "American Intellectuals and Foreign Policy," *Foreign Affairs,* July, 1967, reprinted in *On the Democratic Idea in America* (New York: Harper & Row, 1972).
21. "Capitalism 101," *Newsweek,* April 30, 1979.
22. Peter Steinfels, *The Neoconservatives: The Men Who Are Changing America's Politics* (New York: Simon and Schuster, 1979).
23. Robert Nisbet, *The Twilight of Authority* (New York: Oxford University Press, 1975).
24. Daniel Bell, *The Coming of Post-Industrial Society* (New York: Basic Books, 1973).
25. Philip Boffey. *The Brain Bank of America* (New York: McGraw-Hill, 1975).
26. Ida Hoos, "Models, Methods, and Myths—the Mystique of Modern Management," paper delivered at 1975 Winter Computer Simulation Conference, Sacramento, California, December 18, 1975.
27. Ida Hoos, *Systems Analysis in Public Policy: A Critique* (Berkeley: University of California, 1972).
28. B. F. Skinner, *Beyond Freedom and Dignity* (New York: Knopf, 1971).
29. Jose M. R. Delgado, M.D., *Physical Control of the Mind* (New York: Harper & Row, 1969).
30. Charles Merriam, *Political Power,* 1934 (Glencoe, Ill.: Free Press, 1950).
31. Daniel P. Moynihan, "The United States in Opposition," *Commentary,* March, 1975.
32. Walter Laqueur, "The Issue of Human Rights," *Commentary,* May, 1977.

Chapter 10: Friendly Fascist Economics

1. Irving Kristol, "The Worst Is Yet to Come," *Wall Street Journal,* November 26, 1979.
2. Daniel Fusfield, "Introduction," Arthur S. Miller, *The Modern Corporate State.*
3. Robert Theobald, "What New Directions for Society?" *Los Angeles Times,* May 24, 1970.
4. A. W. Phillips, "The Relation Between Unemployment and the Rate of Change of Money Wage Rates in the United Kingdom, 1861–1957," *Economics,* November 1958.
5. Steven Rattner, "Executives Fail Fed's New Policy," *New York Times,* October 15, 1979.
6. Herman Kahn, *The Next 200 Years* (New York: Morrow, 1976).
7. *The Next 200 Years.*
8. Barry Commoner, *The Poverty of Power* (New York: Knopf, 1976).
9. *The Next 200 Years.*
10. Jim Hightower, *Eat Your Heart Out* (New York: Crown, 1975).
11. Mihajlo Mesarovic and Eduard Pestel, *Mankind at the Turning Point* (New York: Dutton, 1974).
12. James Ridgeway, *The Last Play* (New York: Dutton, 1973).
13. Robert Engler, *The Politics of Oil* (Chicago: University of Chicago Press, 1961), and *The Brotherhood of Oil* (Chicago: University of Chicago Press, 1977); and John Blair, *The Control of Oil* (New York: Pantheon, 1976).
14. Quoted by Anthony Sampson in his vivid *The Seven Sisters: The Great Oil Companies and the World They Shaped* (New York: Viking, 1975).
15. Barry Commoner, *The Poverty of Power* (New York: Knopf, 1976).
16. Editorial, "Capping Third World Gushers," *The Nation,* July 28-August 4, 1979.
17. Barry Commoner, *The Closing Circle* (New York: Knopf, 1971).
18. Barry Weisberg, *Beyond Repair* (Boston: Beacon, 1971).
19. *Beyond Repair.*
20. *The Next 200 Years.*
21. Donella Meadows, et al. *The Limits of Growth* (New York: Universe, 1972).

22. *The Next 200 Years.*
23. Robert Heilbroner, "Ecological Armageddon," *New York Review of Books,* May 23, 1970.
24. Ozorio de Almeida, "Development and Environment," *The Founex Report,* Carnegie Endowment for International Peace, 1972.
25. David Burnham, "Presidential Panel Asks Curbs on Chemical Perils," *New York Times,* August 15, 1979.
26. Helen Caldicott, *Nuclear Madness* (Brookline, Mass.: Autumn Press, 1978).
27. Dr. John W. Gofman and Dr. Arthur Tamplin, quoted by Dr. Helen Caldicott in *Nuclear Madness.* Dr. Caldicott also cites the numerous publications of Dr. John W. Gofman.
28. *Nuclear Madness.*
29. Anthony Lewis, "Act Now, Pay Later," *New York Times,* December 6, 1979.
30. Vance Packard, *The Waste Makers* (New York: David McKay, 1960).
31. *Beyond Repair.*
32. *Eat Your Heart Out.*
33. "A. Dale Console," in Ralph Nader, et al., *Whistle Blowing* (New York: Grossman, 1972).
34. Dr. Richard Kunnes, *Your Money or Your Life* (New York: Dodd Mead, 1971).
35. David Burnham, "Presidential Panel Asks Curbs on Chemical Perils," *New York Times,* August 15, 1979.

Chapter 11: Subverting Democratic Machinery

1. Murray B. Levin, *Political Hysteria in America* (New York: Basic Books, 1971).
2. Thomas R. Nye and Harmon Ziegler, *The Irony of Democracy* (Belmont, California: Wadsworth, 1971).
3. Yvonne Karp, *Eleanor Marx,* Vol. Two (New York: Pantheon, 1977).
4. Lawrence Dennis, *The Coming of American Fascism* (New York: Harper, 1936).
5. Robert L. Peabody, "House Leadership, Party Caucauses and the Committee Structure," *Committee Organization in the House,* Vol. 2, Select Committee on Committees, 1974.
6. L. D. Solomon, "For New York a Time of Testing as the Nation Looks On," *New York Times,* February 21, 1976.
7. Roger Alcaly, "New York: Waiting for the Dough," *Seven Days,* October, 6, 1975.
8. "For New York a Time of Testing as the Nation Looks On."
9. Interview by Ronald Steel, "Walter Lippmann at 83," *Washington Post,* March 25, 1973.
10. Barrington Moore, *Social Origins of Dictatorship and Democracy* (Boston: Beacon, 1967).
11. Garry Wills, *Nixon Agonistes* (New York: Signet, 1972).
12. Interview with *New York Times,* November 10, 1972.
13. Murray Edelman, *The Symbolic Uses of Politics* (Urbana: University of Illinois, 1964).
14. *The Rich and the Super-Rich.*
15. Douglas Fraser, President of the United Automobile Workers Union, Public Statement, 1979.
16. Quoted by James Farmer in *The Hired Guns of De-Unionization* (Washington, D.C.: Coalition of American Public Employees, 1979).
17. Karl Polanyi, *The Great Transformation: The Political and Economic Origins of Our Time* (Boston: Beacon, 1957).
18. Debra Hauser, "The Union-Busting Hustle," *The New Republic,* August 25, 1979.
19. James Farmer, *The Hired Guns of De-Unionization* and Phyllis Payne, "The Plot To Subvert Labor Standards," *AFL-CIO American Federationist,* July 1979.
20. Personal comment, reported by Sidney Dean of New York City.

21. *The Rich and the Super-Rich.*
22. Edward Luttwak, *Coup D'Etat* (London: Penguin, 1968).

Chapter 12: Managing Information and Minds

1. Herbert Schiller, *The Mind Managers* (Boston: Beacon, 1973).
2. Arthur R. Miller, *The Assault on Privacy* (Ann Arbor: University of Michigan Press, 1971).
3. William A. Caldwell, *How to Save Urban America* (New York: New American Library, 1973).
4. Adolph Hitler, *Mein Kampf.*
5. George Gerbner, "Communications and Social Environment," *Scientific American,* September 1972.
6. *The Mind Managers.*
7. Aldous Huxley, *Brave New World* (New York: Harper & Row, 1958).
8. Alfred Friendly, *Due to Circumstances Beyond Our Control* (New York: Random House, 1967).
9. Statement to the Author by Theodore Gross, editor of *Boston Phoenix,* and *Boston After Dark.*
10. Daniel Burstein quotation in H. Falk, "The Sound and the Fury," *Wall Street Journal,* September 1971.
11. Statement to the author by Larry P. Gross at Annenberg School of Communications, University of Pennsylvania, January 1976.
12. *The Mind Managers.*
13. Harold Mendelson and Irving Crespi, *Polls, Television and the New Politics* (Scranton: Chandler, 1970).
14. Joe McGinniss, *The Selling of the President 1968* (New York: Pocket Books, 1968).
15. *Transaction,* July-August 1971.
16. Edmund Carpenter, *The Dick Cavett Show,* April 1971.
17. Fred Friendly, "Foreword" to Newton Minow et al., *Presidential Television* (New York: Basic Books, 1973).
18. Felicia Lampert, "Deprivacy," reprinted from *Look* in frontispiece to Arthur R. Miller, *The Assault on Privacy* (Ann Arbor: University of Michigan, 1971).
19. Joseph Meyer, "Crime Deterrent Transponder System," *Transmission on Aerospace of Privacy,* July 26, 1966.
20. Paul Baran, *Hearings before the House Special Subcommittee on Invasion of Privacy,* July 26, 1966.
21. Richard M. Nixon, Executive Order 11605, July 2, 1971.
22. James Mardian, Address to the Atomic Energy Commission Security Conference, October 27, 1971.
23. Kenyon B. De Greene, *Sociotechnical Systems* (Englewood Cliffs: Prentice Hall, 1973).
24. Abraham Briloff, *Unaccountable Accounting* (New York: Harper and Row, 1972).
25. Raymond A. Bauer and Daniel H. Fenn, Jr., *The Corporate Social Audit* (New York: Russell Sage Foundation, 1972).
26. William Nordhaus and James Tobin, "Is Growth Obsolete?" National Bureau of Economic Research, *Fiftieth Anniversary Colloquium,* 1972.
27. Paul Samuelson, *Economics,* 9th edition (New York: McGraw-Hill, 1973).
28. Bertram Gross, "The Social State of the Union," *Transaction,* November 1965; Bertram Gross, *The State of the Nation, Social Systems Accounting* (London: Tavistock, 1967). Also in Raymond A. Bauer, Ed., *Social Indicators* (Cambridge, MIT Press, 1966); and Bertram Gross, ed. A. broad review of social indicators and vindicators appears in Bertram Gross and Jeffrey D. Straussman, "The Social Indicators Movement," *Social Policy,* September/October 1974.
29. Richard Greeman, review of James Ridgeway, *The Closed Corporation: Universities in Crisis,* in Tom Christoffel et al. *Up Against the American Myth* (New York: Holt, Rinehart and Winston, 1970).

Chapter 13: Incentives for Systems Acceptance

1. B. F. Skinner, *Beyond Freedom and Dignity* (New York: Knopf, 1971).
2. Aldous Huxley, *Brave New World,* 1932 (New York: Perennial Classic Edition, 1969).
3. Reimut Reiche, *Sexuality and Class Struggle,* 1968, Susan Bennett, Tr. (London: New Left Review Edition, 1970).
4. *Brave New World.*
5. Norman Podhoretz, *Making It* (New York, Bantam Books, 1967).
6. Lewis Mumford, *The Pentagon of Power* (New York: Harcourt Brace, Jovanovich, Inc., 1970).
7. *Future Shock.*
8. Steffan B. Linder, *The Harried Leisure Class* (New York: Columbia University Press, 1970).
9. John K. Galbraith, *Economics and the Public Service* (Boston: Houghton Mifflin, 1973).
10. Frances Fox Piven and Richard A. Cloward, *Regulating the Poor* (New York: Pantheon, 1971).
11. Walter Sullivan, "Scientists Foresee a Longer Life Span, Mainly for the Affluent," *New York Times,* February 23, 1971.

Chapter 14: The Ladder of Terror

1. *Report of National Commission on the Causes and Prevention of Violence* (Washington, D.C.: U.S. Government Printing Office, 1969).
2. Albert Thayer Mahan, *Time,* August 4, 1958.
3. Herman Kahn, *On Escalation* (Baltimore: Penguin, 1968).
4. *Wall Street Journal,* March 17, 1972.
5. *Wall Street Journal,* May 2, 1976.
6. *Wall Street Journal,* May 2, 1976.
7. Richard Harris, "The New Justice," *The New Yorker,* March 25, 1972.
8. Ronald Reagan, cited by Kenneth Lamott, *Anti-California: Report from Our First Parafascist State* (Boston: Little Brown, 1971).
9. Alan L. Oten, *Wall Street Journal,* April 8, 1971.
10. Thomas Szasz, *The Manufacture of Madness* (New York: Harper and Row, 1970).
11. Eugene V. Walker, *Terror and Resistance* (New York: Oxford University Press, 1969).
12. Diane Henry, "CIA's Clandestine Work Assailed Here," *New York Times,* March 26, 1975.
13. Miles Copeland, "Is There a CIA in Your Future?" *National Review,* March 1975.
14. Walter Sullivan, testimony before Senate Select Committee on Intelligence Activities, *Intelligence Activities and the Rights of Americans* (Washington, D.C.: U.S. Government Printing Office, 1976), excerpted in *New York Times,* April 29, 1976.
15. *Intelligence Activities and the Rights of Americans.*
16. John W. Crewdson, "Ex-Operative Says He Worked for FBI to Disrupt Political Activities Up to '74," *New York Times,* February 24, 1975.
17. Homer Bigart, *New York Times,* "Ex-Operative Says He Worked for FBI to Disrupt Political Activities up to '74," March 23, 1972.
18. Nathan Glazer and Daniel P. Moynihan, *Beyond the Melting Pot,* 2nd edition (Cambridge: M.I.T. Press, 1970).
19. Andrew Hacker, *The End of the American Era* (New York: Athaneum, 1970).
20. Kanti C. Kotecha and James L. Walker, "Police Vigilantes," *Society,* March/April, 1976.
21. Alan Wolfe, "Extralegality and American Power," *Society,* March/April, 1976.
22. George Gerbner and Larry P. Gross, "Living with Television: The Violence Profile," *Journal of Communication,* April, 1976.

Chapter 15: Sex, Drugs, Madness, Cults

1. Wilhelm Reich, *The Mass Psychology of Fascism,* Vincent R. Carfagno, Tr. (New York: Farrar, Straus and Giroux, 1970).
2. Anselma Dell'Oleo, "The Sexual Revolution Wasn't Our War," *MS.,* Spring, 1972.
3. Harrison Pope, Jr., *Voices from the Drug Culture* (Boston, Beacon Press, 1971).
4. Dr. Marshall Dumont, "Mainlining America: Why the Young Use Drugs," *Social Policy,* November/December, 1971.
5. Henry L. Leondar and Associates, *Mystification and Drug Abuse* (San Francisco: Jossey-Bass, 1971).
6. Charles Witter, *Trans-Action,* July/August, 1971.
7. *New York Times,* September 5, 1971.
8. Kenneth Clark, "Leadership and Psychotechnology," *New York Times,* November 9, 1971.
9. *Journal of the Cincinnati Lancet Clinic, 1889.*
10. Sigmund Freud, *Civilization and Its Discontents* (London: Hogarth Press, 1953).
11. Thomas Szasz, *Law, Liberty and Psychiatry* (New York: Collier, 1968).
12. Dr. Gerald Klerman, quoted by David Brand in "Beyond the Blues," *Wall Street Journal,* April 7, 1972.
13. Dr. David Rosenthal, *Report for National Institute for Mental Health,* April 1972.
14. G. Brock Chisholm, "The Psychiatry of Enduring Peace and Social Progress," *Psychiatry,* January 1946.
15. "Religious Cults," *U.S. News and World Report,* June 14, 1976.
16. Berkeley Rice, 'The Fall of Sun Moon," *New York Times Magazine,* May 30, 1976.
17. Leo Litwak, "Pay Attention, Turkeys," *New York Magazine,* May 2, 1976.
18. Carey McWilliams "The New Fundamentalists," *The Nation,* June 5, 1976.

Chapter 16: The Adaptive Hydra

1. Noah Chomsky, *American Power and the New Mandarins* (New York: Vintage, 1969).
2. *Inside the Third Reich.*
3. Phillip Selznick, *TVA and the Grass Roots* (Berkeley: University of California Press, 1949).
4. *Socialism.*
5. Mary McGrory, "Pleading and Bleeding," *New York Post,* May 6, 1972.
6. Joseph Clark, *Congress: The Sapless Branch* (New York: Harper and Row, 1964).
7. Samuel F. Yette, *The Choice* (New York: Putnam, 1971).
8. Alphonso Pinkney, Personal statement to the author.
9. *Terror and Resistance.*
10. Friedrich and Brzezinski, *Totalitarian Dictatorship and Autocracy.*
11. Paul Goodman, "1984," in Harold Jaffe and John Tytell, *The American Experience, A Radical Reader* (New York: Harper and Row, 1970).
12. Leopold Tyramand, *The Rosa Luxembourg Contraceptives Cooperative* (New York: Macmillan, 1972).

Chapter 17: The Myths of Determinism

1. Karl Popper, *Unended Quest: An Intelligent Autobiography* (Glasgow: Fontana/Collins, 1976).
2. Corliss Lamont, "The Cassandra in America," *New York Times,* July 25, 1971.
3. Theodore Draper, Letters from Readers, *Commentary,* April 1972.
4. *Without Marx or Jesus.*
5. Friedrich Hayek, *The Road to Serfdom* (Chicago: University of Chicago Press, 1944).

6. Bertram Gross, "Friendly Fascism: Model for America," *Social Policy*, November/December, 1970.
7. Franklin D. Roosevelt, Address at Cambridge, Mass., June 19, 1941.
8. Winston Churchill, Speech on Dunkirk, House of Commons, June 4, 1940.

Chapter 18: It Hasn't Happened Yet

1. Sidney Hook, "The Fallacy of the Theory of Social Fascism," in Louis Filler, ed. *The Anxious Years* (New York: Putnam, 1963).
2. Felix Greene, *The Enemy: What Every American Should Know About Imperialism* (New York: Vintage, 1971).
3. Richard Grunberger, *A Social History of Nazi Germany, 1933–1945* (Holt, Rinehart and Winston, 1971).

Chapter 19: The Long-Term Logic of Democracy

1. William H. Hastie, quoted in George Seldes, ed., *The Great Quotations* (New York: Pocketbooks, 1967).
2. Bernard Smith, Introduction, *The Democratic Spirit* (New York: Knopf, 1941).
3. United Nations Educational, Scientific and Cultural Organization, *Democracy in a World of Tensions: A Symposium*, Richard McKeon, ed. (Chicago: University of Chicago Press, 1951).
4. Harold L. Wilensky, *The New Corporatism, Centralization and the Welfare State* (Beverly Hills: Sage, 1976) and G. David Garson, *The Future of American Public Administration*, A Working Paper, Center for Urban Affairs and Community Services, North Carolina State University, Raleigh, North Carolina.

Chapter 20: The Democratic Logic in Action

1. Vladimir Dedijer, "A Letter to Jean-Paul Sartre," *New York Times*, February 6, 1971.
2. Mary Parker Follett, *The New State* (New York: Longmans, Green, 1918; reprinted Gloucester, Mass.: Peter Smith, 1965).
3. Representative Jim Weaver (D.Ore.), "Weaver on the Draft," *The Reporter for Conscience's Sake*, Washington, D.C., April 1979.
4. James Fenimore Cooper, *The American Democrat: Advantages of a Democracy.*
5. Louis B. Brandeis, *Labor*, October 17, 1941.
6. Robert L. Heilbroner, "The Inescapable Marx," *New York Review of Books*, July 29, 1978.
7. E. F. Schumacher, *Small Is Beautiful: Economics As If People Mattered* (New York: Perennial, 1975).
8. *Economics and the Public Purpose.*
9. *The New State.*
10. Harry Boyte, "A Democratic Awakening," *Social Policy*, Special Issue on Organizing Neighborhoods, September/October, 1979.
11. Hazel Henderson, *Creating Alternative Futures* (New York: Berkeley, 1978).
12. Frank Riessman, "Will Local Populism Lead to a New Progressivism?" *In These Times*, June 13-19, 1979.
13. Karl Marx, Preface to *Capital*, Vol. 1.
14. Ralph Nader, "An Anatomy of Whistle Blowing," in Ralph Nader, et al., *Whistle Blowing* (New York: Grossman, 1972).
15. *Political Hysteria in America.*
16. S. M. Miller, "Police and Science," *Journal of Social Policy*, January 1974.
17. *The Pentagon of Power.*
18. Alfred North Whitehead, *Dialogues of Alfred North Whitehead*, as recorded by Lucien Price (New York: Atlantic Monthly Press, 1954).
19. *Small Is Beautiful.*
20. Mary Parker Follett, *Creative Experience* (New York: Longmans, Green, 1926).

21. Charles E. Lindblom and David K. Cohen, *Usable Knowledge: Social Science and Social Problem Solving* (New Haven: Yale University Press, 1979).
22. Bertram Gross, *The Managing of Organizations* (New York: Free Press, 1964) and "Planning in an Era of Social Revolution," *Public Administration Review*, May/June, 1971.
23. *Labor and Monopoly Capital.*
24. *Small Is Beautiful.*
25. Barrington Moore, Jr., *Reflections on the Causes of Human Misery and Upon Certain Proposals to Eliminate Them* (Boston: Beacon, 1970).
26. Barrington Moore, Jr., *Reflections on the Causes of Human Misery and Upon Certain Proposals to Eliminate Them.*
27. Story first told by Gerhard Colm, "Technical Requirements (for Full Employment)", in "Maintaining High Level Production and Employment: A Symposium," *American Political Science Review*, December 1945.
28. Roland Huntford, *The New Totalitarians* (New York: Stein and Day, 1972).
29. Eric S. Einhorn, "Denmark, Norway and Sweden," in Itzhak Galnoor, *Government Secrecy in Democracies* (New York: Harbor Colophon, 1977).
30. Dankwort A. Rustow, "Transitions to Democracy: Toward a Dynamic Theory," *Comparative Politics*, April 1970.

Chapter 21: What Can You Do?

1. Oliver Wendell Holmes, Jr., Memorial Day Address, 1884.
2. James Weinstein, *Ambiguous Legacy: The Left in American Politics* (New York: New Viewpoints, 1975).
3. John and Barbara Ehrenreich, "Work and Consciousness," *Monthly Review.*
4. Staughton Lynn, "Workers' Control in a Time of Diminished Workers' Rights," *Radical America*, September/October, 1976.
5. Lerone Bennett, Jr., *What Manner of Man: A Biography of Martin Luther King, Jr.* (New York: Pocket Books, 1965).
6. *What Manner of Man. . . .*
7. E. Victor Wolfenstein, *The Revolutionary Personality: Lenin, Trotsky and Gandhi* (Princeton: Princeton University Press, 1967).
8. Christopher Lash, "The Narcissist Society," *New York Review of Books*, September 30, 1976, p. 5.
9. Edwin Schur, *The Awareness Trap: Self-Absorption Instead of Social Change* (New York: Quadrangle, 1976).
10. Peter Marin, "The Human Harvest," *Mother Jones*, December 1976.
11. Thomas Jefferson, Letter to M. de Meunier, January 24, 1786.
12. Thomas Jefferson, Letter to Horatio G. Spafford, March 17, 1814.
13. Francis W. Coker, "Patriotism," *Encyclopaedia of the Social Sciences* (New York: Macmillan, 1933).
14. *Militarism, U.S.A.*
15. Kalman H. Silvert, *The Reason for Democracy* (New York: Viking, 1977).

About the Author

BERTRAM GROSS is a Distinguished Professor of Public Policy and Planning in the Urban Affairs Department of Hunter College, and a Professor of Political Science in the Graduate Program of City University of New York. He has served in government office, and has written extensively on political and social topics. Among his books is *The Legislative Struggle:* A Study of Social Combat, which won the Woodrow Wilson Prize of the American Political Science Association.

During the Roosevelt and Truman administrations, he served as an advisor in the areas of public housing, war-time price controls, small business, and post-war planning. He was the major architect of the orginal full-employment bills of 1944 and 1945, and of the Employment Act of 1946. With Rep. Augustus Hawkins and the Congressional Black Caucus, he developed the original versions of the Humphrey-Hawkins Full Employment and Balanced Growth Act of 1978. From 1946 to 1951, he served as Executive Secretary on the President's Council of Economic Advisors.

While working on legislation in Congress and the President's office, he wrote *The Legislative Struggle.* After this, he was a visiting professor at the Hebrew University. He has subsequently taught at the University of California, Berkeley, has been a fellow at the Center for Advanced Study in the Behavioral Sciences, a Leatherbee Lecturer at the Harvard School of Business Administration, and a Professor of Administration at Syracuse University's Maxwell School, where he completed work on his two-volume *The Managing of Organizations.* He was the founder of the Center for Urban Studies at Wayne State University, and has been the president of the Society for General Systems Research. In 1978, he received a Fulbright travel grant, which he used to travel and lecture extensively in India. As a consultant to the UN Division of Public Administration and Finance, he has written and traveled extensively in the Third World.

Bertram Gross has edited numerous books and publications in his field, and has contributed scores of articles. He helped to write *Toward A More Responsible Two-Party System* for the American Political Science Association. As a leader in the social indicator movement, he published *The State of The Union: Social Systems Accounting,* and edited a series of issues for The Annals, which were brought together in *Social Intelligence for America's Future.* As editor and contributor to a special issue of the *Public Administration Review,* his article on "Planning in an Era of Social Revolution" won the William E. Mosher Award of the American Society for Public Administration.

Bertram Gross has written for the *New York Times* and *Social Policy,* where his first piece on Friendly Fascism appeared. He is a regular contributor to *The Nation.*

Index